The Forgotten Bentley Boy

By the same author

MARINE BOOKS
The Boat Owner's Maintenance Book
The Boat Building Book
The Marine Electrics Book

LOCAL HISTORY
Secretive Southwick – Domesday to D-Day
Southwick – The D-Day village That Went To War

TRAVEL
GROC's Candid Guides to Greece and The Greek Islands (9 in series)
GROC's Terra Firma Guide to the Ports and Harbours of the Solent

THE FORGOTTEN BENTLEY BOY
Tom or 'Scrap' Thistlethwayte

Geoffrey O'Connell.

Published by Willowbridge Publishing.

© Geoffrey O'Connell 2008
The right of Geoffrey O'Connell to be identified as the
author of the work has been asserted by him in accordance
with the Copyright, designs and Patents Act 1988.

First published in hardback in Great Britain in 2008
by Willowbridge Publishing
enquiries@willowbridgepublishing.com
www.willowbridgepublishing.com

All rights reserved. Apart from any use permitted under UK
copyright law, this publication may only be reproduced, stored
or transmitted, in any form, or by any means, with prior
permission in writing of the publisher or, in the case of
reprographic production, in accordance with the terms of
licences issued by the Copyright Licensing Agency.

A CIP catalogue record for this book is available from
the British Library.

ISBN 978-0-9560265-0-7

Design and typesetting by
Ted Spittles of Pen and Mouse Productions Ltd.

Typeset in Minion and Gill Sans light

Every effort has been made to fulfil requirements with regard to
reproducing copyright material. The author and publisher will
be glad to rectify any ommissions at the earliest opportunity.

Contents

Illustrations.		vii – ix
Introduction.		1
Chapter One.	Tom or 'Scrap' Thistlethwayte. Who and Why He and Why 'Scrap'?	5
Chapter Two.	Tom. His Introduction to the Sport. 1924. Count Louise Vorow Zborowski. Romney, Hythe and Dymchurch Railway. Capt. 'Jack' Howey.	19
Chapter Three.	Tom. Marriage and Motor Racing. 1925. Capt. Clive Gallop. John Godfrey Parry Thomas Jack and Clive Dunfee.	35
Chapter Four.	Tom. His Le Mans Year. 1926. Bentley Motors. Capt. Richard Barstow Howey. Sammy Davis. Dr Dudley Benjafield. George Edward Duller. Frank C Clement. Capt. John F Duff.	55
Chapter Five.	Tom. The Lost Year. 1927. Capt. Henry Ralph Stanley Birkin. The Hon. Dorothy Paget. Bernard Rubin. Jean Chassagne.	95
Chapter Six.	Tom. His Reappearance. 1928. Capt. GET Eyston. Humphrey Wyndham Cook.	131
Chapter Seven.	Tom. The Penultimate Year. 1929. Cmdr. George Pearson Kidston.	167
Chapter Eight.	Tom. The Last Racing Year. 1930. Woolf Barnato.	207
Epilogue.		243
Postscript.		248
Acknowledgments.		249
Index.		251

Tom or 'Scrap' Thistlethwayte.
COURTESY OF MERCEDES BENZ

ILLUSTRATIONS

		Page
Plate 1.	Tom aboard his Mercedes S-36/220 probably in 1929.	x
Plate 2.	Tom's 3 litre Bentley, in more recent years.	2
Plate 3.	Tragedy – cartoon.	4
Plate 4.	Southwick House, the Thistlethwayte family residence.	6
Plate 5.	Southwick Village.	8
Plate 6.	Solomon Barnato Joel and Maiden Erlegh Mansion.	10
Plate 7.	Segrave, Mays, Parry Thomas and Campbell.	12
Plate 8.	Punch Cartoons.	14
Plate 9.	Brockbank Cartoons.	16
Plate 10.	Higham House.	18
Plate 11.	Brooklands Circuit.	20
Plate 12.	Count Zborowski and Clive Gallop.	22
Plate 13.	Zborowski and his 'groupies'.	24
Plate 14.	Chitty 1 and Chitty 11.	26
Plate 15.	Chitty 111 and The Higham Special.	28
Plate 16.	Countess Zborowski.	30
Plate 17.	Capt. John Howey.	32
Plate 18.	Tom's 30-98 and the Hispano-Suiza once owned by Zborowski.	34
Plate 19.	Tom's 1925 Frazer Nash and the Boulogne Circuit.	36
Plate 20.	The 1925 Boulogne Automobile Week.	38
Plate 21.	Tom's ex 30-98 and Parry Thomas in his 'Flat Iron' Thomas Special.	40
Plate 22.	Construction details of the 'Flat Iron' Special.	42
Plate 23.	Zborowski and Gallop in 1922 and 1923.	44
Plate 24.	Tom and Gallop in their respective 30-98 and 3 litre Bentley and Parry Thomas in the Leyland Eight.	46
Plate 25.	Parry Thomas and sundry of his motors, including 'Babs'.	48
Plate 26.	Jack Dunfee, Woolf Barnato, Clive Dunfee, Sammy Davis and Cyril Paul celebrating various Bentley victories.	50
Plate 27.	Birkin, Barnato, BO Davis and Clive Dunfee.	52
Plate 28.	The 1926 Le Mans.	54
Plate 29.	The Le Mans Circuit.	56 & 57
Plate 30.	Detail of the 1926 Le Mans.	58
Plate 31.	The 1926 Boulogne Race Week.	60
Plate 32.	Capt. Richard Howey's fatal accident.	62
Plate 33.	Capt. Howey's obituaries.	64
Plate 34.	Barnato's first Bentley.	66
Plate 35.	Capt. Richard Howey.	68
Plate 36.	Davis and Zborowski at the 'helm' of a Miller.	70
Plate 37 and 38.	Sammy Davis' racing 1925–1927.	72

vii

Plates 39.	More Davis and Bentley 'Old No.7'.	73 & 74
Plate 40.	Sammy Davis 1928 and 1929.	76
Plate 41.	The 1930 Brooklands Double Twelve.	78 & 79
Plate 42.	The 1930 Le Mans.	80
Plate 43.	Sammy Davis – the Brooklands 1930 500 Mile and 1931 Easter Races.	82
Plate 44.	Benjafield, the 1927 Le Mans line up and Duller and Davis.	84
Plate 45.	Clement, as well as Clement and Duff and the 1923 Le Mans.	86
Plate 46.	Duff Record Breaking.	88
Plate 47.	Duff and Clement, the 1924 Le Mans.	88 & 89
Plate 48.	The 1925 Le Mans.	90
Plate 49.	Clement and the 1926 – 1930 Le Mans'.	92
Plate 50.	Countess Zborowski's Yachts.	94
Plate 51.	'Tiger Tim' Birkin.	96
Plate 52.	Birkin's DFP and some flights of his inventive fancy.	98
Plate 53.	Some of Birkin's track exploits.	100
Plate 54.	The popular press reports of the 1928 Le Mans.	101
Plate 55.	More Birkin and the 1928 Le Mans.	102
Plate 56.	And more Birkin.	104
Plate 57.	Miss Cunliffe and Birkin and Barnato.	106
Plate 58.	Some of Birkin's 1929 season.	108
Plate 59.	Birkin and the Hon. Dorothy Paget.	110
Plate 60.	The 1930 Le Mans.	110 & 111
Plate 61.	Birkin's 1930s Irish Races.	112
Plate 62.	Birkin at Pau and Brooklands in 1930.	114
Plate 63.	Rubin – 1928 to 1929.	116
Plate 64.	Birkin in 1931.	118
Plate 65.	The 1933 Mille Miglia.	120
Plate 65 & 66.	More Mille Miglia and the 1933 Grand Prix of Tripoli.	122
Plate 67.	Birkin's commemorative plaque.	124
Plate 68.	Chassagne's Races.	126 & 128
Plate 69, 70 & 71.	The Ards Circuit and the 1928 Tourist Trophy Race.	130, 132 & 134
Plate 72.	Tom's Schooner Charmian.	136
Plate 73.	Tom's 'whoopsy' in the 1928 Tourist Trophy Race.	138
Plate 74.	The 1928 Boulogne Automobile Week.	140
Plate 75.	Big Game Hunting and J Murphy in the 1921 French Grand Prix.	142
Plate 76.	Capt. George Eyston, Kensington-Moir, Zborowski and Gallop.	144
Plate 77.	Eyston and Aston Martins.	146
Plate 78.	Eyston and early Races.	148
Plate 79.	Eyston's boating interests.	150
Plate 80.	Eyston and his 1926 Motor Racing exploits.	152
Plate 81.	Eyston and 1927.	154
Plate 82.	The Brooklands 1928 Six Hour and 200 Mile Races.	156
Plate 83.	The 1929 Belgian and Irish Grand Prix.	158

Illustrations

Plate 84.	Eyston Record Breaking.	160
Plate 85.	Eyston and 'Speed of the Wind'. Humphrey Cook and 'Rouge et Noir'.	162
Plate 86.	Humphrey Cook.	164
Plate 87.	Tom's Mercedes S-38/250 and the 1929 Brooklands Six Hour Race.	166
Plate 88.	Phoenix Park and the 1929 Irish Grand Prix.	168
Plate 89.	The start of the 1929 Irish GP.	170
Plate 90.	The 1929 Irish GP battle of the supercharged giants – Tom and Tim.	172 &173
Plate 91.	'The Charioteer'.	174
Plate 92.	The Grineau sketch of the 1929 Tourist Trophy personalities.	176
Plate 93.	Tom and onlookers at the 1929 TT.	178
Plate 94.	The 1929 TT Mercedes Team – Tom, Caracciola and Mertz.	178 & 179
Plate 95.	More 1929 TT.	180
Plate 96.	Tom.	182
Plate 97	The Shelsley Walsh Hill Climb.	182
Plate 98.	Glen Kidston snapshots.	184
Plates 99 &100.	Royal Navy Ships on which Kidston served.	186 & 188
Plate 101.	The 1925 Kidston stable of vehicles.	190
Plate 102.	Kidston's GP T35 Bugatti.	192
Plate 103.	The 1929 Le Mans and Tourist Trophy Races.	194
Plate 104.	Kidston's close escape and the 1930 Monte Carlo exploit.	196
Plate 105.	The 1930 Le Mans.	198
Plate 106, 107 & 108.	Kidston's aircraft, flying exploits and death.	200, 202 & 204
Plate 109 & 110.	Tom's nuptials and the 1930 Summer Season.	206 &208
Plate 111.	A magazine interview with T. Thistlethwayte.	210
Plate 112.	Tom's 1930 Sand Racing.	212
Plate 113.	Tom and power boat racing.	214
Plate 114, 115 and 116.	Woolf Barnato.	214, 216 and 218
Plate 117.	June Trip – Barnato's 'femme fatale'.	220
Plate 118.	Barnato's power boating exploits.	222
Plate 119.	The Bertelli motor car.	224
Plate 120.	Ardenrun House.	226
Plate 121.	The second Mrs Barnato.	228
Plate 122.	Barnato's early race days.	230
Plate 123.	Barnato's first Bentley – a 3 litre.	232
Plate 124.	More Barnato racing exploits.	234
Plate 125.	The 1928 Le Mans.	236
Plate 126.	Barnato and 1929.	238
Plate 127.	1930 and Barnato's swan song.	240
Plate 128.	The Motor magazine Bentley cover of 1929.	242
Plate 129.	The S-38/250 Mercedes, photographs and technical illustration.	244 and 245

Plate 1. Tom aboard his Mercedes S-36/220 Reg. No. YU 1908, probably in 1929.
COURTESY OF MERCEDES BENZ

Introduction

Tom or 'Scrap' Thistlethwayte.

'British designers have nothing to learn from this brand of design.'
THE BRITISH FORD PRESIDENT COMMENTING ON THE VW BEETLE IN 1946.

Scanning the title page, some prospective readers may be inclined to opinion – Tom or 'Scrap' Thistlethwayte – who he? Or possibly, how came he to be termed and or regarded as one of the Bentley Boys? Or, for that matter, one of the Mercedes Boys?

To these enquirers it is only necessary to point out that Tom was, for an admittedly comparatively short period, a very serious Bentley owner and racing driver. And that was before such luminaries as Sir Henry Stanley Tiger Tim Birkin, Cmdr. Glen Kidston or Bernard Rubin, had placed their orders, and then their bottoms on one of the hallowed seats of a WO Bentley product. Even Woolf Babe Barnato was only an owner and competitor one year before Tom. Incidentally, when I write serious, I mean serious – for his first ever race, in his newly delivered 3 litre, was nowhere else other than Le Mans. Yes, the 1926 Le Mans, with only the pre-race practice session to accustom him to the car, let alone the track! Furthermore, it is worth recalling who was his co-driver at this hallowed venue. Step forward Capt. Clive Gallop, a veritable legend of the 1920s racing scene. What's more they had completed 105 laps after 18 hours racing and were lying joint third, before being struck down by the cursed duralumin rocker arm 'disease'. That's how much a Bentley Boy he was.

A couple of other parameters may require some explanation. In the main I have chosen the years of Tom's involvement in the sport as the 'book-ends'. That is the years between 1924 and 1930. To set Tom in context I have also included many of his fellow competitors, those with whom he both raced and socialised during this period.

In carrying out the research certain characters from this long-ago period drift in and out of the racing scene. Many are familiar, attention-grabbing names. They include such worthies as David Brown, he of tractor, specialist gears and Aston Martin fame. Or Harry

Tom's 3 litre Bentley Reg No. KM 4250, Chassis No. 1179, Engine No. 1165, in more recent years.

Plate 2a. At Le Mans celebrating the 50th Anniversary of the 1926 Le Mans Race.
COURTESY OF STUDIO 3.

Plate 2b. A triumphant Nigel Mansell celebrating a victory.
COURTESY STUDIO 3

Plate 2c. On show at Kensington Gardens.
COURTESY JOHN ADAMS – RAY ROBERTS COLLECTION

THESE PICTURES APPEAR IN THE PUBLICATION BENTLEY SPECIALS & SPECIAL BENTLEYS. RAY ROBERTS. PUBLISHED BY FOULIS HAYNES.

INTRODUCTION.

Ferguson, the Ulsterman who was also 'big' in tractors. Capt. Drummond, surely of Drummond's Bank (now swallowed up by one of the other Scottish banking giants) and with whose grandson (?) I used to race, back in the not so distant 1960s. Another star name of the 1960s, with whom I was lucky enough to be competing at the same race meetings, was Patsy Burt. Her father Eric, a director of the civil engineers Mowlems, was instrumental in keeping Frazer Nash afloat in the late 1920s. Major L. Ropner in his Vauxhall OE 30-98 *Silver Arrow*, who was probably one of the Ropner (Shipping Company) family, once based at West Hartlepool. A certain Tony Vandervell (who William Body does not index but mentions in his *Brooklands – The Complete Motor Racing History*) for whom my father carried out much precision engineering work, in the late 1950s, early 1960s. That was when Vandervell Products Ltd of Thin-Wall Bearings and Vanwall GP racing car fame had an Acton factory. The Konig who was the previous owner of Woolf Barnato's Ardenrun Mansion, and Mark Konig who was surely a relation and with whom I also raced in the 1960s. As I did, in recent VSCC events, with Tom Delaney, still competing until 2006. Or Sidney Allard, one of whose breakdown trucks pulled me in at Goodwood, in the 1960s, on my only 'off', ever (in those days), damaging the nose-piece of my Jaguar engined AC Aceca. And I only went 'off piste', as it were, following the brake lights of the car in front, as the rain was so torrential. Honest! The name Percy Lambert and his $4^3/_4$ litre Talbot means more than a little to me. Long ago I owned chassis No. 3, to his chassis No. 1, in which he achieved the 100 miles in the hour, at Brooklands. But then when young I also owned, amongst other vintage machines, the likes of a Trojan (I was very young), a 1925 Fiat 501, a 3 litre Bentley and a 1938 four wheel Morgan. Until recently my garages were 'oil deep' in vintage and PVT racing machines.

As in any history, I am totally indebted to those authorities who have gone before. Those scribes who have researched and written about this period with varying degrees of intensity. If any badge, banner or prize had to be awarded for one specific book in respect of this age it must go to William Boddy, MBE, author of, amongst other articles and publications, the 'Bible'* of pre-WW2 motor sport in England. Other authors and publishers are acknowledged where appropriate. Professional bodies that must be acknowledged and thanked include: The Research Department of the National Motor Museum, Beaulieu; The Brooklands Society; The Bentley Drivers Club; the Vintage Sports Car Club; as well as research professionals including Tim Cooper of British Ancestral Research and various picture libraries. A complete list is to be found at the end of the book.

Without Ted Spittles, who supervised the make-up of the book, its illustrations and layouts, as he has any number of my previous publications, I would still be in a garret!

Lastly, my thanks are due to friends and others who have put up with my obsessive behaviour during the gestation period of this publication. None more so than Christine Aston, my PA, and Rose, my 'unfortunate' partner. Both were very reluctant bystanders, having to put up with the side-effects experienced with an author in the process of giving 'birth' to such a project as this. An old friend and 'pit lane' supporter, Robin Cotton (and that is not to forget his delightful lady, Maria) wishes to be mentioned. I do not know why but he does own a classic Austin Healey BN 6. Perhaps that's why!

---

* Brooklands. The Complete Motor Racing History. William Boddy. MRP.

TRAGEDY

**That morning, when my wife eloped
With James, our chauffeur, how I moped!
What tragedies in life there are!
I'm dashed if I can start my car!**

Plate 3.   This cartoon and caption appeared in The Shell Book of Motoring Humour introduced and edited by Nicolas Bentley. Published by Michael Joseph.

Courtesy Harry Graham: Most Ruthless Rhymes

CHAPTER ONE

Tom or 'Scrap' Thistlethwayte. Who and Why He and Why 'Scrap'?

'Nothing has come along that can beat the horse and buggy'.
An American businessman advising a relation not to invest $5,000 in the Ford Motor Co.

'Our hero' Tom or 'Scrap' Thistlethwayte was absolutely and utterly representative of a pantheon of first, second and third division sporting amateurs, who flowered after the final last post of the First World War (WW1). Those exponents carried on the pre-war, chivalrous traditions of 'playing up and playing the game'. A field of activity and sportsmanship that was perfected in the last years of the late 1800s and the early 1900s. A period prior to the carnage that was to change once and for all the strictures and structures of European society.

They occupied centre-stage for in excess of a decade, bursting out from the wings, almost immediately post-WW1 and spilled over into the 1930s. Their years in the limelight were enacted against a society backcloth of cocktails, Charleston's, foreign excursions, dances and weekend house parties, gaming and gambling, in an age of great personal wealth – and great personal deprivation! This was a decade when eccentrics could afford to be eccentrics and when affluence usually represented enormous, mind-boggling riches. The unspoken, unwritten motto and lifestyle of the 'cast of troupers' was probably best expressed as *play and party very fast, die young*. And for motor racing, one of the more exotic of sports, death was often never too distant. The list of players was made up of ladies and gentleman, now mainly unsung and largely forgotten, that is apart from the male and female leads, the 'superstars' of their day. These celebrities were backed up by a wide-flung 'chorus' of 1920s enthusiastic

Plate 4.   Southwick House in the 1930s. Tom inherited the family 'pile', as well as some 8,000 acres of southern Hampshire in 1924, aged 21. It had been in the family for approximately 386 years, since the Dissolution of the Monastries in Henry VIII's reign. The mansion and village were to achieve their finest year in history during World War II, in 1944. That was the year when Southwick House hosted the military leaders who plotted and executed the plans for D-Day – the invasion of Europe that would culminate in the annhilation of Hitler's Germany and the Nazi Empire.

COURTESY SECRETIVE SOUTHWICK. DOMESDAY TO D-DAY. GR O'CONNELL

performers who fuelled the overall social and sporting scene. Lacking this supporting cast of stage-hands, the 'gofers', the 'roadies' of their day, there would have been a much smaller backdrop against which the major participants could display their talents.

Without doubt, the decade and a 'bit', commencing 1919/20 and petering out in the 1930s, spawned the most amazing crop of sporting super stars. Due to the then not so recent advent of the internal combustion engine, and 'sacks of groats', they indulged themselves in an orgy of flying, power boating, yachting and motor racing. Although the last mentioned activity was the most popular and attracted the majority of contestants, the fascinating aspect of their almost frenetic activity was the interlocking aspirations of this 1920s 'fast set'. Many, many dedicated exponents of motor racing used up any leftover energy, time and money in a farrago of equally enterprising, if less dangerous deeds. These included an admixture of the aforementioned sports, of which yachting was seemingly the least popular. It was probably not fast or dangerous enough!

And a no more representative example of this genre existed than Arthur Donald Claude Thomas (Tom) Thistlethwayte, born 17th December 1903. Now largely forgotten, he was definitely motor racing in 1925, the very same year as he married (for the first time) and a year after inheriting the family Hampshire Estates. In 1926, he was the entrant and driver of his 3 litre Bentley in the Grand Prix d'Endurance de 24 Heures du Mans Coupes Rudge-Whitworth (*Le Mans*). Divorced in 1927, the year 1928 marked the onset of his most serious motor racing period, driving a near 7 litre supercharged Mercedes. Towards the end of the decade Tom was also power boat racing, yachting and flying. During this fairly demanding schedule of hedonistic activity, he somehow managed, in 1930, to squeeze in his second marriage, to a wealthy, pretty young socialite. There's busy!

Incidentally, these latter nuptials bought to an end his motor racing days. But then this stricture would appear to have been an unwritten marriage vow for so many other newly-weds of that era. He did continue, admittedly at an almost sedentary pace, to pursue some other sporting activities, even if, by the middle 1930s, his last remaining serious recreational interest was his yacht. But what a yacht. More a schooner really. It was large enough, weighing in at 175 tons, for Tom to be able to load his Mercedes racing car on to the deck, in 1928. This was in order to sail over the Irish Sea to compete in the Ulster Tourist Trophy Race meeting staged at the Ards Circuit, Belfast. There's a player and a yacht!

And let it not be thought that Tom's comparative obscurity signified he was not deserving of inclusion in the annals of the motor racing rosters of the period. No less an authority than Sir Henry Ralph Stanley Tiger Tim Birkin, of Bentley fame, wrote in his racing autobiography *Full Throttle*.*

> 'Scrap Thistlethwayte… drove brilliantly; he had marked out his course as an expert, before the race and adhered to it with an expert's regularity. He drove faster than any one else, continually lapping at… But took no risks nor by reckless cornering endangered the cars behind. This I can attest, as I was so long behind him…'. *and* 'The last months of that year (1930) were a little sad, for the end of the great Bentley combination was in sight. …I

---

* 'Full Throttle'. Sir Henry (Tim) Birkin Bt. GT Foulis & Co., Ltd.

Plate 5. Just to add lustre to Southwick village's place in history, the Thistlethwayte mansion was the place chosen from which to launch the then greatest military invasion in history.

Courtesy Secretive Southwick, Domesday To D-Day.
& Southwick The D-Day Village That Went To War.
GR O'Connell

question if we shall ever see again as cheery a crowd as the so-called 'Bentley Boys' – Glen Kidston, Babe Barnato, Scrap Thistlethwayte, Sammy Davis, Bernard Rubin, Beris Wood, Jack and poor Clive Dunfee and myself. We were always seen together; we had the same manner of speech, the same jokes among ourselves'. *That was quite a close-knit clique in which to be considered one of the chaps!*

Some 29 years ago, after a particularly unpleasant 'matrimonial', I was fortunate enough to pitch-up at the then sleepy Hampshire village of Southwick, at the south end of the Meon Valley. Here I was lucky to be able to lease a centuries old house – still my present dwelling. There are occasions in the life of anyone, but I would suggest more so of authors, when the hairs actually stand up on the back of your neck. In my case, two coincidences and one unanswered question pushed me into setting out on a somewhat arduous, if immensely enjoyable task. That was the 'loves labour' of compiling the definitive history of Southwick Village – and the family who had owned it for approximately 450 years. The coincidences were based on a couple of WW2 related matters, neither of which is relevant to this book. And the unanswered question? The fact that the village and family had, over the centuries, maintained a discreet wall of silence. Thus, very very little was known about either the Estate or its manorial owners, the Thistlethwaytes. Not one to avoid a challenge, two books reached the light of day, namely *Secretive Southwick – Domesday to D-Day* and *Southwick The D-Day Village That Went To War*. In these I fleetingly referred to one Arthur Donald Claude 'Tom' Thistlethwayte as having been a 'passing' owner of the Estate. Aged 21, he had inherited this portion of southern Hampshire, along with a couple of Domesday villages, in 1924. On hearing of his good fortune he is said to have announced *"That it was not (worth) enough to buy a breakfast with"*!

This aside might justifiably be considered a somewhat ungracious statement, more especially to be made by such an urbane and outwardly charming, if possibly foppish young man. But bearing in mind his antecedents and upbringing, Tom would have been very unusual if he demonstrated anything approaching the common touch. Unsurprisingly, he decided not to take up residence in Southwick House, preferring to leave to others the tedious task of administering this London-distant property. Instead he let it all to his Uncle, Colonel Evelyn Thistlethwayte. This gallant, Boer War serving bachelor already lived in the Mansion. In fact he had resided there for most of his life, together with a scattering of equally aged, mainly unmarried brothers and sisters, as well as a retinue of long serving staff. Southwick House was conveniently set in large grounds and surrounding farmland, then totalling about 8,000 acres. This gracious expanse easily allowed the elderly relatives to live out their aristocratic existence, quite undisturbed by the vicissitudes of the then modern day life. Hunting and shooting continued unabated, even if Tom had rather worryingly taken to 'flogging off' bits and pieces of his inheritance. In the meantime the young rake roared around, racing vast motor cars, power boating, sailing and flying, once to distant Africa for a bit of big game hunting. And why not?

In the 1930s Tom decided to 'offload' Southwick Estate, that is to sell all his Hampshire property. The *raison d'etre* was most likely the necessity to balance his financial status quo, even if only for the time being. He was at this time described as a gentleman of independent

Plate 6a. Solomon Barnato Joel ('Solly Joe'), looking remarkably like King George V, at the helm of his yacht *Eileen*.

Courtesy The Great Barnato. Stanley Jackson. Heinemann

Plate 6b. Maiden Erlegh Mansion.

Courtesy Rural History Centre.

means – not working and earning. But a near decade of racing motor cars, owning a substantial yacht, in addition to the various financial outpourings necessary to maintain a 'man about town' status, would have required a steady, ever available source of 'doubloons'. Despite making a financially sound second marriage in 1930, 'the decks' probably had to be well and truly cleared and the 'books' balanced.

It was rumoured that one 'Solly Joe', a South African race horse owner was about to become the new owner of the Hampshire holdings. When I wrote the aforementioned Southwick books it had crossed my mind that this gentleman was possibly an associate of one or other of Tom's chums. And in a way, I was spot on. During the research for this publication I realised just who 'Solly Joe' was. To fully appreciate the labyrinthine and rather dubious nature of the rumours put about by Tom's agents, in respect of the prospective purchaser of Southwick Estate, it is necessary to digress somewhat.

Without doubt the greatest of the Bentley Boys, if not the most outstanding of the motor racing participants of the 1920s, was Woolf Babe Barnato. He was both a motor racing and a social friend of Tom's. Woolf's father was 'Barney' Barnato, born Barnett Isaacs, in 1852. He had been a one-time boxer, musician and vaudeville artist, described by some as a likable rogue and others as a streetwise rogue – take your pick! In 1873, he arrived, a penniless East-Ender, in South Africa, to seek his fortune. Some ten years later he was a millionaire wheeling and dealing in the heady diamond rush centred on Johannesburg. One of Barney's relations, and a cousin of Woolf's, was Solomon Barnato Joel. On the latter's return to England, in 1903, and also having made an enormous pile of money, he purchased Maiden Erlegh, close to Reading. Here he established the Home Stud Farm horse racing stables.

Solomon Barnato Joel was popularly known as 'Solly Joe'! Thus it does not require a stroke of genius to deduce that this ex-colonial fortune hunter was Tom's so called prospective purchaser. Tom's 'stalking horse' to flush out Uncle Colonel Evelyn Thistlethwayte and hasten him to make his own purchase! Appalled that his extended family's time-warped way of life might be terminated, Uncle Evelyn took the bait – and the train to the City of London. With much muttering, huffing and puffing, about having to sell London properties, earning this, that and the other interest, the gallant Colonel purchased the family pile. Noblesse oblige, but not very 'chappish' of Tom!

Perhaps one of the strangest twists in the story of Southwick Estate is that Robin Thistlethwayte, the present owner, is Tom's youngest son. But that is another tale, as is all of Southwick's history. The latter included the passage of Roman and Norman invaders, the formation of one of the wealthiest Priory's in the South of England, plus the many royal visitors who partook of the dynastic and feudal families largesse, over the years. Amongst these were King John, Henry III, Henry IV, Henry VIII, Charles I, George I, George VI and Elizabeth II. Then there was the Estate's involvement in the Hundred Years War, the Civil War and WW2. Not too bad for a sleepy, backwoods portion of pastoral England.

But back to the plot. It was whilst in conversation with the present-day Squire, in a suitably deferential manner, that he sighted my vintage 12/50 Alvis, ready for another 'trackside breakdown'. He passingly remarked *"Daddy used to race at Brooklands and other venues, don't you know?"* I recalled, when writing the village history, making a passing reference to Tom and his being involved in the sport. It was a matter not pursued at the time

Plate 7a. Major (later Sir) HOD Segrave.

Plate 7b. Raymond Mays in 1927 aboard his Work's sponsored 2 litre, supercharged, 4 cylinder Mercedes Targa Florio.

PLATES 7A, B & C COURTESY BROOKLANDS THE COMPLETE MOTOR RACING HISTORY, WILLIAM BODDY. MRP.

Plate 7c. JG Parry Thomas (left) and Malcolm Campbell, the latter subsequently knighted

as he was somewhat peripheral to the then scheme of things. But now, whilst idly chatting, the hairs commenced to stand upright on the old nape, once again. After Robin 'T' had 'tootled off', no doubt to check my rent was up to date (I jest!), I was able to look-up Tom Thistlethwayte in the definitive William Boddy Brooklands book. Sure enough, there were a few references to him. These I copied and posted to the Squire, who in turn dropped in a package of his father's press cuttings, relating to the late 1920s.

The seeds were sown. I had to know more and more. And the further I delved, the greater my fascination became. It was not simply the sheer width and breadth of his sporting activities and the various giants, and not so giants, with whom he had rubbed (no doubt) spotless, racing 'ovies'. It was not the absolutely outstanding players, whose names will always live on, superstars such as Malcolm Campbell, Raymond Mays, HOD Segrave, Parry Thomas and so on. It was that there were so many now unsung heroes. Participants who had achieved heights of motor racing prowess and performed deeds of outstanding valour, but are nowadays all but forgotten. Sportsmen and women who, if they were able to repeat their 'daring-do' today, would be household, front page, back page, 'in your face' names. But perhaps that is more accurately a reflection of today's puny, self-seeking, game show, so called 'celebs', up with which we now have to put! Surely were the TV jesters and fools of our present day to be transported back in time, to replicate their antics, in the 1920s and 1930s, they would, at the best, be regarded as 'fodder for bedlam'.

'Damned inconveniently' for me, Tom passed away as a comparatively young man, in 1956, aged only 53. Robin, the youngest son, was 19 at the time of his father's demise. The collective recollections of Tom's four off-spring are rather vague, somewhat ethereal and possibly 'secretive'. There's that word again! Apart from the already referred to press cutting albums, which burst into being in 1928 and ceased 'production' abruptly in 1930, there would appear to be very few, if any other family archives. Incidentally, the reason for the bulging folders will become apparent as the plot unfolds. Whatever, it is somewhat strange that Tom should have left so little 'hard' evidence of his sporting activities, achievements and, for that matter, his life. But, as may have been appreciated from previous references to the family, they were by nature – secretive, very secretive.

Thus, even determining the reason for his sobriquet 'Scrap' was a matter for conjecture. As the narrative reveals, during the period covered by this volume, he was without doubt a lean, debonair, very good looking, ladies-attractive, millionaire aristocratic. He was also quite probably a go-it-alone, aloof, single minded, somewhat narcissistic young playboy. No team player, our Tom was obviously not a 'bruiser' or a 'scrapper'. Thus my third or fourth thought was to consider the nickname was due to his being, 'for those days', a mere stripling when he started out motor racing, in amongst many old boys. He was still only 22 when he entered and drove his own special bodied, 3 litre Bentley in the 1926 Le Mans. Really, only 'a scrap of a boy'! Not an expression used very much, if ever, nowadays but quite a common one, in days of yore.

Mention of his Bentley entered for the 1926 Le Mans led to another, more probable reason for the 'moniker'. Late in 1924, a Bentley Motors a press release announced that some thirteen chassis had been damaged by fire, at the South London works of Gurney Nutting. It went on to advise that rogue motor traders (what, rogue motor traders? The very idea!) were

THE FORGOTTEN BENTLEY BOY.

Plate 8a. *The Driver: 'What do you think of these little things?'*
The Passenger: 'Make topping ash-trays.'

Plate 8b. *P.C.: 'You were doing forty miles an hour, Sir.'*
Motorist (whispering): 'Make it seventy, I'm trying to sell him the thing.'

PLATES 8A & B © PUNCH LTD. www.punch.co.uk

'misinterpreting' their output as the genuine Bentley product, based on these written off chassis'. Never! Despite all this righteous indignation and head-shaking, it is reliably and authoritatively stated that Bentley Motors themselves acquired a number of the fire damaged frames. They may or may not have reappeared in 'Bentley clothing', at a later date. Without doubt, several of them were kept around and about the Works and were given the acronym-like nickname *SCRAP*. There were known to be at least two – *SCRAP 1* and *SCRAP 2*. We are nearly there!

Reference to Chapter 4 reveals that Tom's favoured coachbuilder, Martin Walter, was given the almost impossible task of having to 'body' his brand new 3 litre Bentley in time for the 1926 Le Mans Race. The chassis, registered 30th April, was delivered early in May and the finished product had to be ready for racing and at the circuit before 12th June. In the very limited time available, they had the near impossible task of squeezing a 'quart sized', four seater body on to a 'pint sized' Bentley nine foot short chassis. To ease the problem of fitting the finished coach work to the yet to be delivered chassis, Martin's (or more probably Tom) went to the expense of purchasing a bare chassis, from Vanden Plas. This was put to use as a 'former' to which the body could be offered up, as many times as was necessary. Thus, when the actual rolling chassis arrived, there would be as few unexpected surprises as was possible. I suspect the chassis they acquired was one of the damaged (*SCRAP*) items. Thus, to those in the know, the pilot of this particular chariot was for ever afterwards referred to as Scrap Thistlethwayte. Bentley Motors were very touchy about the Gurney affair, so it is no wonder that neither WO Bentley (WO), nor any other executive aware of the situation, let slip how Tom 'caught' his nickname.

The whole cast of players, those who entered the 'lists' during the 1920s, would be too long and boring to be spelt out here, in some endless motor racing liturgy. Some identities are fleshed out as the narrative proceeds. But the following should give a feel of those with whom Tom not only competed, but wined and dined at the various venues he, his friends and acquaintances chose to live out their fast, if not frantic and hedonistic sporting lives. Mention has already been made of Campbell, Mays, Segrave and Parry Thomas. To these luminaries must be added the likes of Capt. Woolf Babe Barnato, Dr. Dudley Benjafield, Sir Henry Tiger Tim Birkin, Jean Chassagne, Frank Clement, Humphrey Cook, John Duff, the Dunfee brothers, George ET Eyston, Capt. Clive Gallop, Cmdr. Glen Kidston, Bernard Rubin and eccentric of all eccentrics, one Count Louis Zborowski (of *Chitty Bang, Bang* fame).

Any register of personalities is subject to personal interpretation, never more so than when dealing with vintage car enthusiasts. For instance Leon Cushman would ring bells with an Alvis enthusiast, whilst Lord Howe or Boris Ivanowski could well be a favourite with Alfa Romeo fans. A Bentley man would have heard of 'Bertie' Kensington Moir and a Bugatti aficionado would be cognoscente of Raymond Mays and Tazio Nuvolari, whilst Frazer Nash devotees would need no introduction to Aldington and Frazer-Nash. Mercedes disciples would revere such names as Rudolph Caracciola and Otto Merz. And so on.

Please do not think this sampling is the total company. Oh no! However, a 'taster' of the other members of the cast might well read as follows: Francis Richard Henry Penn Curzon (later 5th Earl/Lord Howe), Vernon Balls, Jack Barclay, JD Barnes, RA Beaver, Robert Benoist, JR Benson (later Lord Charnwood), Oliver Bertram, EL Bouts, C Brackenbury, the Hon. Mrs

Plate 9a. *"I spy with my little eye another fifty quid coming up."*

Speeding was a much cheaper misdemeanour in the days of this cartoon!

Plate 9b. *"While you're about it, ask him if he knows a good place for lunch."*

PLATES 9A & B COURTESY THE BEST OF BROCKBANK, RUSSELL BROCKBANK. DAVID & CHARLES.

Bruce & Victor Bruce, TW Carson, the Hon. Mrs Chetwynd, John Cobb, Adrian & Denis Conan Doyle (sons of Sir Arthur Conan Doyle), Count Conelli, Earl Cottenham, WM Couper, Miss Ivy Cummings, Baron d' Erlanger, Albert Divo, Kaye Don, Harold Eaton, K Eggar, JF Field, Capt. Fiennes, AW Fox, T Gillett, V Gillow, CRA Grant, WH Green, Kenelm Lee Guinness, Major Halford (*See* Page 155), F Hallam, Tommy Hann (Brooklands workshops and a competitor), CM Harvey, Capt. HE Hazelhurst, RS Hebeler, Gordon Hendy, Dan Higgins, JS Hindmarsh, N Holder, V Horsman, R Jackson, F King, Brian Lewis, ANL Maclachlan, DMK Marendaz, Alfred Moss (Stirling Moss' father), RG Nash, Hon. Richard Norton, RF Oats (OM English concessionaire), Mrs Kay Petre, HW Purdy, V Riley, Major L Ropner, T Rose-Richards, Capt. FHB Samuelson, Saunders-Davies, Mrs WB Scott, Robert Senechal, Chris Staniland, RC Stewart, E Thomas, PH Turnbull, HR Wellsteed, CR Whitcroft, AV Wilkinson, 'W Williams' (aka William Grover-Williams), HF Wolfe, B Harcourt-Wood and Beris Wood. Phew!

It must be noted, as far as Tom's fellow competitors are concerned, that this book is not the place to record their various manifold successes and record breaking activities, in all the events, over the years. Other books and publications do that so very much better.

Plate 10a. Higham House, the Zborowski Mansion.

Plate 10b. The Stable Block.

Plate 10c. The Coach House.
PLATES 10A, B & C COURTESY THE BROOKLANDS SOCIETY.

CHAPTER TWO

Tom. His Introduction to the Sport. 1924.

*'The actual building of roads devoted to motor cars is not for the near future,
in spite of many rumours to that effect'.*
HARPERS WORLD. 1920

If not previously, 1924 was the year during which Tom Thistlethwayte was introduced to the joys of motor racing. As has been explained, much of his life is shrouded in mystery. This is no more so than as to when he 'went' motor racing. I hope those readers I am lucky enough to ensnare will make due allowance for any omissions. I can only assure them this is not a plea to excuse sloppy research or effort. Whatever, I am sure some facts and figures that have eluded me, and or I have managed to omit or muddle, will subsequently come to light. They always do!

Thomas George Thistlethwayte (1859-1912) married Henrietta Louise James (aged 20 or 23, depending! There are discrepancies in the records) on 26th May 1900 and 'our' Tom was born on 17th December 1903. Tom's father passed away in 1912, when he was nearly nine years of age. His mother remarried a Col. William Stopford, one time of Rathmore, Kinsale, County Cork, on 10th September 1913. The Colonel was 57 and 'Master' Tom was a page at those formalities. Aged 68, the retired Colonel of the Kings Royal Rifles died on 10th January 1924, leaving Tom's mother a widow once again, aged 44 or 47 – depending!

Tom's country address, in the early 1920s, when he was a tender 21, was Gorsley House, Bridge, close by Canterbury. At that time, the village of Bridge and the surrounding area was a hotbed of motor racing activity. This was due to a certain Count Louis Zborowski also being domiciled in Bridge, at Higham Park. Amongst many other motor racing sportsmen (and women) who gathered at the latter mansion, Capt. Clive Gallop was a regular. He was the engineer responsible for overseeing the construction of the Count's enormous racing cars and was later to drive for Tom in the 1925 Boulogne Cup Grand Prix and to co-drive with

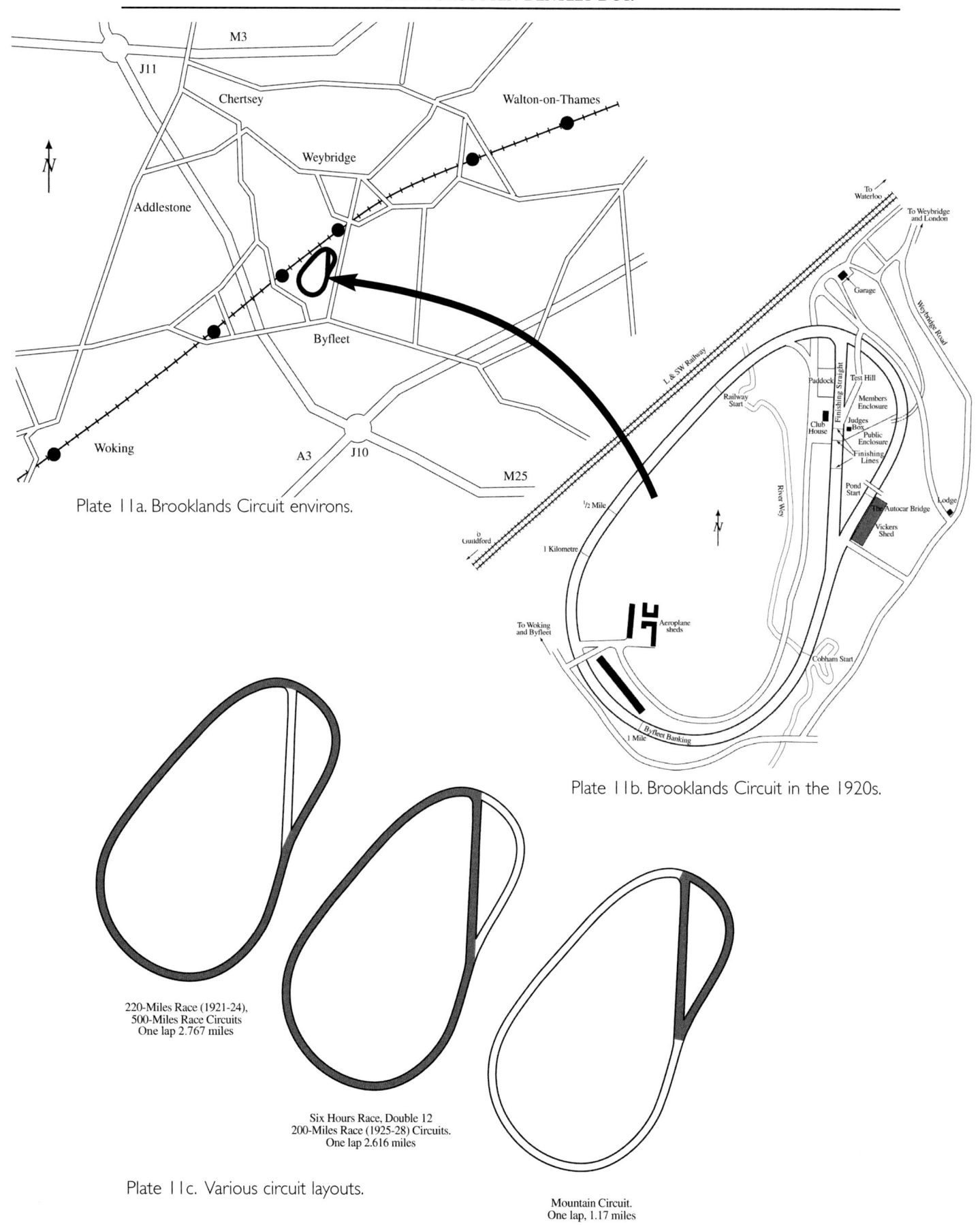

Plate 11a. Brooklands Circuit environs.

Plate 11b. Brooklands Circuit in the 1920s.

220-Miles Race (1921-24),
500-Miles Race Circuits
One lap 2.767 miles

Six Hours Race, Double 12
200-Miles Race (1925-28) Circuits.
One lap 2.616 miles

Mountain Circuit.
One lap, 1.17 miles

Plate 11c. Various circuit layouts.

him at the 1926 Le Mans. Other visitors included the Count's fellow miniature railway enthusiast and racing driver chum, Capt. JE Howey, as well as his brother Capt. RB Howey. Furthermore, both the Count and Parry Thomas were believers in competing in leviathan motors. So, no doubt, Tom, even if only a trackside spectator, was part of the 'Canterbury school of racers'. As a youngster he is reported to have careered around his step-father's Kinsale Estate. He may well have been 'motor-mad' before coming into contact with the heady mixture of like-minded, if more mature, Kentish based gentlemen of the track. It can come as no surprise that he subsequently entered the motor racing 'lists'.

All British circuit racing during the 1920s (and most of the 1930s* for that matter) took place at Brooklands, close to Weybridge, Surrey. Thus it is appropriate to include a few explanatory paragraphs in respect of the venue and its procedures. Most of my knowledge in respect of this subject has been gleaned from the pages of the 'Bible' – *Brooklands. The Complete Motor Racing History* by William Boddy.

BROOKLANDS RACING CIRCUIT. This historic location was the only track to host continuous British motor racing between 1907 and 1939*. That is apart from an understandable intermission due to the 'inconvenience' of the WW1 hostilities. Its creation and inception was entirely due to one man, Hugh Fortescue Locke King Esquire, who owned most of the surrounding land. To write that this was a very bold, courageous and expensive project, is almost an understatement. The 100 foot wide sweep of concrete surfaced track, with extensive banking, was approximately $2^3/_4$ miles round the centre line and is understood to have cost in excess of £150,000 to build. Quite a tidy sum in the early 1900s. The job commenced in 1906 and the first race meeting took place in the middle of 1907. The work force fluctuated between 300 and some 2,000 'navvies' and engineers.

To appreciate the benefits of this facility, it is only necessary to compare the track surface of Brooklands, to say that of Le Mans, in the 1920s. Weybridge offered a wide sweep of comparatively smooth concrete. Le Mans, for instance, was another story. There, in places, the track was nothing more than a corrugated, dry-dusty, wet-sludgy, stony flint and gravel, narrow cart track with uncertain verges. The differences were especially germane when considering the average vehicle raced in those days. Apart from cycle cars, which incurred their own specific problems associated with their comparatively light weight and flimsy construction, many of the racing cars were large and heavy, with high centres of gravity and uncertain suspension. Vehicles with inherent difficulties in handling, tyre wear and keeping the latter on their rims. Not only were tyres and wheels a great concern, but fuel and oil pipes, petrol tanks and headlights were all at risk from flying stones.

The venue was organised by the BARC (*Brooklands Automobile Racing Club*) and until 1914 drivers were distinguished by the jockey style, coloured smocks they wore. This latter stricture was not surprising when it is realised that many of the staff first drafted into assist in the organisation were Jockey Club officials. As the smocks were discarded, the practice took root of painting the car bodywork in distinctive colours, a practice still in evidence in the early 1920s. Individual numbers slowly emerged as the principle method of identifying a specific vehicle and driver.

---

* Donington Racing Circuit opened in 1931, but was initially only used for motorcycle races.

Plate 12. Count Zborowski and Capt. Clive Gallop prepare for the 1921 Brooklands 200 Mile Race to be held on the 22nd October. The engine of their Aston Martin was a prototype 16 valve, single overhead camshaft, 4 cylinder 1486cc unit, which proved to be unsuccessful. They finished in tenth place. However, the race marked the association of the Count with Aston Martin's, which lasted until his death in 1924. He invested some £10,000 to procure two new cars and engines in which to compete in the French Grand Prix at Strasbourg, in 1922.

COURTESY THE RACING ZBOROWSKIS. DAVID WILSON. VSCC LTD.

To ensure the racing was not processional, a system of handicapping evolved under the guiding hand of Mr AV Ebblewhite. He was entrusted with this duty from 1908, all the way through to 1939. The track-wise drivers were more often than not attempting to fool 'Ebby', in order to achieve an advantageous handicap. Nothing new there then! The timing systems were very sophisticated and reliable. As far as I have been able to ascertain, the handicapping was founded on a set number of minimum speed levels. As a generalisation, the finally accepted arrangement came down to 'Short' and 'Long Races', based on speeds of 75, 90 and 100 miles per hour (mph). A for instance being the '90 Long' – that is a long race lapping at an average speed of 90 mph. I stand ready to be corrected! In addition, there were 'Scratch Races', based on the RAC (*Royal Automobile Club*) horsepower rating, as well as 'Lightening Races'. The latter were for the fastest cars where a limited number of entrants were allowed on the grid and out and out speed was the order of the day. In addition, there were measured 'Distance' and 'Time Races' for cars within set swept cylinder bore dimensions. Of these events, two became very popular. One was the 'Six Hour Endurance Race', for production sports cars, in the Le Mans style of operation (dash across the track, hood up, put in some laps and then 'pit' to take the hood down). The other was the '200 Mile Race' (more correctly 180 miles), for vehicles up to 750cc, 1100cc and 1500cc. During the decade the 'Double Twelve Hour Race' evolved, being a two day event with the cars locked away over-night and operated under similar regulations to the 'Tourist Trophy Races'. This 'double twelve' procedure had to be followed as the local residents would not allow non-stop, 24 hour races to take place. Incidentally, the self same spoil-sports also enforced strict regulations in respect of the silencing of engines. Shades of modern day Goodwood. However, these indications and definitions are only that, as a variety of enterprising organisers and motor car clubs were forever tweaking the basic offerings. Additionally, they were wont to devise various innovative races, all depending on their continuing spectator popularity. In closing this subject, it would be remiss not to draw attention to the pivotal place occupied by Brooklands in the business of establishing a myriad of speed and distance records. During its lifetime the circuit was always being utilised for this and that endeavour, which are not only outside the scope of this book, but are very well documented elsewhere. But back to the narrative.

Fellow Performers.

Due to the recently ceased WW1 hostilities, the 1920s motor racing history was 'littered' with serving and 'demobbed' Armed Forces officers and gentlemen. Amongst these was Capt. Gallop (*See* Chapter 3) who would have been regarded as a star, if only for his undoubted engineering genius. Heady compliments? Well, not if it is appreciated it was he who engineered three monster racing cars (collectively and popularly nicknamed *Chitty Bang Bang*) as well as the *Higham Special*, all with and for the legendary:

COUNT LOUIS VOROW ZBOROWSKI (1895–1924). Despite the Zborowski family fortunes being based on American investments, Louis' father, Elliott, and mother, Margaret, enjoyed the English good life, more especially hunting to the hounds. Thus, a country estate

Plate 13a.   Count Louis Vorow Zborowski.

PLATES 13A & B COURTESY THE RACING ZBOROWSKIS. DAVID WILSON. VSCC LTD.

Plate 13b.   The 1921 Easter Brooklands Meeting with the Zborowski 'racing groupies' flanking *Chitty 1*. The 'caps' have it with from left to right: mechanic Godfrey Wigglesworth, a 'Miles', the Count, Capt. John (aka Jack) Hartshorne-Cooper and Major Richard 'Shugger' Hartshorne-Cooper MC. Jack, who was usually down to his last penny, was to die during practice for the subsequent Whitsun Meeting driving his Cooper-Clerget. This latter monster had a 20 litre, 200hp V8 Clerget power unit dropped into the chassis of his 1908 GP Mercedes.

was acquired close by Melton Mowbray. Elliott's wealth was founded on ownership of great swathes of the 'right side of the tracks' Manhattan, New York. And Mummy was no pauper. She was an Astor, the family of fabulously wealthy, American financiers, land owners and philanthropists. Enough said really.

In retrospect, it was not a good day for the Zborowski family when father Elliott decided to take-up motor racing, competing in the 1902 Paris to Venice junket. His new found enthusiasm came to an untimely end on 1st April 1903, whilst driving a new, 4 cylinder 60 hp Mercedes at the La Turbie Hill Climb Race, Nice. One of the reasons given for the accident was that his sizable cuff-links, coupled to large, stiff, double shirt-cuffs, caught up in the steering column mounted throttle and over-rode his attempts to slow down. As with many 'matters Zborowski', the event was presaged by a soothsayer warning of impending doom. The fortune-teller is alleged to have advised the Count that it was not a propitious day for him, that the omens for the 1st April were not good! Exactly! Louis was only eight years old when this disaster overtook the family. Years later this tragedy was to prove a ghastly omen, a 'hairs on the back of your neck' portent.

In 1910, widow Margaret decided to move herself and son Louis to Higham Park House and its extensive grounds, close to Bridge, near Canterbury. Although appearing to be a Georgian or even an early Victorian pile, the mansion had been constructed in 1904. Disaster struck again when Margaret died the following year. Louis now aged 16, Eton educated and quite alone in the world, inherited the title and an exceedingly large fortune. Fairly soon on, he came to the conclusion that his aspirations would be best suited by dedicating his life to spending, as fast as he could, on his immediate interests. Apart from a somewhat idiosyncratic propensity to building small dwellings in the Estate grounds, packing them with explosives and then blowing them up, he was also a small scale railway enthusiast. But the latter was no 'loft Hornby 00 set up'. Oh no! The irrepressible Count's railway interests lay in a full 15" gauge layout. His first venture was achieved by creating a railway line around his grounds. Over this ran a scale Atlantic locomotive, built by Basset Lowke. This obsession led him to gang-up with a fellow 'scale train nutter' – Capt. Jack EP Howey.

In February 1919 he married Violet (Vi) Ethel Leicester, an actress aged 22. Leicester was her father's stage name, her actual surname being Hiatt. Their union did not survive Zborowski being named as the co-respondent, in a High Court divorce case, in 1923. Subsequently, although apparently keeping up a civilised relationship, the Countess moved out of Higham, setting up home at 47 St. James Court, London. Intriguingly, this charming lady was to become involved with Tom, of which more later. Incidentally, during the period covered by this book, the steps of the Divorce Division of the High Court must have proved a very busy passing place for society girls and boys who had been actively committing acts of marital indiscretion.

But back to the nub of the matter, the motor cars. Aged 25, one of Louis' first recorded outings was in a 1914, 4.5 litre, 4 cylinder, 115hp, GP Mercedes, at Brooklands, on 2nd August 1920. He achieved a second and a fourth place. Thereon followed four years of 'home and abroad' racing, amongst which were a few hill climbs. For instance, on 25th March 1922 he put in an appearance at the Kop Hill Climb. He won his class in the 1919 Indianapolis 5 litre Ballot, previously driven by Jean Chassagne at Brooklands in 1920, where he achieved fastest

Fig 14a. *Chitty Bang Bang No. 1* or *Chitty 1*, as originally 'conceived', in front of Higham House.

PLATES 14A & B COURTESY THE RACING ZBOROWSKIS. DAVID WILSON. VSCC LTD.

Plate 14b. *Chitty II* with the Count seated and Clive Gallop on the far side running board.

lap of that year. A Tony Vandervell weighed in with a spirited performance in a two seater Sunbeam with a 6 cylinder, 4.9 litre 'Indy' engine fitted in a 1921 GP chassis, constructed that year. Also present were Woolf Barnato in his H6B Hispano-Suiza and Humphrey Cook in the *Rouge et Noir* Vauxhall 30-98.

The Zborowski racing band-wagon was more often than not accompanied by a gang of unconventionally attired, 'racing groupies', their clothing topped off with garish, large peaked, chequered American style golf caps. Apart from the monster aero-engined cars, the Count competed in: Mercedes; a 3 litre Talbot; a Salmson; Darracq; a 3 litre straight eight GP Sunbeam; Aston Martins; the Ballot; the rather ancient 200hp Burman-Benz (originally a Blitzen-Benz) which was such an 'interesting' drive as to make the Count think twice – it was eventually scrapped and parts used in the construction of the 'Higham Special'; Bugattis; H6B and H6C Hispano-Suizas* and a Miller. The listing of Aston Martins was very much due to his financial involvement with the firm, for a few years. Despite his rather mixed results with the marque, he was still a Director of the Company at the time of his death. Who knows what would have befallen Lionel Martin if Louis had still been alive in 1925? In May 1923 he competed with four other straight-eight, single overhead cam, 2 litre Type 30 Bugattis, in the Indianapolis 500. The Count had to retire. In fact only one of the team finished due to ill-preparation by the Molsheim factory. Clive Gallop was a reserve driver.

The majority of his motor racing escapades involved a series of Edwardian styled, aero-engined monsters, the construction, of which were organised by Capt. Reginald Clive Gallop. Known as Clive or *Gallô*, he had been introduced to Louis way back in 1912.

CHITTY BANG BANG NO. 1 or CHITTY 1. This chain drive conveyance was the progenitor of the car of music hall and film fame. It was basically a modified Mercedes chassis into which was 'dropped' a 23 litre, 6 cylinder, 300 hp, Maybach aero-engine. The latter engines were originally fitted to WW1 German bombers. This creation caused quite a stir on its first appearance at the Brooklands Easter Monday meeting, on 28th March 1921. To quote THE AUTOCAR. ' *...and thus early on one of the biggest attractions turned out. It was Count Zborowski's goodness-knows-how-many-horsepower Chitty Bang Bang – a huge Mercedes chassis with a nominal 500 hp Maybach Zeppelin engine. It was a pleasure to see Count Zborowski's handling of his car on the banking; he drove a perfect course.*' It was 'billed' to compete with a 350hp V12 engined Sunbeam**, developed and originally owned by Louis Coatelen. As the designated French driver 'did not show', Kenelm Lee Guinness stood in but gearbox trouble eliminated the car. John Duff's 10 litre FIAT was second to *Chitty*, whilst Zborowski's 1914 GP Mercedes, driven by Jack Hartshorne-Cooper, came in third. '*Again Count Zborowski's driving was much appreciated by those who realise that to lap at well over 110 mph is not exactly child's play*'. Zborowski, mixing and matching his rides in *Chitty* and the Mercedes, achieved three firsts and a second place. Also appearing at this event were Woolf Barnato, in his 6 cylinder Locomobile, and HRS Birkin, in his DFP.

It appears the Count was accustomed to drive to and from his home, using the trade plates of the coach work builders, Messrs Bligh Brothers. This St. Radigunds, Canterbury based

---

* See Page 190 for a Hispano-Suiza H6 resumé.
** In this car Malcolm Campbell broke the World Land Speed Record in 1924. It later appeared in the 'hands' of the band leader Billy Cotton (1936), an ERA driver.

Plate 15a. *Chitty III*, which was intended to facilitate touring in Europe with style. Here parked 'somewhere' in France.

Plate 15b. The *Higham Special*.

PLATES 15A & B COURTESY THE RACING ZBOROWSKIS. DAVID WILSON. VSCC LTD.

firm, which he finished up owning, 'threw together' the somewhat crude, angular bodywork of *Chitty*. On its debut, despite the car's unattractive appearance, two firsts were achieved, beating the V12 Sunbeam, as well as a second place. It has been suggested that the original coachwork (or lack of ...) was an attempt to pull the wool over the eyes of Mr Ebblewhite, the Brooklands handicapper. On 28th of September 1922, during practice for the Brooklands Autumn Race meeting, a tyre stripped off its wheel rim causing *Chitty* to hit the banking, spin out of control and crash through an official timing hut. The driver was fine, a track marshal lost a few fingers, another was narrowly missed and the car lost its front axle. Despite being rebuilt, Zborowski did not compete in this vehicle again at this circuit. Later re-bodying did little to solve the styling matter. After the Count's demise *Chitty* 'had a rest', languishing in a Kentish shed. Subsequently, it was purchased from Capt. Jack Howey, by Adrian and Dennis Doyle, the twin sons of the world famous author, Sir Arthur Conan Doyle. They did not achieve any success with it. However, the 'Conan Doyle' boys did compete in various other racing cars, during the 1920s. In 1934 Chitty was reported as being dragged to the Brooklands Circuit, where it was placed on display. Subsequently it was rolled away, to 'hunker down' behind one of the many sheds, prior to being broken up for parts!

CHITTY 11. Closely following on No. 1, *Chitty 11* competed alongside its predecessor, late in the 1921 season. Similarly chain-driven and based on a Mercedes chassis, this vehicle was powered with a pre-war, 18.8 litre, 6 cylinder Benz aero-engine power unit. It was not a racing success. Despite or because of this, *Chitty 11* was utilised as a 'damned' fast road car and, on one memorable occasion, served as a conveyance for the Count, his wife and a coterie of chums to take a well earned rest in the Sahara Desert. Yes the Sahara..., early in 1922!

CHITTY 111. Once again a Mercedes chassis and originally powered by a 15 litre Mercedes engine, but this 'model' was prop-shaft driven. The two seater body allowed for a large luggage space to be 'thrown' on to the chassis. It was completed in time for Capt. Gallop to be able to accompany the *Chitty 11* Sahara party, into the desert. Sounds reminiscent of a plot for one of the Bob Hope and Bing Crosby 'Road to...' films!

CHITTY IV. Due to the Count's death this project did not see the light of day.

THE HIGHAM SPECIAL. Completed for the 1923 season, this truly massive, two seater car was powered by a 27 litre, V12 Liberty aero-engine fitted into a rather skimpy chassis. Originally it suffered from some flexing, which must have proved rather exciting. After the Count's premature demise, this monster was acquired by Parry Thomas. He rebuilt it, renamed it *'Babs'*, and died whilst hurtling over the Pendine Sands, in a World Record Speed attempt in 1927 (*See* Chapter 3).

Before leaving these particular cars, it might be opportune to put in a 'pennies worth' as to the origin of the catch phrase '*Chitty, Chitty Bang Bang*'. It has been suggested that the nomenclature resulted from the sound of the exhaust note of *Chitty 1*. However, bearing in mind the nature of the Count and his band of followers, it was more than likely based upon

Plate 16. Countess 'Vi' Zborowski.
COURTESY WWW.OLD-PICTURE.COM/AMERICAN-HISTORY-1900-1930S
6285-14

a WW1 British Army ditty. Reverting to slang, *'Chit'* denoted a young woman and *'Bang Bang* – crudely described an act of procreation! Sorry to shatter all those film-based illusions. Some point out that *Chit* referred to the pass necessary for officers to escape their war duties for a Paris weekend and the *'Bang Bang …'* take your pick.

It has been noted that 1924 was the year in which the legendary Count Louis Vorow Zborowski met his death. Apart from the sadness of any such occasion, his passing was especially poignant. For a number of years he had wished to equal his father's achievement of being offered a Mercedes Works Team drive. Finally, this came about. The selection was the result of his generally outstanding racing record over the years. This reputation had been reinforced by a particularly fine display of driving his American made, 2 litre, straight eight Miller, in the 1924 French Grand Prix held at the then Lyons circuit. Admittedly, he retired during the race, but only after a virtuoso performance against superior machinery.

Thus it came about that Dr. Ferdinand Porsche offered Zborowski, now aged 29, the chance to join the Mercedes Team. That was to pilot a brand new, 170 hp, supercharged, 2 litre, straight eight Mercedes, in the 1924 Monza Italian Grand Prix. It was reported that the 'projectile' handled badly in the bends. The race was originally scheduled to take place on 7th September. This proposed date was put back to 19th October, in part due to the Mercedes entries not being ready on time. The team of four works drivers included Alfred Neubauer, to become the famed manager of the pre-WW2 Mercedes racing team. The reserve driver was a Rudolph Caracciola. He was to finish up with some twenty Grand Prix wins, plus many other racing circuit successes, and was regarded, by many, as the greatest racing driver – ever.

Eerily, and some say in an act of determined defiance of any superstition in respect of his father's demise, the Count wore the self-same cuff links which Elliott had worn, when he crashed and died in 1903. Furthermore he refused several offers and opportunities to scratch this, his first Mercedes team chance. During the race, on lap 43, while in seventh place and whilst negotiating the Lesmo curve, his car careered off the track. It smashed through some track-side netting, finally crashing into a tree. The Count died immediately. One report stated the impact was so great as to drive his head back into his chest. By a strange quirk of fate, his riding mechanic, crouching well down beneath the scuttle, survived.

Had he lived on during the 1920s some intriguing possibilities might have occurred? Apart from the Aston Martin situation, it is thought-provoking to consider what might have happened at Bentley Motors? That is if not only Woolf Barnato's vast wealth and energy, but also the Count's matching resources and innovative mind, had both been attracted to that particular marque?

The widowed Vi inherited large property holdings and a substantial annual income. Somewhat inconveniently, the will left the Count's erstwhile 'lady friend' a lump sum – for services rendered? She was the reason behind all the 'matrimonial's' and was by now a resident of Mayfair, London. The Countess organised, payment of the inheritance money – with some disdain. She also advised the adulteress to keep a Rolls-Royce motor car. This vehicle had been 'bouncing' back and forth, between the Count and Mrs Marix, depending if a row or reconciliation was the present state of play in their reportedly very stormy relationship! Vi sold Higham House to one Walter Whigham, a banker. Walter's wife did not

SAT ON DEAD MAN'S LAP AND STEERED TO EARTH

British Aviator Tells of Thrilling Fight With Germans in Mid-air

Lieut.-Observer J. E. P. Harvey,* an officer of the Bedfordshire Yeomanry, and attached to the Royal Flying corps, who was recently captured by the Germans, has sent the following description of a battle in mid-air, telling how he was treated after his capture:—

"I had a fight with two German aeroplanes when a shell burst very close to us, and I heard a large piece whizz past my head. Then the aeroplane started to come down head first, spinning all the time. We must have dropped about 5,000 feet in about twenty seconds. I look round at once and saw poor —— with a terrible wound in his head, dead.

"Then I saw that the only chance of saving my life was to step over into his seat and sit on his lap, where I could reach his controls. I managed to get the machine out of the terrible death plunge, switched off the engine, and made a good landing.

"I shall never forget it as long as I live. The shock was so great that I could hardly remember a single thing of my former life for two days. Now I am getting better and my mind is practically normal again.

Shook Hands With Enemy Pilot

"We were 10,000 feet up when poor —— was killed and, luckily, it was this tremendous height that gave me time to think and to act.

"I met one of the pilots of the German machines that had attacked us. He could speak English well, and we shook hands after a most thrilling fight. I had brought down his machine with my machine gun, and he had to land quite close to where I landed. He had a bullet through his radiator and petrol tank, but neither he nor his observer was touched.

"Two German officers I met knew several people that I knew, and they were most awfully kind to me. They gave me a very good dinner of champagne and oysters, etc., and I was treated like an honored guest. I then came by train the next day to Mainz, where I was confined in a room by myself for two days. I have now been moved into a general room with eight other English officers, where we sleep and eat. We are treated very well and play hockey and tennis in the prison yard."

Plate 17a. This was No. 6 Squadron flying FE2a aircraft on 22nd March 1916. The dead pilot was 19 year old 2nd Lieut. Kelway-Bamber. Howey either escaped or was transferred to a Swiss interment camp in 1917 and repatriated later that year.

COURTESY CALGARY DAILY HERALD.

• actually Howey.

Plate 17b. (Capt.) John Edward Presgrave Howey driving a Greenly designed Atlantic scale locomotive at his Staughton Manor Estate. The dog seems to be enjoying the ride!

COURTESY RH&DR. HISTORY, WWW.RHDR.ORG.UK

wish to be known as Mrs Whigham of Higham (!), thus the place was renamed Highland Court. 'Damned' strange people these banker's wives. Possibly, of more interest was that Walter was Uncle to an Ethel Margaret Whigham, later and more famously to become Margaret Campbell, Duchess of Argyll. She is germane to our story due to her brief involvement with another of our star performer's. This was Cmdr. Glen Kidston, who was to be Tom's best man on the occasion of his second marriage. But to return to the matter in hand. After some years, the Countess married Pat Singer, one of the Sewing Machine dynasty and in the early 1930s decamped to the USA.

Before 'departing' the Count, it would be remiss not to detail his involvement in probably his most enduring monument, namely the:

THE ROMNEY, HYTHE AND DYMCHURCH RAILWAY. Whilst all the motor racing was roaring on, the Count and Capt. 'Jack' EP Howey were planning to construct a 13½ mile long, part double-tracked, coastal railway line, running from Hythe, south of Folkestone, all the way round to Dungeness. Yes, a …! Howey had already commissioned Basset Lowke to build a scale Pacific 'loco', for his Staughton Manor railway project. The Captain was not only a small gauge railway enthusiast but, you've guessed it, a racing driver. Once again the coincidences keep going round to come round! For his part Zborowski ordered two new railway engines for the proposed scheme. These were to be built by the Colchester based firm of Davey, Paxman & Co. His death (obviously) precluded him from proceeding with the Romney project. Notwithstanding which, 'Capt. Jack' determined to commence and complete the arrangement. He was of 'sufficient', if possibly lesser means than the Count. His financial strength was fortunate as the construction proved to be very costly. Work started in 1926 and was completed in July the following year. Still part-finished, the project was opened, with much fanfare and a short trip for such dignitaries as the Duke of York (later to be King George VI) and Sir Nigel Gresley, designer of the famous LNER Pacific locos. This was no fly-by-night, here-one-day, gone-the-next whim. Allowing for a period when the line was commandeered, during WW2, Howey's ownership continued until he passed away in 1963. It is said, during his lifetime, that he would not invest any more money in the scheme, maintaining it had been built to last a life-time! Subsequently, his wife Gladys sold the remarkable enterprise.

CAPT. JOHN 'JACK' EDWARD PRESGRAVE HOWEY. (1887-1963). Born at Amersham, Buckinghamshire, Presgrave was the maternal surname. His wealth apparently originated from family land investments in and around Melbourne, Australia. It may well be that he inherited the central business district of that city. His wartime experiences demonstrated and foretold his amazing native grit and tenacity. His motor racing career was almost entirely tied-in with his friendships with Zborowski and Parry Thomas. In 1923 he appeared in a Leyland Thomas, in 1924 in *Chitty 1* (which he acquired or at least took responsibility for, after the Count's death), in 1925 in a Leyland Thomas and in 1926 in *Chitty 111*. He ceased competing for a year or two following the death of his brother, Capt. Richard Barstow Howey, during the August 1926 Boulogne Race Week (*See* Chapter 4). His lasting testament must be the near heroic completion and ownership of the aforementioned railway.

Plate 18a. Tom's Vauxhall 30-98 Reg. No. NM 6417. Factory erection date 23/4/25. Chassis No. OE 233. Engine No. OE 233.

Plate 18b.   To the left is the two seater, Kellner bodied 'Monza' H6C Hispano-Suiza previously owned by Count Louis Zborowski and here the property of Clive Gallop. To the right is Tom's 30-98. This picture was taken by Anthony Heal at Brooklands, circa 1925.

Plates 18a & b Courtesy Vauxhall 30-98 The Finest Sporting Car, Nic Portway. New Wensum Publishing.

Chapter Three

Tom. Marriage and Motor Racing. 1925.

The automotive has practically reached the limit of its development as no new improvements of a radical nature has been introduced this year'.
SCIENTIFIC AMERICAN 1909

Without apparently very much fanfare and, for that matter, pomp or circumstance, Arthur Donald Claude Thomas (Tom) Thistlethwayte, aged 21, quietly married for the first time. On 6th January 1925, he and Ethel Mary ('Nettie') Hickie, a 22 year old spinster, took their respective vows. The ceremony took place in the C12th Church of St. Mary the Virgin, in the attractive Kentish village of Elham. Tom's mother, Henrietta Louise Stopford, was a witness but was alone as her second husband had passed away, almost a year previously. The union resulted in the birth of a son, Thomas Noel, on 8th October that year, but that was probably the only tangible good to come from the arrangement.

Having dealt with the domestics, 1925 was the year in which Tom commenced motor racing in earnest. This was the year when he really got the 'tyre between his teeth', as it were. His initial plan was to proceed with caution. In spite of this caveat, he ordered two cars. One in which he could compete in various low key events, that is other than out and out racing. The other was for his now close chum, Capt. Clive Gallop, to seriously thrash round the circuits. He certainly did not take half measures.

His selected chariot was none other than a Vauxhall 30-98 (Reg. No. NM 6417). The choice of this model was possibly due to his recently near neighbour Louis Zborowski's ownership of one of these fine vehicles. A decision that may well have also been influenced by other similarly mounted competitors such as Humphrey Cook *(Rouge et Noir)* and Major Ropner *(Silver Arrow)*. The coachwork Tom commissioned for the 30-98 was a modish, if classy two

Plate 19a   Tom's 1500cc Frazer Nash being prepared for the 1925 season.

COURTESY FRAZER NASH DAVID THIRLBY. HAYNES. FOULIS.

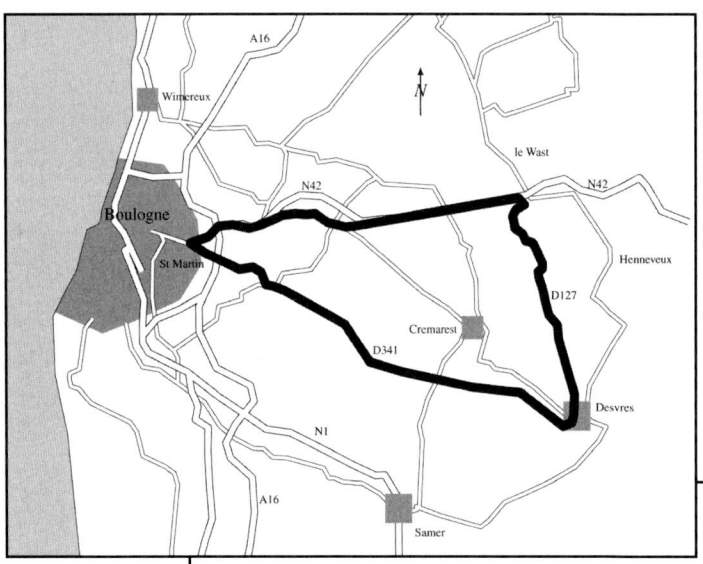

Plate 19b.   The 1925 Boulogne environs and Circuit details.

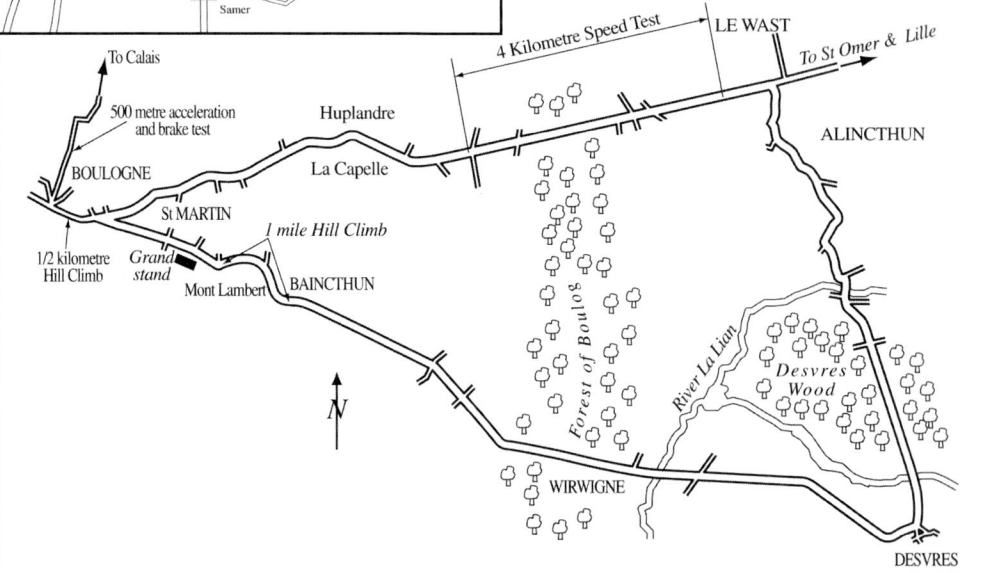

seater sports body from Martin Walter. This choice of the latter business marked the onset of a long relationship with the Folkestone company. The colour scheme was variously described as a dove grey or an ivory body, with red wings but the official registration document details a 'Dove body'. It may come as no surprise to note that the style of coachwork was similar to a Kellner creation 'bolted on' to the two seater, 6 cylinder, 8 litre, 'Monza' H6 Hispano-Suiza that had been owned by the now deceased Count Zborowski (*See* Plate 18b). Well, there's a shock. Incidentally, the Count had also owned a four seater, 6 litre H6 Hispano-Suiza.

The racing machine Tom selected for Clive Gallop to drive was ordered from Frazer Nash (Reg. No. PE 5074). It was to have a lowered, shortened, lightened chassis, fitted with front wheel brakes (a comparative rarity for light cars in those days). Furthermore, it was the first of this company's vehicles to be powered by a 1500cc, side-valve Anzani power unit. Tom advised *"That money was effectively no object"*, which probably encouraged the Work's to build another, similar vehicle. For the latter, Frazer Nash used their usual firm, Love's of Kingston, as the nominated coach builder. The bodywork for Tom's car was once again supplied by Martin Walter. The only noticeable difference in the two Frazer's was that the Martin Walter creation was somewhat slimmer. It will be noted that Tom's 'loner' streak of individuality was prevalent from day one, as it were. I bet a 'sump full of oil' he could be both fastidious and finicky as a customer. Granted, he was the client and was paying the piper.

THE AUTOCAR carried a report of a two-day Skegness Sands Race meeting (12th June). The entry list included Malcolm Campbell, driving his 12 cylinder, 350 hp Sunbeam *'Blue Bird'*. Raymond Mays, having 'signed up' with SF Edge (of Napier fame) and AC Cars was piloting a prototype supercharged 1500cc AC, a project that failed. Other 'notables' included: HS Eaton (Gwynne); H Aldington and A Frazer-Nash, as to be expected in Frazer Nash's; L Cushman (Crossley); and Capt. JEP Howey (Leyland Eight). Also present was EA Mayner, a British Mercedes salesman, driving a supercharged, 2 litre Targa Florio type Mercedes. He achieved Fastest Time of the Day (FTD) in beating off Howey's Leyland, Malcolm Cambell's Sunbeam, Joyce's AC and Tom's 30-98 Vauxhall. On the second day Tom achieved a second in the Handicap, for cars over 1500cc, behind Mrs Christie (Vauxhall 30-98), who had a better handicap, as well as a third in the Handicap for cars of Unlimited Capacity. THE AUTOCAR critique advised '.... *whilst Thistlethwayte's streamlined Vauxhall proved it could travel to some purpose*'. There's damning praise indeed. Mayner also had a good 'day two'. The rising tide terminated the meeting somewhat earlier than expected.

The chosen venue for Tom's grand entrance was the:

1925 BOULOGNE AUTOMOBILE WEEK (27-30th August). This was rather more a four day event, run in and over a very interesting $23^{1}/_{3}$ mile long, almost triangular circuit. On the very wet and wretched Thursday 27th, a number of speed trials were held over a four kilometre stretch of the Le Wast to Boulogne section of the circuit. In addition a series of hill climbs were staged up out of Boulogne town, along a 1 in 10, tram-lined street, towards Desvres. Tom, driving his Vauxhall 30-98, gained a first in the over 3000cc Racing Car Class Speed Trial, as well as the *Crouy Cup* for the fastest Racing Car time overall. A fellow entrant, Parry Thomas, in one of his Leyland-Thomas giants, rather spoilt his chances during practice. Following a dramatic 100 mph skid, he and the car terminated up against a tree.

The 1925 Boulogne Automobile Week.

Plate 20a. Tom 'en-course' in his 30-98 during the 1925 Boulogne Automobile Week.
Courtesy Vauxhall 30-98 The Finest of Sporting Cars, Nic Portway. New Wensum Publishing.

Plate 20b. Clive Gallop (No. 1) in the Frazer Nash with co-driver H Scott checking the grid. To the right is Ringwood's Frazer Nash (more a 200 Mile 1100cc GN), but repainted and rebadged to reinforce the 'British-ness' of the Frazer Nash entry.

Plate 20c. The 'off' with Ringwood (No. 2) ahead of Gallop. Behind and to the right is Lewis (No. 4) in a 1100cc Frazer Nash. This was actually owned by B Eyston and known as the 'Rodeo Special', behind which is Archie Frazer-Nash (No. 3) in the 'sister' car to Tom's Frazer Nash.

Plate 20d. Gallop & Scott celebrating their victory.
Plates 20b, c & d Courtesy Frazer Nash, David Thirlby. Haynes. Foulis.

Result – car wrecked – Parry Thomas – badly bruised and pretty 'browned-off'. Competing in the Hill Climb, Tom's Vauxhall is reported *'To have made a fast, clean and impressive climb'*. Just so! Friday was the day of the *Concours d'Elegance*, in which the Vauxhall was entered. Saturday the 29th heralded the onset of the Grand Prix de Boulogne. This turned out to be yet another damp, horrid day. The race was of 12 laps or 280 miles duration and was for light cars of no more than 1500cc. There were two classes, one up to 500kg and the other up to 650kg. The organisers assumed that the heavier vehicles would provide the winner and thus offered a separate prize for the lighter cars, namely the *Boulogne Grand Prix de Voiture Legere*. Gallop set the fastest record-breaking lap of 67.72 mph but due to a 6½ minute plug-change pit stop was piped at the post by S Marshall, in a Brescia Bugatti, by some two minutes. And that in a race lasting 2 hours 20 minutes. Thus, Capt. Gallop, and his riding mechanic Harold Scott, finishing second, won the race and Marshall, finishing first, only won the 'Voiture Legere'. Rather unfair really! It has to be admitted there were conflicting reports as to whom finished first and second. THE MOTOR magazine reported *'... that Frazer-Nash, accompanied by CW Johnstone, disappeared for about one and a half hours, due to cornering in such a manner as to rip two tyres off their rims'*. Despite this incident, Archie was of the opinion that he had been able to reach 75 mph – on the rims alone! Frazer Nash won the Team Trophy, the eponymous *Pickett Cup*. It was named after FN Pickett*, known as the uncrowned 'King of Boulogne' and the driving force behind creating the event, in 1921. He also caused much of the circuit road track to be resurfaced. There are grounds to maintain this event could have been renamed the *Frazer Nash Benefit*. Gallop's companion HR Scott was both chief draughtsman of Frazer Nash and AG Frazer-Nash's right-hand man, whilst Mr Pickett was a director of Frazer Nash. There's cosy! Before leaving this event it is worth reporting that a B Ivanowski competed in a 1 litre SCAP engined BNC (the French manufacturer Bollack, Netter et Cie). Ivanowski was to achieve much fame later in the decade (*See* Chapter 7). Capt. Gallop's win gave him a Gold medal for the fastest lap and Tom an eighth place in that year's *National Drivers Championship for Voiturette, Light cars & Vetturettes (Unofficial)* Max. Capacity 1.5 litres Minimum Mass 650kg. The press had one or two comments in respect of Tom's performance as follows: *'...Thistlethwayte's beautiful ivory Vauxhall, a svelte, streamlined streak that flung high sheets of spray from its whirling wheels and roared over the crest of a hill, down into a hollow, and out of sight, in an incredibly short space of time, over the next ridge'*. And *'This...on the Vauxhall (who had been transferred to the racing car class) failed to see the finishing line, cut out too soon, saw his mistake and raced on again'*. Yet another report, but not 'Tom based', advised that: *'The hissing, hooting and stoning* (by the spectators) *of a wretched little black dog from the top to the bottom of the hill provided more excitement than did any of the hill climbs'*. Report it as you find it, but those 'johnny foreigners' never were animal lovers. The Sunday Race was for the Georges Boillot Cup Race. Although neither of our 'heroes' were entered in this event for touring trim vehicles, it is worth reporting a couple of the incidents which occurred. R Senechal in an 1100cc Chenard-Walcker (the '*Invincible Chenards*') overcooked the Desvres village corner and crashed through the

---

* Francis Pickett owned a construction company but became a millionaire due to a post WW1 contract to deactivate the millions of tons of unused and unexploded ammunition and their dumps. In pursuit of this activity he operated some nine factories, employing up to 10,000 staff in the Boulogne area.

Plate 21a.   Actress Carita Redmayne in June 1931 at which time she was owner of Tom's Vauxhall 30-98 .
COURTESY VAUXHALL 30-98 THE FINEST OF SPORTING CARS, NIC PORTWAY. NEW WENSUM PUBLISHING.

Plate 21b.   Parry Thomas seated in the second of the 'Flat Iron' Thomas Specials in 1926…

Plate 21c.   …and a front view.
PLATES 21B & C COURTESY PARRY THOMAS DESIGNER DRIVER, HUGH TOURS.
BATSFORD LTD.

temporary barriers into the entrance of a cafe-bar. Another 'eye-catching' moment was recorded in the pages of *The Motor*, wherein was captured a photographic image of the 2 litre Type 30 Bugatti of Chandon de Braille. The dramatic picture detailed his mechanic gripping on for dear-life, as he scrambled alongside and over the bonnet and front wing. This was to make adjustments, whilst the Bugatti roared along at full speed. Yes, just as prescribed in the official manuals! Rather less amusingly, a Mr Matthys, in a 2 litre Bignan, experienced a carburettor backfire. The resultant flames accessed the fuel tank, with the result that the scuttle became a blazing inferno. The riding mechanic leapt out at some 70 mph, fracturing his skull and subsequently succumbed to his injuries. The driver appeared at the pits rather badly burnt, carried in by the other Bignan which was competing.

After the 'high' of the comparatively 'Thistlethwayte successful' weekend, a Folkestone 'boy in blue' apprehended Tom for speeding in his Vauxhall. He was fined £10.00. Typical!

Sometime towards the end of this propitious year, he 'offloaded' his beautiful Vauxhall 30-98. Nic Portway, author and publisher of the quite outstanding book *Vauxhall 30-98 The Finest of Sporting Cars*, advised that a vehicle which exactly fitted the description of his car was advertised for sale, by a London dealer, in *The Autocar* issue of 6th May 1927. Nic also reports that the next time it turned up, in June 1931, it was in the possession of a *'sometime actress, Carita Redmayne'*. The 'how and when' of the disposal of the Frazer Nash is not known. The car was returned to the works for a horseshoe style radiator to be fitted, on the instructions of Mr Thistlethwayte. It may well be that it was 'recycled' by the firm to another client as Tom was to completely rethink his chosen steeds for 1926.

In fact his next racing car purchase was probably the most interesting, expensive and, as it turned out, unsuccessful competition decision he ever made. An order was placed with Parry Thomas for one of his brand new, very innovative and comparatively complex designs. This was the 1.5 litre, supercharged, 8 cylinder, 'Flat Iron' Thomas Special. I believe the *Flat Iron* 'nickname' was to do with the very advanced shape of the car – low, rectangular and squat (rather reminiscent of the 1960s racing machines). It was reported that Tom was guided in this decision by his friend Capt. Gallop. Due to the comparatively recent demise of Count Louis Zborowski, Clive was probably still at a loose end. Delivery was planned for the 1926 season. Parry Thomas depended on private client orders and that of Tom's was presumably a godsend. Without doubt, it enabled him to operate what is nowadays known, if somewhat misquoted, as the *'SOGOF'* principal – sell one, get one free! That is, Tom's purchase helped pay for the second car, which Parry Thomas built and competed in himself. However, it may well be that the deal did not entirely cover the cost of the second car, because Parry Thomas's Special ran unblown during his lifetime.

The Autocar intoned as follows:

> The first Thomas Special, which is the property of T Thistlethwayte, is almost complete. The second, which is for JGP Thomas himself, is far from ready when one considers that the race is as near as the first week of next month. Both cars have ingenious chassis distinctly in the Thomas manner. The engines are straight-eights of 52 by 88mm. bore and

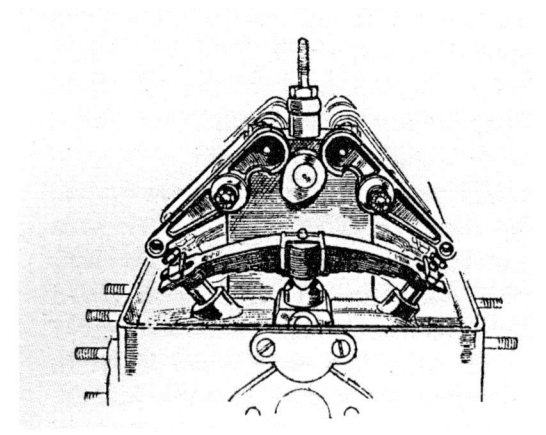

Various construction details from the Autocar of the 1.5 litre 8 cylinder 'Flat Iron' Thomas Special.

Plate 22a.   Central camshaft and leaf spring operated valves.

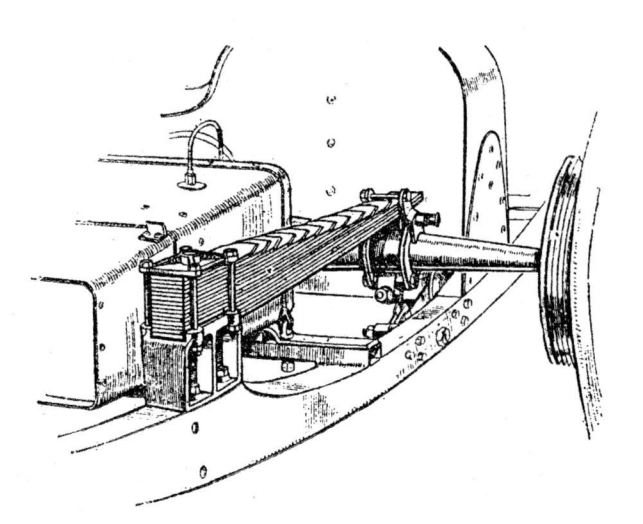

Plate 22b.   Rear axle and suspension.

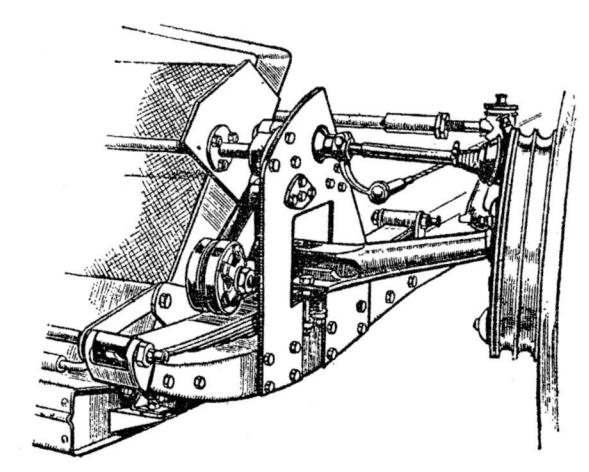

Plate 22c.   Front axle and brake layout.

PLATES 22A, B & C COURTESY AUTOCAR.

stroke, cylinder barrels and jackets being of aluminium with steel liners for the pistons. There is a detachable head, and in the place of the connecting rod and eccentric drive for the camshaft, a train of spur gears has been employed. The valves, of which there are two to each cylinder, have the typical leaf spring of the Thomas design, and the same type of operating mechanism as the Leylands. Both engines have plain bearings, though the white metal used is not the same in each case, and both have a Roots supercharger at the front end of the crankcase *(this was not to be, for details of which read the previous text).*

In this respect there is an unusual point in that the superchargers are water cooled, the water passing round the inside of the casing from the engine, while, as is modern practice, the supercharger sucks from the carburettor instead of blowing through it.

As the engine is high relative to the frame, though low relative to the ground, a separate water tank is fitted in the scuttle to maintain sufficient head for the radiator, which is inclined backwards at a sharp angle. For the lubrication a separate pump is employed, the crankcase being scavenged by a second oil pump. The very ingenious fabric multi-plate clutch which Thomas has used with success for some time is naturally embodied in this design, and behind the clutch there is only a single universal joint.

The gearbox mechanism is interesting because the gear lever movement from first to second involves the passage of the lever through the gate, yet the change from third to top entails another movement through the gate so that the path of the lever would be drawn as an X. To anyone except the designer-driver, this would seem likely to introduce considerable difficulties.

The frame is underslung, the engine and other components therefore, being maintained at their proper height by brackets. The purpose of dropping the frame to this extent is to bring the position of the driving seat much lower than usual; the centre of gravity of the car, in fact, is extremely low. All four brakes are operated by the pedal, but can be actuated also by the hand lever, which, again in accordance with Thomas's usual custom, pushes forward instead of pulling back.

The Motor, not to be outdone, advised:

As the minimum weight for Grand Prix racers has been increased for next year, there is no longer the same need to cut down weight to the utmost. Consequently, Mr. Thomas has decided to take full advantage of the superior rigidity of a cast-iron crankcase, as compared with one made of aluminium. Large inspection plates permit of easy examination of the big end bearings.

The cylinders are separate units of cast-iron, and fit into aluminium jackets, which are cast in pairs. The head is of cast-iron, with all the combustion chambers machined to a perfect hemispherical form and provided with two tulip valves per cylinder. The joint between the cylinders and the head is a copper-asbestos washer, while rubber and linen rings separate the head and water jackets. This arrangement allows for the expansion of the cylinders and water jackets when the engine reaches normal running temperature.

The rockers are of large size, as indeed are most of the parts of the engine. The Thomas Special power unit is, in effect, what Strickland would term "a large engine with small

Plate 23a. Clive Gallop, driving Zborowski's 5 litre Ballot, achieved a first whilst the Count gained a third in the same car at the 1922 Brooklands October Race meeting.

Plate 23b. Count Zborowski seated in his special bodied straight eight, 2 litre Type 30 Bugatti, with Clive Gallop to the right and Major Richard 'Shugger' Hartshorne-Cooper to the left. They were one of five Type 30 Buggatis entered in the 1923 Indianapolis 500. The Argentinian agent, Martin de Alzaga, purchased three of them, which formed the factory Works Team to be driven by himself, P. de Vizcaya and R. Riganti. Zborowski's and de Cystria's Type 30s were private entries. Despite all being made race-ready at Molsheim (the Bugatti factory), they were totally unprepared for the special requirements and rigours of the American 'brickyard' circuit. Only one finished, in ninth place. Zborowski went out on lap 47 with a broken con. rod.

PLATES 23A & B COURTESY THE RACING ZBOROWSKIS. DAVID WILSON. VSCC LTD

cylinders". It is hoped to get a speed of some 6500 rpm and this naturally necessitates large bearings and a relatively heavy crankshaft.

The clutch, which is of the multi-disc type and only about 3½ ins. In diameter, consists of a large number of die-pressed Ferodo plates, from the edges of which the drive is taken direct, and steel plates. A massive spherical universal joint, supported in a phosphor-bronze housing, transmits the power to the gearbox, which is mounted on the forward end of the torque tube. Giving four forward speeds and reverse, the box is designed on very robust lines, all gears being of large dimensions. The constant-mesh pinions are at the back. The back axle is of unorthodox design and very interesting, but we are not at present permitted to divulge the secret of its design. Let it suffice that it is of the fully floating type, the driving shafts being of very substantial dimensions.

The chassis frames, constructed by Messrs Rubery, Owen & Co., resemble sledges, for the dumb-irons curve upwards at each end. The whole frame thus passes under both axles while the driver's seat is a steel cross-member measuring about 20 ins. from the back to front, placed at a height of only 5 ins. from the ground. Owing to the chassis design, the front axle, which is equipped with brakes of the Perrot type, is dropped much less than the usual. The frame is curved so as to provide a perfectly streamlined foundation for the body, while the bottom of the vehicle will be perfectly flat and parallel to the ground.

Incidentally, the cars utilised steel bodywork in order to bring the overall weight to in excess of the legal minimum, weighing in at 1700 lb, when ready for the track.

Fellow Performers.

CAPT. CLIVE 'GALLÔ' GALLOP (1892-1960). If one individual had to be selected from this decade of motoring superstars then Capt. Clive Gallop would have his 'racing overalls in the circuit'. A big statement? Possibly, but consider his *curriculum vitæ*. In 1910 he was working with Peugeot's, in their competition department, driving in some hill climbs and sprints. From this period of his life came his wish to be popularly known as *Gallô*. During WW1 he was commissioned in the Royal Flying Corps, and later in the hostilities was attached to the Air Ministry. On leaving active service, in 1919, WO Bentley (WO) employed him to work on the valve gear of *EXP 1* (the original development 3 litre Bentley). In fact, unbeknown to WO, Clive Gallop, accompanied by the engineer 'Nobby' Clarke, was the first man to drive *EXP 1*. They were seated on a board laid across the chassis, with the body held on by clamps. Gallô gingerly edged out of New St. Mews into Baker Street. On their way back his dust-coat caught in the prop-shaft and commenced to wind him in, prior to the garment's stitching parting. Whilst with Bentley's, Clive helped tune the then Mr Henry Birkin's 2 litre DFP (Doriot Flandrin et Parant). This motor was the product of a French manufacturer, the English sales of which WO and his brother had handled, prior to WW1. Apart from other peculiarities, Tim Birkin's particular vehicle had a wooden, Vickers Aerofirm body (*See* Plate 52a).

On leaving WO's employment, and having known Count Louis Zborowski for many years, he joined forces with him, early in 1921. *Chitty 1* was completed during March that

Plate 24a.   To the left, Clive Gallop in his 3 litre Bentley (KM 2321) and on the right Tom in his Vauxhall 30-98. Circa 1926.

Courtesy Vauxhall 30-98 The Finest of Sporting Cars, Nic Portway. New Wensium Publishing.

Plate 24b.   Parry Thomas 'helming' a Leyland Eight Standard, four seater tourer.

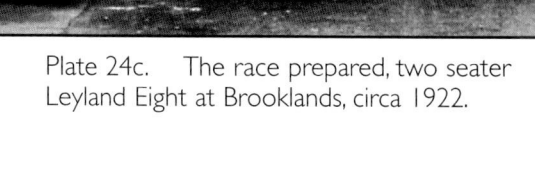

Plate 24c.   The race prepared, two seater Leyland Eight at Brooklands, circa 1922.

Plate 24d.   Count Zborowski 'overseeing' Parry Thomas carrying out fine tuning to his Leyland in 1923.

Plates 24b, c & d Courtesy Parry Thomas Designer Driver, Hugh Tours. Haynes. Batsford Ltd.

year. Due to Zborowski having a two year interest in Aston Martin, Gallop also worked on the preparation and racing of the Count's Astons. So much so, that in conjunction with Sammy Davis and 'Bertie' Kensington Moir, he set up some 22 Light Car and ten World Records, at Brooklands, in *'Bunny'*, the 1.5 litre side valve engined Aston Martin (Reg. No. AM 273). Zborowski loaned his 5 litre Ballot to Clive who competed in the car during the 1922-1924 seasons, mostly at Brooklands. Thereafter it was purchased by Capt. Richard Howey.

After the Count's death, Clive next appeared 'holding' the hand of and advising Tom Thistlethwayte. This encompassed competing in Tom's various cars, including the 1926 Le Mans 3 litre Bentley foray. By 1929 he was Works Manager and Production Superintendent at Birkin's Welwyn Garden City Works. Here were constructed and maintained the racing team of supercharged 'Blower' 4.5 litre Bentleys (*See* Chapter 5). A contributory reason why this venture was not as successful as it might have been was that *Gallô* was reportably unable to see eye-to-eye with Amherst Villiers. The latter had been employed to design the superchargers. Whatever, the outfit was only able to stay solvent whilst bankrolled by the unbelievable Hon. Dorothy Paget. With the almost inevitable closure of the enterprise, Clive Gallop resurfaced early in the 1930s, once again competing in an Aston Martin, sometimes with Leo Cushman.

In the 1930s he was recruited into the world of commerce. With the outbreak of WW2, he subsequently served in a military position, achieving the rank of Lieutenant Colonel. In 1960, aged 68, he died in a motor car accident, inexplicably swerving across the road and crashing into a lamp post.

JOHN GODFREY 'TOMMY' PARRY THOMAS (1885-1927). Probably one of the 'angels', if not the 'God' amongst the post WW1 motor racing fraternity. He was a motor car genius responsible for the manufacture, preparation and racing of cars. This judgement is more especially relevant considering his, 'oh so short' period of participation – just some five years. Additionally, no less a judge than William Boddy wrote '*…the greatest Outer Circuit exponent Brooklands ever had*'. Enough said!

Parry Thomas, sometimes known as Tommy, gained his qualifications at London University. After 'passing out' from College, and working for several companies, he set up his own consultancy/design firm. Subsequently he 'met' Leyland's on one or two projects, as well as working on their Ministry aero-engine development, during WW1. Thus, they were no strangers to each other. In fact they knew each other so well that he first came to prominence as the Chief Engineer of Leyland Ltd., manufacturers of large, luxury conveyances and lorries. He occupied this prestigious post from February 1917, officially through to 31st December 1923. However, in effect, it would appear he had settled in at Brooklands as early as the beginning of 1923.

When he first joined Leyland, it was reported that he could not drive, learning the 'black art' in one or three of the firm's lorries. There's hope for everyone then. By 1921 he had mastered high-speed motoring. Despite this newly acquired skill, he had a very difficult job encouraging the Directors of Leyland's to let him race one of their products, at Brooklands. Finally, Parry Thomas managed to persuade the powers-that-be to embark on a program of motor racing. In 1922, it is recorded that H Spurrier, Senior, who was one of the Leyland

Plate 25a. The Marlborough Thomas with the bonnet off to show the Hooker Thomas power unit. Parry Thomas' passenger is Kenneth Thomson.

Plate 25b. The Hooker Thomas powered Thomas Special. The engine was a 4 cylinder unit of 1493cc.

Plate 25c. *Babs* on the left, the Leyland Thomas No. 1 centre and 'Flat Iron' Thomas Special No. 2 on the right.

Plate 25d. The *Higham Special* as it was at Zborowski's demise.

Plate 25e. *Babs* at Brooklands prior to Pendine Sands.

Plate 25f. Parry Thomas driving *Babs* on to Pendine Sands.

Plate 25g. No caption required.

All plate 25 pictures feature in Parry Thomas, Designer Driver. Hugh Tours. Haynes. Batsford Ltd.

management team, entered a Leyland Eight for Thomas to 'transform' and race. It was stipulated that the vehicle had to be a 'bog' standard car, with full touring gear. The Directors comforted themselves with the thought that it would prove to be an excellent selling feature if he and the car could perform well. It was reported that 'Tommy' ignored these stipulations, 'at the last practice pit stop', removing all the appendages he considered unnecessary, prior to venturing forth. This decision was vindicated as he finished the year with three firsts, eight seconds and three thirds. During these Brooklands outings, Parry Thomas met many other like-minded parties, one of whom was TB Andre. Mr Andre operated out of some of the Brooklands based sheds and was making a name for himself with the Andre Hartford shock absorbers. In fact Thomas utilised them to assist control the Leyland Eight's handling problems. 'Tommy' was no snappy dresser, being renowned for his familiar Highland sweater and grey flannels, resembling a big, cuddly bear. When racing this ensemble was topped off with a brown leather flying helmet. By the beginning of 1923, Thomas and his London University friend Kenneth Thomson were firmly ensconced in The Hermitage Bungalow and adjacent workshops within the Brooklands circuit. Leyland's were very good to him. They packed up a collection of complete chassis', as well as all the spares and parts he could be expected to require! I cannot envisage that sort of glad-handed attitude prevailing nowadays.

One of his first commissions was to build a sister car to the existing racing Leyland Eight for Capt. JEP Howey. At about the same time TB Andre was constructing the Malborough, a vehicle of French origin. So it was not surprising that Thomas should fabricate a racing version – the Malborough Thomas, with a 1493cc engine. This latter development was followed through by taking the Malborough Thomas, adapting a 1982cc engine, in conjunction with the taxi manufacturer, Peter Hooker Ltd., of Walthamstow – thus the Hooker Thomas. The year 1924 also saw the creation of the Thomas Special, fitted with the Hooker Thomas engine. Confused? Incidentally, it has been suggested that the Hooker engines bore a remarkable resemblance to and were almost a miniaturised version of the original Leyland Eight power units. Surely not?

By 1925 the business of Thomas Inventions Development Co. was employing some six mechanics, amongst whom may well have been Dudley Froy, who crops up later in the narrative. Following Zborowski's death, Thomas acquired the *Higham Special* for £125 and towed it from Kent to Brooklands. Not to be left behind on the development front, he announced the new 1.5 litre, straight eight 'Flat Iron' Thomas Special, available with or without a supercharger.

By 1926 his racing and record breaking career was in full-swing. The ex *Higham Special* had been rebuilt, restyled and rechristened – *Babs*. In 1927 various other record breakers were also at work. They included Malcolm Campbell, in his Napier Campbell, at Pendine Sands and Henry O'Neal de hane Segrave, who was shipping his 1000hp twin engined (each of 12 cylinders and 22.45 litres) Sunbeam out to Daytona Beach. The pressure was on Thomas to get on with it. And he did, arriving at Pendine Sands with *Babs* on 1st March. By 3rd March *Babs* was a wreck and John Godfrey Parry Thomas was dead. The records of the flowers, wreaths and tributes did not detail any offering from one Arthur Donald Claude Thomas Thistlethwayte. There would appear to be no excuse for this oversight, although I am fairly certain Tom had his hands rather full that year!

Plate 26a. The 'Old No. 1' Speed Six Bentley with Jack Dunfee and Woolf Barnato celebrating a win in the 1929 Brooklands Six Hour Race. Side on and facing towards Barnato is Wally Hassan, whilst back to camera, at the bonnet end, is Stan Ivermee. Between them is Nobby Clark.

Plate 26b. Clive Dunfee dismounting to hand over 'Old No. 1' to Sammy Davis at the 1929 Brooklands 500 Mile Race in which they achieved a second place.
Courtesy An Illustrated History of the Bentley Car. WO Bentley. George Allen & Unwin.

Plate 26c. Clive Dunfee and Cyril Paul in 'Old No. 1' in which they won the October 1931 Brooklands 500 Mile Race.
Plates 26a & c Courtesy Brooklands The Complete Motor Racing History, William Boddy. MRP.

JACK (1901-1975) **and CLIVE** (1904-1932) **DUNFEE.** In and amongst the practitioners who commenced racing seriously in 1925, was Jack Dunfee. Despite an initial flirtation with a Calthorpe, his first serious appearance was at the Bank Holiday Monday Brooklands Race meeting, aboard a 1100cc, twin overhead cam, 4 cylinder Grand Sports Special Salmson. He achieved a first and a second place. The *Societe des Moteurs Salmson* started out life manufacturing aircraft engines and the car was originally based on the GN cycle car. By the early 1920s the racing versions had a beefed-up chassis, fitted with a 4 cylinder, twin overhead camshaft, 1100cc power unit, coupled to a 4 speed gearbox and conventional propshaft. In this guise the car notched up many class wins. Thus encouraged, Jack acquired a San Sebastian Model.* Over the next three years he achieved successes in the Salmson, a 2 litre Austro-Daimler and a 3 litre Ballot, mixing it with celebrities such as HW Purdy, Dudley Benjafield, Parry Thomas, Capt. Douglas, Woolf Barnato and Malcolm Campbell.

The year 1927 was when brother Clive Dunfee commenced competing in a 3 litre Targa Florio Austro-Daimler. By 1928 Jack was at the wheel of both a 1500cc Alfa Romeo and a 4.9 litre, 6 cylinder, 'Indy' Sunbeam first driven by Tony Vandervell. The brothers were 'working boys' and had to prove their worth by the dint of their skills and not an ability to buy their way into the sport. Jack, in later life described as a Company Director, had been the Manager of a Wandsworth based paper mill. Being interested in the stage and a great favourite with the ladies, he became a very successful theatrical agent. He was the outgoing one of the pair and quite a live-wire, whilst Clive, a member of the London Stock Exchange, was the more introspective brother. To keep costs down they often shared vehicles.

In 1929 Jack acquired the ex May Cunliffe GP supercharged 2 litre Sunbeam, but was also still aboard the Alfa Romeo and the Ballot, whilst Clive was recorded driving both Austro-Daimler's and the Ballot. That year Jack was included in the 1500cc Alfa Romeo Team for the first Brooklands Double Twelve Hour Race (10-11th May). He drove his 1928 'Alfa', sharing with PK Bamber, whilst the rest of the chaps were piloting 'bang-up-to-date' models. At the end of the first day, he was in seventh place but had to retire, with engine trouble, after $2^{3}/_{4}$ hours on the second day. This was also the year in which the 'Brothers Dunfee' joined the Bentley Boys. Co-driving with non other than Cmdr. Glen Kidston, Jack achieved a second at Le Mans (15-16th June) in a 4.5 litre Bentley. This was followed with a first in the Brooklands Six Hour Race (29th June), sharing with the 'boss', Woolf Barnato, in the *Old No. 1 Speed Six* Bentley. For the Irish Grand Prix (13th July) he finished his first (and only) day driving an 1100cc Speed Model Riley into seventh place. The end of the year was rather a let down. Jack was forced to retire whilst driving the original *Old Mother Gun* 4.5 litre Bentley, privately entered by the Hon. Richard Norton, in the Brooklands 500 Mile Race (12th October). It has to be taken into account that this car had been in almost continuous action since 1927. Not to be left out, Clive partnered Sammy Davis in the latter event, piloting the *Old No. 1 Speed Six*. They achieved FTD and Fastest Lap, despite which they were robbed of first place by an inordinate amount of tyre troubles, settling for an honourable second.

The year 1930 saw both Clive and Jack driving an Austro-Daimler, Ballot and the 2 litre supercharged GP Sunbeam. Now well established in the Bentley equipage, both the brothers

---

* The San Sebastian Salmsons (GP) had factory developed racing engine units with twin plugs per cylinder and were leased to the individual country importers or selected individuals.

The Forgotten Bentley Boy.

Plate 27a. Tim Birkin and BO Davis on the right of the picture, after retiring from the 1931 Double Twelve Race, driving Humphrey Cook's Speed Six. Having broken down after only two hours, Davis did not get a drive. Barnato, second from left, appears to be commiserating Birkin's bad luck whilst reaching for his legendary cigarette box. Legendary? Well it was always suggested that to get a cigarette out of that case was as difficult as the proverbial pushing a camel through the eye of a needle! To the left is a smiling Clive Dunfee.

COURTESY BENTLEY THE VINTAGE YEARS. MICHAEL HAY. HM BENTLEY & PARTNERS.

The Autocar. 30th September 1932.

Plate 27b. A touching obituary in respect of Clive Dunfee. Penned by 'Casque' who, as Sammy Davis, had been a co-driver of Clive's a number of times.

COURTESY AUTOCAR.

The Sport by Casque

THE fatal accident to Clive Dunfee is a thing difficult to write about, especially as Clive was my team-mate on two great occasions. That the end, when it came, was swift and exceedingly merciful, is something. That it was so, giving the driver no time whatever to feel the horrors of impending certain disaster, or any pain whatever when that disaster was fact, I am one of the few people living who can have certain knowledge.

✻ ✻ ✻

Clive was all that was best of his type, a very gallant gentleman, an enthusiast for the game he loved, anxious to play that game absolutely and entirely by its rules. Anxious to succeed, yes, but anxious to succeed only if, in success, he could win the approval of those experienced in such matters, and making no attempt to blame his car for failure, caring not a wit for the curious publicity earned so easily to-day.

Certainly he was of the material of which a great driver could have been made when experience had been acquired and its stern lessons well learned. Certainly he was a man not easily spared, nor ever forgotten by those who chanced to know him well. It sounds trite, maybe, to say that he died a man's death driving at a speed that might have been a record for all races, but, though one could have wished that the end had not been so early, nevertheless the fact does remain that it was a manner of death which most of us would prefer but few of us will attain if, in the fulfilment of time, Nature has her way.

✻ ✻ ✻

When we were driving together it was to me most curious that every act of Clive's, aye, and the manner of its doing, brought back, as no one else has done, those days of great enthusiasm that were the beginning of my own racing career; and the bitter part of life, as one grows old, is just the very fact that one must pen such small tribute to departed friends as may ease, perchance, their passing to "Valhalla," though in the doing one's own loneliness increases.

To one who knew Clive better than all of us little chance of comfort can there be from man, but if a genuine and deep sympathy may in any way suffice, that, at least, is offered in all sincerity.

put in an appearance in the Brooklands Double Twelve Hour Race (9-10th May). Jack partnered Kidston in one of the Paget entered 'Blower' 4.5 litre Bentleys. They had to retire with a broken valve spring. Clive co-drove with Sammy Davis, in a Speed Six Bentley and, despite a broken valve, broken valve spring and broken oil pipe, they achieved a second. For Le Mans (21-22nd June), Clive was again sharing a Speed Six with Sammy Davis (*See* Chapter 4). Having taken over from Sammy, who had come in with glass splinters in his eye, Clive had a 'whoopsy' and 'stuffed' the car into the sandbank at Pontlieue. The next month Clive appeared in the Irish Grand Prix (19th July) in a 'works' supercharged 1500cc Lea-Francis. Despite a very smart and swift getaway, he had to make many pit stops, prior to retiring.

With Bentley Motors out of action, for 1931 Jack was in evidence in the GP Sunbeam and partnered Cyril Paul in the Brooklands 500 Mile Race (3rd October), driving the now Barnato entered *Old No. 1* Speed Six. They won.

The 1932 Brooklands 500 Mile Race (24th September) found Clive and Jack sharing the Barnato entered *Old No. 1*, now powered by an 8 litre Bentley engine. Jack was first out, prior to handing over to Clive. He maintained the impetus until … the sound of the exhaust cut out and he failed to appear. Clive was lying dead beside the top of the banking, having put a wheel over the edge and, out of control, 'clouted' a tree. The car careered off down the reverse side of the track banking. Clive had married the actress Jane Baxter, reputably once a 'Woolf playmate', in December 1930. With the usual caveats to the fore, he had not raced for a year or so, this being his comeback event. Jane was a spectator. She first performed on stage, aged 16, in 1925 and was described as being feisty, fun, gracious and a pleasure to be with. She sounded as if she must have been a 'smasher'. Apart from some films, she appeared as late as the 1970s in the TV drama *Upstairs, Downstairs*.

Jack did not race motor cars again, but did put in some time in and around power boats.

The 1926 Le Mans.

9 BENTLEY SUPER SPORTS
4 cylindres en ligne, 2998 cm³

Courtesy L'Automobile Club de L'Ouest, Besançon Le Mans, France.

Tommy THISTLETHWAYTE
Abandon 105ᵉ tour (moteur)

Plate 28a.   Tom and Gallop pre-race.

Plate 28b.   The Hotel Moderne stable yard and the Bentley Team Cars with the Works support crew in attendance. Tom's car is on the left.
Courtesy WO Bentley Memorial Foundation

Plate 28c.   "The short chassis Bentley which will be handled by T Thistlethwayte and RC Gallop. A streamlined underpan is provided and all the brake shoes can be brought into use at once. The windscreen shown in the illustration is, of course, only temporary, and will be replaced in the race by a wire screen." *The Autocar.*
Courtesy Autocar

CHAPTER FOUR

Tom. His Le Mans Year. 1926.

'God would not have invented the automobile if he had intended me to walk.'
IB.

This was the year in which Tom came of racing age, his Le Mans year. Between 1925 and 1926 he made a competition car change of direction. Previously owning a Frazer Nash and a Vauxhall 30-98, he acquired a special bodied 3 litre Bentley and one of the (two) Parry Thomas 1.5 litre, 8 cylinder, 'Flat Iron' Specials. These were to form the springboard for his future competition – at least for that season! The disposal of the Vauxhall is explained by no less an authority than WO (in his autobiography*). He wrote, explaining Tom's purchase of the Bentley, that it was '*…as a result of Scrap Thistlethwayte's dissatisfaction with his OE 30-98 Vauxhall, which he never seemed to be able to make go so fast as Clive Gallop's standard 3 litre (Bentley)*'.

Le Mans or (more correctly) The Grand Prix d'Endurance de 24 Heures Le Mans. Coupes Rudge-Whitworth**) (12-13th June). Of all Tom's sporting exploits, the facts of his 1926 Le Mans outing are, for a change, well documented. This was almost certainly because he was an 'unofficial, official' member of the Bentley Team. The Works entered cars were both 3 litre Speed models. Bentley No. 7 was driven by Sammy Davis and Dr. Dudley Benjafield. Bentley No. 8 was piloted by George Duller and Frank Clement. The third car, Bentley No. 9, described as a 100 mph 3 litre Supersport model (Reg. No. KM 4250), was detailed as a 'factory entry, privately owned'. That is owned by Tom Thistlethwayte.

---
* WO. The Autobiography of WO Bentley, Hutchinson of London.
** It is worth noting that from the outset of the sports car race in 1923 through to 1927, officially there was no winner of the particular year's race. In fact, initially, there was a three year competition based on engine size and a set distance to be covered in the 24 hours with a Triennial Cup awarded by Rudge-Whitworth. After one year this was reduced to a two year competition and Rudge-Whitworth again presented the award, now the Biennial Cup. In the meantime the spectators and press generally elected the first over the line after the 24 hours as to be the winner. Officially, it was not until 1928 that the populist opinion became the accepted winning formula.

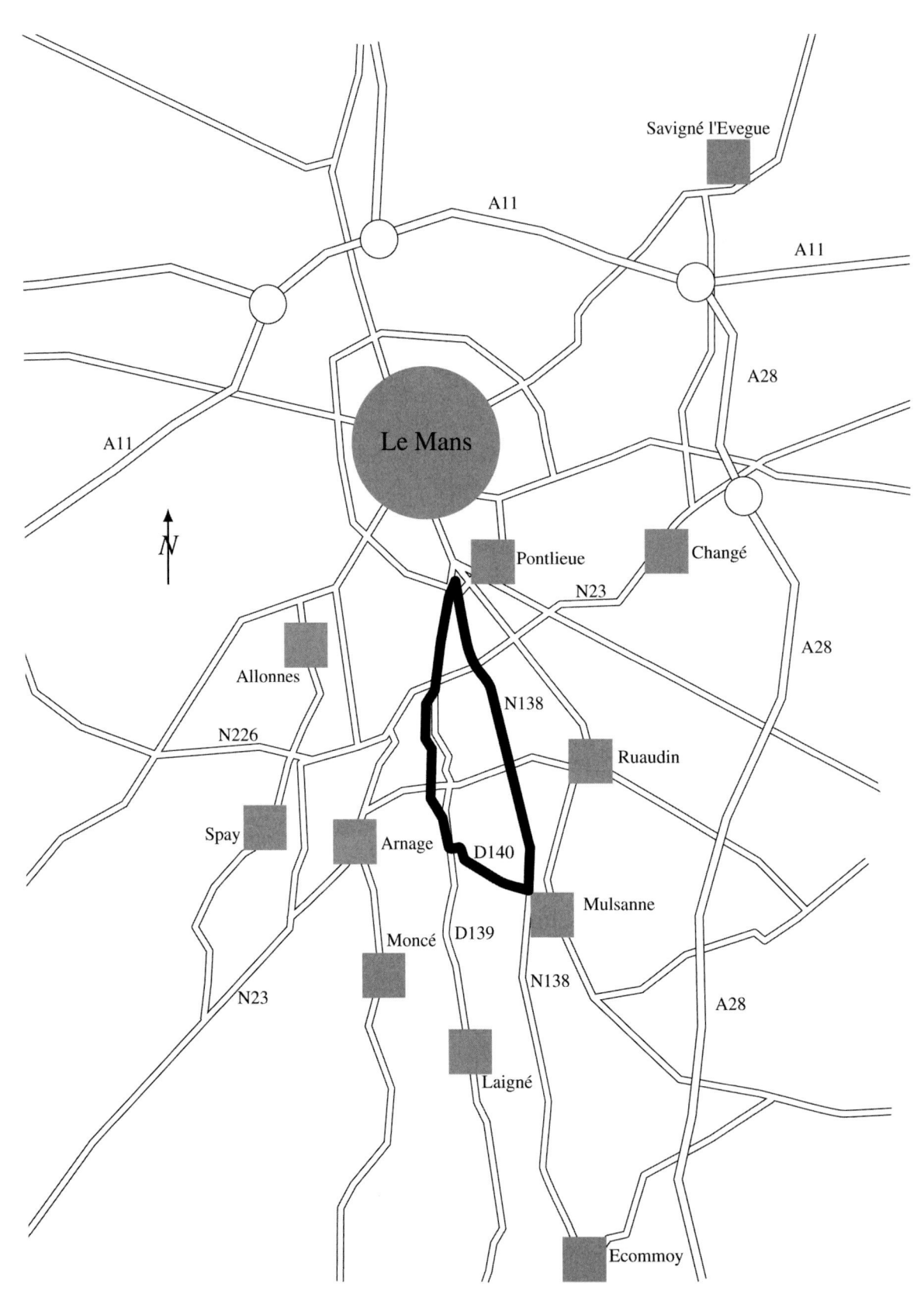

Plate 29a.   The area of Le Mans.

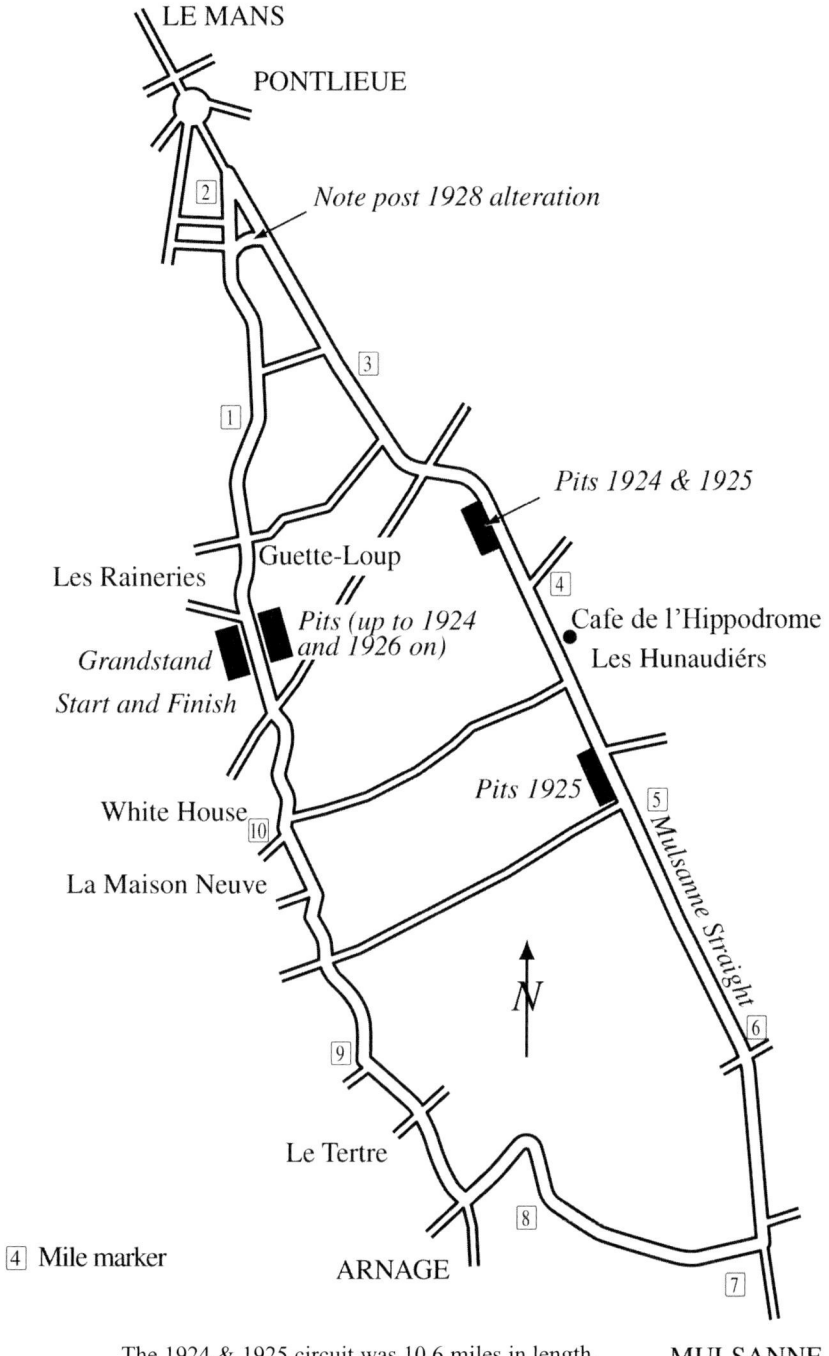

The 1924 & 1925 circuit was 10.6 miles in length.

Plate 29b. The Le Mans Circuit.

Plate 30a. A snapshot of the Le Mans circuit road surface – or lack of!
COURTESY WO THE AUTOBIOGRAPHY OF WO BENTLEY. HUTCHINSON.

The 1926 Le Mans continued.

Plate 30b. "An impression of Thistlethwayte's Bentley on the straight." THE MOTOR.

Plate 30c. Tom's 3 litre en route to Mulsanne.
COURTESY AUTOCAR

It appears Tom's friend Clive Gallop, who had driven for him in the 1925 Boulogne Race, invited Tom to 'share a Bentley cockpit (with him)'. Tom, as has already transpired, was quite possibly not really a team player, more a lone autocrat, rather a martinet and certainly one possessed of fixed opinions. He agreed – but with stipulations. He decreed he should own the vehicle, which he insisted must be a short chassis model, on to which had to be squeezed a four seater body. This latter necessity was to comply with the Le Mans regulations. Furthermore, the coachwork 'had' to be built by Tom's selected coachbuilder, Martin Walter of Folkestone. It was agreed that Clive Gallop (*'who had left us'* – wrote WO) would prepare the car, with the assistance of full Works back-up. Once again the 'creation' of this Bentley points towards Tom's rather go-it-alone characteristic, his inability to 'join the gang' and his probable wish to ensure any glory would be his, all his.

Even bearing in mind Tom's personal peccadilloes, it must occasion the question as to why on earth he was so insistent to have a specification and build-plan that would result in so much extra money and effort having to be expended. It was reported that his demands caused considerable problems, most of which have been discoursed about in Chapter 1. Despite this, WO described *Scrap* as a *"…handsome, debonair playboy but no mean driver"* and elsewhere, years later, as *"…another wealthy playboy, better known for racing his Mercedes cars in the late 1920s".**

The 1926 Le Mans followed a distinct lack of Bentley Works success in the 1925 event and a failed 24 Hour Montlhery record attempt. Thus, everyone hoped for great things but this was not to be. Of the three 3 litre cars, Bentley Race No. 8 went out after some 12 hours running, on lap 72, with a broken valve. Tom and Clive's Race No. 9 ran for 18 hours until 9am on Sunday morning. At 8.30am, Clive Gallop took the wheel but wretchedly, some ½ hour later, on lap 105 and whilst lying joint third, the car had to be retired with a broken duralumin rocker arm. In the meantime, Bentley Race No. 7 was lying a very creditable third, after 23 hours. With only 20 minutes to go, motoring journalist Sammy Davis overtook a 3.4 litre, pushrod 6 cylinder 15 CV Lorraine-Dietrich, after which matters took a turn for the worse. Whilst hurtling towards the Mulsanne corner, he found his brake pedal going straight down to the cockpit sole – and beyond. Thus no stopping power! Result – the Bentley finished up well and truly stuffed into a sandbank, with no chance of the driver extricating it. The Bentley Team's race was over and a sense of gloom overlaid subsequent proceedings.

During the Le Mans weekend the drivers and management were ensconced at the *Hotel de Paris*, whilst the mechanics and pit crews 'bedded down' at the *Hotel Moderne*. But not all was dedicated pit-work at Le Mans. Oh, no! The top mechanic was RAC Clarke, better known as 'Nobby'. Prior to the race, it appears Tom, having stripped off the racing 'ovies' and slipping on a cravat, suggested 'Nobby' should clamber into his Bentley and join him for a drink, back at the *Hotel de Paris*. Nothing strange about that then! A 'damned' good thing to hunker down with the 'other ranks'. 'Nobby' advised that it was Tom's decision to take a one-way street, the wrong way, which he found rather disconcerting! That is against the traffic flow, probably because at the far end of the said thoroughfare was the hotel. And why not? The problem was compounded due to this particular byway also being one along which the trams coursed. And, as luck would have it, as they cruised serenely towards the bar stools, a tram

---

* WO. The Autobiography of WO Bentley, Hutchinson of London.

The Boulogne Race Week 1926.

Plate 31a.   "T Thistlethwayte in the Bentley which he will drive in the Ballot Cup Race."

Plate 31b.   "Thistlethwayte at full speed in the hill-climb in his Bentley with which he secured third place in the three-litre class."

PLATES 31A & B COURTESY THE MOTOR.

bore down on them. Tom was not even stirred, let alone shaken. In the face of a total lack of room to manoeuvre, he piloted the vehicle up on to the pavement, missed the tram by the 'proverbial', whilst pedestrians scattered this way and that, only to pull up 'on the steps' of the hotel. Despite Tom coolly and suavely offering to run 'Nobby' back to his accommodation, post 'drinkies', it is said the redoubtable engineer declined the offer, selecting 'shanks pony'!*

A subsequent aside, or footnote, to that particular years' Le Mans involved Doctor Benjafield. After the dust had settled, and back in 'Blighty' for a week or two, he felt inclined to purchase Bentley Race No. 7. That is the very car in which he and Sammy had done so well. Accordingly, he contacted Bentley's, only to be advised that the two Works cars had been sold to a reputable firm, purveyors of luxury motor cars to discerning clients. Pass the sick bag! Not one to dilly-dally, Benjafield visited the relevant showroom and enquired after the two racing machines. A top sales person drew him to the side of what was a very clean and sanitised racer, but obviously Benjys' recent chariot – Race No. 7. On enquiring as to the condition of the machine in question, he was assured it was in tip-top state and a price was suggested. At this point the good Doctor revealed his true identity and proceeded to detail the thrashing the car had endured at the hands of himself and Sammy Davis. Not surprisingly, a lesser figure was agreed and the purchase concluded. Old car salesmen have obviously never changed their ways!

Apart from Le Mans, Thistlethwayte's Bentley was not exactly over-used. It is detailed as being entered for Capt. RB Howey to drive in an early August Brooklands meeting. However, the records only feature Howey as winning a handicap race, in his familiar 5 litre Ballot. Tom's prized, new, supercharged 1.5 litre, 8 cylinder Thomas 'Flat Iron' Special finally surfaced late in July but it was not race-ready for the planned appearance in the Brooklands British Grand Prix, on Saturday 7th August. Clive Gallop was down to drive for Tom, who was retrospectively described as ' …. *a wealthy amateur feeling his way into motor racing …. and remembered for his later spirited handling of the 36/220 Mercedes-Benz and elsewhere*'. The reason given for non-starting was gearbox machining problems. On the other hand,

an almost legendary authority hints that this may have been to cover an initially disappointing performance. Tom must have been extremely 'hacked off', as he was entitled to be. I understand this particular project set him back some seven or eight thousand pounds, and that was in 1926! Even more frustratingly, neither of the *Flat Irons* were ready for the planned end of August onslaught, more correctly the:

BOULOGNE RACE WEEK (26-29th August). This four day event commenced with a speed trial and a couple of hill climbs on Thursday 26th. The Speed Trial was eventually staged over a six kilometre, somewhat pot-holed course with three switchback hills at about half distance. The hill climbs consisted of a one mile ascent up Mount Lambert and a second somewhat shorter 500 metre section. As the Thomas Specials could not appear for the Saturday Light Car Grand Prix, Tom entered his 3 litre Bentley in the Thursday events as well as the Georges Boillet Cup, on the Sunday. Other drivers putting in an appearance were Malcolm Campbell, in a supercharged 1500cc Type 39A Bugatti, and George Eyston in a similar but unsupercharged Type 39, Frazer-Nash in one of his 1500cc products, Benjafield

---

* Extracted from The Other Bentley Boys. Elizabeth Nagle. George Harrap.

Plate 32. Capt. Richard Howey's fatal accident at the 1926 Boulogne Race Week.

COURTESY THE MOTOR

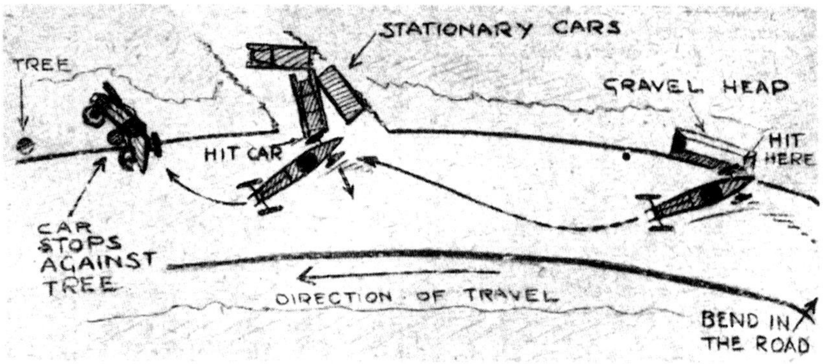

in his 3 litre Bentley and Ivanowski in a Ratier (a what?). The Ratier was a short-lived, production run French car with a 4 cylinder, supercharged 750cc power unit coupled to a 3 speed gearbox. Only a few were produced.

It is worth recording that, despite the wretched turn of events, Benjafield entered *Old No. 7* in the Georges Boillet Cup Race held on the Sunday. Due to a lack of entries, Benjy was in third place with three laps to go and was given 'hurry-up' pit signals in an effort to gain a higher placing. Always one to oblige, the 'good Doctor' applied the accelerator pressure as a result of which he cornered too fast, skidded and spun the car into a tree. The car was bent and Benjy left a number of teeth in the steering wheel. Hearing the public announcement system announce his death, he contacted the pits to advise it was one of those 'old' Mark Twain premature 'jobbies'!

But a tragic event was to spoil the party. On Thursday, in the 4 litre Racing Class, Major HOD Segrave gained a road racing record of 140.164 mph. This was achieved in his 'grass-green', 4 litre 12 cylinder, supercharged Sunbeam*, developing some 450 horsepower. A newspaper report of the day advised:

> '… the Major had established the most remarkable feat in the history of road racing, over six kilometres of hilly ground. From the moment he started he put down the accelerator and drove all out … maintaining the staggering speed of 147 miles per hour. So great was the speed of his car that when traversing the top of the hill it left the ground, and for twenty yards the wheels were six inches in the air. The car came down with a bump that almost flung Seagrave (*sic*) out. Every second he was within a hair's breadth of death. This record is not likely to be exceeded for many years. Major Seagrave (*sic*) confessed afterwards that for the first time in his life he had been really frightened. "I don't know how I did it. I wouldn't have, had I realised my speed. I shall never attempt such a thing again' *I think he did!*

In the 8 litre Class, Parry Thomas was reported as putting in a great run in his Leyland Eight. Capt. RB Howey had a scare when an under-powered motorcycle somehow got on to the course, in front of his flying white Ballot. It pulled into his path, close to the finishing line but by exercising considerable skill Howey avoided an accident. But the portents were not good, not good at all. In fact *The Ides of August* were awful! THE MOTOR magazine stated that '*T. Thistlethwayte's Bentley seemed very fast and was quite reasonably steady despite misfiring setting in on the last half mile of the course*' and '*T. Thistlethwayte made a very fast climb on his Bentley while Dr. Benjafield, who came up next, had a slight skid, …*'. Tom achieved a third in the 3000cc Touring Car Class, behind a Chenard-Walcker and the Benjafield Bentley.

Later that day Howey, in his 5 litre Ballot (*See* Plate 35, page 68), found himself in a terrible and uncontrollable slide, after hitting a pile of stones. His vehicle then bounced off a badly parked car, finally crashing into a roadside tree, killing him and a spectator, as well as injuring four other onlookers. A newspaper advised its readers that:

> 'A grim drama occurred at a motor race meeting at Boulogne yesterday when Captain Howey, who was regarded as one of the World's foremost racing motorists, was killed. In

---

* This was really a land speed record breaker and was later to be developed for this very purpose as epitomised by 'Tiger'.

Plate 33a.   The Motor of 31 August 1926 reported:

> The accident happened to Richard B. Howey in the one-mile hill-climb up Mont Lambert. One by one fast touring models and real racing cars had toured, hummed or thundered up, according to their types. As the faster machines made their attacks upon the dusty, sunlit hill thrills began to multiply in a manner which will later be described. Then came Howey's wonderful climb on his white Ballot racer—an ascent which, up to the fatal moment of his crash, was many miles an hour faster than that of anyone else.
>
> Accelerating rapidly from a standstill, using his gears to the utmost, Howey tore up the hill like a streak of white lightning. The first corner he took fast but skilfully, skidded neatly, with the car in perfect control, round the second, and tackled the third—a treacherous bend of the type that "keeps on" going round—at least 70 m.p.h.
>
> By this time the car was in a long, controlled skid: a mere foot or so out of the straight, when the rear of the car, swinging out, struck a long, low bank of rubble. The blow put him straight again, but immediately afterwards he got into a four-wheel skid, sliding round almost at right angles to the road. He was still sliding, crab-fashion, at a terrific velocity—perhaps 75 m.p.h.—with his steering wheel locked hard over to the right in an attempt to straighten out.
>
> But the tail of the car was well down the camber of the road and off the metalled portion, and a fraction of a second later it struck the side of a car parked just off the road, glanced off, grazing another car as it went, and swung right across to the left.
>
> Then the end came.
>
> Howey, still fighting for mastery, went straight for a mighty tree, hitting it with a crash that was heard, far above, at the top of the hill, and the car turned on its side in the ditch. On the way it gravely injured a gendarme and three spectators, finally hitting an onlooker, who died shortly afterwards. After some little time, and with a great deal of difficulty, poor Howey was extricated from the car and laid on the grass .... with a fractured skull. His death was practically instantaneous and must have been absolutely painless.
>
> Every British man and woman will incline their heads at the passing of this fine driver and, in the finest sense of the word, a gentleman, as well as the unfortunate French victim. We respectfully tender our deepest sympathy to the relatives of the dead.

September, 1926 MOTOR SPORT 91

THE LATE CAPTAIN HOWEY.

IT is with deep regret that we have to announce the passing of a great sportsman, for Captain R. B. Howey was the victim of a fatal accident on August 26th, whilst taking part in the "Course des Cotes" at the Boulogne meeting. Whilst driving his Ballot round one of the bends in the course, Captain Howey skidded and crashed into a tree, passing away without regaining consciousness. A very popular figure at Brooklands, Captain Howey was twenty-five years of age and an Australian by birth. Possessing considerable means he took up motor racing as a pastime with great enthusiasm, being a regular competitor in the principal meetings at the Brooklands track.

He was best known for his performances on the straight-eight Ballot car, which, with several others he purchased from the late Count Zborowski. In October last he created a series of world's records at speeds of 118 miles per hour. Among his successes this year may be mentioned the winning of the Brooklands' Founders Gold Cup at a speed of 106 m.p.h. and the Gold Star race at 110 m.p.h.

Captain R. B. Howey was a thoroughly good sportsman and a man of charming personality who followed the sport of motor racing for the pure love of the game, which sustains a big loss by his death. The sad accident at Boulogne came as a great grief to his many friends and to the public by whom he was rightly regarded as one of the safest drivers on the track.

Plate 33b.   There was an error in the obituary, giving his age as 25 when in fact he was 29 when killed.

the one kilometre, flying start hill test. He preceded Major Seagrave (*sic*) in his "Hush Hush" Sunbeam and Mr Parry Thomas in his giant Leyland. These two were scheduled to follow Howey at one minute intervals. The course was over a steep hill, with treacherous blind corners.

Howey's powerful engine was heard roaring when he took a fierce bend at 100 miles an hour. Howey was noticed twice to be endeavouring to check his speed and then appeared to lose control. He tried to keep his hand on the steering wheel but the strain was too great. It was easy to read the agony on his face. There was a moment of tense silence, then a deafening roar, the monster touched the side of a small car belonging to a spectator, which was swung round like a top. The racing car lurched with appalling speed and crashed into the middle of the spectators. The tail reared up and gashed a great tree then the machine broke up into an unrecognisable mass. One spectator was killed and another frightfully injured, while a policeman's leg was broken.

In the meantime another drama was being enacted at the starting point. Major Seagrave was listening to the time keeper's voice shouting "Fifteen seconds, ten, four, three." Just as the car was about to leap forward a car roared up the hill and pulled up blocking the road, the occupier falling out to advise that "The car ahead's crashed!" This dramatic action might well have saved Major Seagrave's life by seconds. Mrs Seagrave was waiting in agony at the top of the hill, expecting at any moment to see her husband dash round the bend to his death. No more sensational accident has occurred in the history of motor racing here.'

An obituary of the day declared that:

'Capt. RB Howey was a thoroughly good sportsman and a man of charming personality who followed the sport of motor racing for the pure love of the game, which sustains a big loss by his death. A very popular figure at Brooklands, (he) was twenty five years of age *(incorrect)* and an Australian by birth. Possessing considerable means he took up motor racing as a pastime with great enthusiasm'.

The day's events were immediately halted. Tom, in a mark of respect for his friend, withdrew his Sunday Georges Boillet Cup entry, as would be expected of a gentleman.

The end of September heralded the:

BROOKLANDS 200 MILE RACE (25th September). At last the two Thomas *Flat Iron* Special's were ready to race. However, Tom decided to drive himself, rather than Clive Gallop. This necessitated some pretty rapid alterations to the seating and fuel tank installation. Added to which, I suspect, Gallô was pretty miffed at this late switch of driver! After all that, whilst 'tooling' about the paddock, Tom managed to break a half-shaft. Someone recorded the component as being substantial, which was probably a critical sideswipe at Tom's 'ham-fistedness'. Parry Thomas in his still unblown 'sister' car finished eighth overall and fifth in his class.

I think that hereabouts Tom threw-in-the towel and Clive moved on. At the last Brooklands meeting of the year, Parry Thomas was a definite Flat Iron entry, but not Tom.

Plate 34.   Barnato's first Bentley – a 100mph Supersports model (Chassis No. 1106, Engine No. 1109) fitted with a Jarvis of Wimbledon, two seater body.

COURTESY BENTLEY THE VINTAGE YEARS, MICHAEL HAY. HM BENTLEY & PARTNERS.

Hereabouts, Parry Thomas repurchased Tom's car and on the 30th October he set Class 100 Mile and Hour Records – in a supercharged 'Flat Iron Special'. Obviously the ex-Thistlethwayte vehicle. Oh dear me! With that drew to an inglorious end his 1926 season.

BENTLEY MOTORS. At this stage it might not go amiss to sketch in some of the relevant details in respect of the company. More especially after Tom's comparatively short flirtation with the firm. His decision to get rid of the Bentley is made the more unfathomable when it is considered just how much money and effort he had invested in the car. Be that as it may, late in 1925, the financial state of Bentley's was very parlous, so much so that the workforce was well aware of the predicament. Mind you, in my experience, the 'lower decks' more often than not are almost the first to know of all and any organisation's major decisions and well-being. In this particular case the nightmare attendant to the weekly wages being paid – or not – must have been a fairly good indicator!

Outside saviours had to be actively sought – fast. Even William Morris, the guiding light of the more prosaic, mass production, eponymous motor car manufacturer, had been approached. At about the same time, the onset of initially tenuous negotiations were taking place with none other than Woolf Babe Barnato (*See* Chapter 8). In 1925 the latter had purchased his first Bentley. This was a 3 litre model, fitted with Jarvis two seater racing bodywork (the latter costing some £400). Being a very shrewd, streetwise financier, Woolf was obviously aware of the financial black-hole that existed at the company. For whatever reasons, and in the face of strong opposition from his financial advisors, he decided to invest. Early in 1926, Bentley Motors was wound up. Subsequently, Bentley Motors Limited was formed, with a new board of directors, and Woolf injected 'the necessary'. As would have been expected, there was no compassion where even small amounts of money were at stake, let alone large sums. But then this has often been the way of very wealthy men. I recall that a Mr Getty, of oil millions, had a pay-phone installed in his mansion – so as to save guests the embarrassment of having to ask to use the telephone. Oh yes! But back to the plot.

As a result of the takeover, WO, in effect, lost almost everything, except a job, and that was eventually reduced from the Managing Director to Joint MD and Chief Engineer. The other Managing Director was a Cuban banker, the Marquis de Casa Maury, an '…*international sportsman and racing driver*'. Chapter Eight describes how Woolf Barnato came across this gentleman in the pursuit of speed boat racing, certainly by 1924. He was said to be '…*more interested in coachwork, motor racing and women*'! And why not? But it must have been extremely galling for WO. To add insult to injury his salary was halved. Another intriguing appointment as a Director was that of Noel van Raalte. This was the gentleman who had been selected to purchase the very first production Bentley to be sold. However, even this latter statement is subject to much professorial research. Certainly Chassis No. 1 was van Raalte's and he took ownership in September 1921. On the other hand it has been suggested that Chassis No. 3 was received by its owner, some 30 to 40 days earlier, on 3rd August 1921. Before passing on, Nicholas van Raalte was an interesting fellow. His first mentioned involvement with motor sport was his participation in some unofficial University Town racing. He then turned up again, racing a 4.5 litre, 4 cylinder GP Sunbeam in the 1915 'Indy 500', under the *nom de course* N Graham. This was presumably so as not to attract any

Plate 35.   Capt. RB Howey at the wheel of the rebodied ex-Zborowski 5 litre Ballot at the Brooklands Circuit. Richard Howey purchased the vehicle prior to the 1925 Whitsun Brooklands Race meeting whereat he entered the car. Apart from racing, Howey also mopped up some Class C records in 1925 and some more in 1926.

Courtesy The Racing Zborowskis. David Wilson. VSCC Ltd.

*(Page 69) KLG (sparking plugs) was started up by Kenelm Lee Guinness, a member of the eponymous drinks concern. Born in 1887 he was already experimenting with developing a better sparking plug than the porcelain products available in 1912. His venture took place in old outbuildings alongside the then 'Bold Faced Stag' Public House (by the original A3, immediately prior to Kingston-on-Thames), and in which he stored his racing cars. Incidentally the location became an art deco 1930s Road House, complete with swimming pool, but post WW2 had been reduced to a lorry park and is now the site of an ASDA supermarket. Post WW1 he purchased an ex Admiralty craft, which he renamed 'Ocean Rover' and in the holds of which he transported his and others racing cars to the more distant circuits such as the Coppa Florio, Sicily. Despite giving up record breaking and motor racing after a near fatal accident, whilst racing a 6 cylinder, 2 litre supercharged GP Sunbeam in the 1924 San Sebastian Grand Prix, a crash which killed his riding mechanic. he remained very much involved in organising race events. He sold the KLG business to S. Smith & Sons (England) Ltd. (later to become Smiths Industries). Reportedly, becoming increasingly mentally unbalanced, he committed suicide in 1937.

possible WW1 'white feather' commentary. He managed a tenth, if last place, despite which he garnered some prize money. He then went on to a Chicago race track with the same car but to no avail as he had to retire with a broken engine. Apart from inheriting Brownsea Island, he was also a shareholder in KLG (*See* Page 68), the renowned manufacturer of sparking plugs. During the 1920s and 30s he lived at Bursledon Lodge, Bursledon close to the Hamble River shoreline. It can be no surprise that he owned an outboard engine powered speed boat.

With the arrival of Barnato, not only was the future of Bentley's motor car production resolved (for, as it turned out, the comparatively short-term,) but so was the racing programme. The 1926 events had been very touch and go, which may well explain Tom's reluctance to persevere with the marque. And even if he had stayed in the fold, would he have wished his star to have been dimmed by that of Woolf? Whatever, the year 1927 was to see the first full year, of the Bentley Works Team racing plans, under the new owner's guidance. And very successful they were to prove to be.

Fellow Performers.

CAPT. RICHARD 'DICK' BARSTOW HOWEY (1896-1926). This gentleman was brother to Capt. Jack Howey. He joined up aged 17, was given a temporary commission in The King's Own Scottish Borderers and was at the front within a year. He achieved a permanent commission in the Coldstream Guards, serving with gallantry and was injured several times. Post the Armistice, he continued in the Army for another few years, spending his spare time hunting with the hounds. It was during this period, in 1921, that he had a very, very 'close call' in an aeroplane he was piloting. It appears, whilst recuperating, that he was persuaded to take up motor racing – in an effort to divert him from the 'dangerous' sport of aviation. Ho, hum!

When explaining away his ability to very inexpensively purchase Zborowski's white, long tailed, 5 litre Ballot, for the comparatively paltry sum of £500, he is supposed to have described himself as a "*penniless Guards officer and friend of the Count*". He competed regularly in the Ballot. He also engaged in some record breaking attempts, as well as driving other owner's cars, as was common in those days. In the year of his death, he won both the Brooklands Founders Gold Cup and the Gold Star Races. Unlike his brother, he did not make old bones. Aged just 29, he came to a most untimely end at the 1926 Boulogne Race Week, on 26th August. He 'wrapped' the Ballot and himself round a trackside tree' (*See* Plate 32). A poignant obituary of the time described his coffin being accompanied back across the Channel, by his friend Parry Thomas. During the sea-passage, the wrecked Ballot was pushed overboard. Another tribute described him as being:

> '…reckless of his own life …lavish in his generosity to others …a wonderful friend… giving or lending his possessions even to a passing acquaintance. He was…Impossible to ruffle …with a sunny and affectionate disposition …incapable of thinking any evil of others.'

THE FORGOTTEN BENTLEY BOY.

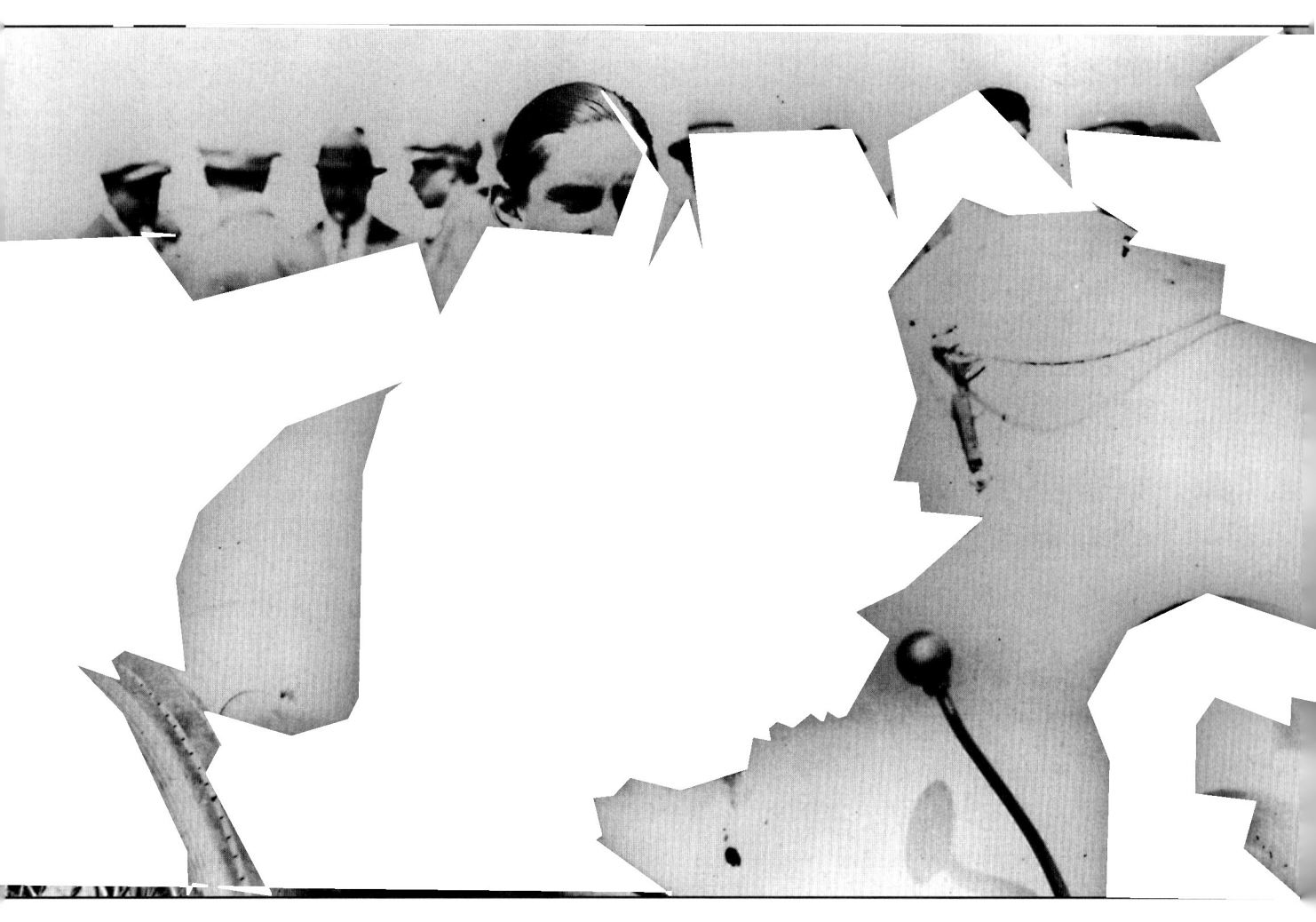

Plate 36. Sammy Davis in the passenger seat of Count Louis Zborowski's American, straight eight, 2 litre Type 122 Miller (Reg. No. FN 5858), prior to the 1924 French Grand Prix, Lyon. Zborowski was prompted to import the car having observed them 'clean up' in the 1923 'Indy 500 in which he competed unsuccessfully in a Type 30 Bugatti (See Plate 23B). In that race Millers took the chequered flag as well as six of the first seven places home.

COURTESY THE RACING ZBOROWSKIS. DAVID WILSON. VSCC LTD.

SIDNEY CHARLES HOUGHTON 'SAMMY' DAVIS (1887-1981). Westminster School educated, from a very early age Sammy was fired with a lifelong enthusiasm for the internal combustion engine. This relationship was cemented by his apprenticeship in 1906 at the Daimler Works, Coventry. He is reported to have entered motor cycling trials, as early as 1907. Quite fortuitously, he came up against WO and his brother HM Bentley pursuing the same aims, more especially in early Isle of Man Tourist Trophy motor cycling events.

On leaving the environs of car manufacture, he took up technical journalism. He was lucky enough to come under the wing of a benevolent Editor, who was starting up THE AUTOMOBILE ENGINEER, to be published by Iliffes. WW1 intervened, during which Sammy worked on aero-engine development – quite coincidentally, from time to time, with none other than WO. On the cessation of hostilities he rejoined Iliffes, but now with THE LIGHT CAR, then progressing to THE AUTOCAR. Fortunately two senior fellow staff members of this magazine were also motoring enthusiasts. They persuaded the Iliffe directors to encourage Sammy in his overweening passion. That was to develop his interests and attend as many major hill climbs, sprints, trials, races and record attempts as he could. Furthermore, to actively participate and compete and or act as riding mechanic, in addition to road-testing new manufacturer's products. Being possessed of a remarkably affable, enthusiastic and enquiring nature, Sammy got to know anyone who was anyone and they got to know him – and his black beret. There can hardly have been a car manufacturer, race, rally, trials or team driver and or team manager, of any consequence, with whom he was not on both friendly and professional terms. Nor, for that matter, a major race in which he did not participate, somehow, 'some-when'. In fact his skills and overall knowledge resulted in him acting as a race and or pit team manager on a number of occasions, over the years. His aptitude at this job was such as to enable him to write a treatise on the subject. In addition to becoming the Sports Editor of THE AUTOCAR, he was an author of a number of books, as well as a humorous cartoonist using the *nom de plume* 'Casque'.

Sammy's track experience appears to have commenced in 1921, piloting, without much success, an AC. That was until the year-end when a new 1.5 litre racing engine allowed him to gain some class speed records. The year 1922 saw him in the driving seat of an Aston Martin, ('Bunny' – Reg No. AM 273)* again involved in record breaking. However, as he raced so many varied machines during this decade, only the highlights are detailed.

His first serious outing was as a riding mechanic to none other than Count Louis Zborowski. The latter was driving his straight eight Miller in the 1924 French Grand Prix, held close by Lyons. During the race, the front axle unfortunately parted company with the rest of the car, resulting in an 'early bath' for the participants. Sammy would appear to have formed a close relationship with the Count. Thus, in addition to Clive Gallop, his wife accompanied the party. Incidentally, the day-time hack cars were the Count's two seater Monza H6C Hispano-Suiza, a Vauxhall 30-98 and a Packard. Yes, a Packard named 'Peter'...!

Sammy partnered Jean Chassagne at the 1925 Le Mans, in a 3 litre, 6 cylinder Sunbeam. As the car was being driven from the Channel ferry port to the circuit, the chassis cracked. Subsequently the Darracq Works collected the vehicle and managed to return it to the track, in time for practice. Scary as that had proved, the Le Mans circuit was showing serious signs of deteriorating, and that was prior to the race commencing. As an aside, it is interesting to

---

* *See* page 47.

Plate 37a. Jean Chassagne with Sammy Davis as his co-driver in the 3 litre Sunbeam in which they finished second in the 1925 Le Mans. This year marked the inception of the traditional Le Mans style starts – drivers dash across the track, leap in, often with hood up and down rules, press the starter and (hopefully) away.
Courtesy Sunbeam Racing Cars, Anthony Heal. Foulis/Haynes.

Plate 37b. Sammy Davis accompanied by LV Head (also of Autocar) at the finish of the first Brooklands Six Hour Race, 1927. The start was a Le Mans dash across the track, hoods up for ten laps after which they could be stowed. They finished second over the line in their duck's back 12/50 Alvis to Duller in a 3 litre, 6 cylinder Sunbeam but won the *Autocar Cup* on handicap – from Sammy's employer!
Courtesy The Vintage Alvis Peter Hull & Norman Johnson. Macdonald

Plate 38a. Busy, busy. The coachyard of the *Hotel Moderne*, Le Mans in 1927. The three Bentley entries are undergoing pre-race preparation. To the fore is the 4.5 litre of Clement & Callingham (No. 1), in the middle the 3 litre of Duller & d'Erlanger (No. 2) and to the rear is the 3 litre of Benjafield & Davis (No. 3).
Courtesy WO Bentley Memorial Foundation.

Plate 38b.   Sammy in his 3 litre Bentley (No. 3 – *Old No. 7*) joins the 'White House Party' in the 1927 Le Mans, desperately trying to avoid the 3 litre Bentley of Duller & d'Erlanger (No. 2) who had crashed into the 4.5 litre Bentley of Clement & Callingham (No. 1). Sammy had slowed somewhat, alerted by a headlight 'searchlighting' the sky, then observing in the glow of the lights specks of chestnut paling glinting on the road surface followed by heavy tyre skid marks.

Courtesy The Bentley at Le Mans, Dr. Benjafield.
Motor Racing Publications.

Plate 38c.

Plate 38d.

Plate 38c, d & e. Sammy's 3 litre Bentley (No. 3 – *Old No. 7*) being prepared for the grand Savoy Hotel appearance.

Plates 38a, c, & d. Courtesy The Autocar.

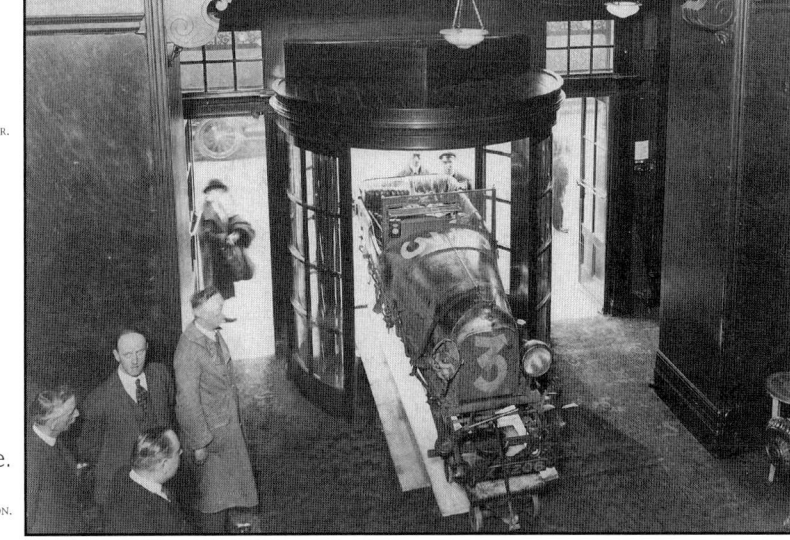

Plate 38e.

Courtesy WO Bentley Memorial Foundation.

Plate 39. *Old No. 7* making its final Savoy ascent.

note that the *Café de l'Hippodrome* was providing an interestingly informal breakfast and tea rendezvous, for the crews and drivers, all those years ago. Despite experiencing pot-holes, flying stones, dust-obscured lighting, being forced off the road (which caused the front axle to take a good thumping), the throttle jamming wide open and the brakes fading badly, Chassagne drove the car over the line in second place. They were only eight miles adrift of the lead car after 24 hours.

The 1926 Le Mans (Tom's year) had Sammy partnered with Dr. Benjafield in the Works 3 litre Bentley ('Old No. 7'). As has been recorded elsewhere in this chapter, a shower and lack of braking power resulted in Sammy 'sandbanking' the machine. Incidentally, as an aide memoir, and as has been detailed previously, it was this self-same car that Benjafield 'tree'd' at the Boulogne Race Week, later in the year.

There is no doubt that Mr Davis spread his talents about, as he was driving a 'duck's back', Super Sport 12/50 Alvis in the 1927 Brooklands Six Hour Race. This was the original event of its kind and it was with some embarrassment, he accepted first prize. The discomfort? Well, it was his employer who donated the cup and had formulated the regulations! You can imagine the banter. Later in the year, for Le Mans, all was as for the 1926 event. That is he was co-driving the self-same 3 litre Bentley, with the good Doctor, but now Race No. 3. However, this was the infamous year of the massive, night-time Bentley pile-up, at White House Corner. The initial cause of the accident was a Monsieur Pierre Tabourin. On lap 34 he crashed his 4 cylinder, 2 litre Theo. Schneider, whereat he, and it, lay across the track. Into this careered Callingham, in a 4.5 litre Bentley, closely followed by the 3 litre Bentley of Duller, then another Schneider and finally a 4 cylinder, 1100cc SARA. Sammy Davis arrived on the scene, also piling into the accumulation of 'scrap metal'. With great good fortune, and much effort, this 'late arrival' was extricated to 'crab' its way back to the pits. Here the 'necessary' repairs were carried out to the front end, in order to keep the car on the road. The lead 4 cylinder, 3 litre Aries, being driven by Laly, started to slow but wily 'old Jean Chassagne' took over the helm. He increased its advantage over the Davis and Benjafield Bentley, which was being nursed round the circuit. At this stage Benjafield was urged to speed up, after which the Aries came to a halt – only to restart. The tension in the pits must have been unbearable. Despite having little or no brakes, the shock absorbers being out of adjustment and the battery-box loose, as well as all the smash associated problems, the Bentley kept motoring on. Then 'Benjy' had to pull-up to re-secure the running board. The Aries stopped again, around about which stage the Doctor came in for Sammy to take over for the last laps – to win at Le Mans. Only eight cars finished. It appears the drinks started at the *Hotel Moderne* and then went on to the *Hotel de Paris*, and so on. At the later, celebratory *Savoy Hotel* dinner, laid on by Sammy's employer and chairman, Sir Edward Illife, the Bentley in question was 'invited' to the meal. Negotiating the ascent to the first floor and back down again proved as difficult a task as getting the vehicle round the circuit! To finish off the year the RAC promoted a Brooklands British Grand Prix (1st October). For this event Sammy was co-driving with George Eyston in a supercharged 1.5 litre Type 39A GP Bugatti, entered by Baron d'Erlanger. They had a lot of problems with the car and had to swap machines. Despite which, and after 'a bit of a scrap' with Benoist, in 1.5 litre, straight eight Delage, and who was to win, they had to retire with an engine fault.

For the May 1928 Six Hour Brooklands Race, Sammy was in a 1100cc Riley Nine

Plate 40a. Harvey & Purdy (No. 27) and Davis & Urquhart-Dykes (No. 28) pose for the camera in their 1482cc unsupercharged FWD Alvis at the 1928 Le Mans. The former pair achieved sixth place, all the first five cars being in excess of 4 litres. Sammy and Dykes came in ninth.

Courtesy The Vintage Alvis, Peter Hall & Norman Johnson. Macdonald.

Plate 40b. On the left Boris Ivanowski, who drove Alfa Romeos (1500cc on Friday and 1750cc on Saturday) and won both day's races in the 1929 12/13 July Phoenix Park Irish Grand Prix. On the right Sammy Davis, driving a 1500cc Lea-Francis, came in a very creditable second in the Friday Saorstat Cup Race.

Courtesy The Autocar.

Plate 40c. Apart from the success of Sammy Davis (third from left), the Lea-Francis Team won the prize for the best Team performance in the 1929 Irish Grand Prix Saorstat Cup Race.

Courtesy Racing in the Park, Bob Montgomery. Dreoilin Specialist Publications Ltd.

Brooklands Speed Model. Not only did he have some trouble with the ten laps, hood-up stipulation, but his race was 'run' when the engine failed. Hallam's Lea-Francis burnt down to the chassis, Ramponi, in a twin cam, supercharged 1500cc Alfa Romeo, was awarded best performance and Birkin won in a 4.5 litre Bentley. At Le Mans, Sammy shared a 1.5 litre, 4 cylinder, front wheel drive (FWD) Alvis with Urquhart Dykes. They had a fright when the car very nearly ran out of fuel, prior to completing the mandatory first 20 laps without making a pit-stop. That night Sammy experienced a rear tyre puncture but managed to claw his way back to the pits. The following day they were still motoring on, but another puncture lost them a few places, finally coming in ninth overall. That was the year Barnato and Rubin, in a 4.5 litre Bentley, triumphed over a strong American contingent and Birkin and Chassagne came in fifth, in another 4.5 litre Bentley. For the Ards Tourist Trophy Sammy was again in a Brooklands Riley. Rain made the track rather uncertain and at Ballystockart, whilst avoiding the crashed Lea-Francis of Newsome, which had been avoiding the crashed FWD Alvis of Major Harvey, he also crashed.

For the (first) 1929 Brooklands Double Twelve Hour Race, Sammy was accompanied by Sir Ronald Gunter, in a 4.5 litre Bentley. They finished the first of the two day event, in joint second place, with Ivanovski's supercharged 1500cc Alfa Romeo behind the similar Alfa Romeo of Ramponi. On day two, the Bentley's oil pressure became a real worry. Additionally, a rain squall caused Sammy to clout a sandbank and a marker barrel. With four hours to go, and Gunter at the wheel, a rear tyre burst. Despite overhauling the lead Alfa, when it pitted to sort out a loose battery box, they burst another tyre. Once again gaining on Ramponi, race control made the Bentley come into the pits, to secure a supposedly loose bonnet strap. Now, running on yet another bald tyre, and with zero oil pressure, they finished almost side-by-side with Ramponi. However, they came second, on handicap – by 0.003 – after 24 hours racing and being 129 miles ahead, on the road. Rather bad luck. That year was somewhat busy for Sammy and the Phoenix Park Irish Grand Prix (12-13th July) followed. The first day was for small engine capacity cars competing for the Saorstat Cup and had him in a 1500cc Lea-Francis. The track surface was very sticky and Ramponi, in an Alfa Romeo, crashed at Gough Corner, whilst attempting to overtake a gaggle of competitors. This let Sammy into second place, behind the faultless Ivanowski in his Alfa. Whatever he tried he could not overtake Ivanowski, finishing 66 seconds adrift – and out of petrol. This excitement was followed by the Ards Tourist Trophy Race. Last event a 'Leaf', this race a Brooklands 1100cc Riley. After a good start, he passed Rubin's 'Blower' 4.5 litre Bentley, upside down close by Glen Hill. After rain, Newtownards Town Hall took at least three 'hits' from various competitors and Cmdr. Glen Kidston's Speed Six Bentley straddled a bank at Bradshaw's Brae, with the bonnet nose down towards the ditch. Perilously close to this latter debacle were the additional hazards of a viewing platform and a telegraph pole, which Kidston had managed to avoid. A difficult pit stop, with clutch disengagement problems, dropped Sammy quite a few places but he won his class and finished 12th overall. The season ended with the Brooklands 500 Mile Race. Sammy was not 'booked' to have a drive, despite which he was persuaded, on the morning of the event, to drive the now re-bodied, ex-Kidston's TT Race Speed Six Bentley. There had been pit murmurings of it being difficult to steer. In fact the day before the event the car was in danger of being scratched. That dangerous! When asked

Plate 41a. The start of the 1930 Brooklands Double Twelve. Hall's Lagonda (No. 12) leads Jack Dunfee's 'Blower' Bentley (No. 5), Davis's Speed Six (No. 3), Barnato's Speed Six (No. 2) and de Durand's 4.5 litre Bentley (No. 10).
Courtesy WO Bentley Memorial Foundation.

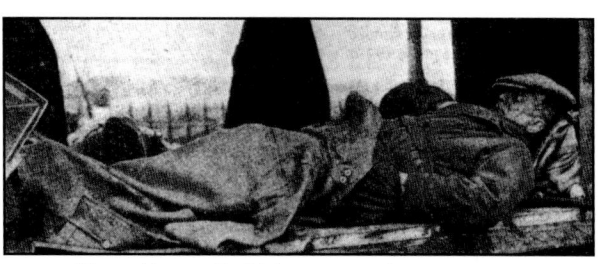

Plate 41c. Earl Howe snatching a nap.

Plate 41b. Barnato & Clement (No. 2), the eventual winners, and Davis & Clive Dunfee (No. 3) who finished second, sweep past de Durand's Bentley (No. 10) and the Hon. Mrs Bruce's 2 litre Silver Eagle Alvis (No. 34).
Courtesy WO Bentley Memorial Foundation.

The 1930 Brooklands Double Twelve.

Plate 41d. Barnato topping up the 'rad'.

Plate 41e. HRH Prince George 'cackling' to Barnato, Davis and WO in the Bentley pit.
Courtesy WO Bentley Memorial Foundation.

Plate 41f. Clive Dunfee & Sammy Davis.
Plates 41c, d & f Courtesy Autocar.

Tom. His Le Mans Year. 1926.

Plate 41g. Earl Howe experienced a difficult, tiresome spell in his 2.3 litre 8 cylinder, supercharged Type 43 Bugatti, having 'attacked' a banking and caused considerable excitement and commotion. Despite these irritations he and Malcolm Campbell finished 22nd overall and first in class.

Plate 41h. The Bugatti's damaged hub required two dashes from the Railway Straight to the pits.

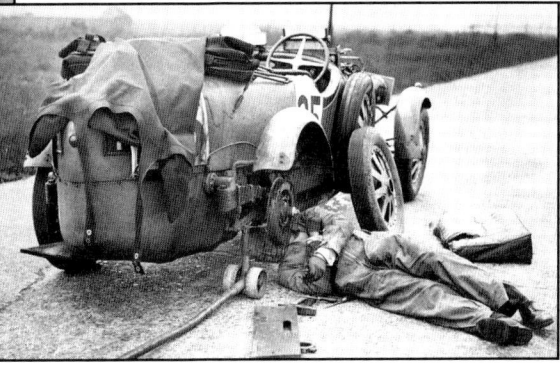

Plate 41i. The Earl at the trot with jack in hand.

Plate 41j. The fire beneath de Durand's Bentley at the pits proved difficult to extinguish.

Fig 41k. Hebeler's '105' Talbot (No. 21) after its fatal collision with Col. Rabagliati's similar Talbot (No. 22).

Plate 41l. Stableford's Riley 'exploring' a ditch. No one was hurt!

Plate 41m. Mechanics dousing the d'Erlanger 'Blower' Bentley fire with little damage to the car.

Plates 41g,h,j,l&m Courtesy Autocar.
Plates 41i & k Courtesy The Motor.

79

Plate 42a. From the start the Speed Six Bentley (No. 4) of Barnato and Kidston, the eventual winners, was already in the lead, followed by the Speed Six (No. 3) of Davis and Clive Dunfee.

The 1930 Le Mans.

Plate 42b. The Speed Six's of Davis (No. 3) and Barnato (No. 4) race past a 4 cylinder 850cc MG Midget.

Plate 42c. "Clive Dunfee's unlucky day. He takes over Bentley No. 3, then lying second, and crashes into the sandbank at Pontlieue."

PLATE 42A, B & C COURTESY OF THE AUTOCAR.

by WO if he would take up the drive, Sammy jumped at the opportunity, despite never having handled a Speed Six – ever. Querying the legality of the driver switch, it appeared it had all been arranged beforehand! His partner was to be Clive Dunfee. The supposedly dangerous 'at speed' handling was overcome by controlling the steering wheel with 'soft hands'. The doughty duo incurred a couple of tyre problems, during the race, and there was a fair amount of general vehicle attrition. Sammy took over for the final spell of the race. Despite putting in the fastest lap of the day, he had to settle for second place to Clement, driving a 4.5 litre Bentley (who achieved his win in spite of his partner's 'wild-west driving' – one Jack Barclay), but in front of John Cobb and C Paul in their 4 litre, supercharged 12 cylinder Sunbeam ('Tiger'*).

The 1930 season started with the Brooklands Double Twelve, in which Sammy was driving a Speed Six Bentley, with his now familiar partner, Clive Dunfee. Apart from the Bentley Team, the Birkin/Paget 'Blowers' were also competing. From reading between the lines, it appears that where both the Bentley Teams were in action, there was some inter-camp rivalry and tensions. The two day event incurred a five minute hail storm, followed by rain, which made for difficult driving conditions. Sammy's car incurred a broken valve spring and two Talbot '105s' collided, the latter accident causing death and destruction. The third Talbot of Max Aitken, son of the newspaper magnate Beaverbrook, retired in sympathy. With the first day over, 19 cars had fallen by the wayside plus the voluntary Talbot retirement. On the second day Sammy's Bentley incurred another broken valve spring and a fractured oil pipe. Prior to the race end, some two hours of torrential rain fell, with Barnato and Clement driving a Speed Six Bentley finishing first and Davis and Dunfee second, some 24 miles adrift. This year's Le Mans saw Sammy and Clive Dunfee again sharing their 'Double Twelve' Bentley. Sammy was first away, harrying the sole S-38/250 Mercedes of Caracciola. That was until he was overhauled by Tiger Tim in his 'Blower' 4.5 litre Bentley, who then took over that task (*See* Chapter 5). Sammy subsequently overtook Tim's car, the latter having suffered from the damaging effects of a rear tyre being torn off, just after overtaking the Mercedes. Later, Sammy's goggles were shattered by a flying stone causing slivers of glass to penetrate his eye. After calmly pitting, whilst lying second, he toddled along to THE AUTOCAR stall, where he partook of a cup of tea and had some of the offending pieces of glass carefully removed – as you do. As has been recorded elsewhere (*See* Chapter 3), Clive then stuffed the car into the Pontlieue sandbank. He alone, and then he and Sammy, attempted to dig the vehicle out, only to discover the steering and front wheels were damaged, beyond repair. Their race was run. Still in some pain, it was discovered Sammy had even more glass left in his eye. How very unpleasant. At the Phoenix Park Irish Grand Prix, he drove the brand new 1.5 litre dry sump Aston Martin, LM4, which appeared to lack the top 300 or more of the top end engine revolutions. Whatever, he finished in seventh place. For the Ards Tourist Trophy Race he competed in a supercharged Lea-Francis. These particular vehicles required a very complicated and precise starting procedure, as well as having a rather hit-and-miss engine oil replacement system. It is interesting to note that a youthful Tom Delaney was very helpful in assisting solving some radiator problems for the 'Leaf' team. He was the son of the Delaney who ran the vehicle radiator and fuel tank family-owned manufacturing firm of

---

* *See* page 63. This model was originally designed for breaking land speed records by such as Henry Segrave.

Plate 43a. Sammy Davis, driving a 750cc Austin (No. 1) in the 1930 October Brooklands 500 Mile Handicap Race with the Earl of March. He had a very close shave when the Dunfee Brothers 2 litre, 6 cylinder supercharged GP Sunbeam (ex May Cunliffe) lost a wheel and half shaft with Clive at the wheel. Having survived the incident Davis went on to win.
COURTESY THE MOTOR

The 1930 October Brooklands 500 Mile Handicap Race.

Plate 43b. Sammy at the controls of 'Blood Orange', so named due to the colour of the paintwork.
COURTESY THE MOTOR.

Plate 43c. The victors, Sammy and the Earl of March.
COURTESY BROOKLANDS SOCIETY.

Plate 43d. The upturned 4.5 litre Invicta of Sammy Davis after his serious accident in the 1931 Brooklands Easter Mountain Handicap Race. Having put in the fastest lap, in inclement conditions, the car and driver skidded down the Members Banking prior to overturning. The Invicta was presumably the S Type developing up to 158bhp from the 4.5 litre, dual ignition Meadows engine.
COURTESY AUTOCAR.

Delaney Gallay. Incidentally, this company had originally been involved in the assembly of imported Delaunay-Belleville motor cars. He was also the Tom Delaney who passed away at the end of 2006, and was a legend in our time, still competing in VSCC events in his historic Lea-Francis Team Car, almost until the very end. But back to the race, which was one of woe for Sammy and the team. His car would not start straight away and then it rained. This deluge caused him to experience a massive slide, just about missing every obstacle he could or appeared to be about to hit. At the next pit stop, too much oil was put into the engine, after which the plugs had to be changed – in the rain. Oh dear me! His mount failed three laps from the finish and the rest of the team were also unsuccessful, leaving Alfa Romeo to sweep the board. His last racing outing of the decade was in the Brooklands 500 Mile Handicap Race. In this he shared a supercharged TT 750cc Austin 7 with the then Earl March. Here again Sammy was a last minute recruit. The weather was inclement but, despite a huge effort by Benjafield in a 'Blower' 4.5 litre Bentley, which was chucking about lumps of tyre, the Austin beat him home to come in first. Behind Benjafield and Hall was the 2 litre, 6 cylinder Sunbeam ('The Cub') of Cushman and Purdy.

Although stretching the parameters of the book's narrative, in the 1931 Brooklands Easter Mountain Handicap Race, and driving a 4.5 litre Invicta, Sammy experienced a nasty crash. He had just made fastest lap when he lost control and rolled down a bank. The car finished up on its side. His leg was badly smashed and he had to spend about a year in this or that hospital. It was a few years before he was able to take up motor racing again. The year 1934 found him assisting the Aston Martin Team with their racing management. The following season saw him back in the 'saddle' to compete in an Aston.

He even had a good WW2, joining the then engineering branch of the RAOC as a Lieutenant. This organisation became the REME. Following D-Day, he embarked with his regiment, from Southampton, to land at Arromanches. *En route* to cross the Rhine, 'his lot' managed to proceed via Le Mans. Here Sammy dutifully 'did' a tour of the old circuit. He reported it had suffered quite a mauling. Well, there's a surprise!

DR. JOSEPH DUDLEY 'BENJY' BENJAFIELD (1880-1957). The Doctor's speciality was bacteriology and he was sufficiently eminent to gain a Harley Street address. Being popular with the other Bentley Boys, he was known as 'our bald headed chemist'! Most of the racing drivers of the 1920s spent some years sorting out their favourite or chosen marque, if ever. On the other hand, Benjy was (fairly) steadfast, plumping first off for a Bentley, as early as 1923. After the Duff & Clement's 1923 Le Mans win, he ordered a long chassis, 3 litre Bentley with a standard saloon body. Whilst having his new acquisition serviced, he made the aside that his car lacked grunt. That it "...*would appear to find it difficult to break its way out of the skin of the proverbial rice pudding*" – or words to that effect. In a trice he was led over to an oil and dirt streaked, red bodied, two seater Bentley. He was then instructed to be at Brooklands the next day, where he would be given, by way of a demonstration, conclusive proof of what one of these cars really could achieve. Reluctant to back down, the game 'medico' agreed to be 'all present and correct and on parade'. And he was. He was apparently given the fright of his life, as a passenger. After his legs lost a rubbery inability to support him, he shakily enquired after the price of the machine. He bought it, there and then, later claiming that he did not know

THE FORGOTTEN BENTLEY BOY.

Plate 44a. The 'good' Doctor Benjafield soon after his purchase of the 1922, ex Clement two seater 3 litre Bentley (No. 2 – Reg. No. MF 330), at the 1924 Brooklands Whitsun meeting. Just forward of the cockpit, cloth capped and facing the camera is Noel van Raalte.
COURTESY THE OTHER BENTLEY BOYS, ELIZABETH NAGLE. HARRUP.

Plate 44b. The 1927 Le Mans pre-race Bentley line-up. From the left: Clement, Callingham, d'Erlanger, Duller, Davis and Benjafield. Behind Davis is the Marquis de Casa Maury alongside whom is WO. Behind d'Erlanger is Barnato…
COURTESY THE OTHER BENTLEY BOYS, ELIZABETH NAGLE. HARRUP.

Plate 44c. …and the overjoyed 1927 Le Mans 3 litre Bentley winning pair of Benjafield and Davis, the latter standing on the driving seat whilst Benjafield comforts Chassagne, whose Aries had to retire.
COURTESY BENTLEY FACTORY CARS, MICHAEL HAY. OSPREY AUTOMOTIVE.

Plate 44d. George Duller and Sammy Davis at Brooklands.
COURTESY THE RACING ZBOROWSKIS, DAVID COLSON. VSCC LTD.

84

why! This was the 1922, Race No. 2, ex-Clement, 3 litre, two seater race car!

During 1924 he had an excellent season in his recent acquisition, reportably enjoying himself immensely. He achieved at least one good win and several places. As a result of this showing, he was approached to co-drive with 'Bertie' Kensington Moir, in the 1925 Le Mans. Incidentally, the pre-race training necessary to lose those few spare pounds weight, as well as finally hone the body and mind, was achieved by digging up 'Bertie's' kitchen garden! As you do! It would be remiss not to report they had to retire on lap 19. The car had run out of fuel due to a serious miscalculation in respect of the petrol consumption, with the hood up, combined with some spirited driving by 'Bertie'. During this year Benjy also raced a new San Sebastian Salmson, in addition to his red Bentley. Long after his demise, it came to light that subsequent to Woolf Barnato's takeover of Bentley Motors, the 'good' Doctor often 'financed' one or more of the race car line-ups. Whatever, thereafter he was a team member at the next four Le Mans, winning in 1927 and achieving a third in 1929. And that was in addition to a number of Six Hour and Double Twelve Brooklands Race wins over the years.

Being a very 'clubable' gentleman, Benjy used to host fairly 'chatty', most enjoyable dinner parties, at his Wimpole Street home, for the great and the good drivers of the day. These gatherings were to lead to the founding of the *British Racing Drivers Club* in 1926.

GEORGE EDWARD 'CROUCHER' DULLER (1891-1962). A most unusual racing driver in that, prior to his taking to the circuits, he was a renowned jockey. And no ordinary one at that. An authority on the subject wrote that he was a *'specialist jockey over the hurdles, a steeplechaser par excellence'*. He was short, stocky and somewhat 'horse faced', with an exaggerated 'trademark hunch' over the saddle – thus *The Croucher*. In 1918 he was the Champion National Hunt Jockey. It is reported he made Sandown's *Imperial Cup* 'his own'. This event was the most prestigious hurdle race of the season, until along came the Cheltenham Champion Hurdle, in 1927. He won the *Imperial Cup* seven times as a rider, three of these on *Trespasser*, reputably the finest hurdling horse of the time. Incidentally, he was still riding the 'gee-gee's' up to 1927. Even after giving up riding, he went on to win this particular event twice, but as a trainer. He was then based at St. Margaret's Racing Stables, Langley Vale Village, due south of Epsom. He also found time to pilot his own plane. Just shows what used to happen, prior to the advent of television.

Despite all this horse-flesh involvement, in about 1921 he commenced racing 'iron' steeds as well. One of his first mounts was a Silver Hawk owned by a Capt. Macklin*. Being a friend of Parry Thomas, it was not surprising to find him aboard a Malborough Thomas, in 1923. This was the same year in which his wife was recorded as racing, in amongst other cars, a Leyland Eight. Over the years Duller competed in any number of vehicles. These included: the ex-Zborowski 'Indy' Type 30 Bugatti; a 3 litre, twin-cam 6 cylinder Sunbeam; a 'Blower' 4.5 litre Bentley, for Birkin's equipage; an Austin 7; an MG; and a Maserati. In the 1930s he drove for, amongst others, Gwenda Stewart, Whitney Straight and Elsie Wisdom. He was still racing in 1938 and 1939, in a Duesenberg. Wherever he was present he enlivened the proceedings, being renowned as an ebullient, mischievous practical joker, who could take it,

* The 10/35hp Silver Hawk was an out and out sports car from the Capt. Noel Macklin stable of car production between 1920–1921. Similar to his earlier Eric-Campbell but with a 1373cc side valve engine. Later on in the decade he was to evolve the Invicta.

THE FORGOTTEN BENTLEY BOY.

Plate 45a. Frank Clement in the driving seat of the 3 litre Bentley (EXP 2), the car later purchased by Doctor Benjafield.
Courtesy Bentley Factory Cars 1919-1931. Michael Hay. Osprey Automotive.

The 1923 Le Mans.

Plate 45b.   The 1923 Le Mans. Clement and Duff driving a 3 litre Bentley achieved a very creditable fourth place, despite a 2½ hour delay caused by a punctured fuel tank. Here Clement is to be seen stemming the leak…
Plates 45 b & c Courtesy WO Bentley Memorial Foundation.

Plate 45c.   …and here post race, the weary duo.
Courtesy WO Bentley Memorial Foundation.

as well as hand it out. It can be no wonder he was a great chum of Woolf Babe Barnato.

He commenced racing for Bentley's in the 1926 Le Mans paired with Frank Clement but they had to retire. In 1927 and prior to the Le Mans, in which he partnered Baron d'Erlanger, and during which race they crashed, he competed in the Brooklands Six Hour Endurance event. Driving a 3 litre twin cam, 6 cylinder Sunbeam, he came home first after an eventful race. Later that year he and Frank Clement came home first in the GP de Paris staged at Montlehery, driving a 4.5 litre Bentley. This was the first win for this model, despite the car catching fire twice. His next Bentley appearance was with Tiger Tim Birkin in a 'Blower' 4.5 at the Brooklands 500 Mile Race (4th October 1930). They finished ninth, but that was the last appearance of the 'Blower breed' as a Team.

FRANK C 'SUNSHINE' CLEMENT (1888-1970). Frank Clement could claim to be amongst the most interesting of all the racing drivers during the 1920s. He was a true professional in that he earned his living through the sport. Rather similar (for those of us old enough to remember) to the days when cricketers were classed as professionals and gentlemen. When the latter had to occupy different dressing rooms and that was only some thirty or forty years ago. In modern-day 'babble-speak', his personal interactive skills must have been supreme. This paid-hand had to intermingle with men of immense power and wealth, many of whom had delicate egos which could easily be bruised and or umbrage swiftly taken. Fortunately for fairly short, squat Frank, he was calm, fast and unflustered, more especially in the pits. Additionally, he was blessed with unlimited technical knowledge and was liked equally by both his fellow workforce and the private clients. Another commentator blessed him with a light hearted, devil-may-care attitude to life. Pass the halo's round!

Born at Tring, his youthful interest in 'all things motoring' had been ignited by the 'goings on' at the nearby Aston Clinton Hill Climb. Jobs at Star Engineering, Napier's and vehicle testing with Vauxhall's, were followed by his joining Straker-Squire. Here, apart from works duties, he also raced their cars. Frank, in a Straker–Squire, and WO, in a DFP, both competed in the 1914 Isle of Man Tourist Trophy Race. His immediate post-WW1 service, in the Royal Engineers, was as head of department, testing aero engines. There's a surprise. Almost all the early-day engineers associated with WO appear to have been in and around wartime aeroplane power units. He joined Bentley's in 1920, initially as Works Manager. When Clive Gallop departed, in the direction of Count Louis Zborowski, he assumed responsibility for the new Experimental Department. He also dealt with the demands of preparing the competition cars. It was whilst in this position that fate dealt Frank Clement one of those rare, pot-beating hands of cards. He met Capt. John Duff. This gentleman, in conjunction with William Adlington, trading as Duff and Adlington, from No. 10 Upper St. Martin's Lane, had at about that time been appointed one of Bentley's London agents. Please excuse a short diversion from Frank to paste in a paragraph or ten in respect of the aforementioned:

CAPT. JOHN F (*Le Capitaine*) **DUFF** (1895-1958). A schoolboy hero if ever there was one. If you were to pen a short biography of this man and send it to *THE EAGLE, THE HOTSPUR* or *BOY'S OWN* or whatever is the modern day equivalent, they might well dismiss the whole extravaganza – as being too ridiculous for words. But here goes. It appears that John's parents

Plate 46a. John Duff seated in his 3 litre Bentley whilst the car is refuelled and oiled, whilst breaking the Double Twelve Hour and Class D records in 1922, at Brooklands.

PLATES 46A & B COURTESY THE OTHER BENTLEY BOYS. ELIZABETH NAGLE. HARRAP.

Plate 46b. Duff during the same achievement, here having a push start. Clement and WO are to the right of the picture.

Plate 47a. The 1924 Le Mans. Duff and Clement's 3 litre Bentley (No. 8) in the pits. Duff, with goggles on his forehead, oversees affairs with Clement about to rejoin the race. This despite the headlight guards being awry and the windscreen missing.

COURTESY WO BENTLEY MEMORIAL FOUNDATION.

TOM. HIS LE MANS YEAR. 1926.

Plate 47b. Bentley No. 8 powers on, night…
COURTESY AN ILLUSTRATED HISTORY OF THE BENTLEY CAR, WOB. GEORGE ALLEN & UNWIN.

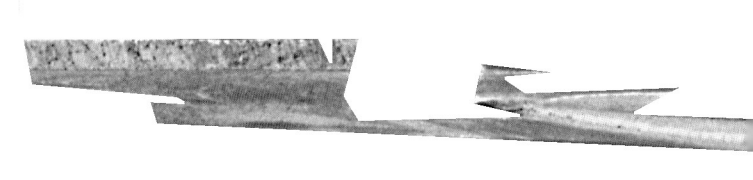

Plate 47c. …and day.
COURTESY THE BENTLEY AT LE MANS, DR. BENJAFIELD MD. MOTOR RACING PUBLICATIONS.

Plate 47d. Duff and Clement celebrate the first ever Bentley win at Le Mans.
COURTESY THE BENTLEY AT LE MANS, DR. BENJAFIELD MD. MOTOR RACING PUBLICATIONS.

The 1924 Le Mans.

Plate 47e. The redoubtable duo in Bentley Race No. 8, parked up in the City of Le Mans after the epic race and now 'all spruced up'.
COURTESY WO BENTLEY MEMORIAL FOUNDATION.

Plate 48a. After the success of 1924, Bentley entered two 3 litre cars, Race No. 9 to be driven by the formidable team of Clement & Duff, and Race No. 10 by Dr. Benjafield & 'Bertie' Kensington Moir. The 1925 start was the first of the 'traditional' kick-offs — dash across the track, hood up, leap in and ignite the engine and off. The two Bentleys were first away.

COURTESY BENTLEY THE VINTAGE YEARS 1919-1931.
MICHAEL HAY. HM BENTLEY & PARTNERS.

CAPT. DUFF'S LE-MANS 3 LITRE BENTLEY SPORTS
COACHWORK BY VANDEN PLAS (ENGLAND) 1923 LTD.

The 1925 Le Mans.

Plate 48b. The Bentley Team had not allowed for the extra fuel consumed by high speed racing with the hood erected for the mandatory 20 laps. Additionally, the first fuel stop could not take place until 200 miles or approximately 20 laps had been completed. The miscalculation, combined with Bertie's spirited competition with Henry Segrave in the 3 litre twin cam, 6 cylinder Sunbeam (No. 15), resulted in No. 10 running out of fuel on the 15th lap. Their race was run! Incidentally Segrave and his co-driver Duller also had to retire, after some 26 laps, with clutch problems,

COURTESY WO BENTLEY MEMORIAL FOUNDATION.

Plate 48c. The off! Bentley No. 9 suffered a broken fuel pipe at about the same time as No. 10 went out but a repair was effected after a 1½ hour delay. However at about 5am Sunday morning, with Clement at the wheel, a carburettor float chamber came adrift and the car caught fire. Their race was also run! No. 4 is a 6 cylinder, 3.5 litre Lorraine-Dietrich driven by Stalter and Brisson which came in third. The 'sister' car of Courcelles and Rossignol won the event.

COURTESY THE BENTLEY AT LE MANS, DR. BENJAFIELD MD.
MOTOR RACING PUBLICATIONS.

departed Canada for China, without father Duff explaining to his 'dearly beloved' he was taking up missionary duties. That is how the young Duff came to be borne close by the Yangtze River. For various reasons the child, now somewhat of a handful, was sent back to Canadian relatives. They and the school authorities, being unable to cope, returned him to the 'bosom of his family', back in China. Hereabouts, in 1914, and aged about 19, he decided to make his way to England, by way of the Trans-Siberian railway. Oh, and at that time Russia was at least on a war footing. On reaching England, once thoughts of his being a spy had been discarded, he joined The Royal Berkshire Rifles as a Lieutenant. He acted heroically, was promoted to Acting Captain and subsequently invalided back to good old 'Blighty'.

The year 1921 marked the onset of John Duff, the racing driver, first with a 10 litre 1910 Fiat. This was followed by another Fiat, a 1908, chain-driven monster of a vehicle nicknamed *Mephistopheles*. It was fitted with 18 litres of 'grunt', a capacity achieved by two linked cylinder blocks of 2 cylinders each. This monster had originally been commissioned from the Fiat factory by Sir George Abercrombie, Bt., a Scottish Guards officer with an Aberdeen estate. The 89.5hp car was to cost £2,500 but Fiat firstly raced it at Brooklands in a match race against Edge's Napier in 1908, which it won, and secondly built a sister car. After litigation Abercrombie had to 'cough up' £1,250 and his costs. Post-WW1 Duff located the leviathan in a London mews garage and, urged on by RF Cooper, Zborowski's chum, purchased it for £100. At the Brooklands Whitsun Race meeting he won a handicap race driving the brute, whilst Frank Clement achieved the first Bentley win in *EXP 2*, in a sprint handicap. In Duff's hands *Mephistopheles* achieved some notoriety, more especially when the engine experienced what was reported at the time as possibly the most immense explosion in the history of motor racing – ever! In an effort to 'beef-up' the performance he had Ricardo's design replacement high performance pistons – despite the latter's misgivings. With Callingham, a Shell Petroleum representative, as a riding passenger, one of the cylinder blocks went into orbit, taking the enormous bonnet and other ancillaries with it. The good Captain, not surprisingly, appeared to lose interest in the vehicle, a state of mind probably accelerated by his running a 21.5 litre Benz, owned by Dunne, over the top of the Brooklands banking, breaking both his ankles. More importantly, he had purchased a short chassis, 3 litre Bentley and was offered a London sales franchise if he could locate a suitable address and showroom. Having met a Mr Adlington, who luckily had such premises in Upper St. Martin's Lane, the business of Duff and Adlington was formed and the Bentley deal done. Astride the newly acquired car, in 1922 he gained the Double Twelve Hour as well as a lot of Class D records. At this stage it might be germane to appreciate that *Le Capitaine* was not only an all round sportsman and a world class fencer, but was an extremely tough fellow.

Following on these successes he approached WO with the suggestion that he should enter the 1923 Le Mans. WO's initial and, for that matter, second and third response was one of total dismissal. But the young man, being a personable fellow, won the day. As a result he was offered the services of, you've guessed it, Frank Clement. The latter was to help prepare the car and be co-driver. And that, as they say, is history. Anyone who has not driven, let alone raced flat-out on old, narrow, unsealed, flint and gravel surfaced tracks can have little if any idea of the state, or lack of state, of the then surfaces, over which the Le Mans race was run. Apart from the dirt, dust, stones and corrugations, there were the deep, very deep potholes

Plate 49a. The 1926 Le Mans. The 3 litre Bentley (No. 8), with Clement seated. Behind him is Gallop beside whom are Benjafield and Davis.

PLATES 49A & D COURTESY THE BENTLEY AT LE MANS, DR. BENJAFIELD MD. MOTOR RACING PUBLICATIONS.

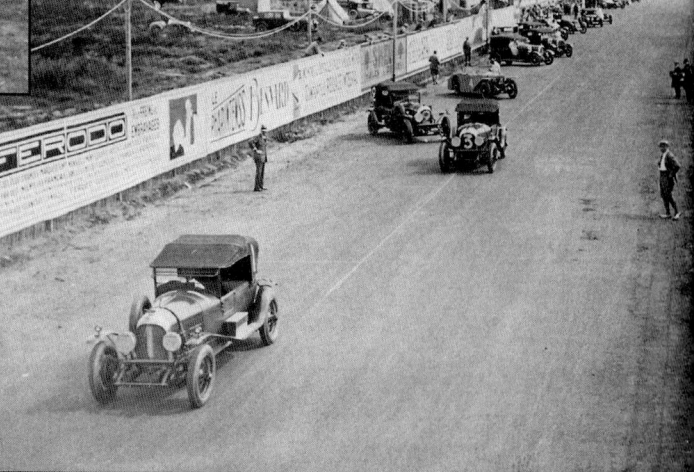

Plate 49b. The 1927 le Mans. Clement & Callingham's (first) 4.5 litre Bentley (No. 1) is away in the lead, followed by the 'Old No. 7' 3 litre Bentley of Benjafield & Davis (No. 3) and the 3 litre Bentley of d'Erlanger & Duller (No. 2). Next out is the 3 litre Aries of Chassagne & Laly.

COURTESY WO BENTLEY MEMORIAL FOUNDATION.

Plate 49c. The 1928 Le Mans. This year the hood up regulation was dropped so full scale windscreens could be replaced by fold flat items. The three Bentleys were all 4.5 litre. Here Clement (No. 2) is followed by the eventual winner, the Bentley of Barnato and Rubin with Rubin at the wheel.

COURTESY WO BENTLEY MEMORIAL FOUNDATION.

Plate 49d. Clement (No. 2) refuelling his Speed Six Bentley which he shared with Watney in the 1930 Le Mans. The gentleman on the right of the car with the seal, is the official "Plombeur" waiting to reseal the radiator cap.

COURTESY WO BENTLEY MEMORIAL FOUNDATION.

dotted about. Taking into account the rather rudimentary suspension of those days, the experience must have been an absolute nightmare. But back to the actual event. One headlight broke, almost immediately the race started, then, some three miles distant from the pits, a stone punctured the petrol tank. Fortunately, at that time there were no restrictions in respect of refuelling. So Duff ran back to the pits and Clement borrowed a bicycle, pedalled back to the car, drove a wooden peg into the hole and topped up the fuel. Despite an 'escape road' excursion and the 2½ hour delay, caused by the fuel tank problems, Clement set several lap records in attempting to make up the lost time and they managed to finish a very creditable fourth. A couple of months later, Duff competed in the GP de Tourisimo Guipusca, at the end of July, staged at San Sebastian. He had the misfortune to take a direct hit in the eye from a flying stone whilst in the lead, on lap 13. This caused him to crash out of the race. It is said he was given the 3 litre class prize to compensate for his bad luck. In September he attended the Boulogne Race Week (30th August-2nd September – *See* Chapter 6) but had to retire after running into a herd of cows!

He entered the 1924 Le Mans with a new Bentley, again with Frank as co-driver. Having learnt from the previous year's lessons, they prepared the car accordingly. WO supplied the full Works backing this time round. To overcome the natural pangs of hunger, during the long hours at the wheel, *Le Capitain* wrapped a sack-full of salad, boiled eggs and jars of honey in a bed sheet. It is not recorded if Frank was allowed to share this 'dorm fest', but they won the event. This was Bentley's first victory at Le Mans. He also cast his gaze over the various speed records, gaining many between 1922 and 1925. Incidentally, that same year, John Duff was a member of the British Olympic fencing team

In 1925 he partnered Frank Clement at Le Mans but the car caught fire on lap 64. A special 3 litre Bentley was prepared for him and Dr. Benjafield to 'have-a-go' at Montlhery (9-10th September). Breakdowns all but ruined the attempt but they achieved 'hits' in the 1,000 kilometre and 1,000 mile records. Not a quitter and with the same car, but now accompanied by Woolf Barnato, some two weeks later in the year, he made another attempt. They took the World 24 Hour Record.

At the end of March 1926 he and Clement gained the 2,000 kilometre record in a 3 litre Bentley, after which, that was that. No more racing in England. He emigrated to the USA in 1926. Outside the scope of this book, I advise any readers (still left) to track down the rest of John Duff's fascinating story.

And so back to Frank Clement. He was the only driver to compete in eight consecutive Le Mans, in the same marque. That was from 1923 through to and including 1930. Apart from his 1924 win, his only other Le Mans places were a fourth with Duff in 1923, a fourth with Jean Chassagne in 1929 and a second, with R Watney in 1930. He would appear not to have competed at a National level in motor racing thereafter. In conclusion it will not go amiss to report that it was said of Frank that he was the most resourceful driver Bentley ever had. Yes, ever had! Furthermore, that to the best of anyone's knowledge, he never crashed a car in his racing life, nor did he wreck or break a vehicle, whilst competing. His last four years with Bentley's, until their closure, were spent sharing his time between the factory, as a driver and working for the Newcastle agent as a salesman.

Plate 50a.   The Motor Yacht *Grey Mist*, Countess Zborowski's first yacht.

Plate 50b.   Schooner *Cynara* was the lady's second yacht.

Plates 50a & b Courtesy Beken of Cowes.

CHAPTER FIVE

Tom. The Lost Year. 1927.

'In my sport the quick are too often listed amongst the dead!'
JACKIE STEWART 1972.

Considering Tom's overweening devotion to matters motor racing, his absence from the 1927 circuits at first appears difficult to comprehend. For instance, why did he not follow the example set by the rest of his chums and stay with the throng of racing Bentley owner drivers? He already had his own trackworthy, racing 3 litre Bentley. Perhaps he might have considered selecting the rather individual route eventually chosen by his friend Tiger Tim Birkin? That is of 'customising' the product. There was no end of scope and many of the then 'racing-rat-pack' were 'Cricklewood-bound'.

In respect of the selection of this or that racing machine, the answer more than likely lay in Tom's individualistic and singular character. As in the past, he appears to have wished to plough his own 'pit lane'. This was as evidenced by his previous choice of mounts and as was to be the case in his notable selection of a supercharged Mercedes' for the following years. His decision to have a lay-over-year and to plump for the German machine may well be considered a very sensible 'chariot option'. But hindsight is such an exact science!

His conspicuous non participation in the year might well be understood if his busy 'off-track' social life, in and around 1927, is taken into account. Tom, it will be recalled, had probably been inspired to go motor racing by his then near neighbour Count Louis Vorow Zborowski. The latter was married to the one-time actress and Gaiety girl, Violet (Vi) Ethel Leicester. The apparent happiness of this union 'ran off the track' in the spring of 1923. For that was when the Count and one Vera ('Pixi') Marix indulged in an injudicious, ill-concealed and public period of infidelity. This passionate fling resulted in the inevitable High Court Divorce proceedings. The Countess moved out of Higham to take up residence in London. Her personal chauffeur trailed along. Not long after this domestic upheaval the Count died, in October 1924, in a horrific motor racing accident.

As an *aide memoir* it will be recalled that Tom married his first wife, Ethel Mary Hickie in 1925. A son was born later that year and by 1927 divorce proceedings were in hand. In the

Plate 51a. A classic Birkin pose.
COURTESY THE BROOKLANDS SOCIETY.

Plate 51b. The doomed marriage of Birkin and Audry Latham in 1921…

Plate 51c. …and the resultant offspring.

Plate 51d. Another classic Birkin study but this time in mufti!

PLATES 51B, C & D COURTESY CLASSIC SPORTS CAR.

meantime, the widowed Countess' chauffeur reported that '…*(the Countess) was encouraged in her vehicle ownership by her friend Tommy Thistlethwayte'*. Another source linked 'Vi' with our Tom, recording that '…*should there have been a liaison, it was conducted very discreetly'*. Well, well, well! It was this friendship that probably encouraged her in the direction of matters maritime and the ownership of not one, but two seagoing yachts. The first was the steel hulled, teak decked, twin screw Motor Yacht/Schooner *Grey Mist* built by Camper & Nicholson of Southampton and Gosport. With an overall length of some 197 ft, a beam of 117 ft, a draught of 19.5 ft and a gross tonnage of 102.5 tons, this was no rowing boat. The craft was powered by a pair of 6 cylinder petrol/paraffin units, manufactured by Thorneycroft's of Basingstoke. *Grey Mist* was followed by the 'out and out', twin screw Schooner *Cynara (ex Jason and Portia)*, originally built by Day Summers & Co. of Southampton, in 1913, with a gross tonnage of 247 tons. This latter vessel accompanied the Countess to the USA, when she married into the Singer family (yes, the sewing machine Singers), in the early 1930s, and was re-registered to Mrs Paris G Singer. It is more than likely that the Countess also owned a third craft. This was a comparative 'tiddler' described as a single screw, wood schooner of some 48 ft length, 9 ft beam and 5 ft draught and a tonnage of 5.5 tons, powered by a single petrol Thorneycroft engine. Constructed at Hampton-on-Thames, this motor launch was originally named *Elfin* but renamed, by her as *Ratcatcher*! Having married and moved to America, she lived until 1948, dying at the comparatively young age of 51. Even the good and not so fast died young!

Apart from the new Mercedes racing machine, planned for the 1928 season, it is quite possible that Tom was simply weighed down by domestic and 'social goings on'. There was the impending divorce, the first marriage coming to an end on 24th October 1927, a ruling made absolute on 9th July 1928. In addition there was the ongoing 'car and yacht advisory liaison service' with the widowed Countess. Day to day life must have been proved far too incident ridden to allow for any of that messy, dangerous, smelly old motor racing. Even the temptation of a 7th May Brooklands Race meeting for as near standard, off-the-peg sports cars, with two or four seater bodywork, and engine sizes of up to and over 1500cc did not entice Tom away from his busy social schedule. On the other hand many of Tom's contemporaries were roaring round as fast as they could go, as when and where they were able to so do.

Fellow Performers.

CAPT. (SIR) HENRY RALPH STANLEY 'TIGER TIM' BIRKIN (1896-1933). He was borne into an immensely wealthy Nottinghamshire aristocracy – and looked as if he had been. His adored Sister Ida nicknamed him 'Tiger'. He only gained the title when his father died in 1931. As has all ready been commented, he could have been plucked straight from the pages of a 1920/50s hero novel. Take your pick. Capt. WE Johns' Biggles, 'Sapper's' 'Bull-Dog Drummond' or one of Bertie Wooster's more cerebral Drones Club chums. Neat, bolt upright, military mustachioed and prone to stutter, he was always painstakingly trim. His racing apparel was almost a uniform. The white leather helmet, inset in which was a St. Christopher's badge, was matched by a pair of flying goggles. Around his neck was either a

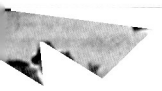

Plate 52a. Tim Birkin's 2 litre DFP in 1921 at Brooklands.
COURTESY BROOKLANDS THE COMPLETE MOTOR RACING HISTORY, WILLIAM BODDY. MRP.

Plate 52b. Miniature Speedway.

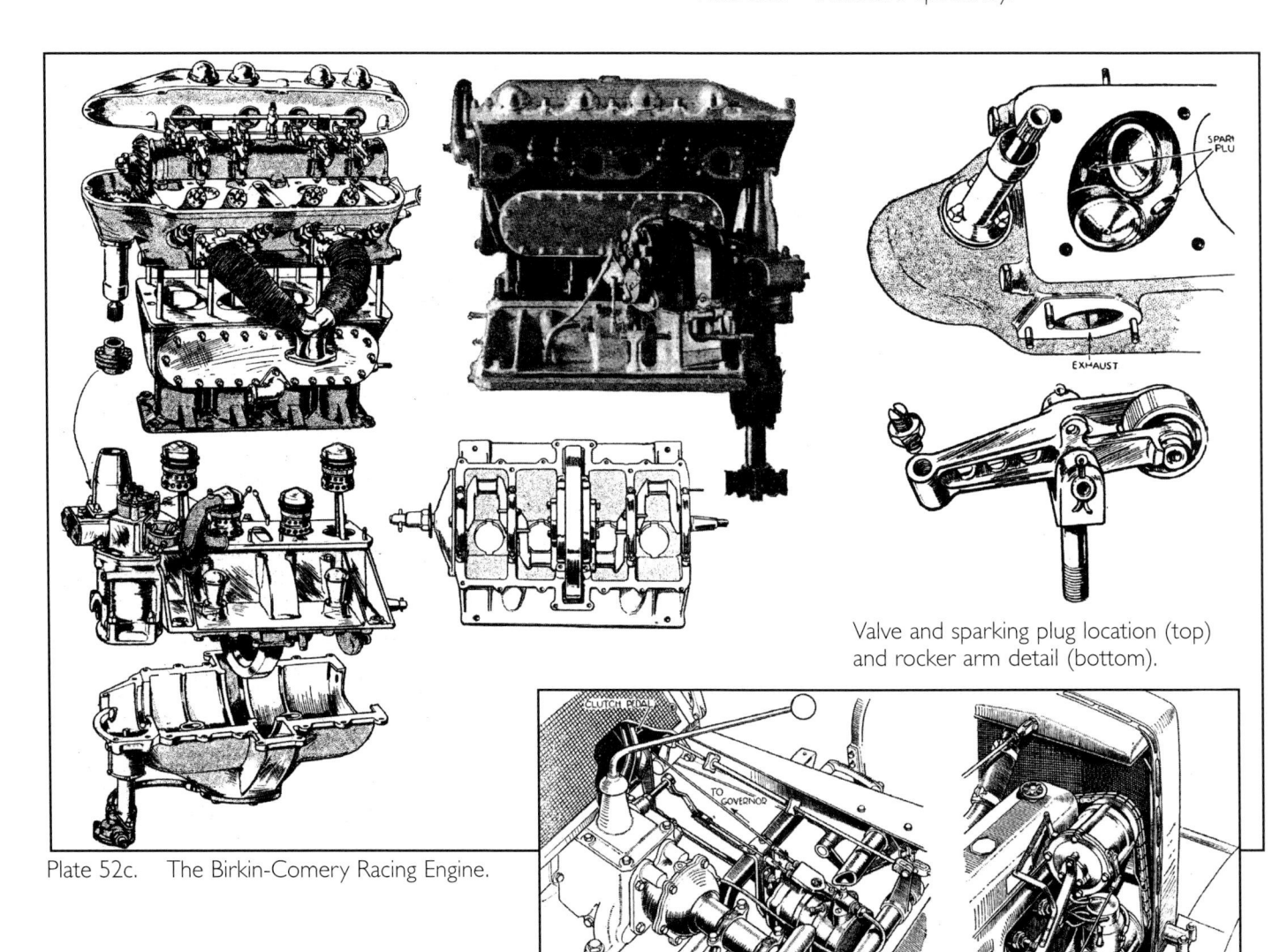

Valve and sparking plug location (top) and rocker arm detail (bottom).

Plate 52c. The Birkin-Comery Racing Engine.

PLATES 52B, C & D. COURTESY THE MOTOR

Plate 52d. The Birkin-Morgan Clutch Control Unit.

98

polka dot kerchief or a streaming white silk scarf. If not wearing white racing overalls, his slacks were matched by a dark cotton or wool shirt, with the sleeves rolled up. When necessary, he donned a tweed country jacket. His waist was kept in shape with a wide, strapped cummerbund.

Between the end of the 19th Century and WW1 the Birkin Lace Company of Nottingham was the largest in the world, but wealth did not bring family longevity. Sir Thomas Stanley Birkin and his wife the Hon. Margaret Diana Hopetoun Chetwynd had four children. They were Thomas Richard Chetwynd (1895), Tim (1896), Margaret 'Ida' (1901) and Charles Archibald ('Archie') Cecil (1905). Thomas died during WW1, whilst carrying out his wartime flying duties over Northern France, Ida succumbed to tuberculosis in Switzerland, in 1923, and 'Archie' died whilst practicing for the 1927 Isle of Man TT motor cycle race. Tim 'handed in his license' aged 33, in 1933.

Ida was a much loved family member, more especially by Tiger Tim. Her teenage war effort was spent helping her mother in nursing the wounded. It is more than likely that it was during this work that she contracted tuberculosis. Once diagnosed with the wretched disease, she was first placed in a Norfolk sanatorium. It is quite possible that Tims' love of this area was as a result of his hospital visits. Subsequently, she moved to Switzerland. To while away her convalescence, she had a fast motor launch constructed, for use on Lake Geneva. It was named 'Ida' and on her death was gifted to Tim.

He had a good war, managing to survive and achieve promotion. But then most who were lucky enough to live through that frightful experience and slaughter gained rank. They deserved it. He endured spells of service in the 7th Sherwood Foresters, the Royal Warwickshire's and the 20th Reserve Wing of the Royal Flying Corps. In Mesopotamia he contracted malaria, an insidious illness which quite possibly contributed to his early demise.

His initial, very brief racing career (started possibly late 1920, ended 1921, and not to be resumed for five years) was in an ex-WO, road-going single seater, 2 litre DFP. Post its previous ownership, it had been 'clothed' in a singular body of copper-sewn, mahogany planking, after the 'Consuta' system. This had been pioneered by Messrs Saunders Roe, of flying boat fame! He turned out for the 1921 Brooklands Easter Monday Race meeting and Clive Gallop is recorded as driving Tim's car in a later Brooklands August meeting.

Capt. Henry Ralph Stanley Birkin's marriage to Audrey Clara Lilian Latham took place on 12th July of that year. As was often the case, in those far-off, more chivalrous days, the marriage vows obviously contained the usual rider. The 'old clause' – *"darling now we are married, you must stop all that dangerous racing with motor cars"*. Additionally, his father was pressing him to be actively involved in the family business. There were two daughters of the marriage. Incidentally, despite his maintaining his absence from motor racing between 1922 and 1927, there is no evidence of his being gainfully employed within the family company. He may have had to forsake the physical pleasures of roaring around with the boys, but his fertile mind was not to ossify in respect of matters 'motor engineering'. Oh no! In 1924 a motoring magazine contained an article announcing the advent of a lightweight, Birkin-Comery, 4 cylinder, 2 litre racing engine, projected to produce 100 hp at 5000 rpm. This was accompanied by fully detailed drawings and pages of technical and construction data. The text advised that at least one of the units would shortly be making its Brooklands debut, in

Plate 53a. The 7th May 1927 Brooklands Six Hour Endurance Race. Tim Birkin and Brother Archie in a 3 litre Bentley (No. 11) are ahead of Randall's side valve Aston Martin (No. 3). Archie's somewhat erratic driving resulted in Clement sharing the drive with Tim for the last two hours.

Plate 53b. A snapshot of the 15th August 1928 Brookland Six Hour Endurance Race. The HE (No. 14) driven by Clease & Keeling is about to be overtaken by Barnato & Clement in a 4.5 litre Bentley (No. 4) with Birkin & Brother Archie following up in their 4.5 litre Bentley (No. 5). The 2.3 litre, 6 cylinder HE, despite a troublesome race, led its class until 20 minutes from the race end, when the timing gear broke.

PLATES 53A & B. COURTESY AUTOCAR

Plate 53c. The start of the 1928 Le Mans. Birkin & Chassagne in a 4.5 litre Bentley (No. 3) are first away, followed by Benjafield & Clement also in a 4.5 litre Bentley (No. 2), Chirron in a 4 litre, 6 cylinder Chrysler, Barnato in another 4.5 litre Bentley (No. 4) and Zehender's Chrysler (No. 6).

COURTESY WO BENTLEY MEMORIAL FOUNDATION.

Tom. The Lost Year. 1927.

Plate 54. As The Autocar advised "The Daily Press does not usually report Motor Races but the importance of this victory (The 1928 Le Mans) was recognised by full reports on principal pages in many journals". The Autocar selected three 'blats' (front pages) as the best accounts to reprint.

More 1928 Le Mans detailing Birkin's exploits.

Plate 55a. Birkin in the 4.5 litre Bentley (No. 3), with the rear tyre shredded, rubs along the sandbanks of the S-bend between Mulsanne and Arnage whilst being closely followed by the 4.9 litre, 8 cylinder Black Hawk Stutz (No. 1) of Bloch and Brisson.

COURTESY THE MOTOR

Plate 55b. Birkin after cutting off the shredded tyre and tube hares towards the Arnage S-bend on a bare rim.

COURTESY AUTOCAR

Plate 55c. The Bentley engineer 'Nobby' Clarke inspects the offending Birkin wheel wreckage.

COURTESY WO BENTLEY MEMORIAL FOUNDATION.

Plate 55d. Birkin completing his last lap, having broken the course lap record, to the onlookers enthusiastic 'plauds'.

COURTESY AUTOCAR

an Aston Martin chassis. After which no more was to be heard*. In fact he was a great innovator and inventor during his comparatively short lifetime. Amongst the other diverse flights of his fancy were the; Birkin-Morgan Unit Clutch Control (1932); Miniature Speedway, a model car racing set-up for up to six cars (1932), and a forerunner of Scalectrix; and a noteworthy style of double-breasted dinner jacket, accompanied by a turned down, pointed shirt collar. In addition there was some chatter about his designing and manufacturing an all British tractor during the existence of Henry Birkin & Couper Ltd. (1931-1932). This latter company was set up by Birkin and WM 'Mike' Couper to operate from the existing Welwyn Garden City premises, after the departure of the Hon. Dorothy Paget. It was liquidated in November 1932, with Couper claiming he was 'robbed'.

Tim's marriage to Audrey was 'wound up' on 29th July 1927, the decree being made absolute on 6th February 1928. He was officially the guilty party. Meanwhile Audrey did not 'hang around' on the shelf, as it were, for too long, remarrying that very year. She must have been 'quite' a lass, marrying a total of four times in her fairly long life. But Tim would appear to have slightly jumped the starting flag in respect of the unwritten marriage vow not to race. He was already back in the saddle, in a 3 litre Bentley, at the 1927 Brooklands Six Hour Race (7th May). Interestingly, he not only shared this drive with Frank Clement, but also his brother 'Archie'. The latter, at one point of his 'circuit promenade', had to be called in, having exhibited some rather wild driving techniques. Despite the brotherly aberrations, the loss of 3rd gear as well as the spare wheel, Tim achieved a meritorious third place! This meeting was to mark the onset of a most impressive and startling motor racing career. From then on nothing was to hold back Capt. Tiger Tim Birkin, apart from an increasingly chronic lack of money! Unfortunately for Tim, and his nascent dreams of manufacturing his own racing machines, the English based, family owned manufacturer of lace was suffering from a long, slow but inexorable post WW1 decline.

For the year 1928 Birkin moved up a size, to a 4.5 litre Bentley, with fair results. The Brooklands Six Hour Race (12th May) was a Le Mans style start with a dash across the track, hoods up and away, the hoods being lowered some laps later. As a portent of 'cars to come', a supercharged S-36/220, 7 litre Mercedes made a mechanically flawed appearance, with Capt. Miller at the wheel. Incidentally, L Headlam's 22/90 (3 litre, 6 cylinder, pushrod operated valves and dry sump lubrication) Alfa Romeo coupe was first away. Despite Tim covering the greatest distance at the race end, he finished third on handicap and a Team prize winner, with Ramponi's supercharged 1.5 litre twin-cam Alfa Romeo declared the first home. Drama was provided by Frank Hallam's Lea-Francis being destroyed by fire. For Le Mans Birkin was partnered by Jean Chassagne, in the same car he had driven in the Six Hour Race (now Race No. 3). After the first lap he was in front but the race pace was fast and furious. On lap 20 a tyre burst, at high speed, resulting in the disintegrated tyre and tube being wrapped tightly around the wheel, brake drum and brake rod assembly. And this was the year and event at which the Bentley Works had decided not to carry a jack. Armed only with clasp knife. he spent in excess of an hour hacking away at the mess. And he was a comparatively slight man and it was a very warm day. When the carnage was finally cleared away and with

---

* However, none other authority than AB Demaus in 'Motor Sport in the 20s' details HRS Birkin driving 'the Birkin-Comery, a 2 litre car with engine designed by WS Comery (one time Chief Designer of Clyno Motorcycles) and financed by Birkin, utilising an Aston Martin chassis!

Plate 56a. The start of the 1928 Tourist Trophy Race. No. 57 was Tom's S-36/220 7 litre Mercedes, No. 56 Watney & Anderson's 8 cylinder, 5 litre Splendid Stutz, No. 54 Cook's 4.5 litre Bentley and No. 50 Viscount Curzon's (Earl Howe) 8 cylinder, 2.3 litre supercharged Type 43 Bugatti.
COURTESY THE AUTOMOBILE.

Plate 56b. Tim Birkin coursing the streets of Dundonald during the 1928 TT. He only finished fifth despite recording the highest average race speed. Handicaps!
COURTESY AUTOCAR

Plate 56c. Tim again in the 4.5 litre Bentley but at the 1928 Boulogne Georges Boillot Cup, again finishing fifth despite, yet again, recording the highest average speed.
COURTESY A RACING HISTORY OF THE BENTLEY. DARRELL BERTHON. THE BODLEY HEAD.

Plate 56d. A well posed scenario reminding one inevitably of the replacement of the light bulb joke – or maybe the exhaust contains 'what the butler saw'? The place is the Welwyn Garden City Works wherin a gaggle of engineers inspect a 'Blower' 4.5 with Birkin in the tweed jacket to the left and Gallop holding the instrument.
COURTESY THE MOTOR

104

the wheels spinning, he set off, apparently at far too fast a speed. As a result, close by the Arnage bends, the wheel and rim gave in, collapsed and the tail end of the comparatively large car finished up in the ditch. Still without any method of lifting the 'brute' of a vehicle, he set off at a gallop for the three mile distant pits. On arrival, he collapsed against the wall. Jean Chassagne, ever the gentleman, and quickly briefed as to the situation, grabbed two jacks and set off on the reverse run for the 'ditched' vehicle. Having to operate within the rules and regulations, and thus without any help (and or hindrance), he managed to extricate the car, fit the spare wheel and tyre, and motor back to the pits. Additionally, he remembered to chuck the useless discard wheel and tyre into the back – rules are rules. If he had returned without the offending item, they would have been disqualified. On arrival Chassagne was greeted with a huge cheer, by all and sundry. However their Bentley was now some three hours or more adrift. The position seemed hopeless if they were to complete the minimum distance required, prior to the race end, in order to qualify for the next year's event. But that was to forget the extremely tenacious natures of both Tiger Tim and Jean Chassagne. As the rest of the day, the night and the next morning wore on, they slowly but inexorably hauled back both position and mileage, steadily clawing their way up the leader board. At 12am on Sunday they were ninth. By 2pm they were fifth overall. Despite which, with only two hours to go, it still seemed impossible for them to finish within the required minimum mileage. This they just achieved, by none other than Tiger Tim breaking the lap record, on the last lap – to finish – and in fifth place. It is said the chassis was cracked, a fault incurred by others in the Bentley Team. Rule Britannia! With Wally Hassan as his riding mechanic, he achieved eighth place in the German Grand Prix, Nurburgring (15th July) and was the first unblown car to finish. The Bentley Works Team entry for the Ulster Ards Tourist Trophy Race (23rd August) was withdrawn, due to the unsuitable handicapping being – a handicap! Notwithstanding, both Birkin and Humphrey Cook privately entered their 4.5 litre Bentleys. WO was proved to be quite correct in assessing this penalty for, in spite of a spirited drive, Birkin could only manage fifth, despite recording the highest speed of the race. Cook took seventh place. The *George Boillot Cup*, Boulogne (8th September) was yet again to prove to be a triumph of the handicapper over Tims' 4.5 litre Bentley's ability to make-up the imposition. The first car away had some 65 minutes start, prior to him being able to apply his boot to the throttle pedal. He finished fifth but had the satisfaction of setting the highest average speed recorded for this event, which was never to be run again. Thus the record stands, for all time. It was during that season that he came to the conclusion that to compete, in 1929, would require some radical rethinking. To have a chance to win against the gathering continental tide of 7 litre Mercedes, 'mit Kompressor' and with drivers such as Caracciola and Merz at the helm, a fundamental change in direction was going to be required.

Thus, he made his singular, if fateful decision to set up his own Works to supercharge 4.5 litre Bentleys. WO believed that greater speed resulted from increased power and chose to develop the Speed Six version of the standard 6.5 litre engine. It has to be pointed out that, apart from the German threat (ever thus!), Birkin was disillusioned with the Bentley Work's race build and preparation. A 'for instance' was his refusal to race a Bentley engine fitted with the duralumin rockers – and rightly so. Mark you it was not his first attempt at motor car manufacture. An article in *The Motor* drew attention to an even earlier piece in *The*

Plate 57a. Miss May Cunliffe, whilst driving her 1924 supercharged 2 litre GP Sunbeam, rolled over at the 1928 Southport 100 Mile Race. Her father, Albert, accompanying her as riding mechanic, was killed and she never raced again. Her car was sold to Jack Dunfee.

COURTESY THE MOTOR

Plate 57b. Prior to the onset of the 1929 Le Mans Race Birkin and Barnato pose for the camera. They were to drive the new Speed Six Bentley (No. 1)…

COURTESY WO BENTLEY MEMORIAL FOUNDATION.

Plate 57c. …and posing again but now as post race winners.

COURTESY WO BENTLEY MEMORIAL FOUNDATION.

CYCLECAR magazine of 1912. This detailed a 16 year old HRS Birkin as having constructed a four cycle wheeled, 5 hp, twin cylinder, air-cooled petrol engined 'box car', with two seats. The fabrication took place in the garages of the family's Aspley Grange Mansion. The chassis was channel steel and the drive was transmitted by a belt arrangement, linked to a lay-shaft and then on to a pulley wheel fixed to the rear driving wheel. Tim was pictured with Sister Ida at his side. It was reported that the first run pulled up short, against a tree.

At this stage, it is interesting to speculate that maybe Tom Thistlethwayte's absence from the 1927 racing season was, in retrospect, a very wise decision. After all, it saved him much time, effort and expense. Whatever, for 1928 he had already taken note of the looming Mercedes invasion – and bought one!

Tims' decision to take his particular racing engine development engine route required the harnessing of an enormous amount of physical effort, relocation, technical knowledge and financial resources. Added to which, and totally necessary to achieve his objectives, it was imperative that Bentley Motors should homologate the 4.5 litre supercharged models by producing a minimum of cars, as a catalogue sales item. This was so he could both compete at Le Mans and achieve the hoped for sales of his Welwyn Garden City Works output. If it had been up to WO – no way! But with Woolf Barnato pulling the 'strings' at Bentley, the deed was done. The technical 'shove' for the 'Blower' Bentleys came in the shape of Charles Amherst Villiers, a supercharger specialist, and our old friend Clive Gallop. The latter was responsible for organizing the new factory and workshops.

WO's dogged opposition to Birkin's proposals to supercharge the 4.5 litre engines may well have been for very different reasons than those he publicly voiced. His stated objections were based on the proposition that supercharging was against the *'natural law of the internal combustion engine'*! That more speed was best gained by increasing the engine capacity and horsepower. Despite which, a Bentley had been supercharged, some years previously, and that adaptation had been carried out at the Bentley Works. Well, well! In the case of Tim's project, WO may well have foreseen that this whole exercise would divert very much needed resources. And this at a time when it was vital to preserve and concentrate all the company's efforts, to ensure the future of the marque. He probably had a very clear realisation that Woolf Barnato's attention was prone to waver and might become sidelined. He was, oh so very right.

Back to the previous supercharging, about which 'improvement' WO had not been so adverse, in earlier years. The first Bentley to receive the 'treatment' was a 3 litre (Chassis No. 221. Reg. No. FR 5189), originally owned by a George Porter. He was the owner of a Blackpool Garage and represented Bentley Motors in the North West, but had a fatal crash in the car in 1924. Subsequently the vehicle was acquired by Miss May Cunliff and the rebuild, including supercharging, was carried out by 1926. Over the years she performed with distinction in this car. This was more especially at the Shelsley Walsh Hill Climbs and various sand races, up to and including the 1928 season. It was reported for the year 1927 and in respect of a Shelsley Walsh Hill Climb meeting that '...*Miss May Cunliffe, who had been building a considerable reputation ... in north-country events, more especially ...on the sands at Southport, drove with great dash and skill her old 3 litre Bentley, now equipped with what appeared to be the world's largest supercharger and a light racing body*'.* Incidentally, at that meeting she clocked up a first in the up to 3000cc Racing Class. Her racing activities

---
* Shelsley Walsh by CAN May. Published by GT Foulis & Co.

Plate 58a. Tim in the prototype 'Blower' Bentley (No. 5) racing in the 1929 Brooklands Six Hour Race. Despite showing pace it was retired.

COURTESY A RACING HISTORY OF THE BENTLEY. DARRELL BERTHON. BODLEY HEAD.

Plate 58b. The start of the 1929 Irish Grand Prix with Tom's Mercedes (No. 1) away first. No. 2 was Birkin's 'Blower' and No. 3 driven by Rubin, was another 4.5 litre 'Blower' Bentley. No. 4 was *Old No. 1* the Speed Six driven by Kidston, No. 7 was the 4.5 litre Bentley of Harcourt-Wood, No. 9 was the 4.5 litre Bentley of Humphrey Cook, whilst No. 10 was Scott's 4.5 litre Bentley.

PLATES 58B&C COURTESY RACING IN THE PARK. BOB MONTGOMERY. DREOILIN SPECIALIST PUBLICATIONS LTD.

Plate 58c. Birkin at pace in the 1929 Irish Grand Prix, finished third behind the supercharged 1750cc Alfa Romeo of Ivanowski and the Speed Six Bentley of Kidston.

Plate 58d. The 1929 Ulster Tourist Trophy Race. This scene depicts the SS-38/250 Mercedes (No. 70) of Caracciola and the 'Blower' Bentley (No. 63) of Birkin, with WO as passenger, almost side-by-side crossing Newtownards Square. Caracciola was to win whilst Birkin came in eleventh.

COURTESY THE MOTOR

came to an untimely end in 1928. The particular event was the Southport 100 Mile Sand Race. Her father, Albert, was acting as riding mechanic in her then 1924 supercharged 2 litre GP Sunbeam. The car became stuck in the deep tyre ruts of other competitors and rolled over and over. Her father was killed and Miss May did not compete again.

The Birkin supercharged or 'Blower' 4.5 litre Bentleys were not available for the onset of the 1929 season. Driving a normally aspirated 4.5 Bentley in the Brooklands Double Twelve Hour Race (10-11th May) Birkin & Holder (whose car it was) had to retire, after some 18 hours, with a rear axle fault. For Le Mans (15-16th June) Tim co-drove with Woolf Barnato to win in a Speed Six Bentley (*See* Chapter 8). This was the first major win for this model and the fourth Bentley Le Mans success. The Brooklands Six Hour Race (29th June) marked the first appearance of a Blower 4.5 litre Bentley. Naturally, there was an enormous amount of interest and speculation in respect of the car. It will come as no surprise that Tim was at the helm. The first impressions were that the hybrid possessed excellent acceleration and was very quick. Unfortunately he had to retire, with an unspecified fault. With that wonderful vision – hindsight – this was to become the 'norm'. However… for the, Phoenix Park Irish Grand Prix (13th July) there were two 'Blower' 4.5 litre Bentleys entered. One for Tim Birkin and the other for Bernard Rubin. This was probably one of the most famous of the supercharged, big motor battles to be fought out. Birkin in his 'Blower' 4.5 litre Bentley and 'Scrap' Thistlethwayte in his supercharged, 7 litre Mercedes. Sections of the track had been resurfaced, but these were melting in the heat, and driving those monster racing cars was proving to be extremely difficult. Neither protagonist could be described as a big, powerful man and the comparatively large and heavy machines, lapping at very high speeds, on uncertain surfaces, really needed some brute handling. The duel went on lap after lap, Birkin just astern of Thistlethwayte, superchargers screaming, the Bentley gaining on the corners, the Mercedes drawing away on the straights. Tom not only drove '…*brilliantly*', but he put in the fastest lap of the day. All good things have to come to an end and Tom's end came on lap 27, when the Mercedes blew a head gasket. Tiger Tim came in third. The Ards Tourist Trophy Race (17th August – *See* Chapter 7) saw four supercharged Mercedes take the grid. Those of Caracciola and Merz were S-38/250's, whilst those of Tom and another were S-36/220's. Up against them were ranged a Works Bentley Speed Six and three Birkin 'Blower' 4.5 litre Bentleys. Tim had WO aboard and experienced a fairly incident-free run, coming in eleventh. Of the other 'Blower's', that of Rubin tipped upside down and he was never to race again (not quite true – read on), whilst that of Harcourt-Wood retired. That was almost the end of any successes for the 'Blower' 4.5s that year. The Brooklands 500 Mile Race (12th October) proved more than interesting for Tim. First he experienced a copious quantity of oil being blown back over the cockpit, causing him to pit. Later, after some 420 miles, a broken exhaust pipe enabled neat flames to play on the fabric body which, not surprisingly, caught fire. Yes, an on board fire, at high speed. Some good comes out of even the worst of incidents. It was this car that was to become the most famous of the 'Blower' 4.5 litre Bentleys. It was re-bodied as a single seater and will always be remembered for its famous Brooklands record lap breaking exploits.

By 1930, the World-Wide Depression was beginning to bite. No totally unrelated customer had purchased a 'Blower' 4.5 Bentley. Tacolneston Hall, Tims' family home, had

Plate 59. Birkin accompanied by the Hon. Dorothy Paget, in order to show the new 'Blower' Team's owner the equipage prior to the rather early start of 8 am for the 1930 Brooklands Double Twelve.

Courtesy An Illustrated History of the Bentley Car. WO Bentley. George Allen & Unwin.

The 1930 Le Mans.

Plate 60a. For the 1930 Le Mans the Birkin Paget Team entered three supercharged ('Blower') 4.5 litre Bentleys. No. 7 was to be driven by Harcourt-Wood and Jack Dunfee but failed to start as there was insufficient time to complete the necessary adjustments required to allow the engine to run on benzol rather than the low grade petrol available.

Plate 60b. No. 8 (Chassis No. HR 3976, Reg. No. UR 6571) was the (fourth) additional four seater car Paget added to the stable when she took over. It was driven by Benjafield and Ramponi. Ramponi being ill during the night hours, meant that Benjafield had to undertake most of the driving, only to have to retire with a broken piston after some 21 hours and 144 laps, whilst lying third.

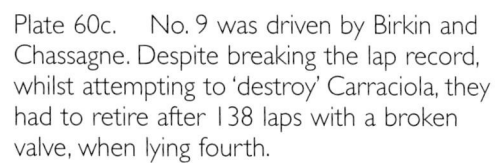

Plate 60c. No. 9 was driven by Birkin and Chassagne. Despite breaking the lap record, whilst attempting to 'destroy' Carraciola, they had to retire after 138 laps with a broken valve, when lying fourth.

Plates 60a, b, & c Courtesy Bentley Fifty Years of the Marque. J Green. Dalton Watson.

110

Plate 60d. This sketch vividly recalls Birkin's epic battle with Caracciola at the outset of the race. Soon after passing the S-38/250 Mercedes, the tyre of the Bentley exploded at the Arnage S-bend damaging the wing, the tread having previously stripped off at Mulsanne.

COURTESY THE AUTOCAR

Plate 60e. Subsequent to the Arnage incident, Birkin changes his ruined tyre and wheel.

COURTESY THE MOTOR.

Plate 60f. Birkin's car making a night time pit stop.

COURTESY FOX

111

Plate 61a. The start of the 1930 Irish Grand Prix. Caracciola's SSK (short chassis S-38/250) Mercedes (No. 3) has gone! Second away is the S-38/250 Mercedes (No. 1) of Campbell, followed by Howe's ex Caracciola's S-38/250 Mercedes (No. 2) and Birkin's 'Blower" (No. 8). Next grid back is the 'Blower' of Beris Wood (No. 6) and the ex Campbell supercharged 6 cylinder 3 litre Sunbeam (No. 9) owned and driven by BO Davis, behind which is Chassagne's 'Blower' (No. 7).

Plate 61b. Close to the end of the 1930 Irish Grand Prix, Birkin is racing down hill, en route to Mountjoy. Behind him is Campari's supercharged 1750cc Alfa.

Plate 61c. Despite setting a class lap record, on lap 23 of a rain effected 1930 Ulster Tourist Trophy Race, Birkin had his one and only racing crash, at Ballystockart. Neither he or the riding mechanic were hurt.

PLATES 61A, B & C COURTESY A RACING HISTORY OF THE BENTLEY. DARELL BERTHON. THE BODLEY HEAD.

had to be sold and his present abode, Shadwell Court, was rented. His money was running out, the pot of 'groats' was dwindling very fast and if capital were not introduced, quickly, the whole Welwyn Garden City outfit would go to the wall. However, a most unlikely saviour was about to come on board.

As an aside, in THE MOTOR of 28th January 1930 it was announced that the: *"…Bentley-Alfa Romeo dual was to be resumed … on Italian territory. Mr HRS Birkin and Capt. Woolf Barnato will definitely compete in the 1,000 mile road race from Brescia to Rome on the 12-13th April … driving a supercharged 4.5 litre Bentley, possibly with cars of the same make entered. In addition two Aston Martins were to be entered by HS Eaton and Sir R Gunter".* This was obviously the Mille Miglia but no such entry took place – more is the pity.

THE HON. DOROTHY PAGET (1905-1960). She was the daughter of Lord Queenborough (a famed race horse owner) and an American lady, Pauline Whitney. Paget was a painfully shy, overweight, 'plain Jane', but was excessively wealthy. For some reason, in 1927, she had purchased the ex Raymond Mays, straight eight, 2 litre supercharged Mercedes, fitted with a 170 bhp engine, capable of exceeding 7000 rpm, with a kerbside weight of 19 cwt. The lady then spent inordinate sums of money making this 'out and out' competition machine suitable for road use.

Fortunately for Birkin, Miss Paget attended the 1929 October Brooklands meeting. Despite the previously referred to fire, which eventually forced him out of the race, his 'Blower' 4.5 litre Bentley was the fastest car at the meeting. With a mission to invest – in something – Miss Paget chose to purchase the Welwyn Garden City racing stable of three 'Blower' 4.5 litre Bentleys and, for good measure, to add another car to the team. Tim must have been convinced there was a God and that it was female! With the financial backing in place, even if no longer the owner or in charge of the money, the forthcoming season must have appeared set fine, very fine. However Miss Paget's financial input was the end of the extremely good news, as far as the 'Blower' Bentleys were concerned, for this and maybe almost all the years left to Tim.

The 1930 Easter Brooklands Race meeting was notable for reasons other than Tim clocking up a win or two. It appears he may well have flown in from Le Touquet to decide a bet made with Woolf Barnato. At stake was a meal, if Birkin could capture the Outer Circuit lap record then held by Kaye Don. Despite there being no other competitors in the particular race, due to attrition, he put in a bravura performance. Subsequently, he is reputed to have flown back across the Channel to claim his prize, as one would. In the Brooklands Double Twelve Race (9-10th May) despite a very distinguished cast of drivers of Birkin & Chassagne, Kidston & Jack Dunfee and Benjafield & Baron d'Erlanger, all three 'Blower' 4.5 litre Bentleys had to retire. It was the same story at the Le Mans (21-22nd June) where Harcourt-Wood & Jack Dunfee non-started, whilst the cars of both Benjafield & Ramponi and Birkin & Chassagne had to retire. It was perhaps this particular race that highlighted the extraordinary 'Jekyll & Hyde' characteristics of Birkin. In private life he was a quiet, prone to stutter, unassuming, diffident man. On the circuit, the trademark white silk scarf streaming out behind him, he became a totally fearless, ruthless extrovert. A man who was quite prepared to drive like the

THE FORGOTTEN BENTLEY BOY.

Plate 62a. The 1930 French Grand Prix held at Pau during which Birkin (No. 18), driving a 'Blower' Bentley, gave the native drivers a bit of a shock…

PLATES 62A & B COURTESY A RACING HISTORY OF THE BENTLEY.
DARELL BERTHON. THE BODLEY HEAD.

Plate 62b. …despite which Birkin appears rather underwhelmed.

Plate 62c. Birkin in the new single seater 'Blower' 4.5 litre Bentley, as it was in 1930…

Plate 62d. …and during the Brooklands Whit Monday meeting.

PLATES 62C & D COURTESY BENTLEY THE VINTAGE YEARS.
MICHAEL HAY. HM BENTLEY & PARTNERS.

wind to destroy the opposition. But back to the 1930 Le Mans. The Bentley Works and the Birkin 'Blower' Teams were up against the potentially awesome might of Rudolph Caracciola's 7 litre supercharged S-38/250 Mercedes. Despite the well known comparative frailty of the 'Blower' Bentleys, of which no one was more aware than Birkin, he decided to 'sort out' the Mercedes. A ferocious battle ensued between the pair. At one point, with Tim hurtling the 2.5 tons of Bentley past the Mercedes at some 125 mph, whilst 'tooling' down the Mulsanne Straight, under heavy braking and one side up on the grass verge, the rear left tyre threw its tread. Regardless of this potential catastrophe, he did not immediately go into the pits, which he should have so done. He pressed on, now down to the bare canvas on one wheel. This was just to keep the pressure on the German, obviously with the hope of breaking his car. Mad or what? Whatever, the ploy succeeded with Caracciola going out early Sunday morning. The 'Blower' Bentleys continued to experience tyre wear problems, as the race progressed, having to pit every so many laps to change their 'boots'. About mid-day on Sunday, and whilst in fourth place, Birkin had to retire with valve problems. He had covered 138 laps, achieved both the fastest lap of the race and broken the overall lap record. An hour later the other supercharged Bentley of Benjafield had to retire, with piston trouble, whilst lying in third place. It is noteworthy that when he was forced to 'throw in the towel', Benjafield had put in a ten hour stint. For the Irish Grand Prix (19th July) Bentley's did not enter a team. However, this was another Mercedes versus 'Blower' Bentley race, but one in which the Bentleys came in – nearly nowhere. By the 5th lap both the 'Blower's' of Beris Wood and Jean Chassagne had retired, with oil pressure problems. In atrocious weather, Birkin's car managed a fourth place. In the rain effected Ards Tourist Trophy Race (23rd August) he did claim a class record lap, but crashed on lap 23 at Ballystockart Bridge. This was the only crash he experienced in his entire action-packed and dramatic racing career. The Team's honour was to some extent maintained as 'Bertie' Kensington Moir came in eleventh, whilst Benjafield had been 'flagged' off. For the French Grand Prix (21st September) at Pau, Birkin entered a 'stripped' down 'Blower' Bentley. The selected course was a triangular, out-of-town, road track, rather than the more well known, round the city circuit. In spite of the less demanding location, the in excess of 2 tons, high centre of gravity, supercharged Bentley was generally not considered suited to the course. Due to the selected date, the Italians had to decline their invitation, leaving Frenchmen to dominate the entries. And most of them were driving low-slung, comparatively lightweight Bugattis, which were eminently suited to this 25 lap race. However, and much to the dismay of the locals, by lap eight Tiger Tim was up to third, and then second. Mon dieu! In the meantime a Type 35C Bugatti driver known as Sabipa crashed and was flung out of his car on to the track. At this moment Birkin arrived on the scene. By the very narrowest of tyre tread margins, and utilizing all his skill and strength, he managed to squeeze his projectile between the prostrate body and the track edge. It is said that Sabipa, who was conscious at the time, reckoned that a tyre brushed his body. There's close! The leading three cars chopped and changed position, but at the race end Tim was second to Etacelin's Type 35 Bugatti. He was only some $2^1/_2$ minutes adrift, and ten seconds in front of Zanelli's Bugatti.

Sabipas' real name was Louis Charavel and he was neither an inexperienced 'rookie', nor a 'spring-chicken'. At the time of the Pau Race he was 40 years old. In 1926 he had been a Bugatti Team member and won the Italian GP, at Monza. He had a close shave in the 1927

Plate 63a.   Barnato and Rubin celebrate their 1928 Le Mans victory in a 4.5 litre Bentley (No. 4). From triumph…
COURTESY WO BENTLEY MEMORIAL FOUNDATION.

Plate 63b & c.   …to disaster: now in a 'Blower' Bentley. Rubin's downfall in the 1929 Ulster Tourist Trophy Race, at Glen Hill.
PLATES 62B & C COURTESY BENTLEY THE VINTAGE YEARS. MICHAEL HAY. HM BENTLEY & PARTNERS.

Targa Florio, when he had to skid off the track to avoid a boulder in the road. He achieved an eighth place in the 1928 Le Mans, in a 6 cylinder, 2 litre Itala and a fourth place in the 1932 Le Mans, in a supercharged, 6 cylinder, 1750cc Alfa Romeo, only to cease racing after the 1933 Le Mans.

But to return to the main narrative. The 1930 Brooklands 500 Mile Handicap Race (4th October) was run in pouring rain. This was to be the last of the Paget entered supercharged Bentley Team races. Tim in the single seater was paired with Duller whilst GET Eyston & Beris Wood and Benjafield & Hall piloted the other two cars. The Birkin car suffered from plugs misfiring, which lost valuable time, but the first and only Team retirement was the 'Blower' of Eyston. The Sammy Davis & Earl March Austin 7 beat Benjafield home, despite the latter putting in the fastest lap, followed by a Sunbeam. Tim came in ninth. But that was that! At the season's end Miss Paget withdrew her support for the Team. She effortlessly moved over to the horses, where she was far more successful. Possibly her most famous 'gee-gee' was *Golden Miller*. To be fair, she did not entirely cut herself off from Tim, continuing to support him by entering the single seater 'Blower' Bentley, during both the 1931 and 1932 seasons.

In addition to Miss Paget's continuing sponsorship, two other guardian angels dropped down from the motor racing equivalent of heaven, to give Tim a leg up, as it were. They were Francis Richard Henry Penn Curzon (Viscount Curzon/5th Earl Lord Howe, 1884-1964), more usually referred to as Lord Howe and probably the only racing driver Privy Councillor. He contributed a 2.3 litre, 8 cylinder Alfa Romeo (8C LM) for Birkin to drive. The other supporter was:

BERNARD RUBIN (1896-1936). Bernard's father Mark, originally from Lithuania, settled in Australia, via Cardiff. His first antipodean stop-off was Sydney, followed by Melbourne and lastly Broome, Western Australia. There he made a fortune in the pearl industry. The family were sent home to London, while Father Mark continued to spend most of his time 'down under'. He then had a stroke of genius. He had the insight to realise War in Europe was almost inevitable. Accordingly, he transferred some of his extensive assets to a number of large sheep stations. His idea was that any conflict would result in a greatly increased demand for wool and that he would be able to cash in, big time. Good thinking. In the meantime son Bernard 'signed on' and was commissioned. In 1917 he was very seriously wounded, being invalided back to England. It took some three years before he was able to walk again. His father subsequently passed away, in 1919, and Bernard inherited everything. Firstly he went hunting 'Big Game'.

Bernard's friendship with Woolf Barnato allowed the latter to persuade WO to permit him into the charmed circle of the Bentley Boys. He commenced racing in 1928. His first outing was with none other than Dr. Dudley Benjafield, driving a 4.5 litre Bentley, in the Brooklands Six Hour Race (12th May). They came in sixth and were included in the winners of the Team Prize. That was the hors d'ouevre. For the main course Rubin partnered his chum Barnato in the 24 hour Le Mans (16-17th June) driving a 4.5 litre Bentley. And they won. And this success despite a cracked chassis. As is well documented elsewhere, this caused the cooling water piping to split and resulted in a red hot engine steaming its way over the finishing line. That was the main course.

Plate 64a. Birkin winning the 1931 Le Mans in an Alfa Romeo 2.3 whilst his co-driver, Lord Howe, cheers him in.

COURTESY ALFA ROMEO A HISTORY. R HULL & R SLATER. CASSELL & CO.

Plate 64b. Birkin in his single seater 'Blower' Bentley at Brooklands.

COURTESY THE BROOKLANDS SOCIETY.

Plate 64c. Birkin during an early October 1931 lap record attempt had the misfortune to experience an engine compartment fire with the flames breaking through the bulkhead. He slowed the car until he was able to bale out.

PLATES 64C & D COURTESY THE MOTOR.

Plate 64d. Sir Henry Birkin at a slightly slower speed, ploughing the fields at his Shadwell Court Estate, near Thetford.

With that 'tasty' year out the way, it was rather downhill for Rubin in the 1929 racing season. For his first outing of the year, he partnered Earl Howe at the Le Mans (15-16th June) in a 4.5 litre Bentley. They had to retire. This was almost certainly due to there being insufficient time for the vehicle to be properly prepared. The previous week Mrs Victor Bruce had used the same car to achieve a 24 Hour Record run. Rubin's Bentley now became a 'Blower' Bentley as he had allowed Birkin to give it the 'supercharger treatment'. Racing at the Phoenix Park Irish Grand Prix (13th July) he clocked up an eighth place. In those days this event was followed by the Ards Tourist Trophy Race, that year held on 17th August. On the first lap his car slid after breasting Glen Hill, broached the banking and flipped right over. He and the riding mechanic had the terrifying experience of being trapped beneath the machine. Very fortunately nothing caught fire and they were both unharmed. Enough was enough. From then on he acted as a fairy godmother, buying cars for others to race. This policy mainly benefited Tiger Tim Birkin! For instance, in 1931 Bernard Rubin purchased for him a 2.5 litre supercharged Maserati Tipo 8C, which Clive Gallop collected from Bologna.

To return to Sir Henry Birkin's remaining years. His 1931 season opened with the Whitsun Brooklands Race meeting, at which the Hon. Dorothy Paget entered her ex Raymond Mays, 1924 straight eight GP Mercedes, for Tim to drive. He gained a third place in a handicap event. Next on was the Phoenix Park Irish Grand Prix (5-6th June) Despite running out of fuel, with all the time that wasted and very heavy rain, he came first in the larger engined class but had to settle for second overall, by a bare 11 seconds. For the Le Mans (13-14th June) Tim partnered Lord Howe in the 2.3 litre supercharged Alfa Romeo 8C LM, which Clive Gallop had very recently collected from Milan. (Clive seems to have spent quite a chunk of hours collecting this or that racing car, from this or that Italian factory). They came first. Next off Tim and George Eyston, in the 2.5 litre supercharged Maserati Tipo 8C, raced at the French Grand Prix (21st June) where they achieved a fourth. Together again, over the weekend of the 4-5th July, they raced the Alfa Romeo in the Belgian 24 Hour Race, at Spa. They certainly clocked fastest lap. A week later Tim, now partnered by BE Lewis, came fourth in the Belgian Grand Prix, again piloting the Alfa. Yet another week on, and Tim, in the Maserati, finished in tenth place at the German Grand Prix (19th July) one place ahead of Lord Howe in his supercharged, 8 cylinder 2.3 litre Type 51 Bugatti. Another week, another race and on to the Brooklands August Race meeting where he put in a record breaking attempt, in the single seater 'Blower' Bentley. The previously referred to Rubin's 2.5 litre Maserati also raced that day. Birkin rounded off the meeting with a third in the 'Blower', in a handicap race. The season ended with the Brooklands Race meeting (3rd October), whereat he excelled himself by gaining a first in the Alfa Romeo, another first in the Maserati and a third in the 'Blower'. Although there is some controversy as to the month, THE MOTOR authoritatively informs its readers that '... *Sir Henry Birkin had a narrow escape when driving the Hon. Dorothy Paget's (supercharged) 4.5 litre Bentley. At a speed of approximately 100 mph the car caught fire. Birkin promptly applied the brakes and switched off, but the flames came through into the cockpit. ...he managed to wriggle out of his seat, on which he stood and steered the car until the speed had been reduced sufficiently before he leapt out none the worse for his adventure*'. 'Biggles', 'Bull-Dog Drummond' where art thou? At the end of 1931 Rubin sold the 2.5 litre Maserati to Whitney

The 1933 Mille Miglia.

Plate 65a.   Marshalling at the 1933 Mille Miglia, Brescia.
COURTESY FOTO-OFFICA.

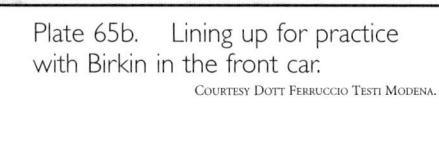

Plate 65b.   Lining up for practice with Birkin in the front car.
COURTESY DOTT FERRUCCIO TESTI MODENA.

Plate 65c. Birkin and Rubin, the first eyeing the surrounds whilst Rubin surveys the rear end of the K3.
COURTESY FOTO-OFFICA ANNIBALE ANNIBALETTO, BRESCIA.

Straight and purchased a more powerful, 3 litre supercharged Maserati Tipo 8C, for the 1932 season. Tim must have felt quite loved.

The onset of the 1932 season was heralded by the Brooklands Easter Monday Race meeting, immediately prior to which Tim 'whacked' in a lap record, in the 'Blower'. During the event he beat Cobb, V12 Delage mounted, in a scratch race. Incidentally, the overseas calendar was nowhere near as crowded as in the previous year. At the 30th April Brooklands Race meeting the highlight was a 100 mile Outer Circuit Scratch Race – the British Empire Trophy. In both the heat and the final race, he had to retire his 'Blower'. In the heat the trouble was tyres, despite which he was still deemed to have attained a fourth place. In the race the problem was the engine. In the Brooklands Whitsun Race meeting (16th May) Birkin, astride the 'Blower', came home first, ahead of Cobb, but had to retire in a later race. For Le Mans (18-19th June) he partnered Lord Howe in the Alfa Romeo, but they had to retire. At the 2nd July Brooklands Race meeting he won a handicap race, in the 'Blower', but had to retire from a later event. The next weekend was the Belgian Grand Prix where he and Lord Howe chalked up a third place in the Alfa Romeo. Then back across the Channel for the 2nd August Brooklands Race meeting. In a three lap scratch race, with a prize of 100 guineas, he won in the 'Blower', again beating Cobb, this time by a fraction of a second. August 20th heralded the Ards Tourist Trophy Race meeting. Birkin, who set a new lap record in the Alfa Romeo, was beaten into fifth place by Lord Howe, driving his other 2.3 Alfa Romeo. It would have been a very different outcome if Tim and his pit crew had not lost valuable time, attempting to cure a sudden drop in oil pressure. And thus ended the 1932 outings.

The only other event of any consequence in 1932 was the publication of Tim's book *Full Throttle**, first published in November. As with seemingly almost everything to which he now turned his attention, this popular publication was not greeted with a fulsome wave of critical acclaim. This was not helped by the text being littered with typo's, grammatical errors and punctuation mistakes. No less an authority than Sammy Davis suggested he would like to '....*take a good Rudge hammer with a heavy head and a long springy shaft and have a detailed chat with the book's editor*', or words to that effect! Interestingly, a few years ago it became apparent that Birkin had not himself put pen to paper. He had employed a ghost writer, but not a professional. Oh, no! The person involved was a young, disaffected undergraduate aged 19, who completed the manuscript in less than three months. No wonder there were grammaticals! It appears Birkin had met the callow youth at a Villa house party, close by Le Touquet. Also present was the then love of his life, Sylvia Ashley (nee Hawkes). She was a cabaret artist, with whom he was besotted. It was the generally accepted opinion that the lady concerned, who was still (inconveniently?) married, at the time, to Lord Ashley, could not match his ardour. He was unable to 'stack up' – on the wealth front, a racing certainty at this period of his life. Poor old Tim! Mrs Ashley had a reputation as a model and actress. Apart from displaying lingerie on the cat-walk, she had been a Cochrane dancer, appeared in the chorus-line of a few musicals, and acted in a number of 1920s plays. Incidentally, once 'shot of' Lord Ashley (and Tim?), the lady managed to marry Douglas Fairbanks, followed by an Edward Stanley (6th Baron of somewhere or other), then none other than Clark Gable and,

---

*Full Throttle by Sir Henry Tim Birkin Bt. G T Foulis & Co., Ltd.

Plate 65d.   During the 1933 Mille Miglia. "High Speed cornering, Birkin at the wheel with Rubin holding on." I bet he was!

COURTESY FUMAGALLI, MILANO.

Plate 66. A poster for the 1933 Grand Prix of Tripoli – 'The Scandalous Race'.
COURTESY WIKIPEDIA.

finally in 1954, a Prince Djordjadze.* No less a judge of womanhood than David Niven is reported to have summed her up as a '... *ravishing blonde beauty ... if selfish ... and a man's woman ...who adored spending money*'. Succinct!

Whatever, there was something as worrying as the young lady's inability to reciprocate his love. It was the book. It had attracted the attention of the legal beavers acting for the Broooklands Estate. This was hardly surprising as he had been rather damning in his condemnation of the state of the circuit. My 'learned friends' passed judgment that he should issue a grovelling retraction, which had to be appended to each and every book.

The year 1933 was to be Tiger Tims' last and only three races dominated the six months left to him. The first was the seventh Mille Miglia, a 1,000 mile Italian race. It was to set out from Brescia, proceed south along the Adriatic coast to Pesaro, from whence down and across to Rome, and then all the way back up north, to return to Brescia. That year it was scheduled to start in the early hours of Saturday 8th April. The planning and preparation started as early as mid-January and occupied almost all the following months. Tim and Bernard Rubin (who had obviously decided to put his racing 'ovvies' back on again) were to race as part of the Lord Howe organised, British entered team of K3 MG Magnettes. The latter cars at that time were powered by the earlier 1087cc engines. The other pairings were Count Lurani & George Eyston and Lord Howe & H Hamilton. Birkin's role was the to-be-expected, 'other' team breaker. In this role he set off at a frenetic pace. This lasted until he broke his MG, beyond Sienna, his job done. It cannot have been much fun for Rubin who had put in all the effort, and no doubt much of the money and owned the car, but did not get a drive. However, the K3 MG Team won both their Class and the Team prize. Next on was the 23rd April Grand Prix de Monaco held at Monte Carlo. Birkin was down to drive the Maserati. However, on hearing that Rubin's next purchase, a supercharged 2.3 litre Monza 8C Alfa Romeo, was to be ready, he decided to switch steeds. Accordingly, he collected it from the Milan factory gates but, whilst driving back, he collided with another car, causing emergency steering and front axle repairs to be carried out – 'tout suite'. The mechanics, in amongst whom was Albert Denly, who had been GET Eyston's co-driver in MG record breaking attempts, were reputed to have had as little as two hours sleep a night for three days. Despite this superhuman effort, Tim had to retire on lap 17 (out of a 100) with a broken differential.

And so to the Grand Prix of Tripoli, to be held on 7th May and which one commentator re-named *'The Scandalous Race'*. It was quite possibly the promise of a large crock of money for the winner and place-men that encouraged Tim to privately enter the Maserati 8C, alongside the Maserati works team. If so, not all was as it appeared. The State Lottery was involved in the selling of the tickets, which were somehow related to the apportionment of the prize money. It appears much skullduggery went on. I have read and re-read the scenario but am still not a lot wiser as to the workings of the general and or specific shenanigans that undoubtedly took place. An added handicap to Tims' particular chances was a little known but vigorously enforced rule which stated that the Maserati Works 'mechanico' could not work on Tims' car – at all. Thus, he had to search out and hire a garage hand, in a land where

---

* This gentleman was yet another of those interesting people who circled the motor racing scene, in this case notably in 1931. An imposing 6ft plus, he was a Georgian nobleman, a Russian emigré. In 1931 he campaigned an SK-38/250 and, with co-driver Zehender, won the Belgian 24 Hour Touring Car Grand Prix, at Spa. He entered the same car in the Brooklands 500 Mile Race with Zehender partnered by WB Scott, from which race they had to retire.

TO THE MEMORY OF A GREAT SPORTSMAN
AND BRILLIANT DRIVER
SIR · HENRY · BIRKIN · Bt
WHO DIED ON JUNE 22 1933 FROM INJURIES
AFTER HIS LAST ROAD RACE AT TRIPOLI
HERE, ON THE SCENE OF HIS MANY VICTORIES
THIS BRONZE WAS ERECTED BY MEMBERS OF
THE BRITISH RACING DRIVERS CLUB

Plate 67.   A commemorative bronze designed by F Gordon Crosby of the Autocar and displayed in the Brooklands Paddock by the British Racing Drivers Club.

COURTESY AUTOCAR.

very few, if anyone, spoke English. Furthermore, the skill levels of the local mechanics were hardly up to the requirements necessary to deal with a sophisticated racing Maserati. This 'fault line' came to a head when he had to 'pit' for oil and water. The fellow could not, or would not, understand even those simple requests. Nor where either were to be obtained, and in what they were to be conveyed! A 'stitch-up'. Fortunately, a native luminary, grasping the situation, leapt into assist and help out. Whilst these intrigues were inexorably grinding on he lost a vital 2^1/$_2$ minutes and Sir Tiger Tim Birkin came in third overall. In front of him were Varzi and Nuvolari and he lost out to the winner by – 1^1/$_2$ minutes. Somehow he managed to win the locals £2,500, so they went off and erected a plaque to him, in gratitude. However, he was to pay the ultimate price for 'enjoying' this event and all the machinations were to matter not at all, compared to that which was to befall him.

During the fateful pit-stop, he had managed to badly burn his arm on the exposed exhaust. Arriving back in England, it was noticed that limb was heavily bandaged. After some six days, he was whisked into hospital. Obviously the Bentley Boys heard of his plight, in amongst whom was the very man for the moment. Step forward Doctor Benjafield. Despite his ministrations and those of the medical staff, the gallant adventurer passed away on the 22nd June, some five weeks after his hospital admission. The official reason for his death was septicemia. Others pointed out that the malaria, with which he had been infected many years before, may well have played a significant role. There were a number of other possible contributory reasons that are more psychosomatic. Here we go, the 'old babble-speak'. Not surprisingly, considering the events of 1932, there can be little doubt that Birkin had started the year 1933 rather out of sorts and in low spirits. Most of us are prone to occasionally wake up in the early morning, cold, dark, low hours and engage in a little introspective soul searching. Those musings when the balance sheet of life is totted up. And if Tim were to have been this self-indulgent, the bottom line could not have looked very good. In essence he had spent a fortune motor racing and was now almost entirely reliant on his close and loyal friends to keep him on the track. Almost everything he touched appeared to turn to failure. Even the book had been gently if critically panned, and that was in addition to the very public apology he had been forced to make to the owners of the Brooklands Circuit. Additionally, his adored lady friend was either on the move, or was soon to so be. Life for him was not exactly a 'bowl of cherries'. It is poignant to note that the rest of his 1933 racing year was planned to take in Le Mans, several major Italian races, the Ulster Tourist Trophy and a 'round the houses' race on the Isle of Man. *C'est la vie* – or not, as the case was to be.

He was married at St. Nicholas Church, Blakeney. Blakeney, the Norfolk coast seaside village so beloved by him. Blakeney where he had honeymooned in the local hotel. The same Blakeney Hotel in which he had been involved in some extra curricula romantic endeavours' and where he had committed the formalities necessary for his divorce proceedings to take place. Blakeney to whence he bought his beloved Sister Ida's power boat*. Blakeney where he had practiced his shotgun prowess, he supposedly being the second best shot in the land. Blakeney where the lifeboat men lay him in his final resting place, reportedly with his feet pointing seawards. His will disclosed total assets of £6,439.00. Tom Thistlethwayte was not listed as a mourner at the Memorial Service!

---

* It will be recalled that this craft came from Switzerland, after Ida had passed away, for Brother Tim to roar round the creeks and sea-ways. It was even hinted he had pioneered an early form of waterskiing.

Plate 68a.   Chassagne aboard a 'fresh off the line' 12 cylinder, 9 litre single seater Sunbeam – 'Toodles V' at Brooklands in 1913. A record attempt was in mind.

Plate 68b. Chassagne and his mechanic on the start line of the 1922 Coppa Florio, Sicily, with their 4.9 litre, 6 cylinder TT Sunbeam 'passing the time of day' with Segrave.

PLATES 68A & B COURTESY SUNBEAM RACING CARS, ANTHONY HEAL. FOULIS/HAYNES.

A short note is probably appropriate to explain why it has been seen fit to list this much detail in respect of Sir Henry Ralph Stanley Tiger Tim Birkin's post 1930 life. Once that milestone had passed by, which included the demise of Bentley Motors, the details of his remaining motor racing years are more often than not shrouded in generalizations*. Apologies are made for the possible overload of facts and figures, but it was considered 'our schoolboy hero' deserved rather more than a few lines to cover the last few years of his most extraordinary life. Were that there were lots more Tim Birkin's, especially nowadays.

One more character should benefit from some 'infill', namely:

JEAN CHASSAGNE (1881-1947). A most interesting man more often than not recognised for his Bentley drives. Sunbeam aficionados will be familiar with him as a very prominent member of their Works Team achievements, earlier in the century. Pre-WW1 he was an aviator as well as a racing driver. In 1910 he is recorded as gaining a third in a Hispano-Suiza at the Copa Catalunya (29th May). This was followed by a DNF, again in the 'Hispano', at the Coupe d'Ostende (4th September). Luckier on the 18th September, he 'bagged' a fourth in the Hispano-Suiza at the Coupe des Voitorettes, Boulogne. From 1913 on he drove almost exclusively for the Sunbeam concern, taking a third place in a 6 cylinder, 4.5 litre GP car at the French Grand Prix (13th June) at Amiens. On 21st September he had to retire a 4 cylinder, 3 litre car from the Coupe de l'Auto, Boulogne but won at Brooklands in October, at the then fastest race winning speed. This was in a 12 cylinder, 9 litre Sunbeam, known as 'Tootles V'. October saw him again at Brooklands where some World Speed Records were wrapped up. No let up for 1914 as March heralded more Brooklands records. On 30th May he gained pole position on the grid at the 'Indy' 500 in a 1913, 4.5 litre, 6 cylinder GP car, only to crash out with a burst tyre. At the French Grand Prix (14th July), at Lyons, he had to retire his 1914, 4.5 litre, 4 cylinder GP car. Annoyingly for him and aged 33, WW1 then intervened. During this unwanted distraction he worked in the aviation department of the Sunbeam Motor Company.

Post the unnecessary and irritatingly time-absorbing hostilities he had a couple of year's 'flirtation' with a 5 litre, straight 8, twin cam Ballot painted pale blue. In the 1920 'Indy' 500 he came in seventh. In 1921 he had to retire from the French Grand Prix, at Le Mans, but achieved a second place, in the Italian Grand Prix, all Ballot mounted. Chassagne sold the car to Count Zborowski, for the 1922 season.

The year 1922 saw him back in the Sunbeam fold. At an April Brooklands meeting he gained a first driving an 18.3 litre, 350hp 12 cylinder car. The Tourist Trophy Race (22nd June) was staged on the Isle of Man and he came in first in a 3 litre, 8 cylinder car, some four minutes ahead of Clement in a 3 litre Bentley. He was less fortunate at the French Grand Prix (15th July), staged at Strasbourg, where he had to retire his 2 litre, 4 cylinder Sunbeam. The Coppa Florio (19th November) was luckier, even if rather stressful. This came about as he had to run the last one or two laps using olive oil as an engine lubrication substitute for his 4.9 litre, 6 cylinder vehicle. In spite of this handicap (or maybe because of this ….) he managed a fourth place. During the year there were some Brooklands appearances and a few drives in a 1.5 litre Talbot-Darracq. At the 1922 August Bank Holiday meeting at Brooklands

---

* That is apart from in the simply superb book, Blower Bentley by Michael Hay. Number One Press 2001.

Plate 68c.   The 4.5 litre Bentley Team prior to the 1928 Le Mans. Birkin & Chassagne (No. 3), Clement & Benjafield (No. 2) and Barnato & Rubin (No. 4) with WO standing by the lead car.

Plate 68d.   Chassagne co-driving with Clement at the wheel of their 4.5 litre Bentley (No. 8) in the 1929 Le Mans. They finished fourth.

Plates 68c & d Courtesy The Bentley at Le Mans, JD Benjafield md. Motor Racing Publications.

he was driving the Talbot Darracq but initially the car stalled on the start line. However worse was to follow. A puncture forced the vehicle into an uncontrollable slide – over the banking. He and his riding mechanic were thrown out but only suffered superficial injuries. Maybe that accident was the reason for my not finding any mention of his competing in 1923.

For 1924 he selected a 2 litre, straight 8, unblown Type 35 Bugatti but at the European (French) Grand Prix held at Lyon, tyre trouble denied him a result. A few weeks later at the San Sebastian Grand Prix, and in the same car, he achieved a fifth place despite a serious engine misfire.

In 1925, co-driving with Sammy Davis, he achieved an excellent second place, in a 3 litre, 6 cylinder Sunbeam, at Le Mans (*See* Chapter 4). On 11th July 1926, and driving a Talbot 70, he crashed out of the German Grand Prix at Avus, Berlin. His month to month race meeting attendances were now falling off. But from 1928 on his time was almost entirely spent 'performing' at the most important races – with the Bentley Boys. And as a gentleman with an enormous amount of experience, he must have been a very welcome addition to the team. He clocked up a fifth place in a 4.5 litre with Birkin in the 1928 Le Mans, a fourth, again in a 4.5, with Clement in the 1929 Le Mans, retired co-driving a 'Blower' with Birkin in the 1930 Brooklands Double Twelve Hour Race, again retiring with Birkin in a 'Blower' at the 1930 Le Mans and finally retiring driving a 'Blower' at the 1930 Irish GP.

The Forgotten Bentley Boy.

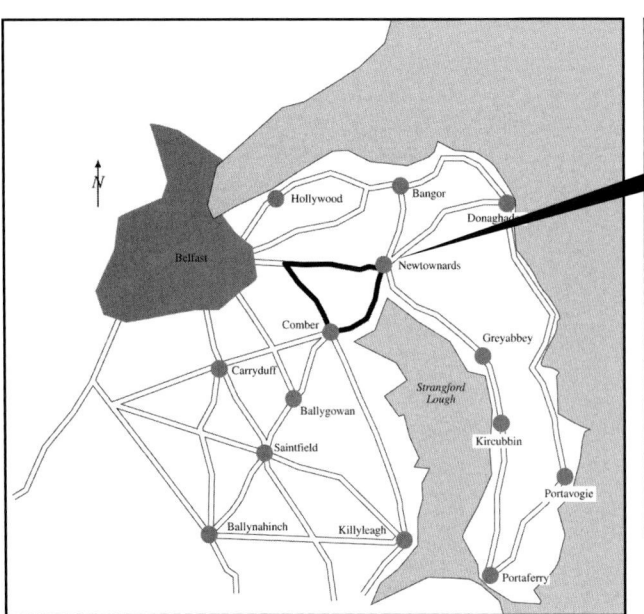

Plate 69a.   The Ards Circuit environs.

Plate 69b.   The Ards Circuit.

The 1928 TT.

Plate 70a.   The 1928 Tourist Trophy ('Le Mans' line up) with Tom's Mercedes (No. 57) in front of Wright's Splendid-Stutz (No. 56), Cook's 4.5 Bentley (No. 54) and Birkin's 4.5 Bentley (No. 53).

Plate 70b.   Hoods up and Cook is first away.

PLATES 70A & B COURTESY ARDS TT. JS MOORE. BLACKSTAFF PRESS.

Chapter Six

Tom. His Reappearance. 1928.

'God would not have invented the automobile if he had intended me to walk'.
Ib.

This was the year in which Tom burst back on to the motor racing scene, after a twelve month long layoff. Notwithstanding this reappearance on the tracks, his social life must have been rather intrusive. It restricted entries, for the year, to a selected few events. The distractions included the finalization of the divorce from his first wife Ethel Mary. She remarried, with 'due haste', very soon after the distressing event. The 'lucky' man was one Mr Addams. They were not to live happily ever after, for she was to pass away, aged 33, in 1936. Also on the list of distractions was some South of France summer 'hols', during which enjoyment he met his second wife-to-be. As one does! In the interim, I suspect the time available for Tom to assist and advise the widowed Countess Zborowski, in the choice of motor cars, yachts and any other personal matters, dwindled to zero

For the 1928 season choice of racing chariot, he had no doubt mused over the previous year's events and listened to the cogitation's of both Tim Birkin and the other Bentley Boys. These meditations led him to order a Mercedes, Model S-36/220* (Reg. No. YU 1908). This was probably placed at the 1927 October London Motor Show, where the Long Acre showroom based British Mercedes Company had a stand. The standard price, complete with body, started off at £2,300. The 36/220 had a 6 cylinder, 6789cc power unit which, 'mit kompressor', produced 180 hp. It had a low chassis and short wheelbase, despite which it

---

*The year 1927 heralded the introduction of the Mercedes-Benz 'S Model', a supercharged sports car. In Britain this was known as the S-36/220, with a 6,789cc 180 bhp engine. Later, in the summer of 1928, it was followed by the 'SS Model', or supercharged super sports car. This was given the nomenclature S-38/250, in the British Isles, and was fitted with a supercharged 7069cc engine, delivering 200 bhp. This latter model was also available with a larger supercharger which delivered some 225 bhp. Other 'pre' and or suffixes were generally as follows: K = short chassis; and L = Lightweight (as in chassis).

Plate 70c. The first lap with Tom harrying the Riley Nine of AV Wilkinson, who must have had a difficulty peering out from that 'lowering' hood.

More 1928 TT.

Plate 70d. Quarry Corner (also confusingly known as Mill Corner) with Tom ahead of the 2 litre Lagonda of Baron d'Erlanger.

PLATES 70C & D COURTESY THE ARDS TT. JS MOORE. BLACKSTAFF PRESS.

accommodated a Le Mans specification, open four seater bodywork. It has to be admitted that the rear seat passengers may well have been more comfortable had they had opted for amputation – of their legs! Certainly, a study of the 'form book' would have revealed this model, first officially competing on 19th June 1927, had been going great guns on the Continent. The 'scribes' of the day were generally ecstatic about the vehicle, if rather critical of the supercharger, tending to be 'all or nothing', and that the brakes were somewhat lacking in stopping power.

Despite rumours and indications of appearances at Brooklands, Tom only entered two events this year. The first was the:

TOURIST TROPHY RACE, Ards Circuit, Belfast (17th August). After many years of lobbying, a group of Ulster worthies, which included Harry Ferguson (he of 'the little grey' tractor fame), managed to persuade the 'powers-that-were' to allow this event to be staged. It was not only amazingly well covered in all the North of Ireland press but was very widely reported in the usual mainland motoring 'blats'. This is quite understandable if it is recalled that from 1907 Brooklands had been the only mainland race circuit – 'on offer'. The last Tourist Trophy car race had been held in 1922, on the Isle of Man.

At stake for this event was a £1,000 Trophy. The original 56 entries were whittled down to 44, by the day of the race. The racing machines ranged from an Austin 7, through to Tom's immense Mercedes.* The latter vehicle and driver (in some of the more 'red top' tabloids) being described as the *'focal point of each and every spectator'*! The local press certainly went into overdrive in respect of the whole 'shebang'. One described Tom's Mercedes *'as being a beautiful cream'* and fawningly advised its readers that *'probably no entry creates quite the interest that does the lovely Mercedes. The young man is a driver who knows no fear and knows about cars'* and *'Tom, the handsome driver received a silk stocking which he tied to the radiator cap'*. Please pass the sick bag! His Mercedes (No. 57) was the sole entry in Class B, for 5000 to 8000cc engined vehicles. It was prepared by the British Mercedes Company, more especially by their chief 'tester', Fred Kindell, who was to be both mechanic and co-driver. Tom's decision to accept the offer of a 'manufacturer's' man, instead of 'leaning on' one of his many skilled friends, probably cost him a finishing place, if not an outright win. After Kindell's 'off' and the resultant time lost, did Tom have to press-on too hard in a vain effort catch up? Of his fellow competitors, Tom's close chums included Tim Birkin & Bernard Rubin, sharing a 4.5 litre Bentley, as well as comrade-at-arms Humphrey Wyndham Cook, in another 4.5 litre Bentley, and Clive Gallop in a Brooklands Riley Nine. Amongst the other entrants were a galaxy of racing stars, amongst whom were: Sammy Davis driving another Brooklands Riley; Kaye Don and George Eyston in Lea Francis; A Frazer-Nash in a supercharged 1.5 litre Frazer-Nash and H Aldington in a specially commissioned, supercharged 1.5 litre TT saloon Frazer Nash; RF Oats in a 2 litre OM; Malcolm Campbell

---

* The approximate chassis cost spread of the entered cars would be as follows: Up to 750cc – a competition Austin 7 at about £150; up to 1100cc – a Fiat £160, an MG £165, a Riley £345 and a Salmson (S) £477; up to 1500cc – a Frazer Nash £325, a Lea Francis £425, an Aston Martin £518, and an Alfa Romeo (S) £975; up to 2000cc – an AC £360, an Alvis £500, a Lagonda £555 and an Alfa Romeo (S) £1,075; up to 3000cc – a Talbot £495, a Lagonda £835 and a Bugatti (S) between £1200 & £1430; up to 5000cc – a Bentley between £1050 & £1475 (S); and up to 8000cc – a Mercedes (S) £1,850 and a Bentley £2,150. 'S' denoting supercharged.

Plate 71a. Tom leading Mason's 3 litre Austro-Daimler (No. 7) at Bradshaw's Brae.

More 1928 TT.

Plate 71b. Tom in the pits.
Courtesy The Motor.

Plate 71c. Tom correcting a slide at the Dundonald Hairpin.
Plates 71a & c Courtesy The Autocar.

and Viscount Curzon (Lord Howe) in Type 43 Bugattis; as well as W Urquhart Dykes, HW Purdy, Major Harvey and Leon Cushman, all driving FWD Alvis.

WO recorded that he was sentimentally attached to the Tourist Trophy and that the publicity value of a success would be well worth while. On the other hand these plus points were negated by the circuit not being entirely suited to the Bentley Works cars and that the handicap formula was – a handicap! Thus there were no official Bentley Team entries.

Without doubt, Tom created an enormous amount of publicity by having his private yacht, the *Schooner Charmian*, sailed from Southampton Water to Bangor Bay. But the really eye-catching headline was that his racing Mercedes was deck cargo! That was style. This craft was certainly 'fit for purpose', being of 175 gross tonnage and built by JM Soper & Son of Southampton, in 1896. Apart from solving the transport problem, the yacht doubled up as 'yer B & B', Tom and his acolytes nightly 'bunking down' on board. *'His arrivals and departures from the quayside always attract an interesting crowd of spectators.'* I bet they did. However Tom had another headline grabbing ploy in his 'glove locker'. When the Mercedes engine urgently required some spares, after one of the practice sessions, it caused a firestorm of newspaper columns when he wired to London and had the parts dispatched – by a specially chartered aeroplane. Without doubt, he knew how to play to the gallery. Incidentally, the local 'rags' also opinioned that *'…amongst the ladies the Mercedes and Malcolm Campbell's Bugatti are the joint favourites for the race'*. That shows how much they knew! The locals were giving the 'bookies' a field day and the pre-race betting was: Campbell 5 to 1; Curzon 7 to 1; Kaye Don 8 to 1; Vernon Balls and Tim Birkin 10 to 1; and Staniland (a Fairey Aviation test pilot) and 'our' Tom 12 to 1. He was not the only competitor to have his boat at Bangor. A Major E Hayes of the 2 litre Lagonda team had a boat moored there, even if it was a smaller craft, described as a motor launch.

The news hounds were having a field day. *'The excitement in Belfast is intense. Tramways, buses, charabancs and donkey carts run to the course all night and thousands of people have arranged to sleep in the open, at night the light of many lanterns spreading hundreds of small pools of light.'* Another reported that *'The driver of the French car Tracta took passage to the Isle of Man, by mistake, and arrived (in Dublin) too late for the official tests, but officialdom relented.'* An additional scribe advised that *'Mr Strachan, a local competitor, (driving a Gwynne) recovered his car's hood* (presumably mislaid in practice) *without which he could not start'*. One expert stated that *'… a quarter of a million people were ranged around the course'*, whilst another, probably well ensconced in a local hostelry, was of the opinion that *'…up to half a million bodies were present'*. Without doubt, many hours before 'the off', ' *…the slopes and stands were full of spectators, so much so as to appear as if an anthill had been upended'*. To help supplement these doughty enthusiasts, six specially laid on steamers were shipping in spectators from England. Oh yes, and Lord Curzon (Bugatti) *'… took all his required spares on board. These consisted of petrol, water, oil, bananas and oranges …proceeding to eat the fruit while travelling (racing).'* As you do!

Of course, the relevant roadways making up the track, as well as the various side lanes and pathways had to be to be closed, blanked off and cleared of every-day traffic. Kenelm Lee Guinness was the marshal appointed to ensure all was empty and secure, prior to the start of the race. It was reported, during this procedure, that he had to apprehend and pursue a

Plate 72. Tom's private yacht *Charmian* – not exactly an end of garden launch!

COURTESY BEKEN OF COWES.

motorist he found tearing towards him. The miscreant was handed over to the 'boy's in blue'. KLG, as he was affectionately known, was a member of the Guinness family and the inventor of KLG sparking plugs. (*See* Page 68). He was also close friends of many of the great and good, of the early 1920s racing set. Apart from winning the 1914 Isle of Man Tourist Trophy in a 3¼ litre, 4 cylinder, 1914 model Sunbeam, he gained the World Land Speed Record, in the 18.3 litre, 12 cylinder, 350bhp Sunbeam, in 1922 (taken away from him by none other than Malcolm Campbell, in 1925), as well as setting several Brooklands lap records and flying measured distance records. He also won a number of prestigious races. His career came to an untimely end when he crashed his 2 litre, 6 cylinder Sunbeam, in the 1924 San Sebastian, Spanish Grand Prix, staged on the twisting, eleven mile long Lasarte Circuit. On lap 11, and lying fourth, KLG hit a rut, then a bank, overturning several times and finished up against a stone wall. Both the driver and his riding mechanic were catapulted over the wall. This incident killed the latter, one Jack Barratt, whilst KLG received head and body injuries from which he never really recovered. Interestingly enough, a few years ago the prestigious Motor Sport magazine ran a One Hundred Best Drivers of the Century series of articles and KLG was listed at eighty nine.

An aside was that the Ards circuit loud speaker system was disappointing and the announcer often absurd, though distinct. One had to feel sorry for the official concerned. No more so than when the massed throng howled for him to 'shut up' after his fourth attempt to advertise the advantages of a certain newspaper's offer of free insurance against road accidents. The event was due to start at 11 am. Each lap was 13⅔ miles long and the race was to cover 30 laps, or some 410 miles. The 'headline' rules were that each entrant had to complete two laps with the hood up and the start was to be of the Le Mans variety. That is the driver and riding mechanic/co-driver had to dash across the track, at the drop of the starter's flag, raise the car's hood, leap in and drive off. After two laps (in this case) the car could (and would) come into the pits, drop the hood, to race off, once again.

One thing was for certain. This Tourist Trophy was not to prove to be an anticlimax, which was rather fortunate, considering all the pre-race hype, suspense and anticipation. The rustling pandemonium of 88 contestants scrambling across the track was followed by an almost deafening silence, whilst the hoods were 'panicked' into place. Once the protagonists had leapt into the cars, the grunt of the starter motors whining over presaged the cacophony and roar of the engines firing into life. True to form, the 4.5 litre Bentleys of Cook and Birkin were first away, followed by the chasing pack. They were somewhat obscured by a pall of exhaust smoke, mingled with the billowing race track dust. The sole car briefly left behind was the Frazer Nash of Aldington. First time round and Tom, bringing up the tail, had 'to pit' to change the sparking plugs, for the second time. At the end of the second lap, the whole show streamed into the pits 'to de-hood'. Birkin was first away this time. This particular stop was somewhat enlivened by the fuel tank of Campbell's Type 43 Bugatti catching fire. As a consequence, his car burnt to the ground, despite the best efforts of the pit crew and marshals. I believe I am correct in stating that the great man was uninsured, a fact made all the more questionable as he was a Lloyds Insurance Underwriter.

The race attrition was steady and spectacular. After ten laps, eight cars had retired. With half the race run, Tom Thistlethwayte handed over to his co-driver, Fred Kindell. The latter

Plate 73a. The 'ditching' of the Mercedes at Quarry (or Mill) Corner. As the giant car slides off, Birkin's Bentley followed by Taylor's Austro Daimler can be seen safely negotiating the bend.

COURTESY THE MOTOR.

And Tom's 'whoopsy' in the 1928 TT.

Plate 73b & c. Silence was probably best!
COURTESY ARDS TT. JS MOORE. BLACKSTAFF PRESS.

COURTESY THE AUTOCAR.

138

had a 'whoopsy', having failed to negotiate Quarry Corner, and finished up well and truly stuck in the brambles covering a steeply sloping ditch. From the contemporary pictures of this debacle, it is impossible to conceive that Tom and Kindell could possibly have extricated the enormous vehicle from it's, as it turned out, temporary resting place. This was especially more so as the regulations stipulated that no outside help could be sort or given. Nothing like being in a sinking ship and only having a leaky bucket with which to bail! It took some $^1/_2$ hour for the doughty duo to get the Mercedes back on the track and a wildfire rumour spread that the driver was dead. Without doubt he was dead, dead tired after digging that brute out of the mire. The language must have been interesting. After about 20 laps the Mercedes blew a head gasket and Tom's race was run. To prove his class, he had put in the fastest lap of the day in 11 minutes 12 seconds, or some 74.39 mph.

The lead was changing consistently whilst spilt sump oil and localised rain showers made for very 'interesting' driving conditions. The FWD Alvis's were especially proving a handful in these adverse conditions. Shortly before half distance, Cushman in his Alvis clouted a bank. His riding mechanic became airborne, 'fell to earth' on the track and was knocked unconscious. Nothing daunted, and in order to fully comply with the race regulations, Cushman shoved the inert body back into the passenger seat and raced on – as you do. A lap later the unfortunate man demonstrated he was still alive, by weakly waving at the spectators. In one series of crashes, close by Ballystockart, Harvey's Alvis, Newsome's Lea Francis and Sammy Davis' Riley all went out. Urquhart Dykes' Alvis turned over on top of him, breaking a leg, rib and collar bone. Lord Howe, bearing in mind Malcolm Campbell's fire, in a similar car, decided to retire his Type 43 Bugatti. This turned out to be a wise decision as the fault was quite possibly a batch of faultily riveted fuel tanks. Clive Gallop, after one or three rotations, shot through a hedge and came to an abrupt halt, standing his Riley on its radiator. Fascinatingly, the race was regarded as being reasonably accident free!

Kaye Don in a Lea Francis was the eventual winner taking 5 hours 58 minutes 13 seconds. He had held the lead position from the fourth hour, on lap 20. Despite what was hailed as a brilliant drive, he was only 13 seconds ahead of the second placed Leon Cushman in his Alvis. Both were very, very low on oil and fuel, the latter car running out of 'fluence', some 300 yards beyond the finishing line. Apart from all these heroics, the really truly amazing results were the third and fourth places which went to the 3 litre Austro-Daimlers. These vehicles had been designed by Dr. Porsche (as was Tom's Mercedes – with a few years in between the two drawing boards) and were 'Uprights'. They were no more than standard tourers and beat the mighty Tim Birkin's 4.5 litre Bentley into fifth place. Talk about the tortoise and the hare. To rub salt into the wounds, the Austro's won the Team Prize, with fourth, fifth and tenth places. Tim took a Class win and Humphrey Cook came in seventh, in their 4.5 litre Bentleys.

One other appearance for Tom was at the:

BOULOGNE AND LE TOUQUET SPEED TRIALS AND HILL CLIMBS (6-8th September). This was an enterprising, two centre, 25 kilometres' apart, Automobile Week, based on Boulogne sur Mere and Le Touquet-Paris-Plage. A 900 metre High Speed Trial was held along the sea promenade of Le Touquet. The Wimille Hill Climb was to the north of Boulogne and the three kilometre Flying Start Speed Trial was staged in the forest close by

The 1928 Boulogne Automobile Week.

Plate 74a.   Baron von Wentzel-Mosau 'foot hard down' in his S-38/250 Mercedes.

Plate 74b.   Bielovuci's accident in his 2 litre supercharged Bugatti.

Plate 74c. Miss Maconochie and her 1100cc, twin overhead cam, supercharged, 6 cylinder Amilcar C6.

Plate 74d.   Birkin and his 4.5 litre Bentley negotiating Desvres.

PLATES 74A, B, C & D COURTESY THE MOTOR.

and to the east of Boulogne. The aggregation of the three events would give the overall placings. A newspaper of the day announced that Capt. Malcolm Campbell was entering both a Type 43 Bugatti and his 1.5 litre, straight eight Delage and that other British entrants included Miss MJ Maconochie, Miss Violet Cordery, Mrs Urquhart Dykes, Kaye Don, A Frazer-Nash, T Thistlethwayte and CJ Birkin *(sic)*.

The fastest time for the Le Touquet High Speed Trial was put in by a Monsieur Bielovuci, in a 2 litre supercharged Bugatti. This gentleman was supposedly the first aviator to fly over the Alps, in 1910, in a Bleriot aeroplane. Unfortunately he was to have 'one of those days'. In the Flying Start Speed Trial, at well over 100 mph, his car struck a kerb, shot at right angles across the track, through a coppice and cut a swathe over the spectators, thereabouts. Two brothers were killed and the Bugatti careered on, before inverting itself. Bielovuci was thrown out, but apart from some cuts and bruises he was simply shaken. The car burst into flames. Back at the promenade, Tom was third behind a Madame Jennky and a 1/5th second in front of a Baron von Wentzel-Mosau. The latter two were listed as piloting '38/220' Mercedes. Without doubt Tom was still using his S-36/220. The next model in progression, as it were, was the S-38/250. No need to take your pick, the Baron was driving a S-38/250. The latter, a dashing amateur and quite often a class winner, was 'Mercedes dedicated' having entered the 1927 Boulogne Week in a 33/180hp car.

An intriguing entrant was Miss Maconochie in an 1100cc Amilcar C6, gaining a second in Class. That year she also won a handicap race at 21st June Brooklands Race meeting, in a Salmson, a further win in the August Brooklands Race meeting, in the Amilcar Six, and a third in a handicap event at the Autumn Brooklands Race meeting, again in the Amilcar. More interestingly, Miss Maconochie would appear competing in the 1929 Ards Circuit Tourist Trophy Race, but in an S-36/220 Mercedes. Quite some step up.

The Hill Climb passed without incident but, as has been described, the Flying Start Speed Trial was to prove somewhat deadly. In fact, immediately prior to the Bielovuci debacle, another Bugatti lost its un-strapped bonnet, which struck and killed a lady spectator. Not unnaturally, the last incident called a halt to the proceedings. For some reason Tom only made one run out of the three required, namely two Speed Trials and one Hill Climb. (Incidentally, the first was the 900 metre Speed Trial which was followed by the Wimille Hill Climb and the 3 kilometre Speed Trial). Thus he did not finish nor was he listed but the sole time recorded probably indicated mechanical problems. Nonetheless the British flag was kept flying by Tim Birkin (4.5 litre Bentley) and Mrs Urquhart Dykes (Alvis) in the incident packed *Georges Boillot Cup Race* in which much skullduggery was reported to have taken place. Tim beat all the records but the handicapping pushed him into fifth place. Mrs Urquhart Dykes came in ninth and was the first woman ever to finish this event.

It must not be thought that Tom's overweening interest in all things motoring precluded him from dipping his toes in other madcap pursuits. Oh, no. By now a firm friend of Cmdr. Glen Kidston (for more details of whom *See* Chapter 7), they decided to go Big Game Hunting. And why not? Earlier in 1928, millionaire Alfred Loewenstein, a somewhat mysterious Belgian financier, was the owner of a Lynx engined, Fokker aeroplane. In this transportation, he was accustomed to make daily flights, to and from the airports of Croydon

A crowd waving as the aeroplane in which big game is to be hunted in Kenya Colony left Croydon Aerodrome yesterday. It is the machine from which Captain Loewenstein, the millionaire, lost his life in the English Channel.

Plate 75a. 'Big Game Hunt in the ex Loewenstein's Plane'.
COURTESY THE MIRROR.

Plate 75b. The group before take-off. Left to right: Captain Ronald Drew, the pilot; Mr Whatley, mechanic; Mr Brand; Lt Cmdr Glen Kidston, leader of the expedition, and Mr Thistlethwayte.
COURTESY GETTY IMAGES.

Plate 75c. 'Jimmy" Murphy piloting his straight eight, 4.2 litre Duesenberg to win the 1921 French Grand Prix staged at Le Mans.
COURTESY FLAT OUT GET EYSTON. JOHN MILES PUBLISHING, LONDON.

142

and Brussels, accompanied by a staff of four. This procedure came to an abrupt halt when he 'carelessly' fell out of the machine, whilst over the English Channel. Captain Ronald Drew stayed on as pilot and Glen Kidston, 'in cahoots' with Tom, purchased the plane. The plan was to fly from Croydon Airport to the then Colony of Kenya. Apart from the aforementioned, a Mr Brand and a Mr Whatley made up the aircraft's compliment. The flight was not without incident and there were tales of a forced landing, somewhere in a river in the Sudan '…*only the skill of the pilot avoiding damage to the plane*'. Part of the purpose of this 'jolly' was to make a film of wild life being hunted. I am not sure how the party returned, because the Fokker was reported to have been dismantled and crated-up, prior to being returned to the factory for repairs.

Fellow performers.

CAPT. GEORGE EDWARD THOMAS 'GET' EYSTON (1897-1979). During WW1, George Eyston served as a machine gun officer in the then Royal Field Artillery, taking part in the 1915 Battle of Loos. His gallantry won him the Military Cross and he remained in uniform until after the Armistice was completed. Demobbed, he gained a BA degree at Trinity College, Cambridge. University life saw him become a crack oarsman and a member of the Leander Rowing Club. After formal schooling he took an engineering course at a Fareham (Hampshire) College.

Before and after the unnecessary wartime interruption he achieved a measure of success racing motorbikes, having owned an early Triumph, when aged 13. This particular acquisition caused much parental dismay. But 1921 was the year in which his future destiny was to be determined. Driving a GN and on his summer 'hols', he was staying in a French chateaux, close by the Sarthe circuit. As fate would have it, this vacation coincided with the opening stages of the French Grand Prix which was being held at Le Mans that year.

This was the first post war French Grand Prix (Monday 25th July) to be staged. The Works Teams commenced practicing by mid-July and the race was to be of 30 laps or 321.78 miles. Not unnaturally, the event attracted an enormous amount of interest. Having banned the Germans from competing, the French had high hopes of re-establishing their national motoring pride. This was more especially desirable as the Mercedes team had come in first, second and third in the last French Grand Prix to be staged in 1914, just one month or so prior to the onset of the European hostilities. But this dream was not to be. An American straight eight Duesenberg driven by the 'all-Yankee' Jimmy Murphy won. He beat a 3 litre, 8 cylinder Ballot driven by Ralph de Palma into second place. In third and regarded as having driven a sensational race, more especially taking into account the lack of 'grunt', was the first Frenchman home, one Jules Goux. He was also in a Ballot, but the 2 litre, 4 cylinder model. The French hosts failed to suppress their dismay at not achieving a home win by omitting to play the American national anthem and by all but ignoring the winning team at the subsequent reception. Oh dear! Incidentally, the Italian team of three FIAT's had to withdraw due to national unrest in their country. It is also worth a mention that the track was in an appalling state '…*being littered with stones the size of tennis balls, which unrelentingly peppered the cars and drivers alike*'. It was reported that at least two riding mechanics were knocked

Plate 76a.   Capt. George Edward Thomas Eyston aged 29, in 1926.

COURTESY MOTOR SPORT.

Plate 76b.   Kensington-Moir in the prototype 1.5 litre side valve Aston Martin whilst record breaking at Brooklands in 1921. He had joined Aston Martin from the Zenith Carburettor Co., prior to which he had been at Straker-Squire, being a nephew of Sydney Straker. Famously, he subsequently moved to work with Bentley's.

Plate 76c. The two 1.5 litre, 16 valve, twin overhead camshaft engined Aston Martins (TT1 & 2) at the July 1922 Strasbourg Grand Prix . Zborowski to the right , Gallop to the left.

PLATES 76B & C COURTESY ASTON MARTIN 1913-1947. INMAN HUNTER. OSPREY AUTOMOTIVE.

unconscious by flying rocks. A certain Kenelm Lee Guinness achieved a seventh place, in an English built, 1.5 litre, 8 cylinder Talbot, ahead of a Major HOD Segrave in a Talbot-Darracq. Also down to drive a similar Sunbeam Talbot-Darracq was Zborowski with Clive Gallop and Sammy Davis as his support team. It was reported that he failed to make the start line due to his car's brake shoes having been 'borrowed'!

The practice stages and event gripped Eyston's imagination. So much so that on returning to his Bournemouth home he leapt out and purchased a pre-war GP Sunbeam. The seeds were sown. Subsequently, in 1922, he acquired a second-hand 4.5 litre Vauxhall 'racer which was 'a bit of a pup'. Having had some tuning carried out, he gave the car a run at Brooklands. Here he fortuitously (or not, as the case may be) bumped into Lionel Martin of Bamford & Martin, manufacturer of Aston Martin motor cars. In Eyston's own words they were constructing '...*a perfectly lovely little car of 1.5 litre capacity*'. Observing 'Bertie' Kensington-Moir compete in an Aston Martin (No. 1) his attention was well and truly concentrated. The seeds were germinating.

Thus, Capt. Eyston, whom Lionel Martin rated as '....*a good and useful prospect*', purchased not one, but two ex-works cars. One was the car he had seen Kensington-Moir driving, fitted with a side valve engine. The other was reputably the racing machine Count Louis Zborowski had driven at Strasbourg, although at least one commentator maintains it was actually Clive Gallop's car. The latter ex-Grand Prix car was for sale but without the power unit. The idea was for George to swap the engine into whichever chassis was to be used for road or track racing, as the occasion demanded. Thus were cultivated the seeds of what was to turn out to be a perfectly outstanding, if possibly under-appreciated racing record. This may well be due to his record breaking becoming so prominent as his career progressed, post 1930. At the end of 1922 he attended a private motor cycle meeting at Brooklands and won a race in one of the Aston's. The seeds were now bearing fruit

Incidentally, no more different characters can be imagined than on the one hand George Eyston and on the other the archetypal, outward, flamboyant, part-party, Bentley Boys. He was somewhat introspective, self-effacing, rather large and lumpy, with owl-like, old fashioned spectacles and a small 'tach', 'stuck' under his nose. Sometime in the early 1920s, he set-up a business manufacturing air compressors (and another to do with artesian wells). It was no giant leap to connect compressors to superchargers and thus to *Powerplus Ltd.*, manufacturers of car engine 'blowers'.

The year 1923 was to be a very busy and successful racing season for Eyston. Admittedly the Easter Brooklands Race meeting did not rate highly, as his car incurred plug troubles. During this year's Brooklands season he achieved several first, second and third places. In amongst the circuit racing he attended a number of hill climbs, sprints and speed trials. These included the Caerphilly Hill Climb, near Cardiff, followed by a Porthcawl Speed Trial, the Spread Eagle and South Harting Hill Climbs, all with mixed results, and the Southsea Esplanade Speed Sprints. At the latter he drove a single seater Aston Martin – known as *'Razor Blade'* (first known as *'Oyster'*) – with a body by the de Havilland Aircraft Company. This particular pet name was initially due to the snug cockpit. Incidentally, this habit of giving specific cars a 'moniker' was a habit shared, for instance, with the Sunbeam Car Company. At Southsea he gained a first, second and a third place. Incidentally, at the Spread

Plate 77a. The single seater Aston Martin, originally known as *Oyster*, on show to the press and public at Brooklands in July 1923.

PLATES 77A & B COURTESY ASTON MARTIN 1913-1947. INMAN HUNTER. OSPREY AUTOMOTIVE.

Plate 77b. After some modifications the same car was renamed *Razor Blade*.

Plate 77c. Eyston and his riding mechanic. The latter is changing the spark plugs of the 16 valve, twin overhead cam GP Aston Martin during a pit stop, whilst competing in the 1923 Brooklands 200 Mile Race.

COURTESY THE MOTOR.

Eagle Hill Climb he became acquainted with Malcolm Campbell, driving a 'big Sunbeam'. George was really getting his 'feet under the chassis', as it were, for he next attended Brooklands to accompany and assist Sammy Davis in tuning the Aston Martin *'Razor Blade'*. This heralded an attempt on the 1500cc, 1 hour Record, somewhat spoilt by the offside front tyre bursting and cart-wheeling-off along the track. In the meantime Eyston entered the Boulogne Automobile Week (30th August - 2nd September). In practice his 'svelte-green' car incurred quite extensive front end damage. At first the havoc appeared unrepairable but, locating a vehicle pit in a close-by farm building, closer inspection changed his mind. Thus, still in his racing 'ovies', and begrimed and oily, he ran the five miles to Boulogne Harbour. There he boarded a Cross Channel boat, caught a train to the Capital, and picked up the necessary bits and pieces, including a spare front axle, from the Abingdon Road, W8, London premises. He then retraced his route, made the necessary repairs and was back on the track the next day. Such actions are sufficient to prompt one to break into a rendition of *'Rule Britannia'*! But he was not the only Englishman to experience problems. Early Sunday morning John Duff in his 3 litre Bentley had a moment, prior to the start of the 'big event', the Georges Boillet Cup Race for the larger engined cars. At speed he ran into a herd of cows, killing three or five, depending on who was counting! This deprived the Bentley of front shock absorbers which rather upset the handling. That and an engine compartment fire whilst racing, doused speedily by the riding mechanic, coupled later on to a broken petrol pipe, not surprisingly put him out of the results. His Bentley colleague, 'Bertie' Kensington Moir (No. 26), did at least finish. But back to George. He was down to compete on Thursday in a speed test which was to be followed by a hill climb. He achieved a seventh overall and first in class. Parry Thomas in his Leyland Eight would have won but he was disqualified for changing tyres, after a protest by the originally second placed man. Swine! On Saturday George competed in the 1500cc Racing Class of the Grand Prix de Boulogne, awards for which included the *Pickett* and *Bulletin de l'Automobile Cups*. After some four hours racing he finished third overall behind the winner Segrave, in a Talbot, and RC Morgan in a side-valve Aston Martin. And all this after the earlier disasters which befell him, when communications were of the 'forked-stick' variety. No wonder we had an Empire in those far-off days. Where would the multi-vehicle transporter 'comforted' boy-racers of today have been then? The season ended with the Brooklands 200 Mile Race meeting (13th October). After practice, Lionel Martin approached Eyston, advising he had an instant buyer for his car, if it 'came with' the race entry. Furthermore, he could sell him a brand new car, at that moment being completed and scheduled to be ready the night before the race started. However matters then became rather complicated as the Talbot-Darracq Work's Team pulled out, at the last minute. This left Major Henry O'Neal de hane Segrave without a drive. Accordingly, he pitched up on Aston Martin's door step, asking for a vehicle. To Martin's everlasting credit he advised Segrave that the only available car was committed to Eyston, whom it appears was prepared to stand aside. 'Golly gosh', they were chaps and men of honour in those far off days. The race had two classes: up to 1100cc and up to 1500cc engine capacity. In some quarters there was confusion in respect of Eyston's fate in the senior class. Despite some reports of his demise, at some stage during the race, he did finish. Honest! The pre-race hype was all about the threat to the 'Brits' from two supercharged 1500cc Fiats, one

Plate 78a.   Bad luck for Eyston and his Aston Martin in the 1924 Grand Prix de Boulogne.

COURTESY THE MOTOR.

Plate 78b.   The 1922 ex-works, originally side valve Aston Martin known as *Green Pea* and raced with effect by RC Morgan, often accompanied by Mrs Agnew.

COURTESY ASTON MARTIN 1914-1940. INMAN HUNTER. OSPREY AUTOMOTIVE.

Plate 78c.   Eyston reported as 'putting up a plucky fight' in an Aston Martin.

COURTESY MOTOR SPORT.

of which was being driven by Malcolm Campbell. Of the Aston Martins drivers, Eyston was favourite but he was suffering from a badly poisoned hand. Count Zborowski was down to drive one of the other Aston's but did not appear to feature. Without doubt, the Fiats were quick and in the lead for the first few laps. But by lap 13 they had fallen by the wayside and George was in the lead. At about lap 39, his engine commenced to misfire and he pulled into the pits. Fearing irreparable valve troubles, he sped off again. This delay cost him some two places, a situation which worsened as his inability to keep going at the car's notional top speed continued to cost him places. The pit crew put out a 'come in now' sign but his short-sightedness meant he could not read the signals. (That gives one food for thought!). For some inexplicable reason his riding mechanic waited another 16 laps to point out the instruction. On coming in, Lionel Martin insisted the plugs and leads were changed. Hey presto, the engine regained its full power. The referred to mechanic, in pushing the reluctant-to-start vehicle, lost a boot as he scrambled back into the cockpit, when the engine suddenly burst into life. George was now seventh but commenced to claw his way back up the leader board. By the 61st lap he was fourth, where he stayed until the finish. The delays and lap-after-lap reduced speed cost him the race. It is poignant to consider the sporting nature of Lionel Martin's altruism. Unable to fill one of his planned entries, he allowed Alvis to take the slot – and the latter marque won! In its 200 Miles Jottings THE AUTOCAR noted that *'the catering did not seem any the worse than usual. Determined people got their money back if they couldn't get the food they had paid for. But it required firmness'.* Nothing new there then! Seems to me this was a ghastly portent of the offerings 'up with which' the modern motorist has to contend, at this or that roadside catering establishments.

For 1924, the Boulogne Automobile Week (28-31st August) was on the 'menu' once again. Generally, the weather varied between the awful and the appalling. Confusingly, Eyston entered a Marseal 'for fun' and to be driven by an RL Barnett! It appears this vehicle was used to tow-start George's Aston Martin – his 'proper' entry. Despite the Marseal* having front spring trouble THE MOTOR reported it to have ' ...*covered the course at a fair speed'* and *'...Barnett appeared to treat the whole thing as a huge joke, beating his car on the flanks to make it go faster'.* (Maybe I will try that!). Of the two Aston's down to compete, the other one was driven by RC 'Bobby' Morgan. He was accompanied by Mrs Agnew, a 'very active' *mecanicienne.* I am sure she was! The lady, who was an enthusiastic and gifted driver, was to marry 'Bobby' and they owned the side-valve Aston, named *Green Pea.* They were to have a legal 'falling-out' with Lionel Martin, in 1925, after they had inserted a 1.5 litre Hooker-Thomas engine into the car, which thereafter raced as a *Thomas Special.* But back to the narrative. In the speed trials and the hill climb, George's car was misfiring badly and he did not feature in the results. In the Saturday Grand Prix de Boulogne, and despite the appalling weather conditions, he was driving like the wind. By the end of the second circuit of ten he was well in the lead. On the other hand 'Bobby' Morgan was experiencing ignition problems. Later, when the magneto was found to be at fault, sabotage was imagined, a view reinforced when it became apparent that the spare unit was also suspect. On the third circuit of the race, bad luck struck Eyston. He had been shadowing and desperately looking for a way past a

---

*As a matter of interest the Marseal (Marseel) was manufactured between 1919 and 1925 by DM Marendaz and Seelhaft. This Marseal was probably the 1500cc model. The former gentleman was to go on to subsequently manufacture the eponymous Marendaz.

Plate 79a. Eyston's powerboat *Miss Olga* in a storm off Calshot, the Solent.
COURTESY FLAT OUT, GET EYSTON. JOHN MILES.

Plate 79b. The caption reads 'Motor Boat Racing is another of Mr Eyston's pursuits'.
COURTESY MOTOR SPORT.

rather erratically driven, slower Marechal. Approaching Wirwignes, he made to pass. At that precise moment the Frenchman's car hit a pile of stones and shot back into George's path, forcing him into a ditch. The car careened on to smash up against a telegraph pole, badly damaging the front end. His race was run. Poor old 'Bobby', still suffering from ignition problems and the wretched weather, decided his own attempt was a waste of time. Thus, he gallantly picked up George and his mechanic and bought the dispirited duo back to the pits. Thus 'endeth' that year.

At the outset of 1925, George had married. Accordingly, it will come as no surprise if the usual, often self-inflicted, but to be expected caveat came into force. *No more motor racing!* Being a bit of a fidget, his attention turned to other sporting activities, one of which was flying. He gained a pilot's license, flying for pleasure and occasionally taking part in air races. It appears he advertised his plane for sale and a prospective purchaser arrived, took the machine up for a trial flight and 'forgot' to return! It is said George was grateful to unload the thing as he had lost interest in it and the sport. Mmmmh! Hunting, shooting and fishing were also part of his chosen leisure pursuits but that which really turned him on was power boat racing. Ye gods! At some stage the Duke of York's Trophy Race, for 1.5 litre hydroplanes, over a Putney to Mortlake course, came to his attention. Accordingly, he contacted the Walton-on-Thames Launch Works, just along the road from the Brooklands Circuit, and had CW Burnard build a racing hydroplane in which was installed an Aston Martin engine. Lionel Martin supervised the work and, as there was another similarly powered boat, he was able to watch over George's first test outing. The craft was named *Miss Olga*. Incidentally, the other Aston engine powered craft crashed and foundered. In the preliminaries *Miss Olga* had a flying start and he finished second over the line, behind a certain Miss Betty Carstairs.* She was a star of power boat racing and was aboard her latest Saunders (Roe) Sunbeam (engined) craft. Only four entrants qualified for the race, in which George had a three lap scrap with a Fred May, and his craft named *Green*, which was passed when the latter's engine blew up. *Miss Olga* finally finished second to none other than Woolf Barnato, in his Sunbeam engined *Ardenrun*. Next off was the Southend Regatta where he won one race and came second in another, despite an engine room conflagration, caused by a backfire. This was followed by the Royal Motor Yacht Club meeting at Hythe, Southampton Water, where he was up against more 1.5 litre Sunbeam engined boats. He gained a place. Often Eyston's riding mechanic was Val Clark who gained noteworthy regard for being able to change sparking plugs whilst an engine was actually running. (Also *See* Chapter 8, Woolf Barnato for more Eyston).

However, you cannot keep an oil-immersed man away from the *Castrol R*. Later in the year, the 1925 Boulogne Week (27-30th August) drew a strong English entry, including Clive

---

* This extraordinary character demands a footnote. Known as 'Betty' or 'Joe', she was born Marion Barbara Carstairs in 1900 and inherited a 'chunk' of Standard Oil from her wayward mother. Tattooed, she claimed to have been born a lesbian, dressing as a man for most of her life. She achieved fame on both sides of the Atlantic as a power boat owner and competitor, being undoubtably the fastest female racer of her time. After giving up the sport, in the early 1930s, she purchased Whale Cay in the Bahamas, where she lived for some forty years. Apart from a string of lesbian lovers, amongst whom was Marlene Dietrich, at the outset of WW2 she offered her yacht and island's facilities to the British Navy. They were rejected. Amongst a constant stream of notable visitors were the Duke and Duchess of Windsor, after the Duke had been effectively banished from wartime Britain, to be Governor of the Bahamas in 1942. She died in Florida, a solitary figure, in 1993 aged 93. Her lifetime companion, a doll named Lord Ted Wadley, was buried with her. Yes – her lifetime…!

Plate 80a.   Eyston piloting his straight eight, unsupercharged 1.5 litre Type 39 Bugatti around the course of the 1926 Boulogne Grand Prix…

Plate 80b.   …and post race and the winner.

PLATES 80A & B COURTESY MOTOR SPORT.

Plate 80c. Eyston accompanied by his wife (?) posing for photographs after winning the 1926 Boulogne Grand Prix. Perhaps the flowers have been planted?

COURTESY FLAT OUT, GET EYSTON. JOHN MILES PUBLISHING. LONDON.

Gallop and Tom Thistlethwayte (*See* Chapter 3). The event gave drivers a choice of hill climb, speed trials and a race. In amongst the entrants was – George Eyston. So the 'old' unwritten marriage vows clause was dead and buried! During the Speed Trial he had a spectacular slide in his *'pretty little, dark blue 2 seater'* Aston Martin, at the very hollow where, some two years previously, Parry Thomas had very nearly met disaster. A misplaced gully was the fault. George's younger brother, Basil, in a Frazer Nash, nicknamed *Rodeo*, was *'putting up an excellent, although somewhat blood curdling* (Rodeo?) *show. His skids from side to side were horrible to behold but he had the tiny car all the while under control'*. Basil finished up with a first and a second (both in the 1100cc Class). However, once Boulogne was over George put in another power boat race, once again organised by the RMYC, in which he was, as in the past, up against Betty Carstairs, and won. Not bad for a first season power boat practitioner. The Aston engine was pulled out of the boat and put back into a racing car preparatory to the Brooklands 200 Mile Race (26th September). George Eyston shared the now twin overhead camshaft engined Aston Martin with Basil, but with no success. A fellow Aston driver supplied the not so funny 'entertainment' when he crashed through some railings, on the first lap, badly injuring his mechanic. Whatever, it was not surprising that George's close connection with Aston Martin did not survive the Company's almost inevitable receivership, in November 1925. In the meantime, the now engine-less power boat had a British Anzani marine power unit installed. It was designed to be able to accept a 'Powerplus' supercharger, which he had designed and manufactured himself. All this effort was in preparation for next year's Duke of York Power Boat Challenge Race.

By-the-by, the year 1926 marked the arrival of Renwick and Bertelli at Aston Martin's. At the Whitsun Brooklands Race meeting, George achieved a win and a third in a side-valve engined Aston Martin. He also gained a win when Dr. Benjafield miscalculated the number of laps left until the race end. Haven't we all? He picked up another third at a later May Brooklands Race meeting. But back to boats and the Duke of York Trophy Power Boat Race. The start line was opposite Duke's Meadow, Barnes. George only finished rebuilding the boat engine, for bench testing, two days before the start of the event. The craft was finally completed on the morning of the race, a mere 40 minutes prior to the 'off'. I write finished, but the propeller required changing, which had to be carried out, beside the waters edge. After all this effort, and despite a rubbish-fouled 'prop', he finished in second place. It is interesting to note that Parry Thomas was preparing a boat for this event, into which one of his engines was being fitted. So back to motor racing. In preparation for the Grand Prix des Voitures Legeres, Boulogne (27-29th August), George toddled along to have a chat with Malcolm Campbell and purchased his unsupercharged, straight eight, 1.5 litre Type 39 Bugatti. This car had originally been built specifically for the Monza GP, to be driven by the Italian ace, Constantini. Other Boulogne competitors included Parry Thomas, in his straight eight, *Flat Iron Thomas Special* (problems), Campbell in a new, supercharged straight 8 Type 39A Bugatti (threw a con-rod), Miss Ivy Cummings in a new 4 cylinder 1.5 litre Type 37 Bugatti and a scattering of Talbot-Darracqs. Brother Basil was piloting an Aston Martin, to which had been fitted George's ex-power boat, supercharged Anzani (marine) engine. Despite a track-side breakdown, whilst lying second, George passed Ivy Cummings' car, up against a tree, to win the race. Towards the year end he appeared in the Brooklands 200 Mile Race (25th

Plate 81a. A marvellously evocative Brian de Grineau plate "The Bugatti race and records", depicting Eyston at the wheel.

COURTESY FLAT OUT. GET EYSTON. JOHN MILES PUBLISHING. LONDON.

Plate 81b. The 1927 Formula Libre Race, Montlhery whereat Eyston gained a third. The plate details Eyston far side in his Type 35C Bugatti (No. 20) and Chirron centre stage in his Type 35B Bugatti (No. 16). One row back and on the left is the 'Indy' Guyot Special (No. 2) of Henry de Courcelles who was to die during the race. Behind him and up against the Grand Stand wall is the supercharged 4 litre, 12 cylinder Sunbeam (No. 12) of (Grover) Williams. The fellow on the pole must be a photographer. One hopes he did not suffer any splinters!

Plate 81c. The start of the 1927 Grand Prix de Boulogne – in the pouring rain. Eyston's 1.5 litre Type 39 Bugatti is on the left, pulling away from the Frazer-Nash's eponymous car.

PLATES 81B & C COURTESY THE AUTOCAR.

September), in the aforementioned Bugatti. On the first lap another competitor drove into the tail of his car. As a result he had to pull into the pits with a rear wheel obviously bent. Despite this he attempted to drive back on to the track, before being retired by an officious marshal.

By the 1927 Brooklands Whitsun Race meeting he had acquired and drove the ex-Baron d'Erlanger's supercharged 2.3 litre Type 35B Bugatti, as he did again in a Brooklands June Race meeting, scoring a win. Subsequently he entered a straight 8, 2 litre, supercharged Type 35C Bugatti in the Formula Libre Race, Montlhery (2nd July), near Paris. This was staged the day before the French Grand Prix, being held on the same road circuit. The scheduled start was delayed for a couple of hours, due to a howling gale raging over the course. When this inclement weather calmed down to heavy rain squalls, the flag dropped. At this stage the track was still almost flooded with running water. Then it commenced to sheet down once again which made handling the larger powered cars very difficult. Although rather processional, some excitement was caused by the fatal accident to Henry (Henri) de Courcelles. He had been a distinguished WW1 Sopwith fighter pilot and was possibly the first lover of the later notorious Heléne Delangle – aka 'The Bugatti Queen'. Henry was driving an unsuitable, single seater, ex-Indy, 6 cylinder Guyot Special which proved to be rather unmanageable. So unmanageable that he skidded off the track at in excess of 100 mph and smashed into a tree, reportedly with the noise of an exploding round of ordnance. He died instantly. *THE MOTOR* reported *'A great pool of oil lay in the middle of the track and debris and blood strewed the ditch'*. Quite! In the rush to bring up the emergency services, the official rescue vehicle raced to the scene of the accident – the wrong way round the circuit! And this whilst the race was still in progress. Understandably, the competitors left in the event found this somewhat alarming. Fortunately that is all it caused. George managed a third to the current day Continental race aces, Divo in a 1.5 litre Talbot and Chiron in a similar Bugatti to Eyston's. The following day was reserved for the French Grand Prix in which he entered the 6 cylinder Halford Special*, which proved to be rather uncompetitive. Next on the list was the La Baule Grand Prix (25th August) organized by the Automobile Club de l'Ouest. La Baule, in those days, was the venue for a then Europe-famous sand race held on the encircling bay. On this occasion the course was a distance of 100 kilometres. In order to compete, George, in his race Type 35B Bugatti, and his mechanic, driving the 'shopping' Type 35 Bugatti, boarded a boat at Southampton, bound for St. Malo. The major hazard of this type of racing was that the lead man hurled sand at the following pack, sometimes with a violence emulating a grit-blaster. Despite Bourlier, in his 1.5 litre Delage, getting away first, George 'stuck in' and after a great race piped the Frenchman home, to take the winning flag, as well as a number of cups and prizes. As usual, the annual Boulogne-Le Touquet Automobile Week (8-11th September) attracted well-supported fields. That year the event had a rally on the preceding Tuesday, based at Le Touquet. This drew entries from various starting points, including John O'Groats, Chamonix, Nice and Berlin. Thursday was the day for the speed trials and hill climb and Friday was reserved for the *Concours d'Elegance*.

---

* The 1.5 litre, 6 cylinder, twin overhead camshaft, twin plug and ignition, supercharged Halford Special was the brainchild of Major Frank Halford. He was an aero engine designer responsible for the de Havilland Gypsy and subsequently the Napier Sabre engines, the latter powering the Hawker Typhoon and Tempest fighter aircraft. The car emerged in 1923 and was based on a crashed Aston Martin chassis (Eyston's 1924 Boulogne car) with the engine designed, unsurprisingly, by the 'gallant Major – in line with best aircraft practice!

Plate 82a.   GET Eyston in an 1100cc Riley (No. 45) leads the early stages of the 1928 Brooklands Six Hour Race, followed by F Hallam in a 1500cc Lea-Francis and Payne in a 2 litre, 6 cylinder OM.

COURTESY THE AUTOCAR.

Plate 82b.   FJ Clarke in a 1100cc Salmson (No. 20) leads GET Eyston in a 1.5 litre Type 39A Bugatti and Higgins in a 1.5 litre Talbot in the 1928 Brooklands 200 Mile Race. Overhead are a flight of RAF biplanes.

COURTESY THE MOTOR.

Saturday heralded the Grand Prix de Boulogne. The course for this measured 23$^1/_3$ miles and was to run for 12 laps, a total of 278 miles. The three classes were for (three wheeled) cycle cars, and four wheeled vehicles fitted with engines up to 1100cc and up to 1500cc. George was entered in the latter class in his Type 39 straight eight, 1.5 litre Bugatti. His fellow competitors included A Frazer-Nash in a Frazer Nash, George's Brother Basil in a Bugatti, as was Sabipa, the Rumanian Prince Ghica and Malcolm Campbell (a supercharged 4 cylinder Bugatti). In the 1100cc class were some four supercharged Salmson's, three supercharged Amilcar's and one or three other entries. The weather was absolutely appalling. But when was it not during a Boulogne Race week? The end of the first lap and George was ahead of Sabipa (*See page* 115), by one second, with Campbell eight seconds adrift. The Frazer Nash suffered a race long battle with its ignition and Brian Eyston retired. Sabipa then took over the lead, all three cars going 'like the wind', more especially so considering the appalling conditions. To keep the crowd on their toes Prince Ghica added Grand Stand spectator interest by executing some interesting gyrations as he whooshed past, sliding wildly from side-to-side and around and about. One of these passes was dangerously close to a 'pit stationary' car. He finally managed to control the heart-stopping moment or ten. But he was not to give up. Not he! Beyond Le Wast he overturned the car and it was assumed his race was at an end. But oh no! He managed to right the vehicle, only to crash it again, this for the last time. He was dragged off to hospital with broken ribs. At least he tried. But even more drama ensued. With only one lap to run and in the lead, Sabipa came into the pits to have his clutch adjusted – only to find his assistants did not have the appropriate tool. *Sacre bleu!* He is supposed to have raged and in his fury attacked the pit counter in an effort to maul his crew. Meanwhile, Campbell and George were bearing down on his placing. The requisite implement was sent across from Eyston's 'corner' but despite this chivalrous action Sabipa lost the lead. Campbell swept past and just as Sabipa tore out of the pits to rejoin the race, George went by. Driving like a madman Sabipa scraped past George but had no chance of catching the leader. Thus Campbell came in first with Sabipa second and George Eyston third, $^1/_2$ second adrift. The Sunday Boillet Cup Race being for Sports Touring Cars did not involve him. The year end was marked by the Brooklands 200 Mile Race (15th October). George and Campbell, driving straight eight, supercharged 1.5 litre Type 39A Bugattis, were the official Works Team. Despite the main threat appearing to be a three car team of supercharged, 6 cylinder 1100cc Amilcars, by lap ten George was in the lead, ahead of Campbell. From then on they took turns but as predicted the Amilcars were never far away. On lap 38 George had to pull out with broken valve gear. Campbell went on to win, despite having to nurse home a 'not-so-well' car, followed by the Amilcars of Morel and Balls.

The year 1928 saw him renew his relationship with Aston Martin for the Le Mans. He was down to co-drive with 'Bert' Bertelli, in *LM1*, one of two 4 cylinder, 1.5 litre Works entries. The other car, *LM2*, was to be driven by Jack Bezzant, the Service Manager, and Cyril Paul, an amateur of proven ability. The vehicles were driven to the circuit. However the auguries were not good. En route, *LM2* incurred a cracked rear axle casing. Doom and gloom! However, Messrs Leon Bollee of Paris came to the rescue and strengthened the rear-end assemblies of both cars – but to no avail. During the race, *LM1* went out, after an off-circuit excursion, necessitated by having to avoid another competitor. In so doing, the underside

Plate 83a. Eyston partnering Ivanowski and driving a supercharged 1.5 litre Alfa Romeo gained a second overall and first in the 1500cc Class in the 1929 24 Hour Belgian Grand Prix.

COURTESY THE MOTOR.

Plate 83b. Eyston (No.46) was a member of the Riley Team for the Friday *Saorstat Cup* Race at the 1929 Irish Grand Prix. Despite this side-on moment with his fellow team member, Whitecroft, at Mountjoy Corner whilst Poppe's Austin smoothly passes by, he finished fourth overall and first in the 1100cc Class.

Plate 83c. In the main Saturday event of the 1929 Irish Grand Prix, the *Eireann Cup*, Eyston was driving his 2.3 litre Type 35B Bugatti (No. 14) here again experiencing a Mountjoy moment and no doubt giving Higgins in his 3 litre Austro-Daimler a fright.

Plate 83d. However, Eyston's race in the *Eireann Cup* effectively came to an end when his car caught fire. The augeries for this event were not good. Pre-race his brother Basil had crashed after weighing in, skidding on recently watered tram lines into a passing van, from the roof of which a young lad was thrown into the River Liffey and drowned. Reportedly this was the only fatal, let alone serious accident in the three year history of the Irish Grand Prix.

PLATES 83B, C & D COURTESY THE AUTOCAR.

struck a concealed obstruction – which cracked the rear axle. Oh dear! *LM2* motored on until lap 81, when a broken gear lever ended its race. However, the team did receive an award for the fastest 1.5 litre entry over the first 20 laps. Perhaps everyone received a prize? The sporting calendar included the Brooklands 200 Mile Race (21st July). The Saturday was very hot and caused some competitor's cars to suffer overheating and lubrication problems. George and Brother Basil were once again in the 8 cylinder 1.5 litre Bugatti. They were up against the likes of: Campbell, in a straight eight, 1500cc Grand Prix Delage; HW Purdy in the straight eight *Flat Iron Thomas Special*; Dr. Benjafield in his ex Campbell, Boulogne winning, 4 cylinder supercharged Type 37A Bugatti; RF Oats in a straight eight, supercharged OM; Kaye Don in a Lea-Francis who finished third; Frazer-Nash's Frazer Nash being either driven by himself or another, depending on which authority you read, as he was ill; and Vernon Balls in the 6 cylinder 1100cc, 'not out-and-out racing' Amilcar. On the first lap Basil Eyston managed to 'tweak' the tail of Purdy's *Flat Iron*, whilst they were 'cruising' along at about 100 mph – with disastrous consequences for Purdy. He and his machine spun several times before finishing up smashed sideways into the corrugated iron fence. Basil on the other hand was able to proceed, without any undue damage. It was said that the unhurt but aggrieved party was – very aggrieved! Most of the race was spent with George trying to catch the unstoppable Delage. Benjafield made one of those 'silly old counting errors' and had to be urged back on to the track, having come in a lap too soon. The finishing order was Campbell, who was some seventeen miles ahead of the Eyston's, who were followed in by Kaye Don. It is worth mentioning the heroic drive of Vernon Balls in his Amilcar. He came fourth overall and first in class, despite a close encounter with a sandbank and several time-wasting pit stops. For the Brooklands Autumn Race George appeared in a straight eight OM, where he won. I did wonder why, out of the blue, he selected such a car but obviously he was of the opinion the OM would win. So that's why he appeared in an … !

From 1929 on, much of his track racing was 'aboard' a 1.5 litre, 6 cylinder, supercharged Alfa Romeo. For the Brooklands Double Twelve Race (10-11th May) he was paired with Kaye Don but their car failed, with engine trouble, after $3^{3}/_{4}$ hours. At the Belgian Twenty Four Hour Grand Prix (6th July) he co-drove with Boris Ivanowski in the 1.5 litre Alfa, as a private entry. The three strong Works Team were piloting 1750cc Alfa Romeos. With the advantage of steady rain and very wet surfaces, after some 12 hours the Eyston & Ivanowski car was in the lead. The rain eventually stopped and, as the road dried out, Benoist, in a Work's Alfa, started to overhaul them. He achieved this after another five hours, at 9 am. He was not to loose the lead and at the finish Benoist & Marinoni were first with Eyston & Ivanowski an extremely creditable second, some two laps adrift. For the Irish Grand Prix (12th July) George was a constituent of the Riley Team, the other members of which were Kaye Don, Jack Dunfee and Brother Basil. George came fourth in the *Saorstat Cup*. Saturday was the major race of the weekend and he was competing in his 2.3 litre Type 35B Bugatti. He may not have achieved a placing but he did supply a spectacle. Some three hours into the race, and immediately after a fuelling pit stop, his mount burst into flames as he roared along the straight. He came to an abrupt stop in the middle of the track. Here the authorities struggled to put out the inferno, whilst fellow competitors took avoiding action as they bore down on the flaming vehicle. Despite this unfortunate happening, some reports state that he managed to restart but had to

Plate 84a.   'Capt. GET Eyston with Albert Denly, his co-driver and mechanic.' I hope George's tailor was looking the other way.
COURTESY MOTOR RACING AND RECORD BREAKING, GET EYSTON & BARRIE LYNDON. BATSFORD, LONDON.

Plate 84b.   Another publicity shot after achieving 140.52mph in 24 hours.
COURTESY SPEED ON SALT. GET EYSTON & WF BRADLEY, BATSFORD, LONDON.

retire almost immediately with continuing fuel problems. The following week saw the dawn of the Ards Tourist Trophy (17th August). For this event George was part of the official Alfa Romeo Work's Team, driving one of the 1.5 litre cars. This was Alfa's debut at the TT and they had a total of eight supercharged entries, five of which were powered by 1.5 litre engines and three had 1750cc units. He finished in fifth place. Unaccountably, for the Brooklands 500 Mile Race (12th October) he competed in the 2 litre, supercharged, 6 cylinder Sunbeam, known as *Cub*. Despite leading at about half distance, he had to pull out with a broken suspension.

As to be expected, for the 1930 season he was Alfa mounted. For the Brooklands Double Twelve Hour Race (9-10th May) he was part of the Work's Team, again co-driving with Ivanowski, but now in a 1750cc Alfa. They won the 2 litre Class. At the Whitsun Brooklands Race meeting he picked up a third place. In the Irish Grand Prix (18-19th July) he was again team driving, now in a 1.5 litre Alfa, in the *Saorstat Cup* event. He was reported as starting off slowly but finished up with the fastest average speed and second place overall. He lost out on handicap to the 1100cc Riley of Victor Gillow who had a '...*thoroughly wild drive involving considerable hedging and ditching*'.* And so 'endeth' this lesson.

Well, not quite. During all these years George had been record chasing, a pastime in which he was to achieve much fame and success. On the other hand, these activities are outside the scope of this book and are covered in detail so much better by others. However it will not go amiss to sketch one or two specific incidents, if only to give a flavour, an insight into this extraordinary man. Boris Ivanowski introduced him to Mr Ratier, a Frenchman. This gentleman specialised in producing a package of a 'blown' 750cc power unit, a lightweight chassis and aerodynamic body which were ideal for record-breaking. George purchased one, planning to 'bolt on' one of his own *Powerplus* supercharger's. Subsequently, he gave this project up, after a chance meeting with Ernest Eldridge, an old University Undergraduate chum. This gentleman had spent much of his motor sporting life involved in developing record-breaking vehicles. He suggested George take the 'MG route'. Thus he met Cecil Kimber Esq., the Managing Director of the MG Car Co. The latter was very interested and supportive of George's record breaking plans. Initially utilizing an unsupercharged power unit, resleeved back from 847cc to 747cc, this car was known as *EX 120*. He was in business. On the 31st December 1930, at Montlhery, he took three records, after which the valve gear incurred problems. He then fitted 'his' *Powerplus* supercharger and within some four weeks was 'hot seat', back on the course. On 16th February 1931 he took four records, all at in excess of 100 miles an hour. This led to a plan to assault other records at Brooklands '*due to Montlhery's inability to time the planned mile and kilometre record attempts*'? In spite of troublesome carburettor settings he took both. Thus, further encouraged, and 'despite the previous comments', he was back at Montlhery, in late September. Here he broke three more records – before his car was engulfed in flames. The popular, rather romanticised folklore account reported that, notwithstanding the conflagration, he calmly assessed the situation. Being in sight of both the finishing line and another record, and not wanting to jeopardise his chances, he dropped the gearbox into neutral. He then wriggled his comparatively bulky way out of the extremely snug cockpit, on to the tail section of the car. From this vantage point he could still steer the flaming projectile, until the last moment, finally bailing out at

---

*Alfa Romeo. A History by Peter Hull & Roy Slater. Cassell & Co.

Plate 85a.   Eyston, his team and others after he had won the world's 24 hour record, with a distance of 3,372½ miles, in 1935 at Bonneville Salt Flats, USA. *Speed of the Wind* was powered by a 12 cylinder unsupercharged Rolls-Royce Kestrel aircraft engine.

COURTESY SPEED ON SALT. GET EYSTON & WF BRADLEY, BATSFORD, LONDON.

Plate 85b.   Humphrey Cook in the original bodied Vauxhall 30-98 *Rouge et Noir* at Brooklands, circa 1921.

COURTESY VAUXHALL 30-98 THE FINEST OF SPORTING CARS. NIC PORTWAY. NEW WENSUM PUBLISHING.

about 50 to 60 mph, leaving the vehicle to 'scumble' along the track edge. By this time his clothing was fully alight, with his boots and socks already burnt off. A passing circuit performer stopped and beat out the flames engulfing his by then torch-like body. In the meantime, and whilst all this was going on, the car crawled over the finish line and he took the 1 hour record at 101 mph. Bravo! His support team, finding a driverless, burnt-out car, were more than somewhat perturbed! As you would be. However a very authoritative guru* suggests this interpretation of events may not be correct, in every detail. It appears Eyston elected to complete one lap more than was really necessary, just to make sure he had the record in the 'toolkit'! It was during this last circuit that the flames took over so it was not necessary to line up the MG for the finishing line, with all the accompanying legend. But why spoil a good tale? On the other hand he did have to bring the car's forward motion down to a reasonable speed, to allow him to bail out, prior to being 'barbecued'. And his crew did arrive to find a blazing car 'sans' the pilot. His injuries took three months to heal. During his recovery, a single seater MG *(EX 127)*, the *'Magic Midget'*, was being prepared. As soon as he had recovered sufficiently, he was off again, just prior to Christmas for yet another Montlhery bout of record attempts. No turkey, trimmings and Christmas 'pud'. That's just a snapshot of our George – to wet readers appetites.

HUMPHREY WINDHAM COOK (1893-1978). He was a quiet and unassuming man who would not tolerate failure but was not one to throw his weight about. Despite which, he was probably to exercise as great an influence on the pre-WW1 motor racing scene as WO and or Barnato, to name but two big hitters (*See* Epilogue). His early career and formative motor racing years did not really foreshadow the influence he would bring to bear on the circuits, in the late 1930s. He appeared as early as 1914, at Brooklands, in a 10.6 litre, chain driven, Type KM, 100hp Isotta-Fraschini. Post WW1, he showed up in 1921 in his first Vauxhall 30-98, known as *'Rouge et Noir'*, which he also ran in 1922, achieving a remarkable success rate in hill climbs and speed trials, despite it being in his words 'a pretty standard vehicle mechanically'. However, Nic Portway in his quite remarkable book** states:

> 'In competition probably the most consistently successful 30-98 driver … was Humphrey Cook … A wealthy sportsman who had competed in a Prince Henry Vauxhall before the Great War, and on 7th May 1921 appeared at Kop Hill with a stark black and red 30-98, (E347) – 'Rouge et Noir'. Cook proceeded to climb the hill faster than any other car present, setting the pattern of performance which was to repeat itself many times. The car had been prepared at the Luton factory for competition use and boasted two light racing seats and a bolster petrol tank. No mudguards were used and the car had two small 'Aero' screens.
>
> Cook then proceeded to enter a motoring competition of some sort most weekends for the next three seasons. In 1921 he entered four principal BARC Brooklands meetings, taking first place in the 27th 100 mph Short Handicap at the September meeting and gaining two second places and a third place in other races during the season. …That year he also took 3rd place in the open class at Shelsley Walsh in September, …and achieved

---

* William Boddy's excellent 'Montlhery. The story of the Paris Autodrome'. Veloce Classic Reprint Series.
** Vauxhall 30-98. The Finest of Sporting Cars. Nic Portway. New Wensum Publishing.

THE FORGOTTEN BENTLEY BOY.

Plate 86a.   Humphrey Cook's *Rouge et Noir* Vauxhall 30-98 with its later bodywork.
PLATES 86A & B VAUXHALL 30-38 THE FINEST OF SPORTING CARS. NIC PORTWAY. NEW WENSUM PUBLISHING.

Plate 86b   A 'top shot' clearly showing the pointed tail of *Rouge et Noir*.

Plate 86c.   Cook in his 4.5 litre Bentley (No. 54) leading Harvey's 1.5 litre FWD Alvis (No. 31) in the 1928 Ards Tourist Trophy Race.
COURTESY THE MOTOR.

many placings at other venues. For 1922 a new, streamlined body was fitted at Vauxhalls with a handsome pointed tail but although Cook continued to achieve more Brooklands places, as well as numerous successes in hill climbs and speed events, the car was not discernably faster than 1921.'

As a host to fortune, it is worth noting he possibly met one Raymond Mays, driving his 1.6 litre, side valve Hillman, in May 1921, at Irondown Hill, on the Deddington to Chipping Norton road. In 1922 he also drove a straight eight, 1919, 5 litre Ballot, similar to that owned by Count Zborowski. The year 1923 saw him driving the 30-98 again, reinforcing his fearsome reputation at both hill climbs and speed trials. He recorded FTD at, amongst other venues, the Hill Climbs of Aston Clinton, Holme Moss, Kop, South Harting and Sutton Bank, as well as the Speed Trials of Madresfield and Skegness. For 1924 and 1925 more often than not he drove the ex-Eyston track car, known as *Razor Blade*, fitted with a 1.5 litre, 16 valve, twin cam GP engine. This was the only works racing car left from that period and the handling was unpredictable. Unsurprisingly, Cook did not 'hold the back page' whilst mounted in this steed and in fact retired from racing, if only temporarily as it turned out.

In 1922 the Vauxhall factory designed and built three, 3 litre racing cars to enter Grand Prix events, but a late change in formula made them obsolete. Having acquired No. 2 of the three TT Vauxhalls, Cook requested Amherst Villiers to supercharge the same but an accident in *Razor Blade* resulted in his selling the car to Jack Barclay. Villiers subsequently acquired it but his involvement with Birkin resulted in his passing it on to Raymond Mays. With Cook's financial aid and Villiers' input of knowledge, Mays raced it on the hillclimb circuit and renamed it the 'Vauxhall Villiers'. The developed power was harnessed by fitting twin rear wheels and in this guise a number of hill records were gained, more especially at Shelsley Walsh. The Vauxhall factory car No. 3 finally passed into the ownership of David Brown who also had Villiers supercharge the racer. That arrangement was a natural fit as David Brown's Huddersfield-based gear manufacturing business already made various components for the Villiers superchargers.

For the 1928 season Cook was listed at the Brooklands Six Hour Race (12th May) in which he entered a privately owned 3 litre Bentley, managing an 18th place. This vehicle may well have been loaned to him to see how he 'felt about life'. Whatever, thus encouraged, on 28th July he took delivery of a 4.5 litre, Le Mans Sports Model Bentley which he raced in the Ards Tourist Trophy (18th August). Despite a rather patchy practice session, he managed a seventh place in the race.

In 1929 he shared Birkin's 4.5 litre Bentley with Frank Clement in the Brooklands Double Twelve Race (10-11th May). They had to retire. He was down in the lists to compete in that year's Le Mans. Unfortunately for him the late absence of the Birkin 'Blower' 4.5 litre cars meant the Bentley entries had to be compressed, Cmdr. Kidston & Jack Dunfee taking over his car. Bother! In the Brooklands Six Hour Race (29th June) Cook shared his car with Callingham, and achieved third place. His good showing continued with a fifth in a 4.5 litre Bentley at the Phoenix Park Irish Grand Prix (13th July).

Plate 87a. Tom's new S-38/250 Mercedes receiving the racing car coachwork treatment at his favoured firm, the Martin Walter coachwork business based at Folkestone.
COURTESY A TO Z OF BRITISH COACHBUILDERS. NICK WALKER. BAY VIEW BOOKS.

Plate 87b. After ten laps the hoods could be lowered in the 1929 Brooklands Six Hour Endurance Race. Grineau's cartoon sketch vividly depicts the battle of the superchargers on the Byfleet banking. Tom's S-36/220 Mercedes (No.1) is 'outboard' of the 4.5 litre 'Blower' Bentley of Birkin (No. 5), which is 'laying smoke'. Closely following is Barnato's Speed Six Bentley (No. 3), all three cars hurtling by Wyndham's 2.3 litre Bugatti (No. 8).
COURTESY THE MOTOR.

CHAPTER SEVEN

Tom. The Penultimate Year. 1929.

'Since the early days of motoring there have been many changes in the apparatus designed to keep drivers posted as to any sensational developments under the bonnet. In the first cars there was little or none of this form of affectation. Steam coming out of the radiator, or elsewhere, indicated that the water was boiling, and a radiator that slowly became incandescent showed that it had finished doing so. This was all there was to go on …
In those days motorists were motorists.'

IBIS.

This was the year in which Tom and his bride-to-be announced their intentions, but that was not until December 1929. At least this end of year formality kept 'all that betrothal stuff' out of the way of the serious things of life – motor racing. And 1929 was the year in which he was once again to get into full stride.

Although he planned to replace his existing S-36/220, with the latest Mercedes S-38/250, this did not happen until too late for that year's competition. Thus, apart from a few sand race excursions, the new model was never to be put to use by him on the circuits. More is the pity, as the later model's supercharged horsepower output was boosted to 225 hp, with a very small increase in cubic capacity of 280cc, from 6789cc to 7069cc. The extra horsepower was mainly due to an improved valve configuration, all this extra 'grunt' being accommodated by a more robust crankshaft. The braking system was improved, even if this necessity was still not brilliant. His first outing (and all this year's, for that matter) was in the previous year's Mercedes S-36/220 and was at the:

EASTER MONDAY, BROOKLANDS RACE MEETING (1st April). In his event he was in the lead but had to retire on the last lap. This let through Jack Dunfee in a 3 litre Ballot, ahead of a 21.5 litre Benz and a Bugatti. Tom very rarely had any success at Brooklands.

Six weeks on and his next outing was at the:

SOUTHPORT 100 MILE SAND RACE (18th May). Not one to quibble, but with each lap measuring $2^6/_{10}$ths of a mile and the race being of 35 laps duration, it was more a ninety one mile race. Whatever, it was a hot day, the sands were firm and the event pulled in a crowd of

Plate 88a.   Dublin and the Phoenix Park area.

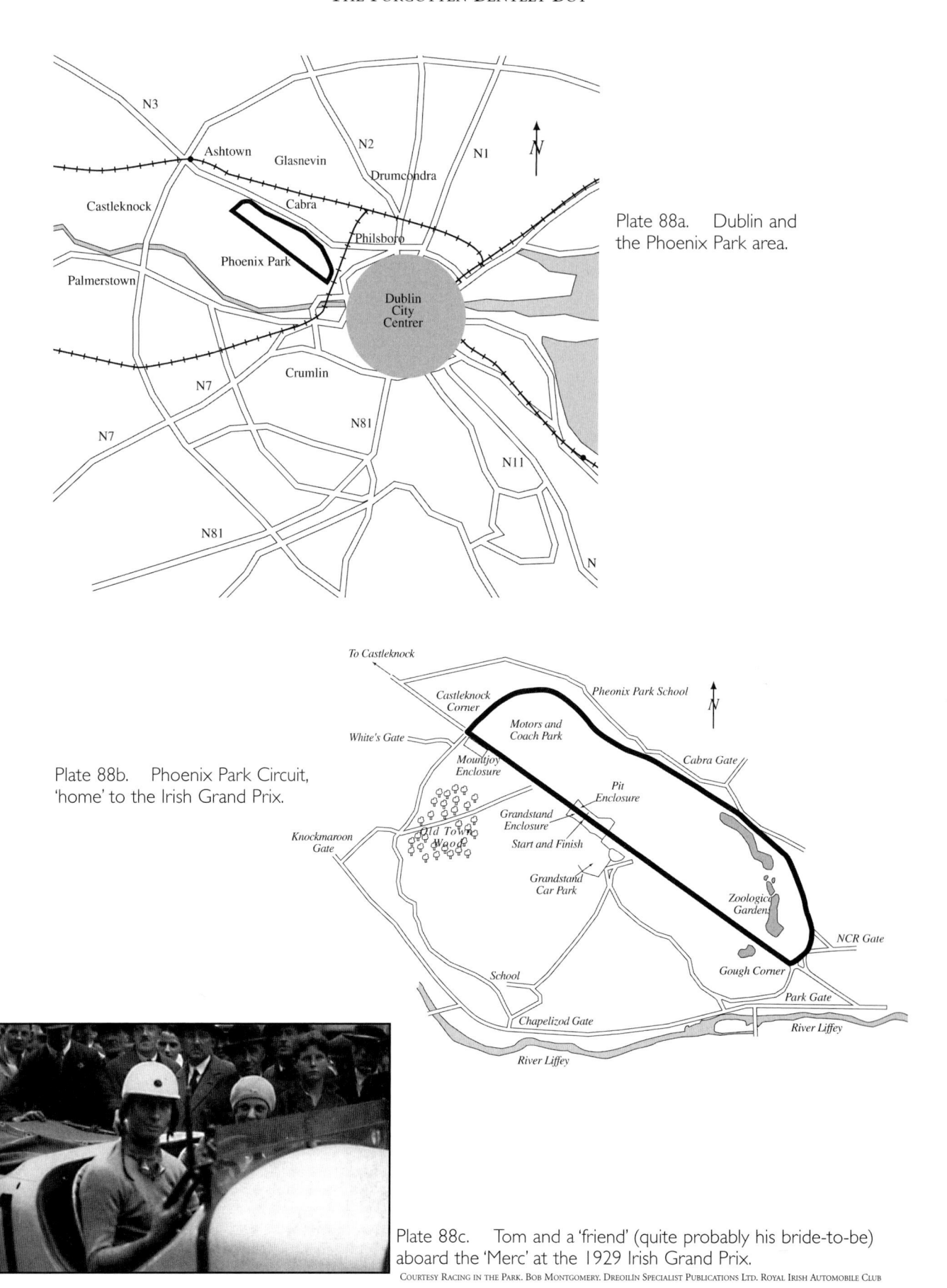

Plate 88b.   Phoenix Park Circuit, 'home' to the Irish Grand Prix.

Plate 88c.   Tom and a 'friend' (quite probably his bride-to-be) aboard the 'Merc' at the 1929 Irish Grand Prix.
COURTESY RACING IN THE PARK. BOB MONTGOMERY. DREOILIN SPECIALIST PUBLICATIONS LTD. ROYAL IRISH AUTOMOBILE CLUB

some 60,000. In addition the entry list included one or three stars – apart from Tom! Raymond Mays was to drive his Villiers Vauxhall, Lord Howe a Bugatti, Don Higgin's was piloting the ex-Segrave 1.5 litre Talbot. Benjafield and Cobb may have failed to appear or DNS. A certain amount of excitement was caused when the Lea-Francis of Ray Mellor threw a tyre and it 'wheeled' into the crowd, 'damaging' three spectators. Undaunted, Tom roared off to win the race and the Daily Dispatch Vase, beating both the experienced local man Higgins and Raymond Mays. To quote the inestimable *Motor Sport* 'The shriek of its (Tom's Mercedes) *supercharger drowning all other sounds, his expression registering scorn, anger and pained surprise as the Austin 7's hounded him, then happiness.*' That's our Tom – well able to express the necessary emotions with simply a curl of the 'old' aristocratic upper lip – especially at speed.

The following month heralded the:

BROOKLANDS SIX HOURS ENDURANCE RACE (29th June). I hesitate to argue with the official Brooklands 'score card'. However, despite the listings, I would suggest Captain JEP Howey was driving an S-38/250 Mercedes and Tom the older Mercedes S-36/220. The field was well supported and star-studded. The body of Howey's car was reported to have shaken itself to bits after much trouble with the hood and exhaust. Tom had a mechanically troublesome race. The third lap saw him changing the plugs. After some hours he was in the pits again 'shouting for oil' but none was readily available. These delays caused him to put in some very quick lap times in an effort to catch up with the leaders. During the fifth hour he had to retire with a broken valve, but he had achieved the fastest lap speed of the race. Birkin's 'Blower' 4.5 litre also had to retire. This meeting heralded the very first appearance of the latter vehicle, which was to become the renowned single seater, as distinct from the other four seater, tourer bodied 'Blower' 4.5's. Barnato & Jack Dunfee won in a Speed Six Bentley, second was L Headlam in his 1750cc, four seater Alfa Romeo, third was the Cook & Callingham's 4.5 litre Bentley, fourth were Benjafield & Ivanowski in a 1750cc Alfa Romeo, Oats was fifth in an OM, whilst George Eyston & Ramponi were sixth in a 1500cc Alfa Romeo. It will be noted that some interesting names cropped up at this event.

Having run the now long defunct Whitehall Shipyard at Whitby (for a couple of years, some decades ago) the name Headlam brought back memories of that wonderful north-eastern coastal seaport. The Headlam family owned and operated a couple of inter-linked coastal shipping companies, as well as some middle-distance fishing boats. Father William Headlam had three sons. The eldest died during WW1. The second son, Leonard, raced during the 1920s, dying in a road accident in March 1930, supposedly whilst en-route to Brooklands. As will be observed he came fourteenth overall in the 1929 Tourist Trophy Race. William, the third son, purchased one of the most beautiful Aston's ever made. That was the one-off, 1.5 litre, fixed head coupe constructed by 'Harry' Bertelli, the engine of which he had bored out to 1750cc, a year or so later. He also owned and raced the ex-Bira Aston Martin Ulster, competing at Spa in 1936, where he gained a class win.

There is no doubt that Tom enjoyed the big canvas, the major event at which to display himself and his chosen chariot and nowhere could supply a better stage than the:

Plate 89a.   The start of the 1929 Irish Grand Prix, Eireann Cup Race, Tom's car to the foreground.

PLATES 89A & B COURTESY RACING IN THE PARK. BOB MONTGOMERY. DREOILIN SPECIALIST PUBLICATIONS LTD ROYAL IRISH AUTOMOBILE CLUB

Plate 89b.   Tom's S-36/220 Mercedes (No. 1) was first away in front of the 'Blower' 4.5 litre Bentleys of Birkin (No. 2) and Rubin (No. 3). Kidston was driving the 'Old No. 1' Speed Six (No. 4), whilst Harcourt-Wood (No. 7), Cook (No. 9) and WB Scott (No. 10) were aboard 4.5 litre Bentleys.

IRISH GRAND PRIX, Phoenix Park, Dublin (12-13th July). At the outset of the century, in 1903, the Irish authority's agreed to host the 'return' Gordon Bennett Race. The hidebound, stuffy English had declined to so do. As a result, and to show their gratitude, all the British drivers painted their machines green. It is heart-warming to think this tradition has carried through to this day. Hearts and roses over and back to 1929. The great success of the Ulster Tourist Trophy Race, in the previous year, plus much 'old boy's' influence and favours called in, encouraged the Dublin authorities to host a motor racing event. Thus the Irish Grand Prix. The planned circuit was of a 'D' shape, with a lap measuring 4 miles 460 yards. The race was to last for 70 laps, giving an overall distance of three hundred miles. The two day races were handicap events. Friday, the first day, was for cars up to 1.5 litres, racing for the '*Saorstat Cup*'. Saturday was for cars in excess of 1.5 litres, racing for the '*Eireann Cup*'. The Grand Prix winner would be judged on the placings calculated from the combined average of the two days. With the Alfa Romeo team entering both events, it was to make for very interesting computations to determine the eventual winners and place men. Both Birkin and Campbell were enthusiastic about the venue and the entry list was star-studded. The arrival of the Alfa Romeo team drafted in an almost exotic number of international class, foreign drivers. In the midst of these were Guilio Ramponi, who had won the Mille Miglia for two years running, in conjunction with Cavaliere Giuseppe Campari (sounds like a nice aperitif, n'est pas), and Boris Ivanowski. The latter had recently won the Spa 24 Hour Race and was reputed to have been a former Russian Czar, Imperial Guardsman. It was rumoured that he just evaded death at the hands of the rioting mob, in the 1917 Russian Revolution. These 'johnny-foreigners' were joined by various 'Brit's', some of whom had recently been breaking this and that record. In amongst these luminaries were Malcolm Campbell (World Speed Record and in this event driving a supercharged 3 litre Sunbeam) and George Eyston (1100cc Riley). Some of the other notable drivers included Kaye Don and Jack Dunfee in 1100cc Rileys whilst Sammy Davis drove a supercharged 1.5 litre Lea-Francis. In addition, there were a host of Bentley Boys, the Works Team having recently somewhat conclusively swept through Le Mans with first, second, third and fourth places. No contest, really!

Apart from a massive piece of silverware, the overall winner was to scoop £1,000. The crowds were estimated at 100,000 for the Friday, in front of whom the Free State Irish President Cosgrave was to drop the white starting flag. The 'off' was to be the standard Le Mans style 'get away'. The racing was not made any easier due to the heat of the day. In fact, the blazing sun melted the recently re-laid tar surfaces, more especially at and around Mountjoy. It was here that Ramponi, attempting to make up time, had a moment, crashing into the railings. The first day's results in order of placings were B Ivanowski (Alfa), Sammy Davis ('Leaf'), W Green ('Leaf') and George Eyston (Riley).

Due to Saturday being for the bigger engined, more dramatic cars, there was an even larger spectator turnout. Furthermore, the weather was hotter than on Friday. The 'stars' included: Tom in his Mercedes, and as the largest capacity car, his was the scratch vehicle; the Works Bentley Team was Cmdr. Glen Kidston, in the Speed Six model, known as *Old No. 1*, ably backed up by the privately owned 4.5 litre Bentleys of Cook and Harcourt-Wood, in addition to the 4.5 litre Bentley privateers of Holder and Scot; the Birkin pair of 4.5 'Blower' Bentleys driven by Tim and Rubin; Malcolm Campbell, driving a supercharged 3 litre, 6

Plate 90. The duel of the supercharged giants which was to last for 26 laps, with Tom leading Birkin.

Courtesy Racing in the Park. Bob Montgomery. Dreoilin Specialist Racing Publications Ltd. Royal Irish Automobile Club

The Charioteer.

THERE are tall men striding about the town who are not of it. You can see that at a glance, by their clothes, by their faces, by their general appearance. I recognise it by the way they are built, by the way they carry themselves. There is a certain economy in their bones; the hips are not wide and they have small heads: There is another and a marked characteristic which, now that someone has pointed it out, I can see for myself; 't is very noticeable; but I am afraid to mention it for fear of giving offence—you can see their necks. This, of course, does not mean that you cannot see the necks of other people because their chins cover them or because they are low-built and short. For all I know, there may be people who are glad that they are not long in the neck. Anyway, you can see the necks of the people I am describing because they hold their heads high as men who acquiesce reluctantly; and who are not given to bend either neck or knee. If you get nearer you will find that they smile seldom; and yet they are not pre-occupied, because to be pre-occupied is to be to some extent detached from the present, to be dreamers, maybe. These men are occupied. They are purposeful and bent on something, the Motor Race, of course. And since they are grave, since they take sport seriously, they are Englishmen undoubtedly. Englishmen of a type, the type I like to think about. Fat, brown Englishmen, too, there are about the place; but then there is a man with a Russian name who is being claimed as an Italian, so we must not be surprised at the proselytism and strange christenings of Sport. The fat-faced, expostulating fellows cannot make my Englishmen less typical: what they may make of England in the long run if they go on multiplying and gesticulating, I do not know; and I do not care very much, as long as some of the tall men prone to eutrophelia are left to write about and admire.

I have my eye on two of them now. I hope that they will not catch me watching them. Admiration would be the last thing they would give me credit for in this country. And yet it is a sporting country. We have even been accused of overmuch devotion to sport; but that a devotion of this sort should be catholic enough to include English fellow-sportsmen is not regarded as a necessary corollary to our sense of sportsmanship. There is even danger of its being interpreted as snobbery, flunkeyism, or evidence of a slave mind. This would be all very well if an Helot were to admire a Spartan athlete. I am not a Helot; and I feel that, inasmuch as I admire a fellow-sportsman, I liken myself to him. I know the seriousness which marks the companions of danger; and I love the men who, crowned with life, choose danger as the only adversary worthy of them; and try a fall in his very courtyard with Death. These are the protagonists of Destiny. These are the men who are not content to wait ingloriously to grow old. These are no hollow nuts who hang on wishing to be cracked. Their fine bodies and indomitable hearts are informed with an inborn spirit which was a gift; and their reliance on it is their best thanksgiving. Perhaps this explains what, on first-sight, always seemed to me to be rather absurd; why we should take most credit to ourselves for the very qualities in which we had the least say, such as our stature, our appearance, and our strength. It is our gratitude and our trust in God which is intrinsic in these very qualities themselves, in beauty, in strength, in comeliness. So these splendid fellows cast true to the character of the Parent who is Master of Life, whose subordinate is Death with whom it is their pleasure to try a fall. "The starry essence brooks no mortal Lord."

Let us go on to the Games.

The sun is up. It is not yet six a.m., and the blue mists are yet between the oaks. Far to the south the long line of hills shows green like a background in an Italian landscape. And from the hidden road comes the well-toned boom as the cars designed for speed are trying out on the curves of the back leg of the course. And what a course! No city in the world can claim the like of it. A few minutes from the centre of our town, the fastest road-race way in the world! We have so few things which are the best in the world, and, of even the few we have, we are loath to make anything: our position in the Atlantic, for instance, with Galway Bay, has not been dreamt of yet with all the potentialities of its link with another continent; nor the magnificent aerodrome which the Fifteen Acres offers; so near, when one thinks of the distance of Croydon and Le Bourget from their capitals which almost stultifies the advantages of flying.

The Royal Irish Automobile Club is our best patriot for the moment, and the modest Walter Sexton our greatest philanthropist. But what is that high and increasing note? It is something new in the sounds motors make: a clear, long, rising cry. Has speed become audible? Have the Muses of Metal, the dreaming metallurgists given a new voice to their creations? There it is again! It is coming nearer in intermittent calls like a proclamation that some unimagined triumph, something unprecedented in space reduction has been achieved. Here he comes! I aim at him with my camera. Before I can press the shutter-stud, he has gone.

I have gazed on the Charioteer, that serene statue coloured with a green which is the colour of Eternity, the patine of Greek bronze. I have wondered at the straight fall of his long, pleated skirt, and at the cool, extended hand from which Time has taken the rein. That was at Syracuse. There is a copy at Delphi. It is this which I see more clearly now; and now I understand why there was no attempt made to represent the action of the wind on the garment, nor to suggest the forward straining of the steeds. No; the great Greek knew better! By the light of his genius he saw what I have only now beheld. Two thousand five hundred years have passed before it was apparent: The Idea of Speed.

When young Thistlethwayte flashed past at 124 miles an hour, I realised in a flash that there is something permanent in instantaneity: there is something unmoving at the root of motion, rest at the axis, on Mount Ida calm above the strife. Of old when a god moved there was a special tense to express his motion, which was not continuous or imperfect: his speed was beyond time and mortal thought. There was a "time-frame" for Heaven long before Einstein. It was not "he came down from Olympus," but "down he was." And Thistlethwayte sat effortless and serene as the immortal Charioteer who looks out from Syracuse where they bred Pherenikos the race-horse; as he looks out on the speed-way of Delphi, and no wind disturbs his robe.

And now I am sitting beside him! A car is somewhere in front of us. I saw it rush past as I was getting in. The bursting gases roar in the delicate chambers. The walls of pressed steel resist the maelstrom of comet flame, and direct it into speed. We pass into our own breeze. Can we slacken speed enough to get round the corner? It is on us now. I am pressed forwards, gently, gradually, strongly as the brakes take off our way. As we round it I can see the car that left us at apparently unconquerable speed. With a note quite different when heard from within, a note such as the barred heraldic Eagle of Germany might make, we abolish the straight spaces of the winding back course. Three times the white Mercédès barks, and we have caught up. And now we pass the car. It is all so effortless and still. No more sense of motion than in an aeroplane. Less vibration and nothing to hear but a constant blowing sound, save when the Eagle barks and stoops on Space.

We stretch the eye ahead to where the long blue straight is lost in the distance, and the trees that hedge that uttermost point are in a moment reached and gone. On the left a little blur which was the Grand Stand. But oh! there is another car! There is no room to pass. To my eye unaccustomed to judge at such speeds it seems that we shall be smashed now; but somehow such a feeling of unreality accompanies the thought, that it does not intimidate the consciousness; we cannot imagine that anything is solid, deadly and material any more. Unbodied, our "race has just begun." In a mood of detachment we watch and are somewhat curious to see what the end will be. We steal a glance at our companion. Behind his visor, transparent as glass, the curved, black lashes never stir. There is a little ripple in the long muscles of the bare forearm. The unblinking eye looks out and the engine whines and stretches to new ecstasies of speed. Unscathed we pass between the barrier and the unskilful driver who encroached too far into our way. Those who fled from their rails return; but we have sped on. The charioteer smiles a little now, and the long, stern note of the supercharger which brought us safely through the narrowing space dies out. You cannot steer a car at great speeds. You can only aim it as you would a search-light. You must be cool under vigilant strain, and a firmer grasp of the forearm does it. You have no time to dally with the idea of death. You are less a person than a projectile. You must play the part. Anyway, you cannot examine your conscience with a supercharger. In the face of such a Present you have no Past. You are transcendantly alive, companion of a young master of life, this instantaneous Charioteer.

For hours to-day that car shall moan and race as if the spirits of the mines were protesting against those who troubled them and brought them forth into the merciless light of day. For hours to-day the Charioteer shall sit serene, and betray not by the motion of an eyelid that he is tempting death unremittingly and evading it by quicker acts of decision than any general has had to exercise on any battlefield. And these are decisions which cannot be revoked, for who can call life back to mutilated limbs? Steel breaks and metal yields in the terrible test; the furious gases may mutiny and break out from their prison walls. But the other engine, the human brain that evolved and materialised these dreams, what of it? Shall it tire? Frail as spider webs in aspic though they be, the fibres of that dreaming engine shall send out infallible commands to guide its tangible and terrible creatures and send them roaring on through space, inspired by Him Who moves the sun and sends his deadal cars along the pathless heavenly way.

Plate 91. Whimsical or what?
COURTESY THE IRISH STATESMAN. DUBLIN 21 JULY 1929.

cylinder Sunbeam; and Ivanowski in a 1750cc Alfa (newly sold, privately owned but loaned to the English concessionaires, for the race), plus some privateer Alfa Romeo owners including Benjafield and Headlam. The flag dropped and after the cross-track streak of white overall clad drivers, Tom was first away, accompanied by the whoosh of the giant Mercedes' supercharger. He was closely followed by Birkin, then Kidston and Ivanowski. Without doubt, the highlight of the race was the some 26 lap, two hour supercharged duel between Tom and Birkin. Their approach was heralded by the piercing crescendo of the grey cream coloured Mercedes which shriek blended into the lower pitched blare of the bright green Bentley. Tiger Tim Birkin was constantly line-astern of Tom, catching him up in and around the bends but loosing ground on the straights. As was an almost 'racing certainty', after a very prolonged high speed chase, the Mercedes finally succumbed to a 'blown' head gasket. This occurred on lap 27 and Tom's race was run. Another race track battle was being fought out between Campbell and Ivanowski, followed by Headlam. The latter's participation finished with a crash induced, damaged steering, following which Campbell's 'steed' lost its clutch. Eyston's Type 35B Bugatti caught fire, somewhat worryingly as he hurtled along the circuit. He, not unnaturally, pulled up centre track, which caused some chaos, what with the Fire Marshals and competitors attempting to avoid each other. Amazingly, Eyston was able to continue for a few laps but the car finally succumbed. It was also reported that as a Lagonda roared out of Mountjoy, the riding mechanic clambered out on to the bonnet, to secure a retaining strap. I can just see the modern day Clerk of the Course contemplating that vignette. Half-way through the race, Birkin was in the lead, followed by Kidston. Despite this, on handicap, Ivanowski was leading, with Kidston second and Birkin in third place. At the race end, after a dramatic five lap Ivanowski and Kidston battle, Ivanowski finished first, Kidston second, some 14 seconds adrift, Birkin third, Harcourt-Wood fourth and Cook fifth. The overall Grand Prix placings were as follows: Ivanowski (1750cc Alfa Romeo), Kidston (Speed Six Bentley), Ivanowski (1500cc Alfa Romeo), Sammy Davis (Lea-Francis) and Green (Lea-Francis).The anomaly of Ivanowski finishing first and third was due to the aggregation of the two day's events. How very Irish!

And so on to the:

TOURIST TROPHY RACE, Ards Circuit, Belfast (17th August). Those who have 'hung in' until this portion of the narrative will recall that the Ulster local press went into journalistic overdrive, in respect of the previous year's Tourist Trophy Race. Well, that was nothing compared to the 1929 coverage. The fourth estate moved from overdrive into absolute orbit, and then some!

Prior to listing the 'riders and runners', some of the more bizarre, sycophantic, ludicrous and banal snatches from the scribblings of the news-hounds might provide some light relief. It has to be stated that our Tom, 'quite a showman really', appears have been the answer to any gossip columnist's prayer. He provided acres of good tabloid copy – a 'sort of' 1920s Hugh Grant.

> 'Thistlethwayte dashed round the course with sleeves up, scorning both helmet and goggles'. 'Tom Thistlethwayte, the good looking millionaire, who is driving his Mercedes

Plate 92. Some of the 1929 TT personalities as sketched by Bryan de Grineau.
Note. Barnato did not put in an appearance, Ramponi was racing a 1.5 litre supercharged Alfa Romeo and Callingham was driving a 1750cc Alfa Romeo.

COURTESY PICCADILLY, LONDON 17 AUGUST 1929.

Benz, was, at one time, in serious danger of injury. Police had to be rushed up to control the frenzied autograph hunters'. 'Mr Thistlethwayte in his Mercedes-Benz is, I believe, the baby of the race as well as the tallest driver'. 'But Mr Thistlethwayte, though a brilliant driver, has the impetuosity of comparative youth'. 'Thistlethwayte, the millionaire, frequently seen in his great black Isotta-Fraschini saloon *(almost certainly the Tipo 8ASS)* has on its radiator a running fox in metal, a noticeable detail'. 'This young man drives with joyous abandon but as a rule his car cannot stand the pace he sets it'. 'Thistlethwayte, idol of thousands reported to have waved to the spectators on a number of occasions'.

To repeat any more of this 'red-top' carry-on would require a very capacious sick bag! Despite which, it should be noted that Tom (No. 67) put in the fastest practice lap, in 10 minutes 58 seconds. An interesting comment attributed to him is that he was of the opinion that an Austin 7 would be the winner, on handicap. As it happened, he was not such a bad judge of form. He also forecast a thrilling contest between '…. *the two wealthy racing drivers*' (himself and Tiger Tim Birkin), which was also an accurate prognostication, if it was not to be a finishing line duel. Practice proved to be quite a killing ground for the local animals, at least three dogs coming to a sudden end, as did a number of chickens. There were also a few, very close encounters with a number of horses.

The event had achieved such a reputation as to gather in a very widespread and interesting list of entrants. These included: Guiseppe Campari, George Eyston, Boris Ivanowski, Attilio Marinoni and Guilo Ramponi, all in supercharged 1.5 litre Alfa Romeos; Dr. Benjafield, Leslie Callingham and Leonard Headlam in supercharged 1750cc Alfa Romeos; Baron d'Erlanger, William Grover-Williams, Count Caberto Conelli and Lord Howe in supercharged 2.3 litre Type 43 Bugattis; Archie Frazer-Nash in an Austin 7, noting there were some four other Austin 7's entered; Sammy Davis in an 1100cc Riley; Kaye Don in a supercharged 1.5 litre Lea-Francis; Rudolph Caracciola and Otto Merz in works entered S-38/250 Mercedes; and Tom and Ms Maconochie in the older S-36/220 Mercedes. Tom was regarded as part of the Mercedes team for the purposes of this race. Other entrants included Birkin, Rubin and Harcourt-Wood in 'Blower' 4.5 litre Bentleys and Cmdr. Glen Kidston in 'Old No. 1', the Works Speed Six Bentley. Of these, it was interesting to note that Tiger Tim had persuaded WO to co-drive with him. An aside to this latter decision was that 'Bertie' Kensington Moir worked himself into a 'right old state' and had to be placated. He was fretting in case WO died during the event, as the Company insurance, on his head, would be null and void in the case of 'death whilst racing'. It is said the document was varied for this specific occasion.

Archie Frazer-Nash was driving an Austin 7's, having lost control of the Frazer Nash manufacturing company. This event took place in one of those mysterious share control shenanigans which occurred whilst he was seriously ill, in 1928. William Grover-Williams, aka 'W Williams', had won, amongst other races and hill climbs, the 1928 and 1929 French Grand Prix', as well as the first ever Monaco Grand Prix, earlier in the year, in a Bugatti Type 35B. A French mother and English father resulted in his being bilingual. An aside is that, having fled to England, at the outbreak of WW2, he joined the Special Operations Executive (SOE). Recruiting another pre-war racing driver and old comrade *de course*, Robert Benoist,

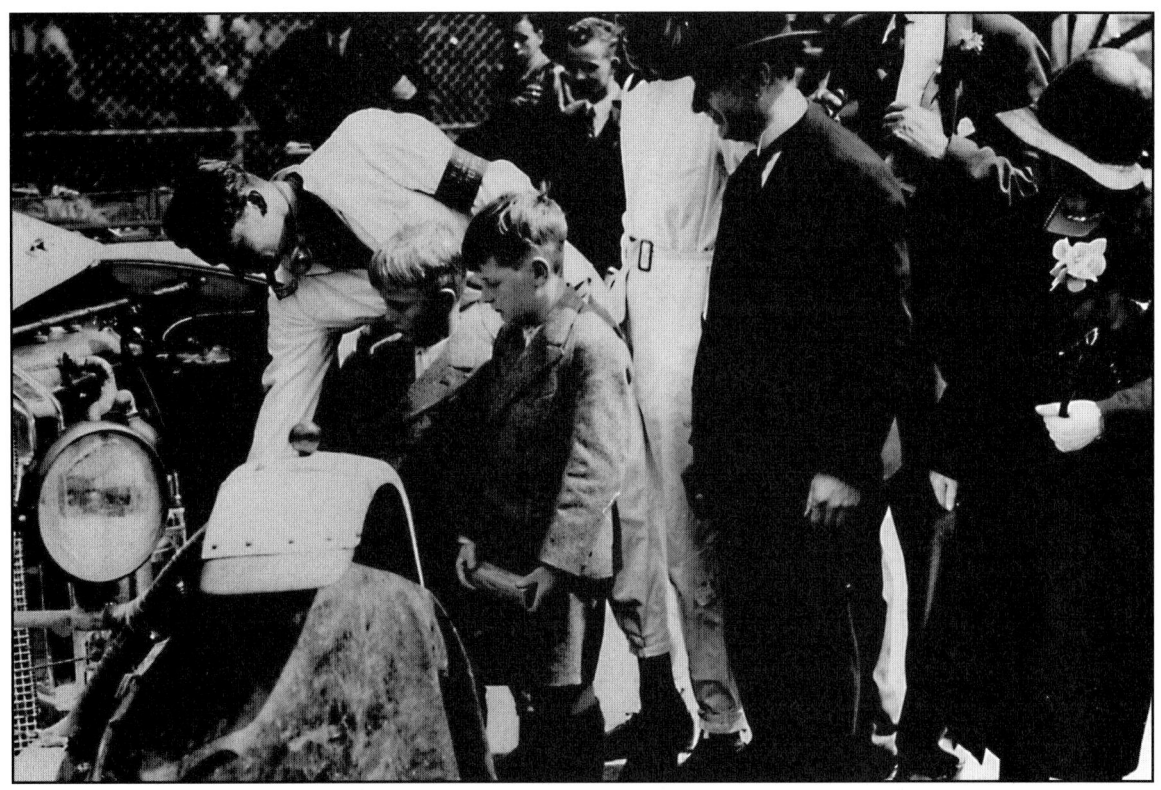

Plate 93.   Tom explains some technicality to a couple of interested lads and the bemused bowler hatted 'gent'.

PLATES 93, 94A, B & C COURTESY OF MERCEDES BENZ.

Plates 94a, 94b & 94c picture the official Mercedes Benz Team. Pictured above, from the left, Caracciola, Tom and Mertz. Tom's car was Race No. 67, Caracciola's No. 70 and Mertz's No. 71.

ON TOP
IN ALL
ROAD
TESTS
PRATTS AT ALL EVEN
71
IIIA-19625

65
70
71

Plate 95a. The start of the 1929 Ards Tourist Trophy, racing across the track to lower the hoods.

PLATES 95A & B COURTESY THE ARDS TT. JS MOORE. BLACKSTAFF PRESS.

Plate 95b. Tom taking a nice line.

Plate 95c. This action packed shot shows Birkin in a 'Blower' 4.5 litre Bentley accompanied by WO (No. 63) first away, followed by Eyston's supercharged 1.5 litre Alfa Romeo (No. 34), Harcourt-Wood's 'Blower' 4.5 litre Bentley (No. 65) and Tom on the inside.

COURTESY AN ILLUSTRATED HISTORY OF THE BENTLEY CAR. WO BENTLEY. GEORGE ALLEN & UNWIN.

they commenced to operate a Paris region based resistance cell. Captured in 1943, 'Williams' was executed, by the SS, in 1945, only weeks before the war ended. Otto Merz, one of Tom's team mates, served his apprenticeship with Mercedes, pre-WW1, training as a racing mechanic and a driver/mechanic. He then joined the Royal Household of the Austrian Archduke Ferdinand, heir to that country's throne. On 28th June 1914, whilst carrying out his chauffeur duties in Sarajevo, the Archduke and his wife were fatally shot by a student assassin. Merz, himself wounded, drove the Royal family out of the range of trouble, only to discover that his Master and Mistress were dying, which they did cradled in his giant arms. Within weeks of this event, WW1 broke out. With the hostilities out of the way, by 1926 he was racing in Mercedes 'colours'. He was renowned for his strength and was reported to be able to drive nails into planks of wood, with his bare palms. He was to die in 1933, whilst practicing for the German GP, at the Avus circuit. Caracciola was the other member of the Mercedes Team. He had not attended the Irish Grand Prix, due to competing in the Nurburgring Grand Prix but flew into Belfast for this event. In describing this race, the great man advised that:

> 'Ireland was an entirely new experience for us and it soon became noticeable that many things were different from Continental habits. There was, for instance, an alcohol restriction which surprised us. Racing drivers are not, cannot be drinkers. But at times it is nice to settle down and have a long drink *(Absolutely. Make mine a very long G & T!)*. Whatever, we thought it would be nice to do this so we accepted Thistlethwayte's invitation to join him in his room where he had installed a private bar* *(As a gentleman would!)*.

Years later he was considered to have been one of the finest motor racing drivers – ever. The latter statement is reinforced if it is realised he won many major Grand Prix and any number of other races, scooping his first victory on a motorcycle in 1922. Despite his twenty four competitive years at the wheel (allowing for the interruption to the sport caused by WW2), he was to die of a liver complaint, in 1959, aged 58, whilst acting as a world wide sales ambassador for Daimler-Benz.

On the day of the race, there were reported to be some 500,000 spectators in place, as early as 7 o'clock in the morning. After some high-level consultation, it was agreed that the 11 am start would be Le Mans style, with the variation that the parked 'for the off' cars would have their hoods already raised and in position. Thus, the 63, 65 or 67 scurrying drivers (depending on who was to be believed) only had to lower and secure the car's hood, prior to leaping in and roaring off. Not really a Le Mans start then! From the 'off', Kidston's Speed Six led Caracciola, followed by Birkin but next time round Caracciola was in the lead. Rubin suffered a nasty 'overturning', which left him and his mechanic pinned underneath their Bentley. Miraculously, neither suffered any damage but Rubin took the hint and subsequently 'packed up' motor racing (as it turned out, only for the time being). Soon after this distraction, the rain 'monsooned' down, the sole driver seemingly unfazed being Caracciola. Admittedly, he came into the pits and fitted the screen with wipers. Whatever, he proved to be the absolute rain-master. On the fifth lap Kidston smashed into the bank at

---
* Tourist Trophy. The History of Britain's Greatest Motor Race. Richard Hough. Hutchinson of London.

Plate 97. The Shelsley Walsh Hill Climb

Plate 96.

Belfast News Letter
Belfast
Date 17 AUG 1929

MR. T. THISTLETHWAYTE (Mercedes).
Blessed—or cursed—with good looks and a whole heap of money, this was one of the most popular drivers in the Ulster "T.T." last year. On his big supercharged Mercedes he had the distinction of putting up the fastest lap average in the race, covering the 13⅜ miles in 11 minutes 1 second— an average speed of 74.39 m.p.h. He also drove in the Irish Grand Prix race in Dublin this year, where average speeds in the neighbourhood of 85 m.p.h. were recorded to his credit. Owing to a defective cylinder-head gasket, however, he was unable to complete the course. In addition to being a capable race driver, Mr. Thistlethwayte is a keen yachtsman.

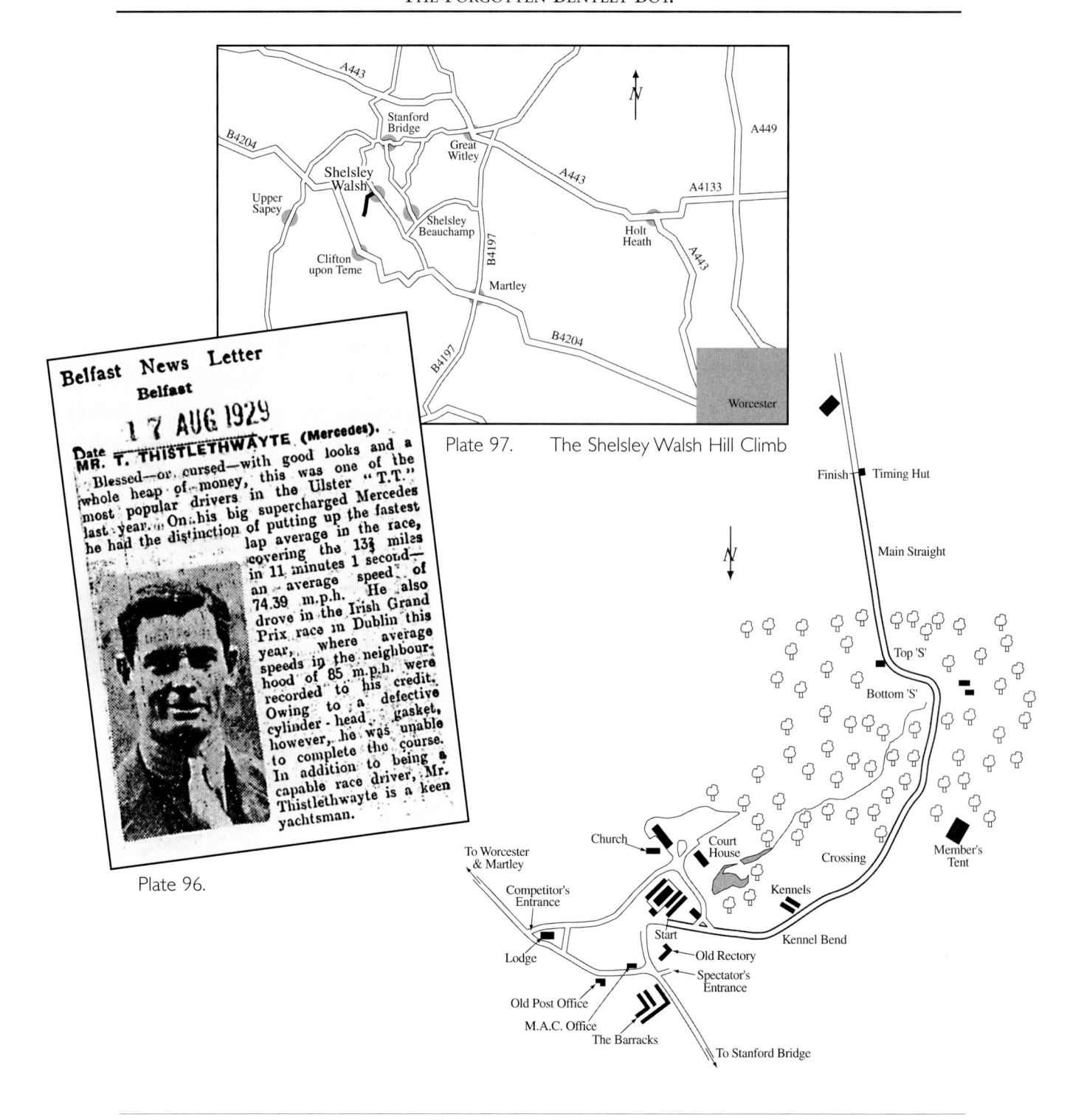

*(Page 183) Lord Howe, the 5th Earl and born Francis Richard Henry Penn Curzon, was yet another fascinating character. Born 1884 and to become an MP, he was probably the only motor racing Privy Councillor – ever. He did not take up the sport until he was aged 44, in a supercharged Type 43 Bugatti recently acquired from Sir Malcolm Campbell at the 1928 Brooklands Six Hour Race, from which he retired with magneto problems. He raced for the rest of the decade, really getting into his stride in the 1930s. Despite all the public and sporting demands he found time to marry three times. His daughter, Georgina Mary Curzon (born 1910) from the first union, married the younger brother of Cmdr. Glen Kidston. His daughter the Hon. Sarah Marguerite (born 1945) from the third marriage was to marry the charismatic racing driver Piers Courage. After the latter's untimely death in 1970, on the circuit, she married the adventurer, gambler and zoo owner John Aspinall, in 1972.

Bradshaws Brae. Merz having skidded into an obstruction, utilised his legendary strength to tear the damaged, front, near-side wing and its attendant stays off the car. Having dealt with that minor inconvenience, he continued racing. All a bit reminiscent of that insufferable chap Jan Ridd in Lorna Doone. The latter was prone to wrench limbs off trees. The Merz incident caused confusion amongst the 'train spotters'. It very much depends whom you read as to whether he was or was not disqualified. Without doubt, he finished over the line, as it were. But the to-be legendary Alfred Neubauer had to apologise to the authorities for whatever Merz said to some hapless official, in respect of this incident and the possibility that he had been flagged off. Towards the end of the race, an enormous effort was made by two of the Austin 7's and Giuseppe Campari's Alfa Romeo to catch the leader. Despite this, Rudolph Caracciola in his Mercedes won. Campari came in second (taking first in class) whilst the Austin 7 of Archie Frazer-Nash achieved third, with another Austin Seven in fourth place. Birkin finished eleventh. Sammy Davis came in twelfth, collecting a Class Win, and Tom, despite a 'race full' of niggling problems, made fifteenth place. Ms Maconchie, another Mercedes competitor, ran out of fuel on the tenth lap and called it a day. The only fatalities occurred when a breakdown lorry attended a side-of-track, crash-wrecked car. This ensemble was run into by another competitor, the impact throwing a young 'truck mounted' assistant to his death in a nearby stream. The driver of the broken down car was also killed. Otherwise it was declared a most successful event, with lots of self-congratulatory, back-slapping and promises of 'see you next year'.

Almost immediately after the dust had settled on the Tourist Trophy Race, Lord Howe purchased the Works Mercedes S-38/250, which Caracciola had driven to victory. The 'belted earl' had the existing body replaced by a creation from Hoopers.

SHELSLEY WALSH HILL CLIMB (15th September). *'Casque'* (Sammy Davis) was in charge of the loudspeaker announcements and Cmdr. Glen Kidston dropped in by Tiger Moth, having flown up from London. Raymond Mays, in his 'super special' 3 litre Villiers Vauxhall, fitted with twin rear wheels, took the record with a time of $45^{6}/_{10}$ths seconds. Lord Howe* was 'climbing' in both his 1750cc Alfa Romeo and the new (to him) Mercedes S-38/250. In the latter car he clocked $47^{6}/_{10}$ths seconds. His time pushed Tom, with $49^{6}/_{10}$ths seconds, in his older S-36/220, into second place in the Sports Car Unlimited Class – 3 litres and over. HB Showell, in a Frazer Nash, caused a frisson of excitement by crashing into some spectators, understandably delaying proceedings. Incidentally, a certain David Brown (later of Aston Martin fame) appeared in a Villiers Vauxhall (*See* page 165) *'…handling his car with precision'*.

Tom's long awaited Mercedes S-38/250 (Reg. No. KP 7678) was originally registered on the 18th June 1929. But as it was having a bespoke Le Mans style body fitted by Martin Walter's, it did not materialise until the end September or early October that year. But all was not lost. Despite tying the knot in the next year, Tom did manage to escape domestic duties, a few times. Perhaps to make up for his disappointment, in October he purchased (in the sales register down as 'Thos') a 6.5 litre Bentley (Reg. No. UM 3280). The rolling chassis was fitted with a saloon body by none other than his favourite coachbuilder, Martin Walter. The car was quite possibly an Olympia Show Car.

* *See* Footnote page 182.

Plate 98a.   Glen Kidston April 1931, just hours after setting the Britain – Cape Town record.   PLATES 98A, B, C & D COURTESY SIMON KIDSTON

Plate 98b.

Glen Kidston

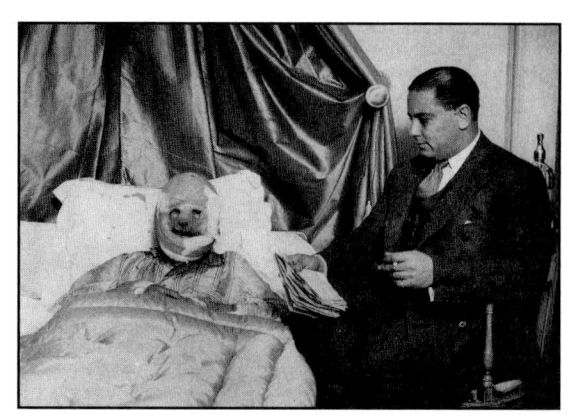

Plate 98c.   Glen Kidston post his horrific 1929 aeroplane crash, with Woolf Barnato visiting.

Plate 98d.

Plate 98e.

Fellow Performers.

CMDR. GEORGE PEARSON GLEN KIDSTON (1899-1931). If all the schoolboy, romantic hero book authors, such as Jack London, GA Henty, Capt. WE Johns, John Buchan and, say, Erskine Childers were to have gathered together to formulate their 'IT' beau-ideal, even they could not have possibly have dreamt up or invented Glen Kidston.

Fortunately for Glen and his grand aspirations, he had impeccably well financed forebears. His grandfather, George Jardine Kidston was born in 1835. When this gentleman was 21, in 1856, his father and uncles purchased the Glasgow based Clyde Shipping Company. In time he became the 'lead' partner, finally residing at Finlaystone, Renfrew. Another family income stream derived from the then well known Glasgow firm of AG Kidston & Co., Metal and Machinery Merchants, *'for well in excess of a hundred years'*. George's eldest son, Archibald Glen Kidston, born 1871, despite working in the family business, joined the Army, becoming a Captain in the Black Watch/3rd Royal Highlanders. In spite of the Scottish associations, Archibald relocated to Gwernyfed Park, Three Cocks, Breckonshire. He married Helene Adeline Blanche Chapman, in 1898, and died, comparatively young, in 1913, having gained a reputation as a local philanthropist. In the meantime the couple sired 'our man Glen', as well as Home Ronald Archibald, Nancy Ellinor, Helene Ellinor (who only passed away in 2005 aged 101) and Audrey. Glen's brother, Home Ronald Archibald Kidston, born 1910, first married Lady Georgina Mary Curzon, daughter of the 5th Earl Howe in 1935 and became Lt. Commander in the Royal Navy.

Notwithstanding the extremely wealthy family background and his father's Army connections, 13 year old Glen 'went' the 'grey funnel' route. He enlisted in the Royal Navy as a non-commissioned Cadet, at *HMS Osborne* in 1912. It would be an understatement to advise that he was to have anything but a very interesting war. By 2nd August 1914, he had joined Dartmouth College, as a Midshipman. With the outbreak of WW1, and within a few days, he was drafted to sea as a Naval Cadet. His billet was *HMS Hogue*, a twin screw, 12,000 tons ship of the Cressy class. These were Armoured Cruisers and when built, at about the turn of the century, were amongst the most powerful ships of their type. At 6.10 am on 22nd September 1914, some 18 nautical miles north-west of the Hook of Holland, a trio of Cressy Class Cruisers, namely *HMS Cressy, Aboukir* and *Hogue*, were steaming NNE at 10 knots. They were supposed to be maintaining 12 to 13 knots, but age was a determining factor. Furthermore, they should have been zig-zagging, but as no submarines had been observed in these waters, this order was (widely) ignored. At about 6.25 am. the German *Submarine U-9* fired a single torpedo at *HMS Aboukir*, the latter rolling over and sinking within 30 minutes. So much for the old 'we ain't seen any of them this year'! The gallant captain of *HMS Hogue*, stopping to pick up survivors, took two 'tin fishes', amidships, and sank within ten minutes. Midshipman Kidston was to have an early bath. *Submarine U-9* then went after *HMS Cressy* and at about 7.20 am fired two more torpedos, only one of which hit its target, but not fatally. However, *U-9* fired its last torpedo which, combined with an exploding boiler, at last managed to sink *Cressy*. The 'good' ship took some 15 minutes to go down. The submarine, having no more shots in its armoury, departed, prior to the arrival of any hostile Battle Ships.

Plate 99a.   HMS Hogue.
Courtesy ©2002 Ships Drawings.

Plate 99b.   HMS Orion.
Courtesy 1998-2006 Worldwar 1.co.uk

In the meantime, Midshipman Kidston had to wallow around in the 'briny', until picked up by one of two Dutch merchant ships. It was 'rumoured' that the Dutchmen threw him back into the sea, to make room for other survivors. But, however inconvenient and less amusing is the truth, he was shipped to and interned in Holland for a few months, prior to being repatriated to 'Blighty'. As neutrals, his 'hosts' should have kept him 'banged up', for the duration. It is noteworthy that in this one action alone 837 men were saved, but 1459 perished. Just one of Glens' many lives! An interesting aside is that *U-9* later sank *HMS Hawke* and was the only one of her class of submarine's to survive the war. However, Otto Weddigen, her captain at the time of sinking the Cressy Cruisers, transferred to *U-29*. This was rammed and sunk with the loss of all the crew, by the British *HMS Dreadnought*, in 1915.

At the end of 1914, or early 1915, Kidston joined the 22,000 ton Battleship *Orion*. So as not to allow boredom to set in, on 31st May 1916, this ship, amongst forty one other British Men of War, engaged with a German fleet of 105 warships, in the Battle of Jutland. So far, so hectic! He was fortunate that although *Orion* fired off fifty one, 13.5 inch shells, the ship suffered no damage or casualties.

By July 1917, he had been promoted to Acting Sub Lieutenant, after which the indefatigable sailor joined the submarine service. The 15th March 1918 saw him confirmed in rank as a Sub Lieutenant and on 15th February 1920 he was promoted to Lieutenant and joined *Submarine L-24* at Portsmouth. This was a 'good ship' to leave as she was "was lost by collision" when submerged, on 10th January 1924. In 1921 he was appointed to *Submarine L-3* and, with a flotilla of other L-Class submarines, accompanied *HMS Titania*, a submarine depot ship, to the China Station. At this time this was the Royal Navy's largest sphere of influence in the world, covering both the East and South China Seas.

In 1923, Lt. Glen Kidston joined the Light Cruiser *HMS Dauntless*. Fortunately, for him the ship was about to set out on a round-the-world 'jolly'. Apologies, that should read – a Royal Naval Special Service Squadron – 'show the flag cruise' bound for Australia, and thence on to New Zealand. The Squadron consisted of the Battle Cruisers *Hood* and *Repulse*, as well as the Light Cruisers *Delhi*, *Danae*, *Dauntless* (on which was billeted 'our man'), *Dragon* and the *Dunedin*. It departed Devonport, England on 27th November 1923 and returned home, a year later, on 28th September 1924. That was when our 'little island' had both an Empire and a 'proper' Navy.

On his homecoming he was appointed to *Submarine X-1*, a one-off, 'white elephant' (based on the unfinished German *Submarine U-173*). It had been completed in late 1925, and was to be scrapped in the mid 1930s. Still a Lieutenant, he was given his first command as Captain of *Submarine H-48* based at Portsmouth. It is said that in one or the other of these submergible 'tin boxes', he spent some hours stuck to the sea bed. Perhaps a second or even third life! On the 15th February 1928, he was promoted to Lieutenant Commander and on 1st May 1928 he joined the Aircraft Carrier *Courageous*. *HMS Courageous* had originally been built as a Large Light Cruiser, in 1917. By May 1928, she was converted to an Aircraft Carrier. This was preparatory to the ship departing Portsmouth, on 2nd June, to take up station at Malta. It was on board this vessel that he was to meet up again with one Owen Cathcart-Jones (OCJ), with whom we shall be reacquainted, at a later date. OCJ was a Fleet Air Arm pilot and was the first such officer to be given a Royal Navy ranking. This was to enable him

Plate 100a.   Submarine L-20 – a sister ship to L-24.
Courtesy www.pbenyon1.plus.com.

Plate 100b.   Submarine L-3.
Courtesy MPL Photograph.

Plate 100c.   HMS Titania.
Courtesy 2006 Clydesite.

Plate 100d.   HMS Dauntless.
Courtesy Wikipedia.

Plate 100e.   Submarine X1.
Courtesy The Romance of a Submarine. GG Jackson.

Plate 100f.   HMS Courageous.
Courtesy www.fleetairarmarchive.net.

to command the flight of six aircraft (Flight 404) aboard the Carrier. Incidentally, Glen stowed his Tiger Moth aircraft on board, in amongst sundry goods for others including a pack of fourteen couples of foxhounds (for disembarkation at Gibraltar), as well as twenty six motor cars, a small yacht and two motor boats. As you do! Having achieved and enjoyed all this, he retired active service in September/October of that year.

In the meantime, and as and when the Royal Navy allowed, he had been pursuing a private life. This took in a spasmodic, if ever increasing amount of motor racing and a marriage. He announced his engagement in June 1925, and that as a consequence he had decided to give up motor racing. Oh, yes, that old chestnut! The lovely Bugatti, detailed later, was sold to a fellow competitor, George Duller (of horse racing and Bentley fame. See Chapter 4). To make up for this loss he reportedly purchased a 14 ft National Morgan Giles dinghy. Not much of a swap. He duly married Nancy Muriel Denise Soames (1907-1997), in November 1925, at St. Margaret's, Westminster. The bride was described as a bewitchingly beautiful girl, despite which it was not to prove a very happy union. Their son, Archibald Martin Glen Kidston (1927-1978), was born two years later.

A commentary on the state of their relationship is no better expressed than in the affair of the 'Bride's Trousseau'. This reached the hallowed steps of the King's Bench Division of the High Court. The rather bizarre case took place in and around June 1927, just over a 1½ years after they had tied the knot. It involved a firm of Court Dressmakers claiming against Glen Kidston's wife, Nancy, and her father, a Mr Edward Roland Soames. The action was in respect of the long overdue balance of the money due on the wedding 'kit'. It appeared £288/9/6 remained outstanding from the overall invoiced account of £419/17/0. Please note the latter sum would have purchased a new, semi-detached house, in those far off, halcyon days.

'Daddy' Soames admitted being a director of various companies and that he had given his then 19 year old daughter, permission to purchase a trousseau. On the other hand, he alleged he had restricted the 'spend' to a maximum of £250. The defendants had to agree that the marriage was very, very good for the Soames family, whilst denying any responsibility for the bill. Everyone wriggled, that is apart from the husband, who was strangely absent from the proceedings. Or perhaps not so strangely? Obviously Glen was dissociating himself from the action and was not going to be saddled with this particular bill. The bride's father denied having any money, the bride claimed she was under age and was not liable in law, for anything – ever. She did admit not daring to tell 'Mummy' or 'Daddy' how much everything was costing. You bet! Mrs Kidston was questioned by the prosecuting counsel about the *fantastic tales in respect of the riches and wealth of her husband*, as well as 'rumours' of much foreign travel and the ownership of a motorboat'. Bless her, she managed to distort the facts admirably, probably well guided by her legal team. She claimed that the motorboat had sunk. Indeed it had, splitting in half, in May that year, whilst Glen and his wife were smashing their way along the Solent at 50 knots. They subsequently had to spend ½ hour in the 'briny' awaiting rescue. She added that her husband was ill and had been sent abroad (for his health you understand – nothing to do with his being 'in the pink' and a serving officer in the Royal Navy!). I hope the 'dear girl' was able to keep a straight face whilst spouting these misrepresentations of the facts. To the detriment of the prosecuting counsel, the matter of Glens' financial affairs were not forcefully followed up. His presiding Lordship found for the

Plate 101a. The Hispano-Suiza, 3 litre Bentley and 2 litre straight eight T35 GP Bugatti 'moored' at the south-east corner of Grosvenor Square were described as the 'fine fleet' of an enthusiastic owner-driver naval officer! Aka Lt. Glen Kidston.

PLATES 101A & B COURTESY THE AUTOCAR.

Plate 101b Hispano-Suiza details. The very advanced specification, 6.6 litre, single overhead cam, 6 cylinder power unit (based on one bank of the WWI, 12 cylinder V6 fighter plane engines) Hispano-Suiza H6 was introduced in 1920. Despite its Spanish origins it was mainly manufactured in Paris and subsequently a few under licence by the Czechoslovakian firm of Skoda. Yes… By 1922 the more powerful H6B (37.2hp) was introduced. A number of H6Bs were constructed for racing with a slightly larger capacity (6860cc), a shorter wheelbase and were known as the 'Boulogne's' after an initial success at that event. By 1924 the 8 litre H6C was brought to the market and subsequently a similar 'racing treatment' resulted in the 'Monza' model.

defendants, but it must have been a rather pyrrhic victory for the Soames family, with all that unflattering, very embarrassing publicity.

There are suggestions that Glen was involved with motorbikes, between 1920 and 1924, but his seagoing duties would have precluded such activities from 1921 to early 1923, and late 1923 and the end of 1924. In September 1924 he purchased a Speed Model 3 litre Bentley, with a four seater Park Ward body (The Reg. No. is detailed as XU 995 in the excellent standard work*, but I would suggest it was XU 895). By 1925, in addition to the Bugatti and Bentley, the stable also included a very tasty 1924, Hispano-Suiza. This was the 45 hp, H6 Boulogne short chassis, Olympia Motor Show car, fitted with a 2 door Hooper body. In July 1926, to this collection was added another Speed Model 3 litre Bentley, this one fitted with a 4 seater, Le Mans, Vanden Plas body (Reg. No. YF 4817).

The year 1925, and prior to his marriage and those 'wretched' no more motor racing clauses, was the 'twelve months' when Glen set out on what was to prove to be an astonishing competition career. Mark you, and totally in character, he started out in and with style. In January of that year he purchased a new, straight eight, 2 litre Bugatti T35, with cast aluminum ribbed wheels. He entered this in the:

GRAND PRIX DE PROVENCE, France (8th March). This event was staged at the Miramas Circuit, some 30 kilometres' from Marseilles. Apart from an artificial hairpin-corner, built up with concrete, the rest of the track was akin to a flat, unbanked highway. The race was 100 laps of the 5.5 kilometre long circuit. There were four classes: non-supercharged up to 1500cc; up to 2 litre; up to 3 litre; and an unlimited capacity. He achieved a fifth overall and a second in class, finishing only some 12 minutes behind the winner, and that after in excess of 500 kilometres. The stars of the event were Major (ex WW1 RAF) HOD Segrave, Caberto Conelli and George Duller, all mounted in 1.5 litre, unsupercharged Talbot 70s, in addition to Marcel Vidal driving another Bugatti 35. The Talbot 70s came in consecutively first, second and fourth overall, with Vidal in third place. But this was only a curtain raiser, for Glen's next event was to be the:

BROOKLANDS EASTER MONDAY RACE MEETING. The Bugatti (No. 1) created quite a sensation, for this was the first appearance of this model at Brooklands. He did not let the side down, bagging' a third in a handicap race and a first in another handicap event, whilst achieving Fastest Standing and Flying Lap in both. This was followed by the:

BROOKLANDS WHITSUN RACE meeting. He came in second to a 'big Fiat' and ahead of the Leyland Thomas of Parry Thomas, in one race and did not feature in another.

SHELSLEY WALSH HILL CLIMB (May). His contribution is probably best summed up as follows (in a loose translation of CAN May**): *'A Lt. Glen Kidston, RN, …showed a tendency for spectacular driving, in win or bust tactics, bashing into the Kennel Bank, followed by a side on slide at the initial corner off the S, peppering the members enclosure spectators with gravel'.*

---
* Bentley. The Vintage Years 1919-1931. Michael Hay. HM Bentley & Partners.
** CAN May Shelsley Walsh. GT Foulis & Co.

Plate 102a. Kidston showing off his newly acquired straight 8, 2 litre Grand Prix T35 Bugatti at Brooklands in 1925.

COURTESY BROOKLANDS THE COMPLETE MOTOR RACING HISTORY, WILLIAM BODDY. MRP.

Plate 102b. This shot vividly depicts Kidston's renowned performance at the 1925 Shelsley Walsh Hill Climb event in his Bugatti.

COURTESY THE BROOKLANDS SOCIETY.

It maybe worth noting that some years later one of the Bentley mechanics declared him to be the wildest (driver) ever and that few would volunteer or opt to ride with him. Enough said. Thus Glen's 1925 season came to an end. From hereon his marriage vows and Royal Naval duties took precedence.

He was not to be seen on the track again until 1929. But what a manner in which to reappear on the international scene for he selected his re-emergence to be at that year's:

LE MANS (15-16th June). It would make for an interesting narrative to report otherwise, but this race was a clockwork walkover for the Bentley Team. It was attended by a full Works entry of Barnato & Birkin, in a Speed Six, and three 4.5's in the hands of Glen Kidston & Jack Dunfee, Benjafield & Baron d'Erlanger and Clement & Chassagne. And that is the order in which they finished. Game, set and match.

Next on the agenda was:

THE IRISH GRAND PRIX, Phoenix Park, Dublin (13th July). (*See* Chapter 7 and this Chapter). Tom Thistlethwayte, in his Mercedes, was first away, followed by Tiger Tim Birkin, in his 'Blower' 4.5 litre Bentley, Cmdr. Glen Kidston, in the Works Speed Six Bentley, and Ivanowski in his 1750cc Alfa Romeo. Glen executed a neat 'off' at Mountjoy, rejoining the circuit a little further on. As the race progressed, the order was Tom, Tiger Tim, Glen and Ivanowski, but the latter was still ahead by his original three lap handicap. With 50 miles to the finish, Glen was really pressing on in a valiant attempt to overtake Ivanowski, and his handicap. Getting more and more emboldened Glen had a second Mountjoy 'moment' which, at the race end, left him in second place to Ivanowski. But only by 14 seconds. This particular Speed Six Bentley, *Old No. 1*, was one of, if not the most successful racing Bentley. Apart from this second place, the car achieved a first in the Brooklands Six Hour Race, a second in the Brooklands 500 Mile Race and won Le Mans, all in 1929. In 1930 it was the winning car again at Le Mans and in 1931 captured the Brooklands 500 Mile Race. Incidentally, Birkin finished in third place.

THE TOURIST TROPHY RACE, Ards Circuit, Belfast (17th August). Described quite fully elsewhere in the Chapter, Glen, once again driving the *Old No. 1* Speed Six, had a monumental, very high speed crash at Bradshaws Brae, finishing up straddling the bank. His 'rescuers' found him quite unmoved and unshaken. Nerves of steel and yet another of his legendary lives!

Aside from motor racing, he was about to have another 'life' granted him. On the 7th November 1929, the newspapers burst into lurid headlines, such as: '*Six Men Perish in Blazing 'Plane*' and '*Man With The Luck Of The Navy*'. Another boldly proclaimed '*Six men perished when a great German air liner struck trees on Whitehill hilltop, crashed and burst into flames, near Caterham, Surrey, yesterday*'. The Junker aircraft in question took off at 10 am. from Croydon Airport on the 6th and was bound for Berlin, by way of Amsterdam. It had only been airborne some 10 or 15 minutes. There were eight passengers on board, only two of whom initially survived the crash – Kidston and the second pilot, Prince Eugen

Plate 103a. The victorious 1929 Bentley Le Mans Team. From left: Baron d'Erlanger, Woolf Barnato, Tim Birkin, Jack Dunfee, Glen Kidston, Dr. Benjafield, Jean Chassagne and Frank Clement.

PLATES 103A, C & D COURTESY THE AUTOCAR

Plate 103b. The Bentley winners, line astern, across the 1929 Le Mans finish. The Race No. 1 Speed Six of Barnato & Birkin followed by the 4.5 litre cars of Kidston & Jack Dunfee (No. 9) and Benjafield & d'Erlanger (No. 10) Out of camera is the fourth car home, the 4.5 litre Bentley of Clement & Chassagne (No. 8).

COURTESY THE MOTOR

Plate 103c. Kidston battling with his 'Old No. 1' Speed Six Bentley (No. 4) having a 'Mountjoy moment' in the 1929 Irish Grand Prix …left, an off …right, back on.

Plate 103d. Kidston's 1929 Tourist Trophy moment at Bradshaws Brae. In focus is the 1.5 litre Alfa Romeo of Attilio Marinoni.

Schaumburg-Lippe. The latter was a relative of Princess Victoria of Scaumburg-Lippe, sister of the ex-Kaiser. There's well connected! Survive they might have, but both were burnt. The Prince's injuries were so severe that he was to die a day or so later. He had been a famous stunt pilot, specializing in flying over *Tempelhoferfeld,* Berlin's airport, with some 'idiot' hanging by his teeth beneath the plane in question. The dead included the first pilot Rod Schika, a mechanic, W Ullrich, a wireless operator, H Niklas, a DL Jones of London, a GTG Milnes, no permanent address, and HJ Gaspar, whose first (and last) flight this was to be. Of all Glens' close shaves, this was probably the very closest he survived. Escaping through a jagged hole in the side of the fuselage, his clothes caught fire and he was in danger of becoming a human torch. Quick of thought and deed, he doused the flames by rolling himself over and over and over. Despite his injuries our hero bustled about and coming upon some boys, sent one of them to telephone for an ambulance, doctor and the police. He then accompanied a passing chap to his home, where he telephoned the Aerodrome to advise them of the disaster. After all this tidying up he found himself in hospital, swathed in bandages. Making a temporary exit, he borrowed a friend's car, dashed back to Croydon, chartered an Imperial Airways taxi plane and had himself flown over Wallington and Carshalton, for 10 minutes. As you do, *'just to steady the nerves and keep my hand in'*. Having studied and written about this amazing man, I am not sure he had any nerves.

Several interviewers and friends who visited him in hospital reported that, through the bandages swathed around his head, all that was visible were two sparkling eyes. The hole where his mouth would have been, more often than not contained a lighted cigarette. During one interview he claimed he was 'a lucky mascot' and that he led a charmed life. Incidentally, whilst in hospital, his personal valet sorted out the congratulatory telegrams, telephone calls and 'smokes'. At the Inquest he was recorded as being pale, but otherwise fit, and accompanied by his wife. Still together then!

At the outset to 1930 he purchased a 6.5 litre Bentley, with a Gurney Nutting saloon body (Reg. No. GC 3661) and entered it in that year's:

MONTE CARLO RALLY. The British contingent had to set out from John O'Groats, Scotland. Without much delay he skidded on black ice and crunched into a fairly solid stone wall, buckling the front axle and ruining the brake mechanism. Undaunted, he disconnected the offending brakes and straightened out the axle – to drive on. The delay caused him to miss various check-points, as well as the designated, scheduled Cross Channel ferry. Not one to be thwarted, he chartered a 'passing' boat, as you do, managing to reach the principality, if somewhat out of time and totally out of the reckoning.

BROOKLANDS DOUBLE TWELVE HOUR RACE (9-10th May). In this event he shared a 'Blower' 4.5 Bentley with Jack Dunfee. They had to retire with a broken valve, whilst Woolf Barnato & Clement came first and Sammy Davis & Clive Dunfee came second, both in Speed Six Bentleys.

But trust Glen, he was going to go out a high, and my goodness did he?

LE MANS (21-22nd June). The Bentley Works entered three Speed Sixes to be driven by

Plate 104a.

MAN WITH THE LUCK OF THE NAVY

ESCAPE FROM BLAZING AIR LINER

A NERVE TESTER

AIR FLIP WHILST STILL SUFFERING FROM BURNS

A thrilling account of how Lieut. Commander Glen Kidston, R.N., escaped from the blazing German aeroplane which crashed yesterday, and then, still suffering from burns, took a flight in another machine, "just to test his nerve," is given in to-day's "Daily News."

Commander Kidston's life story is one of amazing escapes, and he seems to be pursued by all the luck of the Navy.

When interviewed in bed, his face was swathed in cotton wool, and all the "Daily News" interviewer could see were two sparkling eyes and a lighted cigarette.

MAN WITH A CHARMED LIFE

Always Escapes Out of Tight Corners

Not for the first time has the "Luck of the Navy" pursued Commander Glen Kidston, one of the two survivors in the German air liner crash. The "Luck of the Navy" is another way of saying that the Commander possesses that pluck and resource which has got many a naval officer out of a tight corner.

His people say he has a charmed life, but it is more than that. The first thing the Commander did after the crash was to rush to Croydon Aerodrome in a friend's motor car, and, while his face was still aching with burns and his head swathed in bandages, he chartered an Imperial Airways taxi, piloted by Captain G. P. Olley, and flew over Wallington and Carshalton for ten minutes "just to steady his nerve."

"FUNNY LITTLE WAY."

"It's a funny little way I have after little dusts up of this kind," the Commander confessed to me afterwards.

I found him in bed in a blue pyjama suit, calmly smoking a cigarette. The Commander's face was invisible through a heavy mask of cotton wool. All I could see of him was a pair of sparkling eyes, two rather swollen lips, and a nose through little holes in the cotton wool.

Telling the story of the flight, the Commander said: "We left Croydon a few minutes before ten. I was bound on a business trip to Berlin by way of Amsterdam. As we passed up the Caterham Valley towards the eastern end of the Surrey Hills I noticed that the clouds came lower and we were flying below 100 feet from the ground.

"I was not alarmed. At the same time I could not pick out the ground. Twice the pilot had to pull the joystick back sharply, and on one occasion we only just cleared the tree tops. The weather was bad. We knew that at the start.

TERRIFIC CRASH.

"Suddenly I had a sensation of turning, and was under the impression that the pilot, finding that the mist was increasing, decided to return to Croydon. Then, almost immediately afterwards, there was a terrific crash, and simultaneously the machine came to rest in a state of wreckage.

"For the moment I was partly dazed. The cabin was in a complete state of confusion. I was flung about, but, strange to say, I do not remember seeing any of the other passengers.

"I did not know what became of the pilot, Prince Eugen von Schaumberg-Lippe. The first thought that came to my mind was the possibility of fire, and, to my horror, I saw flames breaking out. I caught sight of a hole in the starboard side of the cabin, and, wrenching myself free, I struggled through the opening to the ground.

"Then my own clothes caught fire and my hair was singed. Smoke was all around me, and with the flames growing bigger I threw myself to the ground and rolled over and over, and at last put out my blazing coat.

MASS OF FLAMES.

"I happened to look at my watch at the time of the crash, and it was 10.15. The machine appeared to be flying level, all engines running normally.

"As soon as I had risen from the ground I saw the machine a mass of flames reaching as high as the trees. I went back and attempted to get into the cabin, rushing first to one side and then to the other, but I could not approach on account of the tremendous heat. I then ran down the hill for assistance.

"I have had a few narrow escapes in my time, but I think this was about the narrowest," he said. "When people ask me what my mascot is I just smile and show them the little gap in my front teeth. That is where I breathe in all my good luck.

"I had that same luck in the war when I was torpedoed in H.M.S. Hogue in September, 1914. I was in the water two and a half hours before I was picked up. I was in the battle of Jutland in H.M.S. Oran and we came through all right.

"I and another man, Mr Thistlewait, bought the famous machine from which the tragic Mr Lowenstein fell into the English Channel. We were flying on our way to film a big-game expedition when we had a forced landing in a river in the Sudan. Again I managed to pull through unhurt. We were rescued by boat.

"If anyone wants a reliable mascot,' said the Commander. "Well here I am I shall be about again in a day or two."

COURTESY HULL EVENING NEWS.

Plate 104b. Cmdr. Kidston's Speed Six Bentley with a four seater Weymann Sportsman's Coupe body by Gurney Nutting & Co. Ltd. entered in the 1930 Monte Carlo Rally starting from John O'Groat's

COURTESY THE MOTOR.

Barnato & Kidston (*Old No. 1*), Clement & Watney and Sammy Davis & Clive Dunfee. Also present were a full Team of the Birkin/Paget 'Blower' 4.5 litre Bentleys, whilst a single Mercedes S-38/250 was piloted by Caracciola & Werner. After the first hour the order of the day was Caracciola (Mercedes), Davis (Speed Six), Kidston (Speed Six), Ramponi (Blower 4.5), Clement (Speed Six), Brisson's Stutz, Birkin (in what else?), followed by the Talbot 90s of Lewis & Eaton and Hindmarsh & Rose-Richards. After some 2½ hours the goggles of Sammy Davis were shattered by flying stones. Some shards of glass penetrated his left eye. Now, whereas you and I would have come to a rapid halt and leapt out of the vehicle, screaming the house down, that was not Sammy's style. Foot still hard down, he quietly and calmly changed the eyepieces and drove on round to the pits, for his co-driver to take over! However, Clive Dunfee rather spoilt all this stoic effort when subsequently he well and truly 'stuffed' the Bentley into the sandbank at Pontlieue. Their race was over. After three hours, Caracciola was followed by the remaining Team Bentleys. A certain amount of extra excitement was introduced into the unfolding drama when Rigal's Stutz caught fire. In attempting to grab the extinguisher and jump out, his foot caught on the top of the bodywork and he finished up sprawled across the centre of the track. At this precise moment, Barnato's Bentley hurtled into sight, 'cruising along' at about 110 mph. Had I been Rigal, I would not only have taken a jaundiced view of the possibilities, but would have been praying – very, very hard. By dint of an amazing piece of driving and in the limited space left available, Barnato avoided Rigal's body, by the width of a tyre tread, at which precise moment the fuel tank of the Stutz exploded. Fortunately the blazing car was to one side of the track but for at least two hours the drivers had to steam past the unintentional hazard and on each and every occasion were both temporarily blinded and scorched. After five hours, Barnato snatched the lead from Caracciola but not for long. Soon the positions were reversed – and then reversed again. This ding-dong battle for supremacy went on for another five hours. At 2.30 am Sunday early morning the mighty Mercedes ran out of battery, starter power and lights. Caracciola's race was run. By daylight the pace had told equally on the drivers and the cars, the former being physically exhausted and the latter mechanically worn out. Despite which, Woolf & Glen and Clement & Watney continued to power on, with Lewis & Eaton's Talbot in third place, followed by Callingham in the Lord Howe 1750cc Alfa Romeo and the Talbot of Hindmarsh & Rose-Richards. At the finish the Bentleys of Barnato & Kidston and Clement & Watney steamed over the finish, line astern. In their train were the Talbots of Lewis & Eaton, and Hindmarsh & Rose-Richards, followed by Lord Howe & Callingham, in their Alfa Romeo.

This was to be the end of serious racing for not only the Work's Bentleys, but also for Woolf Barnato and Cmdr. Glen Kidston. A remarkable end to a remarkable era.

In the meantime the Commander was refocusing. Oh yes. Out with racing cars, in with aeroplanes. The speed and horsepower were not widely disparate but the medium was distinctly aerial. He lost no time in transferring his allegiance to flying, and how! He had flown a small Tiger Moth for some years but this was to now become a serious pursuit. He purchased one of the first off the assembly line, DH80A Puss Moth's, from the de Havilland Aircraft Co., Stag Lane, Edgware. The three seater had a top speed of 128 mph, developed

Plate 105a.   The Winners, Barnato and Kidston.
PLATES 105A, B, & D COURTESY THE AUTOCAR.

Plate 105b.   Kidston hurtling past the flaming Stutz of Rigal.

The 1930 Le Mans.

Plate 105c. Crossing not only the finish line. First home Kidston & Barnato's 'Old No. 1' (No. 4) followed by the Speed Six of Clement & Watney (No. 2). The T40 Bugatti ladies are waving them home. Marguente Mareuse and Odette Siko drove this Molsheim product which was basically a 1.5 litre touring car. Despite this they came second in the 1500cc class and seventh overall. COURTESY THE BENTLEY AT LE MANS, DR. BENJAFIELDS MD. MOTOR RACING PUBLICATIONS.

Plate 105d.   The Victors. From left: Dick Watney, Glen Kidston, Woolf Barnato and Frank Clement. R Watney was originally with Rootes Group, founded in 1913 and which company assimilated various car manufacturers from 1929 on. He was to achieve management status, alongside WO Bentley, with LG Motors which arose phoenix-like from the ashes of Lagonda.

from the 130 bhp engine, and cost between £595 and £650. At least there was a monetary saving over and above luxury motor cars! Having made the acquisition, he contacted his old naval friend and fellow shipmate, Owen Cathcart-Jones (OCJ). The latter was a not absolutely 'Mensa class' adventurer whose service career was rather chequered, to say the least. In later life, he washed up in Hollywood, initially as a flying advisor to the film studios. One of his more interesting tasks was to assist his to-be friend Errol Flynn in locating suitable companions, for party, party time.

But back to 1930 and Glen, who wanted OCJ to co-pilot the Puss Moth in the 9th Kings Cup Air Race. This was due to start on 5th July. The race set out on the 753 mile circuit, from and back to Hanworth Airfield. OCJ was of the opinion they were handicapped out of the event. Be that as it may, out of a total field of 88, and starting off 82nd, they finished in sixth place. Glen was absolutely delighted and on 22nd July offered OJC full time employment, as his co-pilot and 'runner', with the intention of *'breaking all the worlds flying records that were appropriate'*. That's our man. You simply have to be in awe of his sheer ebullience, imagination and guts. What a player!

Never one to let aspirations get in the way of revelry, revelry, revelry, between early August and early September 1930, one of, if not the last of the Bentley Boys 'Great Cannes Parties' took place (*See* Chapter 8). By 2nd September, the lotus-life palled for Glen and it was on to more serious matters. On the way back to England, in the Puss Moth, via Germany, he became very interested in Templehof Aerodrome, Berlin. So much so that he wished to establish a similar facility in Hyde Park, London. Yes, an international airfield in ….! For a start, it was so damned inconvenient having to land at the airfields of either Croydon or Heston (the latter to become our very own London Airport) and then endure the slow, forty minute drive into the centre of London. You might, at this stage think an April Fool is on, but oh no! Incidentally, he found it difficult to comprehend why this particular idea was not seized and acted upon, soonest. But then it was not to be his only disappointment with the powers-that-be, in respect of matters flying. From Berlin it was on to Dessau. This was to visit the Junkers factory, as he was now seriously searching for the perfect aircraft with which to achieve his dream of breaking all those world air speed records. It was then a short Puss Moth hop to Hamburg to visit a firm of yacht builders, in respect of a craft they were building for him. Then back to England and Cowes, Isle of Wight, to board his recently acquired Auxiliary Ketch *Pamela*, moored in the Medina River. This craft had been built by White & Son, Southampton in 1928. Fitted with inboard petrol engines, she was 64 ft long by 15.5 ft beam and 10.8 ft draught with a Registered tonnage of 32.83. In the light of events that were to take place, one cannot but help wonder what happened to that Hamburg boat?

On 30th September 1930, Glen ordered an American Detroit-Lockheed Vega Special aircraft, with long range fuel tanks and 'bang up' to date navigation equipment. It was re-registered G-ABGK. This was a serious bit of kit, being a six passenger monoplane. The 450 hp engine allowed a cruising speed of 155/165 mph, with a top speed of 165/185 mph. The first planned record attempt was to be made on the London to Cape Town route. Just to ensure he could not be accused of sitting around, Glen took passage on board the *Liner Europa*, outward bound from Southampton, for the USA. The intention was to visit the Lockheed factory. He returned on the *Liner Berengaria*, inward bound for Southampton. A

Glen and his Aircraft.

Plate 106a. The DH60G Gypsy Moth.

Plate 106b. 'Glen' posing with the Lockheed Vega.
PLATES 106A, B & D COURTESY THE FLIGHT COLLECTION.

Plate 106c. Bodicote House, part Georgian and the Oxford residence of Tom and his wife. The stables housed his Mercedes mechanic and the Park doubled up as an airstrip for the Tiger Moth aircraft he shared with Glen Kidston.
COURTESY MR GEORGE WALKER.

Plate 106d & e. The Times reported that Lt. Cdr. Kidston (actually Cmdr.) flew from Netheravon Aerodrome, Wiltshire, to Cape Town in 6½ days, thereby reducing the previous record for the flight by two days. Cmdr. Kidston was accompanied by WO Cathcart-Jones as second pilot and L Johnson as the wireless operator.
PLATE 106E COURTESY THE TIMES.

fellow passenger was none other than his old chum Woolf Barnato. That must have been fun. Naturally the two men could not land at one place and proceed to another similar address (in this case in 'old London Town'), without making a race of it. Barnato motored a Bentley to Grosvenor Square whilst Glen took a car to Hamble Airfield, from whence he flew to Heston, and then motored to London. Barnato won.

The next destination was to fly to Tiger Tim Birkin's Shadwell residence, for yet another winter month's house party. Amongst the guests were Lady Sylvia Ashley, Tims' reasonably long term lady friend, despite still being married to Lord Ashley (*See* Chapter 5), and Woolf Barnato. Hardly had Glen landed the Puss Moth than he was harrying Tim to construct a landing strip. Thus, the gardeners and general factotums were rounded up and marshalled out to the grounds. The instructions were to generally level the location and fill 'all those rabbit holes'. However, it is doubtful if this particular Kidston 'flight of fancy' went any further. What there can be no doubt about was that Tim had quite enough problems piled up in his 'in-tray', without having to construct landing strips. Sometime in 1930, Glen met and was more than somewhat taken with the then 18 year old Ethel Margaret Whigham. She was to achieve some notoriety in her later life, when much better known as Margaret Campbell, Duchess of Argyll.

At the onset of New Year 1931, the crated Lockheed Vega was placed on board the *SS American Trader* for trans-shipment to Britain. OCJ was dispatched to make the necessary arrangements involved with unloading, transporting, uncrating and assembling the aircraft. In the meantime Glen made for Bodicote House, the Upper Heyford residence of Tom Thistlethwayte and his bride of some six month's (the marriage of which will be caught up with in the next Chapter, and at which Glen had been the Best Man). The Vega was ready for its first test flight on 31st January 1931, following which two further test flights were made. Next off, on 21st February, Glen and OCJ made an attempt on the flight time from Croydon, London to Le Bourget, Paris. They achieved this in the record time of 1 hour 12 minutes. About now he conceived the idea to build the Lockheed Vega aircraft under license, in Great Britain. The British aircraft industry was resoundingly disinterested and all his approaches were met with a deep silence. Not a man to be trifled with, this response, or more realistically lack of response, made up his mind. From now on he determined that his mission in life would be to convince the whole world as to the future of commercial aircraft. More especially to attempt to give Great Britain a wake-up call in this respect. No one can but admit his vision was to be proved correct. Sadly, he was, in effect, a prophet in his own land, and we know what happens to prophets in their own land!

In the middle of March 1931, the long-range fuel tanks were fitted to the Vega and another test flight made. There was much conjecture as to the ideal airfield from which to take off, for the soon to be made Great Britain to Cape Town flight. The choice fell on Netheravon, Salisbury Plain, the very field at which OCJ had originally learnt his 'craft'. The Vega was relocated from Croydon to Netheravon on 28th March and at 6 am, on 31st March, they set off. This was to prove to be a record breaking flight of 6 days and 9 hours duration, during which they averaged a speed of 134 mph. The high profile arrival of Cmdr. Glen Kidston, who was 'billed' as an enormously wealthy man, caused some anticipation in the then Colonies of South Africa and Rhodesia. This was more especially so as he had pre-

Plate 107a.   Kisumu, Lake Victoria. Owen Cathcart-Jones with Mechanic Hills at work on the engine of the Lockheed Vega during the record flight to Cape Town, April 1931.

Plate 107b.   Cape Town, 6th April, 1931. Circling Maitland Aerodrome prior to landing at the finish of the record flight from London.

PLATES 107A & B COURTESY AVIATION MEMORIES OWEN CATHCART-JONES. HUTCHINSON.

announced his intention to invest in at least one local aviation company. In fact he had let it be known he was interested in taking over the firm of Union Airways. In this connection he had teamed up with Tony Gladstone, an ex Cobham/Blackburn manager, whom Glen considered the ideal man to assist him in his stated aims. One of the very interested party's in these intriguing possibilities was the Rhodesian Aviation Co. Ltd. They had been left somewhat in the lurch when the South African interests of the Cobham/Blackburn Company, who were substantial investors in Rhodesian Aviation, were taken over by Imperial Airways. The latter, on completing the deal, immediately pulled the financial rug from under Rhodesian Aviation. Thus, the arrival of a man with 'large sacks' of money, looking for investment in local airlines, must have seemed like manna from heaven.

In pursuit of all this planned activity, he flew the Vega to Johannesburg accompanied by two legal and accountancy 'beavers' and Tony Gladstone. OCJ was left behind – a decision which was to save his life. Once at Johannesburg, Glen and Gladstone initially wished to fly to Pietermaritzburg, over the Drakensberg Mountain range, and then on to Durban. As the Vega was considered too large for the airfields involved, Glen borrowed a DH Puss Moth based at Baragwanath Airfield, from a local owner. I hope this gentleman was insured for third party risks – or 'any other driver', as it were. Thus, on 5th May 1931, the pair took off. But, whilst climbing over the Drakensberg Mountains, the plane plummeted out of the sky. Cmdr. George Pearson Glen Kidston and his passenger fell to their death. Glens' luck had finally run out – there were no more 'lives'. The reasons for the accident were endlessly debated. It was suggested the baggage had been badly stowed and a case had come loose, causing the pilot to loose control. Alternatively, there was much consideration that a wing had failed and been wrenched off. Certainly, it transpired the owner had recently struck a telegraph wire with his plane and the repairing engineer had not inspected the relevant wing for internal damage. On the other hand, the violent down-draughts, often experienced over those particular mountains, were well known and feared by local aviators. OCJ returned to England, on the Union Castle Liner *Windsor Castle*.

The Editor of THE AEROPLANE took a rather unsympathetic, hectoring, school masterly, possibly green-eyed view, declaring:

> 'He (Glen Kidston) was one of those unfortunate young men who have too much money and consequently never develop their real ability. Being so wealthy he had nobody willing to tell him when or where he was wrong, and was made very much a hero by the cheaper newspapers, though the adventures of which they wrote so glowingly were merely those of a young man with the luck and wealth to take part in dashing sports. Had he lived to acquire knowledge and experience, Kidston, with his money and imagination, might well have become a valuable asset to British aviation, but all we can do is regret the loss of a young man of immense energy and courage'. *Well, say it as you see it!*

As a counter-balance the following were rather more representative and heartfelt obituaries. One was from WO Bentley and the other from his good friend and 'co-pilot', Woolf Babe Barnato. WO intoned:

GLEN KIDSTON KILLED

CRASH IN NATAL

HEAVY WINDS AND DUST

FROM OUR CORRESPONDENT

DURBAN, May 5

Lieutenant-Commander Glen Kidston, who recently made the record flight from England to the Cape, was killed when the machine he was flying from Johannesburg to Natal crashed on the Drakensberg Mountains 16 miles north of the Van Reenen Pass, shortly before midday to-day. Captain T. A. Gladstone, who accompanied him, was also killed.

The crash was seen by a country storekeeper named Helman, who came into Van Reenen to inform the authorities of it. Mr. Helman stated that when he reached the aeroplane he found both occupants dead, but a visiting-card lying near revealed the identity of Commander Kidston, it apparently having been jerked out of his pocket in the crash. A high wind was blowing on the mountains, and, as a consequence of the recent dry weather, dust was thick and visibility bad. Commander Kidston had arranged to visit Pietermaritzburg to-day, and was due at Durban this afternoon.

The accident occurred about 11.20 in the morning, close to the mountain known as Tantjiesberg. Local farmers who saw the crash and hastened to the spot found the machine smashed to matchwood, some of the pieces lying among the rocks and in thick bush and others scattered over the veld. One piece was found half a mile from the scene of the crash.

The aeroplane was seen coming southward over the Orange Free State, meeting a heavy wind and heavy clouds of dust. As it passed over Tantjiesberg a large object fell from it. What this was nobody is able to say, but it is presumed to have been a wing, for immediately the aeroplane made a violent nosedive and crashed. The bodies of the dead airmen have been removed to Harrismith. The air route from the Rand to Durban is always regarded as a bad one on account of frequent low-lying clouds on the Drakensberg, which rise in this district to 11,000ft.

LIEUT.-COMMANDER GLEN KIDSTON, the distinguished airman, who was killed while flying in Natal yesterday. He made a record flight to the Cape last month.

Plate 108.　　　　　　　　COURTESY THE TIMES.

A DANGEROUS PASS

FROM OUR OWN CORRESPONDENT

CAPETOWN, May 5

Local airmen say that Van Reenen's Pass, through which the railway from Bloemfontein to Ladysmith descends the precipitous barrier of the Drakensberg, is a death-trap for any airman unused to its peculiar dangers. It is a pass where terrific air currents and pockets abound; it is often blind with fog or dust storms. It winds, a narrow path, among the towering peaks of the Drakensberg, and is confused with innumerable valleys, from which there is no outlet for an aeroplane caught in gale or mist. Lieutenant-Commander Kidston's death is bitterly lamented here, where he made a host of friends during his brief stay, and Captain Gladstone's is lamented with equal sorrow.

A memorial service for Lieutenant-Commander Glen Kidston will be held in St. Mark's, North Audley-street, on Friday at 2.15. An obituary notice appears on page 16.

COURTESY THE TIMES.

COURTESY THE TIMES.

'Glen Kidston was a born adventurer, rough, tough, sharp, and as fearless as Birkin. I think I was the only person never to receive the rough edge of his tongue, which could certainly be very sharp at times, and we always got on well together. Glen was a traditional naval officer type, quieter than most of the others and very amenable to discipline. Thickset, with very powerful shoulders, and good looking, his life seemed to consist of one hair-raising incident after another'.

Barnato lamented the loss as follows:

'He was the beau ideal of a sportsman. The word fear had been expunged from his dictionary … A resourceful and gallant driver with a flair for any kind of mechanism – a combination of tender hands and a keen judgment plus that indefinable will to win that means so much … The most perfect host and good talker and a better listener…A man about town when in the mood, a man of action in another'.

Thus ended one of the truly Elizabethan, buccaneering lives of the 20th Century. Tom Thistlethwayte did not appear to attend the funeral and Nancy, his long suffering wife, remarried that same year.

Possibly outside the scope of this book, but it was alleged that OCJ was somewhat forgetful as to the whereabouts of the Lockheed aircraft. It appears it had to be located and recovered in order to return it to the Kidston family.

The Times, London — 26 May 1930

MR. T. THISTLETHWAYTE AND THE HON. EILEEN BERRY

The marriage arranged between Thomas Thistlethwayte, son of the late Captain T. G. Thistlethwayte and of Mrs. Stopford, and Eileen, eldest daughter of the late Lord Buckland of Bwlch and of Lady Buckland, Bwlch, Breconshire, will take place in London on Thursday, July 3.

Morning Post, London — 26 May 1930

Mr. Thomas Thistlethwayte and the Hon. Eileen Berry

The marriage arranged between Thomas Thistlethwayte, son of the late Captain T. G. Thistlethwayte and of Mrs. Stopford, and Eileen, eldest daughter of the late Lord Buckland of Bwlch and of Lady Buckland, Bwlch, Breconshire, will take place in London on Thursday, the 3rd of July.

WOMEN OF TO-DAY.

HON. EILEEN BERRY TO WED IN JULY.

The marriage will take place at the Chapel of the Savoy, London, on Thursday afternoon, July, 3, of Mr. A. D. T. Thistlethwayte and the Hon. Eileen Berry, the eldest of the five daughters of the late Lord Buckland and of Lady Buckland of Bwlch, Breconshire. Their engagement was announced last December. They first met in the South of France about two years ago, when the Hon. Eileen Berry was on holiday.

Mr. Thistlethwayte is the son of the late Captain Thistlethwayte, R.A., of Southwick Park, Hampshire, and of Mrs. Stopford, of Sherborne, Sandgate. His family is an old Warwickshire one, and he has a shooting-box at Butlers Marston, Kineton, Warwickshire. He is a keen rider to hounds, and in addition to motor racing (he took part in the Ulster road motor race last year) he has done a great deal of flying.

The Hon. Eileen Berry was for some years the youngest M.F.H. in the country, becoming Master of the resuscitated Gelligaer and Talybont Hunt when only fourteen. She was the youngest Master that ever sat a saddle, and throughout her association with the Hunt she showed herself a keen fox-hunter, a hard rider, and a popular Master.

Mr. Thistlethwayte was at Buckland for the Hunt Ball season last winter, and was present with his fiancée at the Brecon Hunt Ball and the Monmouth Hunt Ball. He has already made many friends in South Wales.

Plate 109.

Chapter Eight

Tom. The Last Racing Year. 1930.

'The horse is here to stay but the automobile is only a novelty – a fad.'
President of a USA Bank advising a client not to purchase car manufacturing shares'. The client who ignored these pearls of wisdom sold for a 125% profit.

The 3rd July was the day on which Arthur Donald Claude Thomas Thistlethwayte, more popularly known as 'Tom', married The Honourable Gwladys Eileen Berry. She had been born in 1908 and was aged 22. Cmdr. Glen Kidston was the best man. The ceremony took place at the quaint, little old Chapel of the Savoy, behind the Strand, London. In amongst the guests were Tom's mother, now the widowed Mrs Stopford, and Uncle Colonel Evelyn Thistlethwayte. The latter gentleman was to be somewhat bamboozled into purchasing Southwick Estate from Tom, in a year or so (*See* Chapter 1). In the main, the old motor racing friends were noticeable by their absence. However, dependable Clive Gallop, a co-driver in Tom's early years of competition, was present. Mind you there was some competition on that day, there being, amongst other such gatherings, a Guinness family 'knees up' at St. Margaret's, Westminster, where a Miss Maureen Guinness 'traded' vows with the Earl of Ava.

A fascinating aside in respect of the union was that quite correctly the marriage certificate detailed Tom as being a divorcee. Notwithstanding which, in all the pre-nuptial publicity, which achieved an almost disproportionate amount of press coverage in the daily 'blats', this fact was not mentioned – ever, anywhere. Almost to a journalist, he was never referred to as being divorced. Now call me an old cynic, but it took a little time to understand how this 'sleight of the press cuttings' had been achieved. Possibly, all becomes clear if one casts an eye over the blameless bride's immediate forebears. John Mathias Berry, an estate agent and one time Mayor of Merthyr Tydfil, had three sons (and a daughter). The male issue were: Henry Seymour (1877-1928), to become Baron Buckland; William Ewart (1879-1954), to become

AT EDEN ROC, JUAN-LES-PINS: MAJOR NOEL SAMPSON, MR. AND MRS. THISTLETHWAYTE, AND THE HON. MRS. IAN CAMPBELL

Plate 110a.
COURTESY THE TATLER, LONDON.

Summer Season Draws to Cannes

(Special Correspondence.)

CANNES.—Thanks to the continued fine weather, the summer season is now at its best, all the hotels being crammed and the summer colony increasing daily with the arrival of luxurious motor-cars.

The galas at the Palm Beach Casino are always frequented by well-known people, among those recognized there recently having been: Lord and Lady Portarlington, Lady Ashley, Sir Lewis and Lady Orr Duncan, Major and Mrs. Butler Humphrey, the Hon. E. Harmsworth, Major Jack Coats, Captain Wolf Barnato, Mr. and Mrs. Thistlethwaite, Captain and Mrs. Brooksbank, Captain and Mrs. J. Rodney, Mr. and Mrs. Troup, Captain Norton Richard, Mr. Philip Yorke, R. Kindersley, Mrs. Pearce, Mrs. Royston.

Plate 110b.
COURTESY THE NEW YORK HERALD, PARIS.

1st Viscount Lord Camrose; and James Gomer (1883-1968), to become Lord Kemsley. Older readers may well be grasping the direction and thrust of the possible solution to the question posed above, with 'handles' such as Camrose and Kemsley being bandied about.

Henry Seymour Berry, a director of some 80 companies, was the father of five daughters, amongst whom was the bride-to-be. Henry died comparatively young, in a horse riding accident. By 1927, Gwladys' uncles, through hard work and a succession of shrewd acquisitions, owned the Allied Newspapers, established in 1924. By 1927, when the DAILY TELEGRAPH was added to the stable, they also controlled the SUNDAY TIMES, the FINANCIAL TIMES, the GRAPHIC, the DAILY DISPATCH, the DAILY SKETCH, the MANCHESTER EVENING CHRONICLE and the SUNDAY CHRONICLE. These were in addition to eight provincial weeklies and about 70 periodicals. You could say they had a close control over much of the every day news output. That was more especially so in those far off days of very limited radio output, no television and a discreet 'fourth estate'. The days when journalists were more than prepared to toe this or that newspaper proprietor's required dictates and whims. Thus Tom's previous 'form' remained unmentioned.

With the World spiralling into a financial trough, after the October 1929 Stock Market crash, the summer social scene of 1930 was probably to be the last of the best. On 25th June, Tom was reported as spending the weekend at *The Hermitage*, Le Touquet-Paris-Plage, probably settling those pre-nuptial nerves! Post the wedding, Mr and Mrs Thistlethwayte were detailed as 'late arrivals' at the same hotel. Possibly Tom had been ensuring that everything was going to be 'tickety-boo' on their wedding night.

But this was only a curtain raiser for *La Saison d'ete' a Cannes* which, that August, was going to be quite a social affair. Later in the year, the Thistlethwaytes were based at Juan-les-Pins, on the French Riviera, with other, no doubt very acceptable, desirable and well connected people. Cmdr. Glen Kidston, and his recently employed co-pilot, (OCJ), flew the Puss Moth down to join the fun. Due to the lack of an aerodrome at Cannes, they were 'forced' to fly in and out of the French Naval airbase at St. Raphael. This was halfway between Cannes and St. Tropez. OCJ had to fly to Paris, several times during the month, to collect and deliver various party guests and, on one occasion, to purchase a supply of kippers. This latter delicacy was not only one of Glens' favourite dishes, but they were unobtainable in Cannes. Damned inconvenient, really. On the day of the kipper delivery, Glen had such a 'hots' to get his teeth round them, that he sent one of the various powerboat's over from Cannes to speed up their collection. As you do!

Glen was in a select party that included Woolf Babe Barnato, Babes' golfing partner, Dale Bourne, and a truly large American, one 'Babe White'. Additionally, there was a month long, fluctuating party of like-minded, fun loving 'girls and boys'. The mornings were 'wasted' with Glen and Woolf racing their respective Chris-Craft speedboats from *Palm Beach* to *Eden Roc* and back. En-route they intentionally swamped the swimmers sunning themselves on the raft at Antibes with their wash!' A fellow reveller had a larger, faster power boat so the plane would be deployed to circle his craft, prior to dive-bombing *Eden Roc*! No doubt this high-spirited behaviour would nowadays be termed mindless hooliganism. Tiger Tim Birkin, not to be left out, had chartered Louis Mountbatten's yacht which was anchored in the bay, off-shore from the *Hotel Majestic*. During the afternoons, Glen and Woolf raced their cars from

Plate III.

Cannes to St. Raphael and back. OCJ was often seated alongside his employer, in the very Speed Six Bentley (*Old No. 1*) with which the doughty duo had recently won the year's Le Mans. It was Glens' target to shave a few seconds off the journey time, each and every day. It must have been terrifying to be a passenger.

As one would expect, Glen bored of the aircraft being round the coast, at St. Raphael. Thus inconvenienced, he persuaded OCJ to attempt a landing on the Mandelieu Polo Ground, close to Cannes. One evening, when the conditions were as good as they were going to get, OCJ came in, down wind, through a gap in the tall trees surrounding the 'wretched' field. By good fortune and undoubted skill, the pilot managed to pull up, just prior to the far-end hedge. There is no mention of how the plane was flown out of the polo ground. It may well have had to be dismantled and reassembled elsewhere. In any case, one wonders how the local authorities took to this unorthodox, unauthorised landing. Notwithstanding, the Commander employed his special brand of charm and, in cahoots with a local dignitary, persuaded the Municipality to consider constructing an airfield. They eventually did but not soon enough for Glen who by that time had moved on to celestial airfields.

On 24th August both the *Excelsior Paris* and *Palm Beach Casino* reported the presence of Cmdr. Glen Kidston, Capt. Woolf Barnato and the Thistlethwaytes. On 29th, Mr and Mrs Thistlethwayte and Mrs Kidston were at the Cannes Gala Night. This late in the Kidston's marriage, it was very rare to read their names 'side-by-side'. Perhaps as a result of his spouse's arrival and close proximity, but certainly because he was now tired of the scene, a few days later Glen flew off to other pastures. Not long after, possibly one of the last of the great extravaganza, French Riviera, racing driver summer season's drew to a poignant close.

But back to matters sporting and the beginning of the year. On 31st January 1930, Tom granted an interview to a journalist, from a now long defunct publication, titled THE AUTO MOTOR JOURNAL (*See* Plate 111). If the ingratiating, fawning, bootlicking, Uriah Heap tone of the article were repeated very often, then I imagine the magazine would have choked on its own *mal de mer*. There was reference to an earlier issue of the magazine which had featured a previous article in the series of 'Racing Celebrities'. The 'victim' on that occasion being Capt. HRS Birkin. Without doubt, the most interesting extract from the sycophantic piece with Tom, bearing in mind the date, was his answer to the question ….

'Now, Mr Thistlethwayte, what are your plans at the moment with regard to the coming season? Shall you be entering in all the big events, and driving the Mercedes as usual?' In answer Tom replied … 'Oh, yes in all the leading meetings – the Tourist Trophy, Irish Grand Prix, Twenty-Four Hours and Le Mans, etc., but not alone *(sic)* with the Mercedes, oh no!' 'Oh', the interviewer exclaimed, 'another car entirely?' 'Not exactly', replied Thistlethwayte 'For the coming season I hope to be entering a complete team of cars in all the smaller and more general events – a team of three racing Aston Martin's'. 'By Jove, that sounds interesting', the interviewer replied. 'Shall you, yourself be driving one?' 'Not in a general way, I am afraid, but I shall certainly be driving an Aston Martin on the first day of the Irish Grand Prix. On the second (day), however, I shall return to my Mercedes'.

Well there's a surprise. According to the records of both Aston Martin and the race

Plate 112a. Tom in his 'new' Mercedes S-38/250 (as evinced by the different number plate – KP 7878 as distinct from YU 1908) in the Southport 100 Mile Race.

Tom's 1930 Sand Racing.

Plate 112b. 'Thistlethwayte's Mercedes leads Rogers' Type 37A Bugatti and de Durrand's 4.5 litre Bentley around the turn', in the Skegness two day event.

Plate 112c. 'Dignity and impudence'! A scrap between Thistlethwayte's Mercedes and the comparatively tiny HFB Special, at the Skegness Sand Races.

PLATES 112A, B & C COURTESY THE AUTOCAR.

Plate 112d. Skegness again, with Brayshaw's HFB skidding wide, Thistlethwayte's Mercedes taking a central line and Fish's Bugatti tucking in close to the turn.

PLATE 112D COURTESY THE MOTOR.

meetings detailed, the whole commentary would appear to have been a huge flight of fancy. One presumes Tom's marriage had the usual motor racing caveats attached? Certainly, his entries for 1930 were restricted to three sand race events and a provisional entry for the July Irish Grand Prix, which was scratched. Probably of most note was that his 1930 activities were in his new (well, late 1929 new) much heralded Mercedes S-38/250, as distinct from the older S-36/200 model.

SOUTHPORT HUNDRED MILE RACE (Saturday 24th May). Held on Ainsdale Beach, the planned track had to be moved further along the sands, due to wind and tide conditions. There were five handicap classes, with Tom, in 'a' Mercedes, entered in the unlimited category. THE DAILY DISPATCH of Manchester was co-hosting the race. They promoted the event in their issue of 21st May, announcing that *'Phenomenal speeds are promised ... last year attracted 100,000 spectators ... many of the most famous drivers and riders in the country ...',* and so on. The 'blats' of the day reported a spasmodic start. The race turned out to be a battle between Tom's Mercedes and the 2 litre Type 35 Bugatti of Selby, a protracted and exciting tussle of horsepower versus handicap. Despite the extra 5 litres engine capacity of the German car, the Bugatti had a two lap handicap start. At about half-distance, a storm passed through, and Selby and Tom were well ahead of the pack. As with most racing, especially sand competition, the power of the Mercedes overwhelmed the opposition on the straight. However, the tight hairpin bends, coupled with its overall weight of 2.5 tons, tended to be its undoing. At the finish, after 1 hour 42 minutes, Selby was still ³/₄ of a lap and 1 minute 50 seconds ahead. Tom did achieve first in the Unlimited Class, winning THE AUTOCAR Cup, but he was the only entrant! As an aside, on handicap, he had to concede eight laps or 16 miles to an Austin 7. A David Brown made a showing in his Vauxhall Villiers (*See page 165*) but, apart from a deferred start, he had to retire after eight laps. Another entrant of interest was a BH Davenport in a car of his own design which, despite coming in fourth, was laughingly referred to '*... as being ready for the scrap heap*'. That good! Incidentally, THE JOHANNESBURG STAR carried a report of this event, as late as 11th September, in which they announced that "*.... Captain* (Captain, promotion at last) *Thistlethwayte was second in the race for the Gold Cup recording the fastest time of the day on standard India Super tyres*'!

SKEGNESS ANNUAL TWO DAY EVENT (13-14th June). This event attracted good entries and crowds. Running a two day meeting meant working the tides, which must have made for 'a bit' of a nightmare. This was especially more so with the paddock, starting and timekeepers arrangements all in place on the sands overnight. The incoming tide on the first day very nearly left the timekeepers and starter isolated – for the night. The course was approximately one mile long, with a series of hairpins. Despite the non-appearance of the much trumpeted Malcolm Campbell and Raymond Mays, Tom and his giant, *'magnificent'* Mercedes became the main attraction. The reality proved rather different as reported by THE MOTOR. This august publication advised '*Thistlethwayte's Mercedes Benz was the star turn, but was too unwieldy on the corners compared with cars like the Bugatti*'. THE MOTOR SPORT intoned '*Thistlethwayte's grey Mercedes and Roger's (sic)Bugatti were well matched in classes 6 and 8 but in spite of magnificent driving, the Merc's speed on the straight could not compensate for the*

Plate 113. Three of the competitors in the Hundred Miles Speed Test – a motor boat race held in and around Poole Harbour. From left: Viscount Kingsborough who was the the winner (No. 33), Mr K Miller (No. 9) and Mr T Thistlethwayte (No. 30).

COURTESY THE BOURNEMOUTH ECHO.

Plate 114. Makers of History 1928. No. 7. (A 'brooding') Woolf Barnato.

COURTESY THE AUTOCAR.

small car's nippiness on the corners'. For the first day the Racing or Sports Car Unlimited Class Race was a one lap event. On the second day the same class race was of five lap's duration. In both Tom came a very close second to the Type 37A Bugatti of Roger's. The gap was less than one second a lap on both occasions. In the last event of the second day, the Class Fifteen, five lap Handicap Race, THE AUTOCAR informed its readership *'In the last race Thistlethwayte whose big car was at a disadvantage on the corners when the field was all bunched (up) had the misfortune to damage a piston in the engine of his beloved Mercedes'*. The second day was declared to have been even better than the previous one – except for Tom!

And that was that for one Tom or Scrap Thistlethwayte's motor racing career. He had an entry for the Irish Grand Prix (18-19th July) but scratched. There was also an entry for the next year's 1931 Southport 100 Mile Sand Race (June), but once again he did not show. It was reported *'…the failure to appear of Thistlethwayte on the big Mercedes car … being the cause of much disappointment'*.

Over the years a number of the motor racing fraternity played about with speed boats. Perhaps of this genre Kaye Don was the most famous, but Barnato, Birkin and George Eyston also seriously messed about in the water. Their involvement was probably an attempt to replicate the thrills and spills of motor racing. On a restricted and smaller scale Tom also indulged himself with some power boating. For instance on 17th May 1930 he was in the lists for national endurance race for *The Yachting World Challenge Cup*. This scratch event was to be staged in Poole Harbour over a distance of a 100 nautical miles, each circuit being of four miles. It is amazing to read how many of the car racing fraternity were involved in both the competition and the organisation. Familiar names such as Lord Howe, who was the Judge, and 'Bertie' Kensington Moir, who was in charge of the refuelling arrangements. Apart from Miss Carstairs, some of the competitors were also recognisable with names including Sir Henry Segrave and the Hon. Mrs Victor Bruce, with her husband as the riding mechanic, in the outboards up to 350cc Class. Tom was listed in a 14 ft Speedcraft, powered by an outboard, in the 500-1000cc Class. He was not detailed as a finisher.

Fellow Competitors.

(JOEL) WOOLF 'BABE' BARNATO (1895-1948). Well, where do we start? At the beginning, where else? Woolf's father was Barnett or Barney Isaacs, later to be known as Barney Barnato. He was born in 1852, in an East End slum, to a Jewish father, who owned a second-hand clothing store. As a young man, he and his older brother, Harry, made their living as dance hall entertainers, street musicians, conjurors and jugglers. Barney was also an excellent prize fighter. In 1871 Harry decided to swap the squalid streets of East London for the burgeoning diamond fields of Africa. He was a penniless immigrant, armed only with some stage props and grease paint. Barney joined him in 1873, travelling out 'steerage' on the *SS Anglia*. He carried with him £30 and a stash of 40 boxes of mouldy cigars. The latter were to be traded on a 50/50 profit split, with his brother-in-law, Joel.

Initially, the brothers were to keep body and soul together as entertainers but, in time, Barney became a very successful 'kopje walloper'. The latter term described an 'above ground

THE FORGOTTEN BENTLEY BOY.

November, 1925 — MOTOR SPORT — 159

MOTORING SPORTSMEN.

Mr. Woolf Barnato.

By THE EDITOR.

PROBABLY few men in the world have such opportunities of judging the merits of the world's best cars as Mr. Woolf Barnato, who has recounted some of his views and experiences for inclusion in our popular series of "Motoring Sportsmen," his name being particularly prominent in the motor world at the present time as having shared with Capt. John Duff the honour of capturing the 24 Hours' Record for Great Britain, as recorded by Capt. Duff himself in another part of this issue.

Like so many other prominent motorists, Woolf Barnato started his motoring career with a motor-cycle, but made his acquaintance with four wheelers at the early age of 15 years, when he volunteered to try his 'prentice hand on a two-cylinder Renault car belonging to his brother. Without any tuition, he took the wheel and drove the car through the crowded streets of Cambridge. The first attempt finished with the car facing backwards in a shop window, and young Barnato had to exercise his persuasive powers in extricating himself from the consequences of driving without a car license, being too young to possess one at the time.

On leaving Charterhouse, Woolf Barnato went to Trinity Hall, Cambridge, where he studied for the Bar and was well on with his course when War was declared. Mr. Woolf Barnato joined up with the Royal Field Artillery as a first lieutenant and spent some time in the Ypres Salient (1915), afterwards serving in Palestine on various parts of that front from Gaza to the Jordan Valley.

Though he had motored for many years, Woolf Barnato did not fully appreciate the fascination of real speed until he chanced to notice a sporty-looking Calthorpe when walking down Euston Road one day. The particular car had been built specially for hill-climbing events before the War, but had not actually been used, so it was purchased with the idea of using it as a quick runabout. In 1919 the Calthorpe was entered in the speed trials at Southend, thus Mr. Barnato made his first appearance as a racing motorist.

The next development was when staying with a keen motoring friend, it was suggested that the Calthorpe should be entered for a race at Brooklands, this being done by telegram on the spur of the moment. For a couple of days prior to the race Woolf Barnato did what tuning was possible on the machine, though he had not the remotest idea what it could do in the way of maximum speed. The event was a Private Competitors' Race and to his own and everyone else's astonishment, the Calthorpe romped home an easy winner, with the length of the Finishing Straight in hand at the average speed of 60 miles per hour.

After that the Calthorpe was sent to the works and hotted up, with the result that it put on another 9 m.p.h. and won several other races, until it eventually retired from active service with many successes to its credit.

At first Mr. Barnato took to motor racing merely as a new kind of amusement, without any serious intention of developing his natural ability in this branch of sport; but like so many others he became an enthusiast, and from that time has raced very many of his own cars, besides taking part in numerous speed events and hill climbs.

A very fine collection of cups, medals and other trophies in Mr. Barnato's possession bear witness to his prowess at the wheel, though his modesty prevented more than a passing reference to the events in which they were won.

Among other cars owned and raced by Mr. Barnato are: a Wolseley, Austro-Daimler, Locomobile, the Talbot originally owned by Percy Lambert, and another smaller Talbot which is still used as a hack. His Wolseley Ten, specially built to his order, ran with some success at Brooklands and lapped at 91.6 miles per hour, a very useful average for a car of its limited engine capacity, and was incidentally faster than any other Wolseley Ten at that time or since.

Last year, it will be remembered, Mr. Barnato attacked and broke several records in the 8 litre class, including all distances up to 500 Kilometres, the Three Hours and the 300 Miles, the speeds averaging out at 92¾ miles per hour, which was an excellent performance considering the car was a standard tourer with a sports body. The chassis happened to be a Hispano-Suiza and now, having retired from the track, is used for touring purposes.

Considering Mr. Barnato's skill as a fast driver and a clever exponent of track as well as road racing, it may be wondered why he has not come more prominently to the front in the ranks of racing men; but the explanation is quite simple, for this gifted amateur recognises that real success can only come as the result of consistent practice, for which he cannot spare the time. In other words, he realises that the best car which money can buy is only one factor in racing, the other being a driver who is able to spend undivided attention on the track in order to secure the best results.

At the same time, however, Mr. Barnato appreciates the benefit of motor racing as a recreation, finding it a healthy and invigorating pastime. Besides racing, he makes a hobby of buying sporting cars of all kinds and of studying their individual characteristics from the viewpoint of an owner-driver. As a matter of fact, there are many men in the trade who might well envy Mr. Barnato's knowledge of various makes of cars. At this point it is interesting to note that he considers the Boulogne type of Hispano-Suiza one of the finest sports cars on the road and describes the new "Big Bentley" as the finest car yet produced, a remarkable tribute

---

160 — MOTOR SPORT — *November, 1925*

MOTORING SPORTSMEN—continued.

from such a connoisseur, whose opinions are unfettered in any way.

With his opportunities of sampling all the best cars in the world, it is not surprising to find that Mr. Barnato has a very considerable selection in his private garage at Lingfield, where there is accommodation for twelve cars. At the present time he owns a very fine Rolls-Royce saloon, a Hispano-Suiza sporting tourer, a 3 litre Sunbeam, a 3 litre Bentley, a 2 litre Bugatti racer and a Wolseley Ten racer, as well as various other hack cars, including the ubiquitous Ford.

Mr. Barnato's sporting character is exemplified by the readiness with which he lent his assistance to Capt. Duff in the recent Twenty-four Hours record in

MR. WOOLF BARNATO IS WELL-KNOWN FOR HIS SKILL IN MOTOR BOAT RACING.

answer to a telephone request, and though able to enjoy the good things of this life he keeps himself hard enough to endure a physical test which would try many athletes and took his turns at the wheel of the speedy Bentley without a moment's anxiety.

This, perhaps, is a matter for no great astonishment in view of the fact that Mr. Barnato is a rather useful heavyweight boxer, plays cricket with the lads of his village, hunts with the Old Surrey and Burstow, besides being a keen golfer and tennis player.

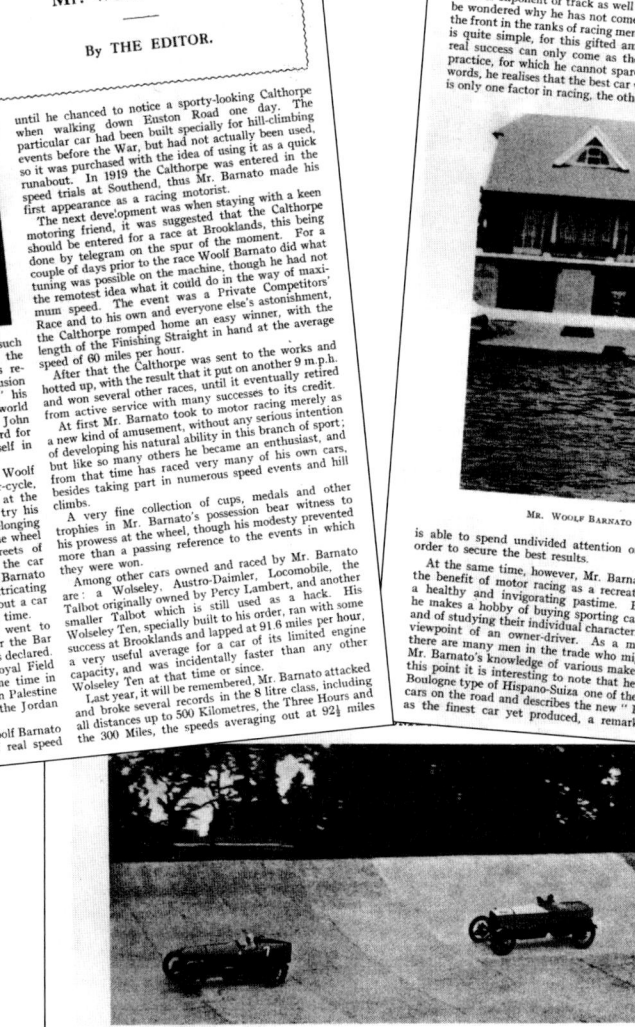

Where motors are concerned, he is equally at home on land and water and takes a keen interest in motor boating, owning two very fast racing boats, one being a 3 litre Saunders hulled Wolseley, capable of 32 knots,

MR. WOOLF BARNATO ON HIS BUGATTI AT BROOKLANDS.

and the other a 1½ litre Saunders Sunbeam with a speed of 40 knots. This year he won the Duke of York's Trophy on the Thames and has many continental successes to his credit.

Speaking of motor boat racing, Mr. Barnato described some very interesting details about cornering on the water and explained how a good helmsman could cause his craft to execute a double skid, so as to cut round the buoys without loss of way, much in the same manner adopted by road racing motorists.

He appreciates the opportunities presented by Brooklands as a training ground for beginners and as a venue for races, but considers that the possibilities of the Track should be developed not only for racing but to provide more of a social rendezvous than is the case at present.

In a brief review it is impossible to do justice to the attainments of this very versatile sportsmen, and we join our readers in the hope of seeing him at the wheel in further record breaking runs as well as in next season's races.

THE 33/140 H.P. SUPERCHARGED MERCÉDÈS SALOON.

Plate 115.

COURTESY MOTOR SPORT.

216

operator' who bought uncut, recently dug diamonds, straight from the miners. Trading fairly, he became well established and trusted. In 1883 Barney gambled on sinking the first ever underground shaft. That was as distinct from the then to-date accepted method of open cast digging to obtain the spoils. He and his family formed the Barnato Diamond Mining Company and gained a dominant position in the huge and immensely profitable Kimberley Mine. This was followed by a titanic struggle with the De Beers Mining Company for control of the total diamond output. De Beers were headed by wily (and devious) Cecil Rhodes, backed by the Rothschild Bank, London. After a long and dirty fight, the two companies merged, in 1888, as De Beers Consolidated Mines. Barney became a major shareholder and one of the richest men in the world. An eccentric to the end, prior to returning for the last time to dear old 'Blighty', he returned to the Music Halls and acted in various amateur dramatics. In 1897 he and the family were aboard the *Liner Scot,* bound for Southampton, when Barney died in extremely mysterious circumstances, falling or being pushed overboard. What a way to make your last stage exit! Incidentally, all sorts of conspiratorial suggestions in respect of the incident were put forward. On the other hand, for some time it was without doubt that he had been both depressed and drinking rather too much.

Woolf, or Babe, as he was affectionately known, was two years old at the time of his father's death. For such an unconventional man, his early life was almost staid and run-of-the-mill – that is a moneyed run-of-the-mill early life. Education at Charterhouse School was followed by Trinity Hall, Cambridge, after which WW1 hove into view. He did his duty, gaining the rank of Captain. As early as 1915 and aged 20, he married Dorothy Maitland Falk, the daughter of an American Wall Street stockbroker. Woolf later said he was 19 (but what's in a year and he was nigh on 20) and that after a short honeymoon he sailed off to join the Royal Artillery – or Engineers, in France. He later served in The Palestine. His wife was described by Woolf as being a home-loving, family girl from a simple, small, New York adjacent community. That did not really square with her father being a Wall Street stockbroker, except for the New York adjacent bit. An interested party, who might have wished to diminish Dorothy and her character, advised she was a pretty American with a flawless complexion.

Woolf and Dorothy's first child, Virginia, was born towards the end of 1916. So 'Daddy' came home, on leave, to find an established, settled family living at No. 39 Elsworthy Road, Primrose Hill, Hampstead. Their second daughter, Diana, was born early in 1918. Post war and 'demobed', first things first. Woolf had a score to settle with his two cousins, 'Solly' and Jack (known as Isaac) Joel. They were the sons of (Woolf's father) Barney Barnato's Sister Kate, who had married a Joel. Still with me?

In line with the terms of his father's will, Woolf became a partner in the London based family firm of Barnato Brothers, in 1917. He had received a sum of £250,000 and a further £274,000, but on joining the business found that the 1897 capital of £8,885,000 had all but evaporated. Not unnaturally he wanted explanations and accounts, none of which were forthcoming. Accordingly, in 1919, a summons was issued to uncover the truth, with (Joel) Woolf listed as the plaintiff. (A note here to explain that Woolf later had his first Christian name, Joel, expunged, by law, and thank goodness for that!). In hindsight, his appointment of *The* Norman Birkett as his QC was fortuitous. The case was won in 1924 and settled in

Plate 116. "My first love, Woolf Barnato, whom we called Babe." – June Tripp.

CAPTION AND PHOTOGRAPH COURTESY JUNE, THE GLASS LADDER, AN AUTOBIOGRAPHY. HEINEMANN.

1925, for a sum not unadjacent to £1,000,000 plus costs – and that was when a million was a million! Despite all this, he was still pursuing the legal costs and interest thereon, as late as 1928. Incidentally, regardless of all this meaningful family infighting, his closest friends, with whom he socialised and partied big time, on his return from the 'wars', were – the Joels. That's Jewish families for you. And party, they did. One of their favourite watering holes, for late night entertainment, was *The Embassy Club*.

Unfortunately for the Woolf Barnato marriage, a performer at this club, in 1920, was one June Howard Trip (1901-1985), a star of stage and screen. Her mother and father were 'of the stage' and mother moved heaven and earth to have her daughter become a top class dancer. Noel Coward was one of her early fellow students, to drop one name in the pool. Later she was taken on as a pupil of the legendary Anna Pavlova. As she had the necessary talent, it was widely expected that June would become a top ballet dancer. Unfortunately, the lack of money, any money in her family, resulted in her having to abandon those high-flown aspirations. She had to settle for a more populist form of the art of dancing, appearing in a Paris Folies Bergere Review, at the tender age of 13. By 1920, June was part of the glittering West End world of the great impresario, CB Cochrane. She was to spend a decade performing in London and Paris shows, making entrances and exits at various smart, society clubs, as well as taking part in a number of films. Despite sounding very glamourous and chic, her chosen profession often meant her having to make as many as two or three separate appearances, in any 24 hour period. This frantic effort was mainly necessary to keep herself and her family from destitution.

But back to *The Embassy Club*. Here June was introduced to the extended Barnato and Joel set, one fateful evening early in 1920. Apart from Woolf (call me Babe), who was *'a somewhat swarthy, extremely good looking, tall but compact young blade with a mischievous smile'* and the various Joels, in amongst the crowd was a 'Dot'. June assumed she was the widow of an oft referred too, recently 'war deceased' brother of Babes'. Also present might well be the latter's mother, Fanny, and Sister Leah. If the party showed signs of having 'legs', 'Dot', who did not drink or smoke, would excuse herself, advising she was both tired and off home to bed. The party would jolly-on. To a fairly impressionable, very young June, Babe must have been irresistible. Now aged 26, he hunted with the North Bucks Whaddon Chase, played a good round of golf at Sunningdale, plucked the ukulele, raced a Bugatti at the Brooklands circuit and had boxed at University. As a result of the latter prowess he was a member of the International Club, the Monday night boxing bouts of which were famed.

One *Embassy Club* night a girl friend, close to the Barnato and Joel party, pointed out to June exactly whom 'Dot' was. That she was Babes' wife, who was infatuated with him and conversely that Babe was infatuated with June. The 'old' eternal love triangle. Allegedly, June fled the scene – never to speak to Babe again, ever. However, love will out and she was persuaded of 'this and that' and that he had already pleaded for a divorce, and more of the same, much more. Of course, at some stage, there has to be a point of no return and that was quickly sped past. To be fair to Woolf, a case before the Probate, Divorce and Admiralty Division (why … and Admiralty? What on earth has the navy got to do with Probate and ….?) sheds much more light on the whole affair. On 18th July 1922, Barnato v Barnato was down for judgment. His Lordship pronounced a decree of the restitution of conjugal rights,

Plate 117a. June watches Babe Barnato at work on one of his cars at Brooklands. It was more than likely one of the Bertelli's

COURTESY THE NATIONAL MOTOR MUSEUM.
JUNE, THE GLASS LADDER, AN AUTOBIOGRAPHY. HEINEMANN.

Plate 117b. Jack Barclay, 'one of the best salesmen to top people' and June who, when this photograph was taken, was Lady Inverclyde, wife to the heir to the Cunard Shipping Line. The car is the 4.5 litre Bentley (Reg. No. YW 5758) which won the 1929 Brooklands 500 Mile Race with Frank Clement and Jack Barclay aboard. It was originally Humphrey Cook's vehicle in which he achieved a seventh place in the 1928 TT Race. In 1929 it was retired from the Double Twelve (Clement and Cook) and gained a third in the Six Hour Race (Cook and Callingham).

COURTESY AN ILLUSTRATED HISTORY OF THE BENTLEY, WO BENTLEY.
GEORGE ALLEN & UNWIN.

in respect of the petition of Dorothy Maitland Barnato against Mr Woolf (Joel) Barnato, son of the late Mr Barney (Barnett) Barnato. The suit was undefended. In the pleading Dorothy advised that they had lived happily together until October 1920, after which matters were not right and she heard of another female being involved. When she challenged her husband, he became angry and would not promise to give up the 'other' woman. The 'lady in question' was, of course, none other than June. In October 1921 Woolf left the family home, never to return. And this despite a very moving, despairing letter from Dorothy, which only elicited a curt response from her husband. In this he argued that the marriage was over and that divorce was not only inevitable but morally the right course of action, in the circumstances. Incidentally, his Lordship's decree had to be obeyed within fourteen days, with costs! But how do you make the unwilling go to bed?

Despite many of the Bentley Boys, and no one more so than Babe, appearing to be persistent and unrepentant womanizers and although June was allegedly referred to as *'that infamous actress'*, their love affair went on through thick and thin for a number of years. And this in spite of June's sometimes life-threatening illness's and their continued time apart. The separations were mainly due to June having to earn a living, in order to keep her family in funds. She declared she was happy to receive gifts, furs and jewellery, but would not be a 'kept' woman, in the accepted sense of the word. Be that as it may, throughout the affair, she continued to work, mainly as a very successful actress, appearing in many West End shows. In the meantime, Dorothy at first decided to play the long game and refused to divorce Woolf. She was of the belief that if he were unable to remarry, the affair would fizzle out. Unfortunately for the family she was correct but her forecast was only to come about – long after she had given up the unequal struggle and any hope of reconciliation. An interesting, character-revealing aside is that June maintained that she was constantly advised that Woolf's wife kept up her refusal to divorce Babe, for some five or six years (until 1927). Perhaps she was not a reader of the more heavyweight newspapers of the day. Had she so been, she would have been able to call Woolf's bluff anytime after April 1923. To be exact, after 19th April 1923. For on that day the undefended suit was presented in the High Court for Mrs Dorothy Maitland Barnato to achieve the dissolution of her marriage, consequent to the failure of her petition to have her conjugal rights restored and in the light of his admitted adultery. Woolf made life easy for the legal process by advising at which hotel he would be resident to commit the adultery and when. To assist in the matter, the chambermaid testified to finding a toothbrush, on which was engraved his name, and the hotel proprietor agreed that the guest was indeed the defendant and that the woman who accompanied him was other than the Mrs Barnato. Job done, mission accomplished.

For a time, during the years 1923 and 1924, June often accompanied Woolf to the Brooklands Race circuit. Here she met the likes of Malcolm Campbell, HOD Segrave and 'Tommy' Parry Thomas. Some two years after they met, Woolf purchased Ardenrun in Lingfield, Surrey. It was a pseudo Georgian 'pile' in the style of 'late grotesque'. It had been constructed about twenty years previously and had been the country 'palace' of one of the Konig family – very successful London bankers. Apart from a huge snooker room and plant-filled conservatory, there was a massive organ and a Minstrels Gallery, the whole being set in about 350 acres. Not content to leave well alone, he ripped out the cellar, within which was

Plate 118a.   Barnato rounding a mark in *Ardenrun*, close by Hythe in August 1923.
COURTESY THE MOTOR.

Plate 118b.   Barnato at the helm in 1925.
COURTESY MOTOR SPORT.

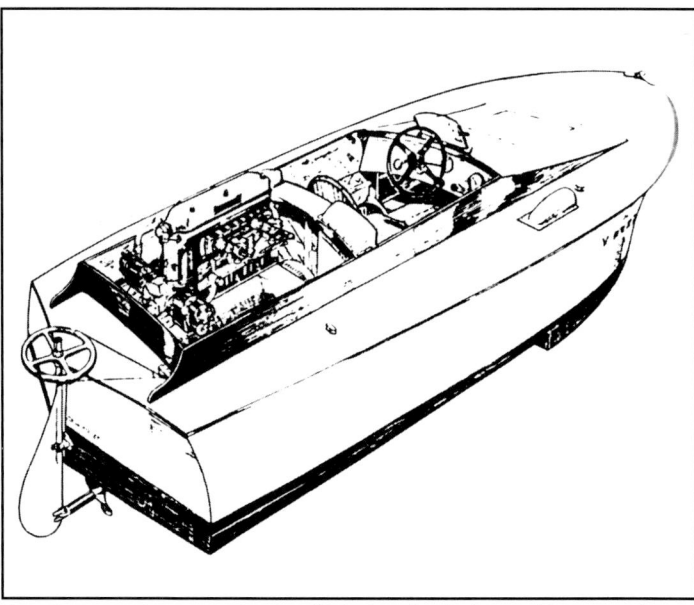

Plate 118c.   Now rather more rounded and somewhat snug in the lifejacket, in *Ardenrun V* competing in the Duke of York International Trophy over the weekend 26-27 June 1930 at Welsh Harp.
COURTESY BENTLEY FACTORY CARS 1919-1931, MICHAEL HAY. OSPREY AUTOMOTIVE.

constructed a mock *'Ardenrun Arms'*, complete with oak beams, open fireplace, Elizabethan type paned glass windows, pewter mugs beer mats and bar cloth's. In addition, the main and back-of-house driveways were adapted to form part of an impromptu, high-spirited race circuit which was pressed into action, often after riotous partying. Woolf added a further 650 acres to the original holding.

The onset of the slow but steady decline in Woolf and June's relationship probably dated to the time when she appeared in the new musical *Toni*. In this she starred opposite the then renowned lady's man, Jack Buchanan. The climax of the show was a long kiss between them, as the final curtain came down. Woolf was in the audience and was of the opinion that this kiss was no stage-driven matter. And surely there was no one better able to pass judgment than our stage-door, motor racing hero! Matters romantic between them were never quite the same again. There was no sudden, abrupt end to their affair, more a slow decline. They both had conflicting interests and obligations and their separations became longer and longer. By the time Woolf decided to admit a divorce had finally came through, it was too late to save the romance. By 1927 it was all over. An aside, made by a shrewd observer, was that most of his conquests came from the stage door or film world – not really the place to meet a 'nice girl'.

Residence at Ardenrun resulted in Woolf hunting with the Old Surrey Barstow Foxhounds. Between 1928 and 1930, he also played six first class matches for Surrey Cricket Club, all but two of them against Cambridge and Oxford University's. His main forte was as a wicket keeper, taking 19 catches and making one stumping. Despite scoring few runs (highest score seven and an average of 3.28), I am surprised in amongst the motor racing and Bentley duties that he had any time left to contemplate playing cricket. Having created an area of practice nets in the grounds, in 1930 he acted as host to the Surrey County Cricket team, including such luminaries as Percy Fender and Jack Hobbs, as well as the whole Australian touring team, then led by Don Bradman. Apart from cricket, Babe was reputed to be a superb shot, a good tennis player and skier, was still sparring as a member of the Fitzroy Lodge Boxing Club, and was an excellent golfer. In respect of the latter sport, his favourite companion and friend was Dale Bourne, who won the English Championship in 1930 and was in the final of the British Amateur event.

If all this sporting ability was not quite 'sickening' enough, 'blow me down' if he was not, over the years, consistently involved in power boat racing. Certainly Tim Birkin kept a craft at Blakeney, Norfolk and was detailed as purchasing a supercharged AC motor car engine to fit into a high speed boat. Mention has already been made of the CW Burnard owned Walton-on-Thames Launch Works, close by Brooklands Circuit. Apart from Birkin being a client of this firm, his father is reputed to have had a craft with the soubriquet *'Frothblower'*. Tom Thistlethwayte dabbled, but in smaller, outboard powered craft, but only after his motor racing days were over. Glen Kidston had a power boat or two, as evidenced in the 'tale of the bride's trousseau' and the 1930, Riviera, month long jolly. George Eyston was a very serious player for a time but Woolf had an even longer history of motor boat racing. In 1923 he was recorded as entering in the 15th Monte Carlo Motor Boat Racing Fortnight (April), at the helm of his Saunders hull, Wolseley engine powered craft, *'Ardenrun'*. Another reference of that year was to his competing in a Royal Motor Yacht Club Regatta (August) at Hythe,

Plate 119a. The place – Ardenrun outbuildings. The car – the Bertelli. From the right Bert Bertelli, then Douglas and, at the bonnet, Barnato. On the left, hovering over the cockpit is Bert's brother, the bodybuilder, Harry.

PLATES 119A & B COURTESY ASTON MARTIN 1913-1947. INMAN HUNTER. OSPREY AUTOMOTIVE.

Plate 119b. Two Bertellis on show at Ardenrun with, from the left, Barnato, Bert Bertelli and Douglas. Incidentally, quite a pagoda!

Southampton, again in *'Ardenrun'*. He won that 12 mile race, at an average speed of 27 knots. The engine was detailed as being very similar to that fitted to the 15 hp Wolseley car. In September he competed in the British Motor Boat Club event at Burnham-on-Crouch where he won his scratch class, beating home a boat named *'Mr Poo'*! The article quaintly concludes that the crowded state of the roads was leading to a number of motorists taking up the 'sister' pastime of marine motoring! Nothing new there then! For 1924 he raced a 1.5 litre Sunbeam engine powered craft, *'Ardenrun 11'*. On the fifth lap of the annual Duke of York's International Trophy (July), staged in Tor Bay, he was reported to have struck a submerged object. Also competing in that event was one Marquis de Casa Maury, representing the French nation (despite being of Cuban origins) and to feature in Woolf's restructuring of Bentley's (*See* Chapter 4). Perhaps Barnato and Maury's relationship was founded on their powerboat endeavours? In 1925, in one of the heats for the final of the Duke of York Trophy Race, held on the Thames, between Mortlake and Putney, he was reported as *'…having come in second to Eyston, despite having to hold his hand over a leak in a pipe for the whole race'*! He won the final ahead of George Eyston who was helming *'Miss Olga'*. Miss Betty Carstairs was also an entrant in this race but would appear not to have survived all the heats. In June 1926 he was once again entered in the same event, now in *'Ardenrun Minor'*. He only managed a third and did not go forward to compete in his craft in the international final. However that was not to see the end of Woolf's involvement in that race, for in the actual event he helmed the craft of one of the selected finalist's, namely *'Newg'* owned by Miss Betty Carstairs. He achieved an easy line finish. In 1930 he competed in the Duke of York International Gold Cup Trophy Race (26th June), which that year was held on the Welsh Harp Reservoir (now named Brent Reservoir and fairly close by Wembley Stadium). He was now helming *'Ardenrun V'*, built by Saunders Roe and powered by a 3 litre Bentley engine. The craft sunk in practice, was finally fished out some seven hours later and the engine quickly overhauled at the nearby Cricklewood Bentley works. But to no avail as the unit dropped a valve in the race. Quaintly, he advised the waiting press he was not going to take up the sport seriously! Well, it had taken him at least seven years to come to that conclusion! But this was the year in which he retired from competing in all engine powered sports.

Woolf Barnato's involvement with Bentley is well documented and recorded but it was not his first attempt at car manufacture. In 1923, the firm of Allday & Onions was in money troubles. They were the owners of Enfield-Allday, which company had constructed a successful 'production' and competition car. The lack of money left the Chief Engineer, Augustus Cesare Bertelli (aka Bert!) out of a job. Incidentally, his brother Enrico (aka Harry) had designed the bodywork of the said car. The year before, in 1922, Woolf had raced an Enfield-Allday in the Brooklands 200 Mile Race, but had to retire with engine trouble. Knowing and liking the 'man and the car', he stepped into the financial breach. A new company was formed, Bertelli Ltd, with the £100 share capital. This was split 50 shares to 'Bert', 30 to Woolf and 20 to a Capt. JC Douglas. 'Bert' thought the plan was to build a production car, but Woolf probably had other ideas. Three Enfield-Allday derivatives (*Bertelli's*) were built at Barnato's recently acquired Ardenrun Mansion, where garaging and workshops were made available. 'Bert' originally lodged at Ardenrun. It is an interesting aside that he had to find alternative digs, due to the late night-time parties and show girl activities.

Plate 120a. Ardenrun House, Lingfield, Surrey
PLATES 120A, B, C & D COURTESY JOHN KONIG ARCHIVE.

Plate 120b. The Games Room.

Plate 120c. Ardenrun's impressive interior.

Plate 120d. The Conservatory.

There's a surprise!

In 1923 the three 'Bertelli' competition cars were entered in the Saturday 13th October Brooklands 200 Mile Race. Barnato, Bertelli and Douglas were nominated drivers and they all went well in practice. Despite this, all three engines failed in the race. They were, rather unusually for the time, sleeve valve units. I think, as far as Woolf was concerned, that was the end of the Bertelli Company. On the other hand, he blamed the election of the first ever Labour Government, led by Ramsey MacDonald, on 21st January 1924, as being the reason for him catching the first liner possible, for the USA. He let it be known he was of the opinion that it was citizens of his ilk who would be taxed out of existence (There is a familiar ring to that statement, even some eighty years on!). However, this sudden departure was without a by-your-leave to the other directors, or any financial arrangements in place, to support the new business. 'Bert' Bertelli was not best pleased. In fact he was very miffed, to say the least. But this would not be the last time that Woolf Barnato would be accused of taking the 'the liner way out' from a company's financial problems. Oh no! As it happened, this was not to be a very long absence. He was once again competing on the track, no later in the year than the 1924 Brooklands Easter Race meeting. He won a handicap event in his faithful Wolseley Moth II.

It is of interest, if outside the scope of this book, that later in 1924 'Bert' Bertelli 'chummed up' with a William Renwick. They formed Renwick & Bertelli Ltd. to manufacture car engine power units. In 1926 this company, with more directors on board, formed another company, Aston Martin Motors. This was to take over the assets of the recently liquidated business that had been producing Aston Martin cars.

There is little solid evidence in respect of Barnato being gainfully employed. In fact it has always been assumed he operated in the commodity markets and traded in the family's basic interest – diamonds. He certainly shared an Albermarle Street office, over the years, with his relative Stanhope Joel (son of Solly Joel). It might have become a little crowded at times, as he had at least two financial advisors and a business manager. Without doubt, his admitted weekly spend of between £800 and £900 per week, on the necessary luxuries of life, required a constant deluge of pennies to be accumulating, at a very steady rate. This was the more so if it is considered that he would appear not to have depleted that which he had originally inherited, at the time of his demise. The necessary luxuries? Well, these included maintaining and running Ardenrun House, the 'party centre' of Surrey, as well as the Grosvenor Square residence, located beside the south-east side, in what was known as *'Bentley Corner'*. The latter nomenclature was due to a number of like-minded individuals such as Glen Kidston, Bernard Rubin and Tiger Tim Birkin, also having side-by-side abodes at that location. In addition there were his motor cars, power boats and racing expenses as well as, to a lesser extent, his other sporting activities. It is always difficult to translate various cost figures of the 1920s period to modern day terms. It very much depends on which multiplier is used. As at 2007, if the Retail Price Index is utilised, then the accepted multiple is 30. On the other hand, if the average manual wage figures is employed, then the multiple is around 100! Depending on which is chosen, then the current day figures, in respect of the £800/900 a week would be either £30,000 or £80,000 per week. Take your pick.

Without doubt, he made one pivotal decision in his amazing, very hedonistic and hectic

Plate 121. Woolf Barnato and his 'new' second wife Jackie. They are pictured arriving back at Southampton, aboard the *Empress of Britain*, at the end of a reportedly ten thousand mile honeymoon driving around the USA.

COURTESY RADIO TIMES HULTON LIBRARY.

life that assured his place in the 'Giants' of the 1920s, let alone the eternal pantheon of the motor racing 'Great's'. It was his resolution to ignore the pleadings of his financial advisors and his subsequent investment in Bentley Motors. The accountants, to a man, counselled him not to get entangled, as it would cost him a lot of money. And boy were they right! Mind you, it did not require massive intelligence or a 'First' in economics to take such a jaundiced view. At the time of his effective take-over, Bentley's trade debts were about £75,000 and there was a mortgage of £40,000. And that was as a starter, for a hundred and fifteen thousand pounds! Without his action, Bentley Motors would have plunged into receivership, in 1926. The motoring world would probably never have experienced the joys of the 4.5 litre, the 4.5 litre supercharged, the 6.5 litre, the Speed Six or the 8 litre Bentley models. Furthermore motor racing history would not have included the 'Bentley shaking' events of the years 1926 through to 1930. There's a thought or three. Taking a cross-section of the pundits, it is estimated that the final bill to his wallet, including the final year's funding the company out of his own 'pocket', was some £150,00 to £200,000, or approximately £4.5/6 million (or £15/20 million) in today's 'groats'. Costly, but this investment assured him everlasting fame, immediate prestige and access to a social place in society that he probably would not otherwise have been able to achieve, at any cost.

His original investment in Bentley's has been covered in Chapter 4. To bring that involvement and the end of the affair to a conclusion requires further elaboration. Come his last race, in 1930, he announced that, as far as Bentley Motors Ltd., was concerned, *'there would be no more money in, but no money out'*. In truth, this statement, combined with the recent Stock Market crash and the onset of the World Wide depression, spelt the death knell for Bentley's. But it was to be a rather protracted, labyrinthine, lingering demise. First, exploratory negotiations with Rolls-Royce to acquire Bentley, as a going-concern, came to naught. Subsequently, the first mortgage holder, London Life Association did not instigate High Court proceedings, to recover interest and principal, due on its first mortgage of £65,000, until 11th July 1931. The action was against both Bentley Motors Ltd. and Woolf Barnato, the latter in effect declining to assist. The inevitable appointment of a receiver followed. But even that was not the end of the machinations. A possible purchaser appeared in the guise of D Napier & Son of Acton. Earlier in the century they had manufactured one of the finest motor cars in the world. This option was very much favoured by WO Bentley and most of his associates and staff. It must have been encouraging that an announcement appeared in the August issue of one of the motoring magazines advising that Napier's and the Receiver were in talks. This was followed by heads of agreement and more November press statements. The only caveat appeared to be that Napier's were not paying enough money. However, not for the first time in his life, Woolf appears to have had a different agenda. Unbeknown to most, parallel negotiations had been going on with Rolls-Royce, in which company he had all ready purchased a significant tranche of shares. In the end, Rolls-Royce triumphed and he became a director of the new company, Bentley Motors (1931) Ltd. Well, well! Machiavellian, or what?

One other matter that requires some clarification is the suggestion that he had 'ducked' the receivership issue, by 'liner'ing off' to the USA, prior to and during the London Life High Court hearing. This was probably a slur and inaccurate. He certainly gave an interview to an

Plate 122a.   Clement in EXP No. 2 in front of Barnato in his Locomobile at Brooklands in 1921.

COURTESY BENTLEY PAST AND PRESENT. RIVERS FLETCHER. GENTRY BOOKS.

Plate 122b.   Barnato's Wolseley Moth II in which he achieved a number of successes during 1923 and 1924 at Brooklands. The racer was based on the Wolseley Ten and its 1260cc, 4 cylinder engine with overhead camshaft.

COURTESY BROOKLANDS THE COMPLETE MOTOR RACING HISTORY. WILLIAM BODDY. MRP.

English daily 'blat', the day before the legal action commenced. During the dialogue he explained his reasons for ceasing to support Bentley's. A decision he explained that had to be made, more especially in the light of the current world state of affairs and the inability of the Company to produce an economy model, rather than luxury cars. He did sail away at the end of August, some say in pursuit of a new wife. If this was his admirable objective, he achieved the same, in 1932, when he married a Jackie Claridge, the daughter of a Californian coal magnate. This union was to follow a familiar, almost depressingly predictable pattern. The possible onset of WW2, coupled with some Woolf transgressions of an 'emotional nature', resulted in our 'all American girl' returning home to the 'good old' USA. He did not make very much of an effort to patch things up. No surprise there then!

Prior to moving on to the really interesting matter of outlining his motor racing career, it might not go amiss to comment upon some of his apparently contradictory characteristics. Despite his undoubted abundance of riches, it became accepted 'folklore' that he was ruthless and in 'matters financial' he was hard and mean, in addition to having short arms and long pockets. Apart from the usual habit of immoderately wealthy people to look after the pennies and spend the pounds sterling, the facts do not entirely stack up. WO not only described him as the finest racing driver Bentley ever had, if not the finest British driver of the time, he also reported that he was a perfect team man, always following instructions. Moreover, he was often asked to drive the 'not so good' car, due to his superior skills which could elicit more performance from less. And all this despite the fact that he owned not only the Company, but probably, in his own name, at the time of any particular race, most or all of the racing cars on the grid! Furthermore, had he been a totally ruthless, money motivated man he would not have ensured Bentley produced the necessary number of supercharged 4.5 litre cars, for sale to the public, so that they could be homologated. But for this unnecessary expense and inconvenience, Tiger Tim Birkin would not have been able to enter a team of 'Blower' 4.5 litre Bentleys in the 1930 Le Mans, for which homologisation was a prerequisite. Lastly, whatever part he had played in the scheming of Rolls-Royce winning out in the acquisition of Bentley Motors, after the closure he paid out of his own (long?) pocket, every bench-hand a week's extra money and every staff member an additional month's pay. If this were not sufficient evidence to destroy the suggestion of his being financially tight-fisted, who paid for all the Ardenrun goings-on? Certainly not the glad-handing free-loaders who were hardly 'forced' to attend the year in, year out party-time. Mean or what?

The first mention I have uncovered of his simply great racing career was the 1919 Essex Motor Club Speed Trial (23rd July) on the sea-front at Westcliff-on-Sea. He was listed as driving his reputably bright yellow, pre WW1, single seater, 10 hp Calthorpe. Interestingly, another amongst the competitors at this meeting was none other than Malcolm Campbell. It has been reported Barnato performed and had a first place at a 1920 Whitsun Brooklands Race meeting, but I cannot vouchsafe this.

Without doubt he was present at the 1921 Essex Motor Club and Southend & District AC Speed Trials, again at Westcliff-on-Sea. He also competed at the March Brooklands Race meeting, entering his newly acquired 8 litre, 6 cylinder Locomobile. He imported this from the USA and had a two seater body fitted. Also present at this meeting were some eye-watering players such as Count Zborowski, Tim Birkin, Raymond Mays, HOD Segrave and

Plate 123a.   Barnato's first 3 litre Speed Model Bentley fitted with a two seater Jarvis body and bearing 'Trade Plates'. The location is the Cricklewood Bentley Works yard.

COURTESY BENTLEY FACTORY CARS 1919-1931, MICHAEL HAY. OSPREY AUTOMOTIVE.

Plate 123b. The Jarvis bodied 3 litre `Bentley with Barnato's mechanic, Leslie Pennel, in the driving seat.

COURTESY THE OTHER BENTLEY BOYS, ELIZABETH NAGLE. G HARRUP & CO.

John Duff. Despite this 'shiny' purchase, Babe also raced the original Calthorpe with which he gained a first place in one of the races. It was notable and prescient that another winner was a Frank Clement at the wheel of the Bentley Motor's *Exp. No. 2*. A later Brooklands event saw him in a Dorsey-Calthorpe – a new chassis, old engine and the body now brown coloured – as well as a recently acquired Austro-Daimler. Neither was successful.

For the 1922 Essex MC Kop Hill Climb (25th March) he competed in his Hispano-Suiza. He again appeared in this car at the Essex MC and Southend & District AC Hill Climb (27th May), staged at Laindon Two Church Hill. This was a few miles south of Billericay, close to the modern day A127. In that year he purchased the ex-Campbell 2.6 litre Talbot, with which he competed at Brooklands, early in the season, but with no success. Later on, at the same venue, he had both an Ansaldo and the Talbot in action. The Ansaldo did not finish its race but he gained at least a second place, Talbot mounted. Same location, but mid-summer, he was rather successful, with the Talbot gaining a second to Zborowski (in an Aston Martin) as well as a win, and another win in the Ansaldo. Yet another Brooklands meeting saw him in action in the Talbot, which had been re-engined, supposedly with an ex-Percy Lambert*, Talbot 4¾ litre power unit, but he did not have success. I think this unit had been doing the rounds, as it were. He also entered the Brooklands 200 Mile Race meeting but did not finish.

By 1923 he owned and raced a Wolseley-Moth, a single seater known as *Moth 11*, the second of this particular 'build-plan'. Capt. Alistair Miller, the competitions manager of Wolseley Motor Company had *Moth 1*. Incidentally, Capt. Miller followed an old motor racing principle of being an officer and gentleman – with an eye for the ladies. It is noteworthy that the latter was assisted in his 1922 and 1923 endeavours to develop the Moth project by a Guy Anthony 'Tony' Vandervell. 'Tony' Vandervell, now there is a name with which to conjure. His father was CA Vandervell, who founded the CAV electrical company, based at Acton. This was sold to Lucas in 1925. He also owned RT Shelley Ltd., which took over the financially troubled Norton Motor Cycle Co., in 1913. It was rumoured that in his youth 'Tony' was somewhat wild and preferred racing to work. Who wouldn't? In 1920 and 1921 he was hill climbing in a 4¾ litre , side-valve, four seater Talbot, succeeding in notching up a few wins and places. During 1923 and 1924 he raced motorbikes, mainly Nortons, the reason for which must be obvious.** Settling down somewhat, he went to work for the family firm and had a good grounding in electrical and engineering skills, as well as business practice. His father's sale of CAV did not go down well with him and he left the business, trying his hand at this and that. By one of those quirks of fates he heard of and went to America to negotiate the rights for a 'world beating' new bearing product. Obviously by then 'chatting' to his father, the latter invested in the necessary machinery and Vandervell Products Ltd., was born. This was of course the same Tony Vandervell who pioneered Thin-

---

* Lambert was the first driver to achieve one hundred miles in the hour, in a 4¾ litre Talbot, Chassis No. 1. Many years ago I owned Chassis No 3, which John Rowley, the now deceased, but once very influential President of the VSCC purchased from me and made quite well known in his time.

** Back in the late 1950's , early 1960's my father owned a very high-class precision engineering firm and carried out quite a lot of work for Vandervell's. Knowing of my 'pere's' interest in motor bikes, and that he had been an amateur Manxman, pre-WW2, Tony Vandervell took him on a tour of the Acton cellars wherein were a number of very 'interesting' Norton Motor Bikes.

Plate 124a. Barnato's 3 litre Bentley speeding down the Railway Straight, leading Purdy's Super Sports 12/50 Alvis and 'Bobby' Morgan's Thomas Special (formerly the Aston Martin known as 'Green Pea' into which had been 'dropped' a 1.5 litre Hooker Thomas power unit) in the September 90mph Long Handicap Race at Brooklands in 1925.

Plate 124b. Barnato sharing a 3 litre Bentley with Benjafield experiencing a problem beyond the Member's Bridge in the 1927 Brooklands Six Hour Endurance Race.

PLATES 12A & B COURTESY THE MOTOR.

Plate 124c. Barnato with his first 4.5 litre Bentley, prior to the 1928 Brooklands Six Hour Race. If looks could maim!

COURTESY BENTLEY FIFTY YEARS OF THE MARQUE. J GREEN. DALTON WATSON.

wall bearings and was responsible for the Vanwall Formula One racing car, which achieved fame in the 1950s. But back to the mainstream of the narrative. At an early Brooklands Race meeting Bert Bertelli, in an Enfield-Allday, beat Barnato in *Moth 11*, whilst later in the day Woolf piped the Works car, *Moth 1*. Mid-summer and again at Brooklands, he gained a second in *Moth 11* and a third driving an Enfield-Allday. The details of the Brooklands 200 Mile Race (13th October) have already been laid bare. (*See* Chapter Six).

The year 1924 saw Babe once again at the 'tiller' of *Moth 11*, in which he achieved a win at Brooklands. Later on in the year he picked up a second to Kaye Don, and a third place. The year ended for him at Brooklands, where he took a first in one of the events.

Now to 1925. As far as I am aware, this particular year was not subject to any galactic upheavals, tectonic plate movements, unusual star bursts, unexpected Comets, solar flares, toads turning brown, a hundred day's rain or even unexpected eclipses of the Sun. There should have been. Why? Because this was the year in which the event occurred that altered the face of British car production and motor racing, from 1926 through to and including 1930. That was the year in which Woolf Barnato purchased a Jarvis bodied, two seater, 3 litre Bentley, that's why. Mind you the onset of the season did not merit any thoughts of 'Three Wise Men' setting off towards Cricklewood. Early in the year he entered his 8 litre, Boulogne model, Hispano-Suiza at Brooklands, without any fireworks. A few weeks on, same place, he appeared in the ex-Duller, 2 litre 'Indy' Type 30 Bugatti without much apparent success. However a later Brooklands meeting had him entering his newly acquired 3 litre Bentley, but once again without yet making an impression. On the other hand, he did steer the Bugatti into a third place. But he was just getting into his stride with a third place in the Bentley, a harbinger of things to come. Another meeting, another car, where he gained a third in the Bugatti. There followed a newspaper sponsored Brooklands Race in which he achieved a third in the Bentley. Towards the year end he took two more third places. Things were hotting up.

So to 1926, the year in which he effectively took over Bentley Motors. He became so busy that he only entered one event, early in the season. Even then he did not drive but had the previous owner, George Duller, race his Bugatti. George gained a first and a second place.

For Woolf, 1927 was not to prove much more active on the tracks than the previous year. He was down to race a Bentley at Le Mans but business affairs intruded. LG Callingham took his place, at the last moment. In the Brooklands Six Hour Endurance Race he shared a 3 litre Bentley with Benjafield but they went out with an engine fault. He only appeared at one other Brooklands event in which he gained a third in the Bentley. Later in the year, his chum Duller achieved a second and a third place, in the now re-bodied 3 litre Bentley. But the following year was to prove much busier on the track, very much busier.

1928 supplied a win at Brooklands and at a later meeting a second and a win, all in his 3 litre Bentley. At the Brooklands Six Hour Endurance Race (12th May) a three car Works Team of 4.5 litre Bentleys and two privately entered Bentleys were entered, but without a clean sweep, just yet. Barnato & Clement finished a comparatively lowly eighth having experienced brake problems. Birkin came in third, despite covering the longest race distance, and Benjafield & Rubin managed a sixth place. The Bentley marque won the Special Team Prize. One or two race incidents at this meeting merit a mention. For instance, the riding mechanic of Peacock's Riley took it upon himself to clamber along the bonnet and stretch

The 1928 Le Mans.

Plate 125a. Barnato in *Old Mother Gun* (No. 4) the first production 4.5 litre Bentley leading the Stutz of Brisson and Bloch. Prior to this the Bentley (Reg. No.YH 3196) had crashed out of the 1927 Le Mans (Clement and Callingham), come first in the 1927 GP de Paris (Clement and Duller) and eighth in the Brooklands Six Hour Race. It was to achieve a second in the 1929 Le Mans (Kidston and J Dunfee) after which it passed into the ownership of the Hon. Richard Norton.

COURTESY BENTLEY THE VINTAGE YEARS. MICHAEL HAY. HM BENTLEY & PARTNERS.

Plate 125b. refuelling Barnato and Rubin's mount.

COURTESY WO BENTLEY MEMORIAL FOUNDATION.

out at full length with the car at full tilt in an attempt to secure the front number plate. With all this is going on, the pilot held on to his heels with his left hand, whilst steering with the right. Just as the race regulations specify! The fire, described as a *'wild mass of evil flames'*, which *'consumed'* the Lea-Francis of Hallam, was not without drama. And this, despite the meticulous attentions of the nearby and handy, *'red coated representative of the Pyrene concern'*. But was there to be jam with the tea? Oh yes! At the Le Mans (16-17th June), and all 4.5 litre Bentley mounted, Woolf & Rubin came in first, Birkin and Chassagne a worthy fifth (for more details of which *See* Chapter 5) but Benjafield and Clement had to retire with a cracked chassis, and subsequent loss of coolant. Incidentally Barnato and Rubin were allocated *Old Mother Gun* as they were novices and this 4.5 litre was the oldest and slowest of the trio. The finishing line-up was not a foregone conclusion as that year's Le Mans entries included a strong American element of one 5 litre Black Hawk Stutz and four in number 4 litre Chryslers, all piloted by 'well run-in' French drivers. It turned out to be a quite close run thing. The Stutz was ahead of Barnato and Rubin from the start, well into the early morning hours, after which they swapped places for the rest of the night. Barnato more or less followed team orders, closely tailing the American car. Come Sunday midday and the Stutz was suffering gearbox problems. The Barnato and Rubin Bentley took what appeared to be a comfortable lead. However …the lead Bentley was beginning to suffer from the same problems that had seen Benjafield and Clement retire. The Stutz pit, realising something was amiss, put out the 'get on with it' signal. It is said that the engine of the in-the-lead Bentley, by now free wheeling where possible, was red hot when it crossed the finishing line. After the 'French connection', it was back to the humdrum of 'Blighty', but Woolf was not to compete again that year. The once Jarvis bodied 3 Bentley by now had a 4.5 litre engine fitted and Dudley Froy drove the car for the rest of that season. He gained a win and set some world speed records Incidentally, Mr Froy is rather an enigma, but was related to the Dunfee's and apparently worked for Parry Thomas, in the early Brooklands days. He was described as being a most versatile driver. He must have been a very safe pair of hands as he raced on his own account and for other owners, cropping up in the Brooklands annals year in, year out. He also owned and raced JEP Howey's old Leyland Thomas which he had sympathetically restored. In the 1930 Brooklands 500 Mile Race his 6 cylinder Delage burst into flames, despite which the driver and mechanic escaped unscathed. Even so Froy had a good attempt to get the car going again. In the 1930s he raced for Barnato in the Barnato-Hassan Special.

By 1929 Woolf solely concentrated on the 'big ones' and only entered the Brooklands Double Twelve Hour Race, Le Mans and the Brooklands Six Hour Race meeting. The Brooklands Double Twelve Race (10-11th May) heralded the competition debut of the very first Speed 6 Bentley, from this time on always referred to as *Old No. 1*. Barnato and Benjafield were at the controls. Despite their leading for some nine hours, they were disqualified due to motoring without the dynamo being connected for a period, thus infringing the rules. Holder and Birkin, in Holder's 4.5 litre Bentley, were similarly unlucky when, after 18 hours, the rear axle gave out. Sammy Davis and Sir Ronald Gunter in another 4.5 litre Bentley managed a magnificent second place. They would have won if they had not incurred a burst tyre, a brush with a sandbank, occasioning an unscheduled pit stop, and an 'end-of-race' very dodgy oil pressure. The latter fault meant they had to slow down towards the finish.

Plate 126a. Barnato taking over the Speed Six Bentley (No. 2 and to be known as 'Old No. 1') from Benjafield on its very first outing at the 1929 Brooklands Double Twelve Race. Unfortunately, due to a technicality – all right, a race infringement, they were 'retired'.

COURTESY THE MOTOR.

Plate 126b. Birkin and Barnato 'lounging' on 'Old No. 1' prior to the 1929 Le Mans. See page 106 for the result!

COURTESY BENTLEY FIFTY YEARS OF THE MARQUE. J GREEN. DALTON WATSON.

Plate 126c. Once again a winners pose. Barnato and Jack Dunfee aboard the Speed Six 'Old No. 1' at the 1929 Brooklands Six Hour Race with Wally Hassan to the left and Stan Ivermee to the right.

COURTESY A RACING HISTORY OF THE BENTLEY. BERTHON. BODLEY HEAD.

Meanwhile, Ramponi in a supercharged 1500cc Alfa Romeo came in first, winning on handicap by the minuscule margin of 0.003. That's close! Clement and Cook in a 4.5 litre Bentley had to retire with engine trouble, whilst the private entry 4.5 litre Bentley of Mr and Mrs Scott came in eleventh place. The pits supplied some worrying drama when fuel was spilt whilst refuelling the Birkin and Holder car. An exhaust backfire resulted in a mechanic being set on fire and rather badly burnt. For Le Mans (15-16th June) Bentley Motors fielded a five car team. Woolf & Birkin were in *Old No. 1*, the Speed 6, whilst Kidston & Jack Dunfee, Benjafield & Baron d'Erlanger, Clement & Chassagne and Lord Howe & Rubin were all in 4.5 litre Bentleys. Benjafield and Howe were late substitutions, because two of Birkin's 'Blower' 4.5 litre cars were unavailable, at the last moment. It was also relevant that the 4.5 litre of Howe and Rubin had only just completed a 24 Hour Record run, in the hands of Mrs Victor Bruce. Due to the lack of available time, this car had not had the full works, pre-race service and overhaul. The Americans were in full force that year, with three Stutz's, two Chryslers and one du Pont, all in experienced hands. One of the Stutz' had a Philippe Rothschild sharing the drive, this gentleman being a renowned French playboy, who raced under the *nom de course 'Philippe'*. At the off, Birkin was away at a great lick and during the race set the year's lap record. After a couple of hours, the Bentleys were one, two, three and four, followed by the 'Yankee' machinery. Overnight, various calamities put out two Stutz's and the du Pont, whilst the Bentleys were forging ahead. As the night wore on, both Clement and Kidston's cars incurred intermittent headlight failure, more especially under heavy braking, at the tighter bends. Nasty! Then Clement's car required brake repairs. By Sunday mid-morning, the Bentleys were back where they should have been – one, two, three and four. Whilst Barnato and Birkin settled down to a steady pace, Benjafield had to accept he had no front brakes. Immediately prior to the finish very, very worryingly the lead Bentleys did not appear. Oh dear! Shades of 1926 and 1927! But not to panic. The Bentley Boys had simply pulled over and arranged themselves in an agreed formation, in 'platoon order', and came across the finish line-astern. How very British. Barnato's last race of the year was the Brooklands Six Hour Race (29th June). As to be expected, Barnato and Jack Dunfee, in *Old No. 1*, came first with Cook and Callingham in third place. Birkin's 'Blower' 4.5 litre Bentley was now a prototype single seater which, rather predictably, had to retire. This was to become the 'Brooklands famous' record breaking vehicle.

For what was to be his swan-song year, Woolf only entered two races in 1930. They were the Double Twelve Hour Race meeting and Le Mans. The Brooklands Double Twelve Race (9-10th May) was a very 'spectator popular' race that year, despite the start not having the traditional Le Mans getaway. Instead the drivers stood alongside their chariots. Some interest was generated by a private entry 4.5 litre Bentley catching fire. Despite this conflagration, the car recommenced racing, only to drop out later with rear axle problems. Another less amusing incident occurred when two Talbot 90s had a coming together, which resulted in one dead riding mechanic and a spectator, as well as eleven or so injured spectators. For the first of the two days, the Le Mans specification Speed Six Bentleys of Woolf & Clement and Davis & Clive Dunfee led the race, line-astern again. The second day they wrapped things up and won the race, in that order. And this despite one of the winning Bentleys incurring a broken valve and the other a seized crankshaft damper. The three 'Blower' 4.5 litre Bentleys

Plate 127a.   Brooklands prior to the 1930 Double Twelve with Barnato and Clement seated in their Speed Six Bentley (No. 2), in which they won that race. Bless the ankle-biter alongside! He was (at the time) the youngest son of JK Carruth, a director of Bentley Motors.

COURTESY WO BENTLEY MEMORIAL FOUNDATION.

Plate 127b.   Caracciola and Werner's S-38/250 Mercedes (No. 12) being hounded by the Speed Six Bentley (No. 4) of Barnato and Kidston in the 1930 Le Mans.

COURTESY THE MOTOR.

retired. That year's Le Mans (21-22nd June) was to be a fight to the death between the sole white Mercedes of Caracciola & Werner and the might of the Bentley Team machines. And there was some six of them. Rather David and Goliath, really. Once again Stutz had a presence with two cars, one of them, as the year before, with *Philippe* aboard. The real action of this particular race has been detailed in Chapter 5, wherein the battle plan of Tim Birkin setting out to destroy the Mercedes has already been described. The 'Blower' Bentley of Harcourt-Wood and Jack Dunfee did not start, only the second time this had occurred where Bentley cars were concerned over all the years. In fact, the other two 'Blowers' did not finish, with Birkin and Chassagne retiring on lap 138, having set the race lap record. Even more disappointing was the retirement of the Benjafield and Ramponi car, after 20 hours and 40 minutes. Whatever, at the start of the race, first away was Caracciola's Mercedes followed by Kidston and then Davis. The Bentley orders were to keep in touch, in sight of the Mercedes and wait. Disobeying these instructions, the Sammy Davis and Clive Dunfee car spent the balance of the race nestled into the substantial sandbank, at Pontlieue. Without doubt the Bentley pit work was very smart. This was very instrumental in conducting the duel with the Mercedes, whose race was run after some ten hours of breathtaking driving. Despite the almost predictable problem of the Bentley radiators losing water, the magnificent machines of Barnato & Kidston and Clement & Watney crossed the finish, yet again line-astern. At the podium, the victors insisted the Mercedes drivers were brought centre-stage, to congratulate them on their *'brilliant display of driving and great sportsmanship'*. A frightfully good show with which the final curtain came down on Barnato, Glen and Tom *et al*.

Plate 128. A prominent motor magazine of the year proclaiming Bentley's 1929 major achievements.
COURTESY THE MOTOR.

Epilogue

*'Of that decade of starters and runners, those who lived fastest
more often than not died youngest.'*
GROC.

Of course there were exceptions to the empirical rule above, but quite a few of the very fast-set did not make old bones. This was as evidenced by the very 'early departure' of, amongst others (and not in order of 'demise') Sir Tiger Tim Birkin, Capt. RB Howey, Cmdr. Glen Kidston, Bernard Rubin, 'Tommy' Parry Thomas (who was an exception to the party, party rule) and Count Zborowski.

The Thistlethwayte's wiled away the 1930s, moving from their first home, Bodicote House, Upper Heyford, Oxford, to Burseldon Lodge Old Burseldon, Hampshire. This was adjacent to the upper reaches of the Hamble River. Incidentally this village was where Noel van Raalte had lived, reputably the first production line Bentley owner. Tom only made the 'column inches', in 1935, concerning the fitting a pair of inboard marine engines to his 175 ton yacht, the *Schooner Charmian*. The article does nothing to dispel the thoughts that he would always pursue some perverse furrow of his own choosing. Deciding to replace the original petrol engines, he selected a pair of 100 bhp marine oil engines. But these were not manufactured by a long-established marine diesel engine maker. Oh no! He toddled off to AEC, who had only very recently commenced marketing marine units. Whatever, this time he would appear to have chosen a winner as he was able to confirm he had completed some 9,000 nautical miles, steaming for 900 hours, at an average of 10 knots with a consumption of three gallons per hour. I bet Messrs AEC had been sweating on those trails proving satisfactory. In August 1936 he purchased a 4.5 litre Derby chassis, for which he commissioned Freestone & Webb to fit a saloon body (Reg. No. DGJ 686). Martin Walter must have fallen from grace! During the WW2 hostilities the family home and gardens, which conveniently edged The Hamble River, were requisitioned for the war effort. In 1943 they became the shore base for *HMS Cricket*, a Royal Marine outfit acting as the centre for Combined Operations and Landing Craft. The base featured in the D-Day landings, but

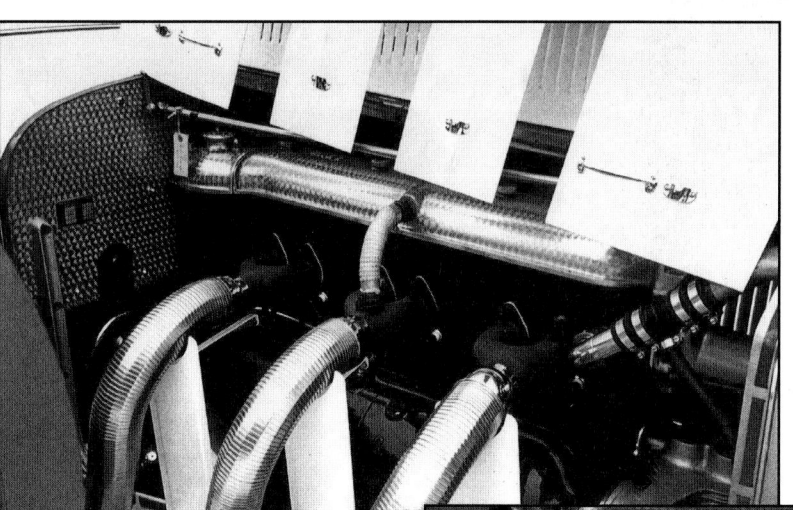

Plate 129.   Photographs of a restored S-38/250 Mercedes Benz and a contemporary technical illustration of the car (Page 245).

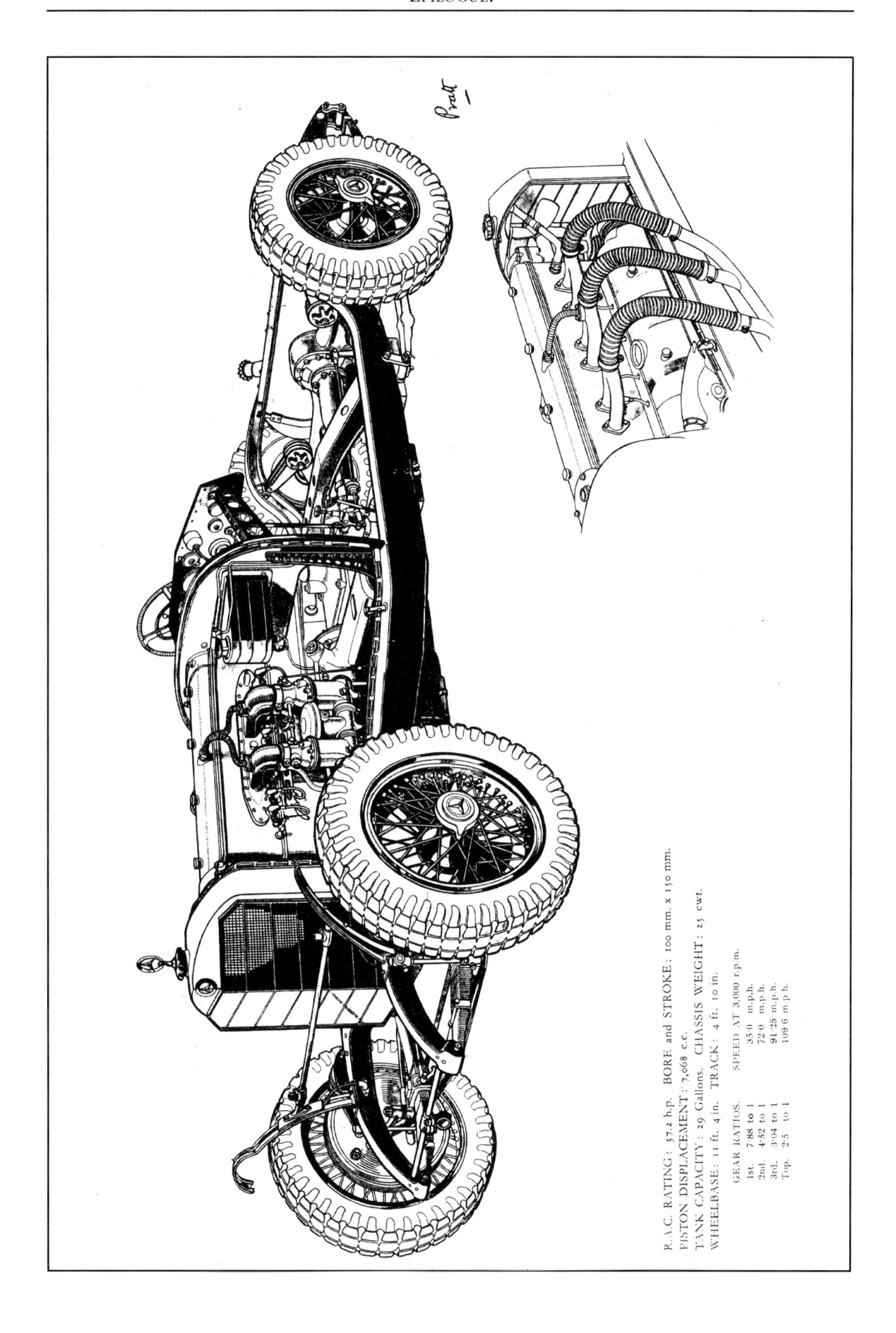

Epilogue.

R.A.C. RATING: 37.2 h.p.   BORE and STROKE: 100 mm. x 150 mm.
PISTON DISPLACEMENT: 7,068 c.c.
TANK CAPACITY: 29 Gallons.   CHASSIS WEIGHT: 25 cwt.
WHEELBASE: 11 ft. 4 in.   TRACK: 4 ft. 10 in.

GEAR RATIOS.	SPEED AT 3,000 r.p.m.
1st. 7·88 to 1	35·0 m.p.h.
2nd. 4·52 to 1	72·0 m.p.h.
3rd. 3·04 to 1	91·25 m.p.h.
Top. 2·5 to 1	109·6 m.p.h.

where on the South Coast did not? War over, *HMS Cricket* closed in May 1946. In the meantime, Tom, having been an RNVR officer in the pre-war years, joined a Special Branch operating out of *HMS Daedulus*. He gained the Temporary Rank of Lieutenant Commander. After he demobilised in May/June 1946, the family reclaimed their home. His wife died on the 14th February 1955, aged only 47. Subsequently, Tom sold up and moved to Temple Usk, Main Road, Colden Common, Hampshire. Here he passed away, a year later, aged 52, in 1956. Not very old bones.

In 1934, Bernard Rubin purchased one of three de Havilland Comet aircraft built to celebrate and participate in the Centenary Air Race from England to Australia. Too ill to fly, he employed none other than Owen Cathcart-Jones to co-pilot Ken Whaller. They finished in fourth place. Bernard passed away in 1936, aged 40, a young man. He simply had not had much luck in his comparatively short life.

When Ardenrun burnt down, late in 1932, Woolf Barnato purchased another great pile, Ridgemead at Englefield Green, adjacent to Windsor Great Park. Post the closure of Bentley's and his avowal never to race again, he employed Walter 'Wally' Hassan, an old Bentley hand, to look after the various Barnato cars. It was Walter Hassan (later of Jaguar and Coventry Climax) who constructed, from the 'ground up' and using lots of Bentley bits, the Barnato-Hassan Special. This was based on the *Old No. 1* Speed Six with the original engine set in a new, narrower chassis. The driver sat to one side of the very slim body. In 1935 an 8 litre Bentley unit was squeezed into place and in 1936 the steering was offset to allow the driver to be centrally located. This projectile was plagued by small-end and connecting-rod failures. Dudley Froy was the usual driver but in 1935 a promising barrister, one Oliver Bertram, became the favoured 'jockey'. In 1939 it was withdrawn from Brooklands racing due to being too punitively handicapped. Walter Hassan, who had also constructed another ex-Bentley giant, the Pacey-Hassan Special, moved on from Barnato to join ERA. Woolf Barnato had a 'reasonable' war. He was promoted to the rank of Wing Commander, responsible for the wartime security of aircraft manufacturing plants and airfields, being answerable to Lord Beaverbrook. As would be imagined, for such a romantic old 'softy', he had one last, if somewhat problematical romance. The affair was compromised by the fact that the lady concerned had promised herself to another. She married that gentleman, realised her mistake, unhitched and finally married Woolf, only for him to die fairly soon after the happy event, in 1948. He was only 53 years old, once again far too young to die. Was Tom amongst the mourners? I think not. The lady remarried a Mr O'Brian.

On the other hand, there were the long-lived. One such was George Edward Thomas Eyston. Born in 1897, he lived until 1979, aged 82, but he was a fairly 'clean' living if highly courageous competitor. Once he took up record-breaking there was no stopping him. From the 100 mph MG record at Montlhery he graduated by 1937 to the huge, six wheeled Thunderbolt, powered by a pair of supercharged V12 Rolls Royce aero engines with a total of 73,000cc giving 4,700 bhp. 'Tanking' this monster about, he held the World Land Speed Record a total of three times between 1937 and 1938 on the Bonneville Salt Flats, Utah, USA. Post WW2, he continued to break records for some years and became a Director of Castrol Oil. He had been an old chum of the original owner of that company, one Lord Wakefield.

Clive Gallop raced on in the 1930s, usually in Aston Martin's and often with Leo

Cushman. He died in 1960 whilst driving on the highways, probably as the result of a seizure of some sort, as the vehicle inexplicably and suddenly veered across the road and hit a lamp post. There was nothing apparently wrong with the vehicle.

Capt. Jack Howey lived to a respectable age, passing away aged 77, in the Folkestone area. Sammy Davis made the grand figure of 94. Dr. Benjy Benjafield achieved 77 years. He may have loved an entertaining dinner party with good food, wine and companions, but on many occasions was probably to be found tucked-up in bed, not too late. Others amongst the exceptions (so why make the empirical rule?) were George Duller, John Duff and Frank Clement. But then the two latter named gentlemen were not always amongst the hot-spots with the rowdy crew.

Post the demise of Bentley Motors, Humphrey Cook continued to race, some of the time with Aston Martin's, but his supreme moment in motor racing history was about to blossom. He was another Englishman who tired of 'johnny-foreigner' dominating the racing scene (as was Vandervell, post WW2). Humphrey longed to be involved in a home-grown outfit manufacturing a competitive vehicle. Then up popped Raymond Mays and his life-long confidante, friend and side-kick Peter Berthon. They had a dream which needed bankrolling. Thus, in 1933, was borne ERA (English Racing Automobiles). Cook put up £75,000 as the capital, Berthon was the Designer Director and Mays the Director driver. Each participant had a share of £2/10/0. The 'work's' were located in Mays back garden, at Bourne. The history and achievements of this remarkable marque are outside the scope of this book but perhaps not the enterprise's demise. Regardless of that which Raymond Mays suggests in one of his book's*, it has been alleged elsewhere that the end of ERA was rather an unpleasant affair. On a visit to the works in 1938, Humphrey was dismayed (to put it at its best) to find some five or so 'well formed' RM sports cars in construction. This diversification had been discussed but he had declined to be involved. His justifiable concern was who was footing the bill. As Mays and Berthon had little funds between them, Cook drew the inevitable conclusion. As a result the firm was wound up, almost there and then (26th May 1939), and all the relevant components removed, via Donington, to Humphrey's London Road, Dunstable premises.

But he was to incur more humiliation. In February 1941 he married Annie Blakely, a 47 year old divorcee, a lady who had herself suffered some emotional grief. With this union came some very unnecessary baggage in the shape of her youngest son, one David Moffett Blakeley. The step-son was to become a rather unsavoury low-life who hung around with the motor racing set, in the early 1950's. In the course of his rackety life he met and became involved with Ruth Ellis. She was a peroxide blond, night-club hostess, who was no better than she 'ought to be'. Pregnant by him and the victim of various beatings, including one which caused her to miscarriage, matters had to come to a head. They did. Aged 28, on the 10th April 1955, Ruth Ellis shot the 26 year old Blakely dead. On the 13th July she made history as the last woman to be hanged. I am quite sure Humphrey Windham Cook did not deserve all that!

---

* Split Seconds. My Racing Years, Raymond Mays. GT Foulis & Co. Ltd.

POSTSCRIPT

Courtesy of and from the Bentley Drivers Club Review of December 1956.

Obituary.

'Scrap' Thistlethwayte.

"It is with real sorrow that one read, quite recently, of the passing of Thomas Arthur Donald Claude Thistlethwayte on the 4th October at the early age of 52.

Always known as 'Scrap', the present writer is uncertain whether this affectionate nickname was due to his many initials or was a retention from childhood. Be that as it may, he was a most affectionate inspiring personality liked by everyone he came in contact with and was always gay and ready for anything.

As neighbours in Kent before the days of traffic density – or by-passes – we got to know each other well and had many fast private point-to-points, the favourite pair of cars being his O.E. 30-98 Vauxhall and the writer's Speed Model 3-litre Bentley.

This led to 'Scrap' wishing to drive a Bentley at Le Mans in 1926 and insisting that it must be one of the short 9ft. chassis, known as the 100 mph Model.

The writer obtained W.O.'s kind agreement to treat this as one of the Team cars and to allow it to run from his pits and under his care. Bertie Moir will no doubt remember it well, W. O. added, with his dry humour, that this was conditional upon the body dimensions being scrupulously to regulations as of course was to be everything on the car. The body presented many difficulties on the 9ft. chassis but thanks to some brilliant work by Messrs Martin Walter of Folkestone all the dimensional coach work difficulties were overcome.

A year or two later saw Scrap driving an S.K. Supercharged Mercedes. This, especially in Ireland, he drove with great verve and very fast indeed. It is indeed no criticism to observe that, at times, he gave the impression of outdriving his own endurance.

Scrap Thistlethwayte had another hobby which loomed as large in his mind or larger than cars – Motor Boats. He bought an M.L. from the 1914-1918 War, in very good condition, fitted with its original open-cockpit 'Sterling' petrol engines.

At one time he had a number of little ships ranging from an Anzani-engined speed dinghy to his very beautiful miniature yacht 'White Lady' with triple screws and first-war Daimler Tank engines.

In the last war he served in the R.N.V.R., with the Little Ships, and held the rank of Lieut. Commander.

Scrap married twice; his first wife was Miss Nettie Hickie and his second The Hon. Eileen Bury (*sic*). He leaves four sons."

R.C.G. (Clive Gallop).

ACKNOWLEDGEMENTS

Books.

Brooklands. The Complete Motor Racing History. William Boddy. MRP.
The Shell Book of Motoring Humour. N. Bentley. Michael Joseph.
'Full Throttle'. Sir Henry (Tim) Birkin Bt. GT Foulis & Co.
Motoring Through Punch. 1900-1970. R. Brockbank. Punch/David & Charles.
The Best of Brockbank. R. Brockbank. David & Charles.
The Racing Zborowiskis. D. Wilson. VSCC Ltd.
Motor Sport in the 20s. A.B. Demaus. Alan Sutton Publishing.
Bugatti. A Racing History. D. Venables. Haynes Publishing.
Vauxhall 30-98. The Finest of Sporting Cars. Nic Portway. New Wensum Publishing.
Frazer Nash. D. Thirlby. Haynes/Foulis.
Parry Thomas. Designer Driver. Hugh Tours. Batsford Ltd.
Bentley. The Vintage Years. M. Hay. HM Bentley & Partners.
L'Automobile Club De L'Ouest. Besancon. Le Mans. France.
Bentley Factory Cars. M. Hay. HM Bentley & Partners.
WO. The Autobiography of WO Bentley. Hutchinson of London.
The Vintage Alvis. P. Hull & N. Johnson. Macdonald.
The Bentley At Le Mans. Dr. Benjafield, MD. Motor Racing Publications.
The Other Bentley Boys. E. Nagle. George Harrap.
Sunbeam Racing Cars. A. Heal. Foulis/Haynes.
Racing In the Park. B. Montgomery. Dreoilin Specialist Publications Ltd.
An Illustrated History of the Bentley Car. WOB. George Allen & Unwin.
Shelsey Walsh. CA. May. GT Foulis & Co.
A Racing History of the Bentley. D. Berthon. Bodley Head.
Bentley. Fifty Years of The Marque. J. Green. Dalton Watson.
Blower Bentley by Michael Hay. Number One Press 2001.
Alfa Romeo. A History by P. Hull & R. Starr. Cassell & Co.
The Ards TT. JS. Moore. Blackstaff Press.
Aston Martin 1913-1947. I. Hunter. Osprey Automotive.
Flat Out. GET. Eyston. John Miles Publishing.
A To Z of British Coachbuilders. N. Walker. Bay View Books.
Aviation Memories. O. Cathcart-Jones. Hutchinson.
Montlhery. The Story of the Paris Autodrome. W. 'Bill' Boddy. MBE. Veloce Publishing.
Motor Racing and Record Breaking. GET. Eyston & B. Lyndon. Batsford,
Speed On Salt. GET. Eyston & WF. Bradley. Batsford, London.
'Tourist Trophy'. The History of Britain's Greatest Motor Race. R. Hough. Hutchinson.
'June'. The Glass Slipper. An Autobiography. Heinemann.
'Split Seconds'. My Racing Years. Raymond Mays. GT Foulis & Co.

Magazines, Newspapers & Photo Agencies.

Autocar, The Motor, Autosport, Motor Sport, Classic Sports Car, The Daily Express, The Mirror, The Times, The Daily Mail, The Morning Post, The Hull Evening News, The Irish Statesman, Dublin, The Picadilly, London, The Belfast News Letter, The Tatler, The New York Herald, Paris, Foto-Offica, Dott Ferruccio Testi Modena, Foto-Offica Annibale Annibaletto, Photo-Reportage, Fumagalli, Beken of Cowes, Fox , LAT .

Clubs, Institutions & Personalities.

Bentley Drivers Club, Brooklands Society, T. Cooper, British Ancestrial Research, National Motor Museum, John Konig Archives, Mercedes Benz, Vintage Sports Car Club.

INDEX

PERSONALITIES.

Plate pages in italic.

A.
Abercrombie, Sir G. 91.
Addams. 131.
Adlington, WJ. 87, 91.
Agnew, Mrs. 148, 149.
Aitken, M. 81.
Aldington, H. 15, 37, 133, 137.
Allard, S. 3.
Anderson. 104.
Andre, TB. 49.
Ashley,
    S. 121–123, 125, 201.
    Lord. 121, 201.
Aspinall, J. 182.
Astor family. 25.
Ava, Earl of. 207.

B.
Balls, V. 15, 135, 157, 159.
Bamber, PK. 51.
Barclay, J. 15, 81, 165, *220*.
Barnato, the family. 215–217, 219.
    Barnet or 'Barney'. 11, 215-217, 221.
    D. 217.
    DM (Dot), Mrs. 217, 219, 221.
    'Fanny'. 219.
    H. 215.
    Jackie. *228*, 231.
    K. 217.
    L. 219.
    V. 217.
    Woolf ('Babe'). 1, 3, 9, 11, 15, 27, 31, *50*, 51, *52*, 53, 66, 67, 69, 77, *78*, *80*, 81, *84*, 85, 87, *92*, 93, *100*, *101*, *106*, 107, 109, 113, *116*, 117, *128*, 151, 163, *166*, 169, *176*, *184*, 193, *194*, 195, 197, *198*, 201, 203, 205, 209, 211, *214*, **215–241**, *216*, *218*, *220*, *222*, *224*, *228*, *230*, 232, *234*, *236*, *238*, *240*, 246.
Barnes, JD. 15.
Barnett, RL. 149.
Barratt, J. 137.
Baxter, J. 53.
Beaver, RA. 15.
Beaverbrook, Lord. 81, 246.
Benjafield, Dr. D. 15, 51,55, 61, 63, 72, 75, **83–85**, *84*, 86, 90, *92*, 93, *100*, *110*, 113, 115, 117, 125, *128*, 153, 159, 169, 175, 177, 193, *194*, *234*, 235, 237, *238*, 239, 241, 247.
Benoist, R. 15, 75, 159, 177.
Benson, JR. 15.
'Bentley Boys'. 1, 9, 11, 51, 83, 117, 125, 129, 131, 145, 171, 199, 221, 239.
Bentley family.
    HM. 45, 71.
    WO. 1, 15, 45, 55, 59, 67, 71, *78*, 81, *84*, 87, *88*, 91, 93, 99, 105, 107, *108*, 109, 117, *128*, 135, 163, 177, *180*, 203, 229, 231.
Berry family. 207–209.
    GE. *See* Thistlethwayte.
    HS. 207, 209.
    JG. 209.
    JM. 207.
    WE. 207.
Bertelli,
    'Bert'. 153, 157, *224*, 225, 227, 235.
    Harry. 169, *224*, 225.
Berthon, P. 247.
Bertram, O. 15, 246.
Bezzant, J. 157.
Bielovuci, *140*, 141.
Bira. 169.
Birkett, N. 217.
Birkin family.
    Audrey CL. *96*, 99, 103.
    CAC (Archie). 99, *100*, 103.
    HRS ('Tiger Tim'), Sir. 1, 7, 15, 27, 45, 47, *52*, 77, 81, 85, 87, 95, *96*, **97–117**, *98*, *100*, *102*, *104*, *106*, *108*, *110*, *111*, *112*, *114*, *118*, **119–127**, *120*, *122*, *124*, *128*, 129, *130*, 131, 133, 135, 137, *138*, 139, *140*, 141, 165, *166*, 169, *170*, 171, *172–173*, 175, *176*, 177, *180*, 181, 183, 193, *194*, 197, 201, 205, 209, 211, 215, 223, 227, 231, 235, 237, *238*, 239, 241, 243.
    'Ida'. 97, 99, 107, 125.
    MDH. 99.
    TRC. 99.
    TS, Sir. 97, 99, 223.
Blakely,
    A. 247.
    DM. 247.
Bloch. *102*, 236.
Boddy, W. 3, 13, 21, 47.
Bourlier, 155.
Bourne, D. 209, 223.
Bouts, EL. 15.
Brackenbury, C. 15.
Bradman, D. 223.
Brand. *142*, 143.
Brayshaw. *212*.
Brisson. 90, 102, 197, *236*.
Brown, D. 1, 165, 183, 213.
Bruce, Mrs & V. 17, *78*, 119, 215, 239.
Buchanan, J. 223.
Buckland, Baron. *See* Berry.
'Bugatti Queen', The. *See* Delangle, H.
Burnard, CW. 151, 223.
Burt family.
    Eric. 3.
    Patsy. 3.

C.
Callingham, L. 72, *73*, 75, *84*, 91, 92, 165, 169, *176*, 177, 197, 220, 235, 236, 239.
Campbell, Mrs Ian. *208*.
Campbell, Sir Malcolm. *12*, 13, 15, 27, 37, 49, 51, 61, 79, *112*, 133, 135, 137, 139, 141, 147, 149, 153, 157, 159, 171, 175, 182, 213, 221, 231, 233.
Cambell, M, Duchess of Argyll. 33, 201.
Campari, CG. *112*, 171, 177, 183.
Camrose, Lord. *See* Berry.
Caracciola, R. 15, 31, 81, 105, *108*, 109, 110, *111*, *112*, 115, 177, *178–179*, 181, 183, 197, *240*, 241.
Carruth, JK. 240.
Carson, TW. 17.
Carstairs, Miss B. 151, 153, 215, 225.
'Casque'. *See* Davis, SCH.
Cathcart-Jones, O. 187, 199, 200, 201, *202*, 203, 205, 209, 211, 246.
Chapman, HAD. 185.
Charavel, L ('Sabipa'). 115–117, 157.
Charnwood, Lord. *See* Benson.
Chassagne, J. 15, 25, 71, *72*, 75, 77, *84*, *92*, 93, 100, 103, 105, *110*, *112*, 113, 115, *126*, **127–129**, *128*, 193, *194*, 237, 239, 241.
Chetwynd,
    Hon. 17.

MDH. *See* Birkin.
Chirron. *100, 154,* 155.
Christie, Mrs. 37.
Clark, Val. 151.
Clarke, RAC ('Nobby'). 45, *50,* 59, 61, *102.*
Clarke, FJ. *156.*
Claridge, J. *See* Barnato.
Clease. *100.*
Clement, FC ('Sunshine'). 15, 55, 72, 73,*78,* 81, 83, *84,* 85, *86,* **87***, 88–89, 90,* 91, *92,* 93, *100,* 103, 127, *128,* 129, 165, 193, *194,* 195, 197, *198,* 220, *230,* 233, 235, 236, 237, 239, *240,* 241, 247.
Coatelen, L. 27.
Cobb, J. 17, 81, 121, 169.
Cochrane, CB. 121, 219.
Comery, WS. 103.
Conelli, Count. 17, *176,* 177, 191.
Constantini, 153.
Cook, HW. 15, 27, 35, 52, *104,* 105, *108, 130,* 133, 137, 139, *162,* **163–165***, 164,* 169, *170,* 171, 175, 220, 239, 247.
Cooper, Hartshorne,
 J. *24,* 27.
 RF. *24, 44,* 91.
Cordery, Miss V. 141.
Cosgrave, President. 171.
Cottenham, Earl. 17.
Cotton, W. 27.
Couper, WM (Mike). 17, 103.
Courage, P. 182.
Courcelles, Henry de. 90, *154,* 155.
Coward, Noel. 219.
Cummings, Miss I. 17, 153.
Cunliff family,
 A. *106,* 109.
 Miss M. 51, 82, *106,* 107–109.
Curzon,
 FRHP. *See* Howe.
 GM, Lady. 182, 185.
 SM. 182.
Cushman, L. 15, 37, 47, 83, 135, 139, *176,* 247.

D.
Davenport, BH. 213.
Davis, BO. *52,* 112.
Davis, SCH ('Sammy'). 9, 47, *50,* 51, 52, 55, 59, 61, *70,* **71–83***, 72–73, 76, 78,* 80, 82, *84, 92,* 117, 121, 129, 133, 139, 145, 147, 171, 175, *176,* 177, 183, 195, 197, 237, 239, 241, 247.
de Alzaga. M. 44
de Braille, C. 39.

de Casa Maury, Marquis. *See* Maury
de Cystria. 44.
de Durand. *78, 79,* 212.
de Palma, Ralph. 143.
de Vizcaya, P. 44
Delaney, T. 3, 81–83.
Delangle, H. 155.
Denly, A. 123, *160.*
d'Erlanger, Baron. 17, 72, 73, 75, *79, 84,* 87, *92,* 113, *132,* 155, *176,* 177, 193, *194,* 239.
Dietrich, Marlene. 151.
Divo, AD. 17, 155.
Djordjadze, Prince D. 123.
Don, K. 17, 113, 133, 135, 139, 141, 159, 171, *176,* 177, 215, 235.
Douglas, Capt. JC. 51, *224,* 225, 227.
Doyle, Conan, family,
 A & D. 17, 29.
 Arthur, Sir. 17, 29.
Drew, Capt. R. *142,* 143.
Drummond, Capt. 3.
Duff, Capt. J. F. 15, 27, 83, *86,* **87–93***, 88–89, 90,* 147, 233, 247.
Duller, GE ('Croucher'). 55, 72, *73,* 75, *84,* **85–87**, 90, 92, 117, 189, 191, 235, 236, 247.
Dunfee family, 237.
 C. 9, 15, *50,* **51–53***, 52, 78,* 80, 81, 82, 195, 197, 239, 241.
 J. 9, 15, *50,* **51–53***, 78,* 82, 106, *110,* 113, 159, 165, 167, 169, 171, *176,* 193, *194,* 195, 236, *238,* 239, 241.
Dunne. 91.
Dykes,
 Mrs. 141.
 U. *76,* 77, 135, 139.

E.
Eaton, HS. 17, 37, 113, 197.
Ebblewhite, AV. 23, 29.
Edge, SF. 37, 91.
Eggar, K. 17.
Eldridge, E. 161.
Ellis, R. 247.
Etacelin. 115.
Eyston,
 B. 38, 153, 157, 158, 159.
 GET. 15, 61, 75, 117, 119, 123, 133, **143–163***, 144, 146, 148, 150, 152, 154, 156, 158, 160, 162,* 165, 169, 171, 175, 177, *180,* 215, 223, 225, 225, 246.

F.
Fairbanks, D. 121.
Falk, DM. *See* Barnato.

Fender, P. 223.
Ferdinand, Archduke. 181.
Ferguson, H. 3, 133.
Field, JF. 17.
Fiennes, Capt. 17.
Fish. *212.*
Flynn, Errol. 199.
Fox, AW. 17.
Frazer-Nash, A. 15, 37, *38,* 39, 61, 133, 141, *154,* 157, 159, *176,* 177, 183.
Froy, D. 49, 237, 246.

G.
Gable, Clark. 121.
Gallop, Capt RC ('Gallô'). 1, 15, 19, *22,* 23, *26,* 27, 29, 34, 35, 37, *38,* 39, 41, *44,* **45–47***, 46, 54,* 55, 59, 61, 65, 71, 87, *92,* 99, *104,* 107, 119, 133, 139, *144,* 145, 153, 207, 246–247.
Gaspar, HJ. 195.
George V, King. 10.
George, Prince. *See* York.
Getty. 67.
Ghica, Prince. 157.
Gillet, T. 17.
Gillow, V. 17, 161.
Gladstone, T. 203.
Goux, J. 143.
Graham, N. *See* Raalte.
Grant, CRA. 17.
Green, WH. 17, 171, 175.
Greenly. 32.
Gresley, Sir N. 33.
Grover Williams. *See* Williams.
Guinness family, 137, 207.
 KL. 17, 27, 68, 135–137, 145.
 M. 207.
Gunter, Sir R. 77, 113, 237.

H.
Halford, Major. 17, 155.
Hall, ER. *78,* 83, 117.
Hallam, F. 17, 77, 103, *156,* 237.
Hamilton, H. 123.
Hann, T. 17.
Hartshorne-Cooper. *See* Cooper.
Harvey, Major CM. 17, *76,* 77, 135, 139, *164.*
Hassan, W. *50,* 105, *238,* 246.
Hawkes, S. *See* Ashley.
Hayes, Major. E. 135.
Hazelhurst, HE. 17.
Head, LV. *72.*
Headlam family. 169.
 L. 103, 169, 175, 177.
 W. 169.
 WS. 169.

INDEX.

Heal, A. 34.
Hebeler, RS. 17, 79.
Hendy, G. 17.
Hiatt, See Zborowski, Countess 'Vi'.
Hickie, EM. See Thistlethwayte.
Hills. *202.*
Higgins, D. 17, *156, 158,* 169.
Hindmarsh, JS. 17, 197.
Hobbs, J. 223.
Holder, N. 17, 109, 171, 237, 239.
Horsman, V. 17.
Howe, (Viscount, Earl) Lord FRHP. 15, *78, 79, 104, 112,* 117, *118,* 119, 121, 123, 135, 139, 169, *176,* 177, 182, 183, 185, 197, 215, 239.
Howey, family.
    G. 33.
    JEP. 21, 25, 29, *32,* **33**, 37, 49, 69, 169, 237, 247.
    RB. 21, 33, 47, 61, *62,* **63–65**, *68,* 69, 243.

I.

Illife, Sir E. 75.
Inverclyde,
    Lady. See Tripp.
    Lord. 220.
Isaacs, See Barnato.
Ivanowski, B. 15, 39, 63, *76,* 77, 108, 158, 159, 161, 169, 171, 175, *176,* 177, 193.
Ivermee, S. *50, 238.*

J.

Jackson, R. 17.
James, HL. See Stopford.
Jennky, Madam. 141.
Joel family, 219.
    J (Isaac). 215, 217.
    SB, Solomon or 'Solly Joe'. *10,* 11, 217, 227.
    Stanhope. 227.
Johnson, L. 200.
Johnstone, CW. 39.
Jones, DL. 195.
Joyce. 37.

K.

Kaiser, The. 195.
Keeling. *100.*
Kelway-Bamber, Lt. 32.
Kemsley, Lord. See Berry.
Kensington Moir, Bertie. 15, 47, 85, 90, 115, *144,* 145, 147, 177, 215.
Kidston family, 205.
    A. 185.
    AG. 185.

AMG. 189.
GJ. 185.
Cmdr. GP ('Glen'). 1, 9, 15, 33, 51, 53, 77, 80, *108,* 113, 141, *142,* 143, 165, *170,* 171, 175, 177, 181, 182, 183, *184,***185–205**, 190, *192, 194, 198, 200, 204,* 207, 209, 211, 223, 227, 236, 239, 240, 241, 243.
HE. 185.
HRA. 182, 185.
NE. 185.
NMD, Mrs. 189, 195, 205, 211.
Kimber, C. 161.
Kindell, F. 133, 137–139, *138.*
King, F. 17.
King, HFL. See Locke King.
Kingsborough, Viscount. *214.*
Konig, 3, 221.
    M. 3.

L.

Laly. 75, 92.
Lambert, P. 3, 233.
Latham, ACL. See Birkin.
Leicester, VE. See Zborowski.
Lewis, BE. 17, *38,* 119, 197.
Locke King, HF. 21.
Loewenstein, A. 141, *142,* 143.
Lurani, Count. 123.

M.

MacDonald, R. 227.
Macklin, Capt. N. 85.
Maclachlan, ANL. 17.
Maconochie, Miss MJ. *140,* 141, 177, 183.
Mansell, N. *2.*
March, Earl. *82, 83,* 117.
Marendaz, DMK. 17, 149.
Marinoni, A. 159, 177, *194.*
Mareuse, M *198.*
Marix, Mrs V. 31, 95.
Marshall, S. 39.
Martin, L. 27, 145, 147, 149, 151.
Mason. *134.*
Matthys. 39.
Maury, Marquis de Casa. 67, *84,* 225.
May, F. 151.
Mayner, EA. 37.
Mays, R. *12,* 13, 15, 37, 113, 119, 165, 169, 183, 213, 231, 247.
Mellor, R. 169.
Mertz, O. 15, 105, 109, 177, *178–179,* 181, 183.
'Miles'. *24.*
Miller, Capt. A. 103, 233.
Miller, K. *214.*

Milnes, GTG. 195.
Morgan, 'Bobby' RC. 147, 148, 149, 151, *234.*
Morrel. 157.
Morris, W. 67.
Moss,
    A. 17.
    S. 17.
Mountbatten, L. 209.
Murphy, J. *142,* 143.

N.

Nash, RG. 17.
Newsome. 77, 139.
Neubauer, A. 31, 183.
Niklas, H. 195.
Niven, D. 123.
Norton, Hon. R. 17, 51, 236.
Nuvolari, T. 15, 125.

O.

Oats, RF. 17, 133, 159, 169.
O'Brian. 246.

P.

Paget, Hon. D. 47, 53, 81, 103, *110,* **113**, 117, 119, 197.
Pavlova, A. 219.
Payne. *156.*
Paul, C. *50,* 53, 81, 157.
Peacock. 235.
Pennel, L. *232.*
Petre, K. 17.
'Philippe'. See Rothschild.
Pickett, FN. 39.
Poppe. *158.*
Porsche, Dr. F. 31, 139.
Porter, G. 107.
Presgrave. See Howey.
Purdy, HW. 17, 51, *76,* 83, 135, 159, *234.*

Q.

Queenborough, Lord. 113.

R.

Raalte, N van. 67–69, *84,* 243.
Rabagliati, Col. 79.
Ramponi, G. 77, 103, *110,* 113, 169, 171, *176,* 177, 197, 239, 241.
Randall, CJ. *100.*
Ratier. 161.
Redmayne, C. *40,* 41.
Renwick, W. 153, 227.
Rhodes, C. 217.
Rigal. 197, 198.
Riganti, R. 44.
Riley, V. 17.

253

Ringwood. *38.*
Rogers, PB. *212,* 213, 215.
Ropner, Major L. 3, 17, 35.
Rose-Richards, T. 17, 197.
Rossignol. 90.
Rowley, J. 233.
Rothschild, P. 239, 241.
Rubin,
    B. 1, 9, 15, 77, *92,* 101, *108,* 109, 116, **117–119,** *120, 122,* 123, *128,* 133, *170,* 171, *176,* 177, 181, 227, 235, *236,* 237, 239, 243, 246.
    M. 117.

S.
'Sabipa' See Charavel.
Sampson, Major N. *208.*
Samuelson, FHB. 17.
Saunders-Davies. 17.
Schika, R. 195.
Scott,
    WB. 17, *108,* 123, *170,* 171, 239.
    HR. *38,* 39.
'Scrap' Thistlethwayte.
    See Thistlethwayte, ADCT.
Schaumburg-Lippe,
    E, Prince. 193–195.
    Victoria, Princess. 195.
Schika, R. 195.
Seelhaft. 149.
Segrave, Sir HOD. *12,* 13, 15, 49, 63, 65, 81, 90, *126,* 145, 147, 169, 191, 215, 221, 231, 233.
Selby, TBG. 213.
Senechal, R. 17, 39.
Showell, HB. 183.
Siko, O. *198.*
Singer, P. 33, 97.
Soames family. 189, 191.
    ER. 189.
    NMD. See Kidston, Mrs.
Spurrier, H. 47.
Stableford. 79.
Stalter. 90.
Staniland, C. 17, 135.
Stanley, E. 121.
Stewart,
    G. 85.
    RC. 17.

Stopford,
    Col. W. 19, 35.
    HL, Mrs. 19, 35, 207.
Strachan. 135.
Straight, W. 85, 119–121.
Straker, S. 144.

T.
Tabourin, P. 75.
Taylor. 138.
Thistlethwayte family, 9, 19.
    ADCT, 'Tom' or 'Scrap'. *vi, x,* 1, 2, 5–17, 19–21, 25, 33, 34, *35*–41, 36, *38, 46,* 47, 49, *54,* 55–67, *58, 60,* 75, 95–97, *104,* 107, *108,* 109, 125, *130,* 131–143, *132, 134, 138, 142,* 153, *166,* 167–183, *168, 170, 172–173,* 174, *176, 178–179, 180,* 181, *182,* 193, 200, 201, 205, *206,* 207–215, *208, 210, 212, 214,* 223, 241, 243, 246.
    Col. Evelyn. 9, 11, 207.
    EM. 35, 95, 131.
    GE, Mrs. 167, 201, *206,* 207, *208,* 209, 211, 246.
    Robin. 11, 13.
    TG. 19.
    TN. 35, 95.
Thomas,
    E. 17.
    JGP ('Parry'). *12,* 13, 15, 21, 29, 33, 37, 39, *40,* 41–43, *46,* **47–49,** *48,* 51, 63, 65, 67, 69, 85, 147, 153, 191, 221, 237, 243.
Thomson, K. *48,* 49.
Trip, JH. 218, 219, *220,* 221–223.
Turnbull, PH. 17.

U.
Ullrich, W. 195.
Urquhart-Dykes. *See* Dykes.

V.
Vandervell family,
    CA. 233.
    GA ('Tony'). 3, 27, 51, 233–235, 247.
Varzi, 125.
Vidal, M. 191.
Villiers, CA. 47, 107, 165.

W.
Wadley, 'Lord' T. 151.
Wakefield, Lord. 246.
Watney, R. 92, 93, *104,* 197, *198,* 241.
Weddigen, O. 187.
Wellsteed, HR. 17.
Werner. 197, 240, 241.
Wentzel-Mosau, Baron von. 140, 141.
Whaller, K. 246.
Whatley. *142,* 143.
Whigham,
    W. 31, 33.
    EM. *See* Campbell, M.
        Duchess of Argyll
White, 'Babe'. 209.
Whitecroft, CR. 17, *158.*
Whitney, P. 113.
Wigglesworth, G. *24.*
Wilkinson, AV. 17, *132.*
Williams, W Grover. 17, *154,* 177–181.
Windsor, Duke & Duchess. 151.
Wisdom, E. 85.
Wolfe, HF. 17.
Wood,
    Beris. 9, 17, *112,* 115, 117.
    Harcourt. 17, *108,* 109, *110,* 113, *170,* 171, 175, 177, *180,* 241.
Wright. *130.*
Wyndham. *166.*

Y
Yorke, Duke of. 33, 78.

Z.
Zanelli. 115.
Zborowski family, 23, 25.
    Count Louis V. 15, 19, 21, *22,* **23–33,** *24, 26, 28,* 34, 35, 37, 41, *44,* 45, *46, 47,* 48, 49, 64, 68, 69, *70,* 71, 85, 87, 91, 95, 127, *144,* 145, 149, 165, 231, 233, 243.
    Elliot. 23, 25, 31.
    Margaret. 23, 25.
    Countess 'Vi'. 25, *30,* 31, 33, 94, 95, 97, 131.
Zehender, G. *100,* 123.

CARS, COACHBUILDERS, COMPANIES, ENGINES, PLANES, SHIPS & YACHTS.

Plate pages in italic.

A.
Aboukir, HMS. 185.
AC. 37, 71, 133.
   Aceca. 3.
   1500cc, supercharched. 37.
   Engine. 223.
AEC. 243.
Alfa Romeo & Team, 15, 51, 83, 113, 133, 159, 161, 171, 175.
   1500cc. 51, 76, 77, 103, *158*, 159, 161, 169, 171, 175, *176*, 177, *180*, 183, *194*, 239.
   1750cc. 76, 108, *112*, 117, 159, 161, 169, 175, 176, 177, 183, 193, 197.
   2. 3 litre 8C LM. 117, *118*, 119, 121, 123.
   22/90. 103.
Allday & Onions. 225.
Alvis. 15, 133, 141, 149.
   12/50. 11, *72*, 75, *234*.
   1.5 litre FWD. *76*, 77, 135, 139, *164*, *176*.
   2 litre Silver Eagle. *78*.
American Trader, SS. 201.
Amilcar,
   1100cc. 159.
   C6 six cylinder supercharged. *140*, 141, 157.
Andre-Hartford. 49.
Anglia, SS. 215.
Ansaldo. 233.
Anzani engine, British. 37, 153.
Ardenrun power boats. 151, *222*, *223–225*.
Aries. 75, 84, *92*.
Aston Martin & Team, 1, 22, 27, 31, 47, 83, 113, 133, 144, 145, 147, 149, 153, 157, 169, 183, 211, 227, 233, 247.
   Chassis. 103, 155.
   Engines. 151, 153.
   Side Valve (ie. AM 270). *100*, *144*, 145, *147*, 148, 153.
      'Bunny', (AM 273). 47, 71.
      'Green Pea'. *148*, 149, *234*.
   Single Overhead Cam, 1.5 litre. *22*.
   Twin Overhead Cam, 1.5 litre. *144*, 145, *146*, 153.
   LM1 & LM2 (4 cylinder 1. 5 litre). 157, 159.
   LM4. 81.
   'Oyster' (later 'Razor Blade'). 145, *146*, 147, 165.
   Ulster. 169.
Aston Martin Motors. 227.
Atlantic Locomotives. 25, *32*.
Austin 7/750cc. *82*, 83, 85, 117, 133, *158*, 169, *176*, 177, 183, 213.
Austin Healey BN6. 3.
Austro-Daimler.
   2 litre. 51, 233.
   3 litre. *134*, *138*, *139*, *158*.
   3 litre Targa Florio. 51.

B.
'Babs' See Higham & Thomas Special.
Ballot.
   2 litre. 143.
   3 litre. 51, 143, 167.
   5 litre (Indy). 25, 27, *44*, 47, 61, *62*, 63, *64*, *68*, 69, 127, 165.
Bamford & Martin. 145.
Barnato Bros. 217.
Barnato Diamond Mining Co. 217.
Barnato-Hassan Special. 237, 246.
Basset Lowke. 25, 33.
Bentley & Team/Works, 1, 7, 15, 45, 51, *54*, 55, 59, 69, 75, 81, 87, *90*, 93, 103, 105, 107, 109, 113, 115, 127, 128, 133, 135, 144,165, 171, 176, 177, 189, 193, *194*, 195, 197, 201, 223, 225, 231, *232*, 235, 241, *242*, 243.
   'EXP 1'. 45.
   'EXP 2' - Race No. 2. *84*, 85, *86*, 91, *230*, 233.
   3 litre. 1, *2*, 3, 7, 13, 15, *46*, 47, *54*, 55, *58*, 59–63, *60*, 66, 67, *72*, *73*, 75, 83, *84*, *86*, 87, *88–89*, *90*, 91, *92*, 93, 95, *100*, 103, 107, 127, 147, 165, *190*, 191, *232*, *234*, 235, 237.
   'Old No. 7'. (3 litre). 63, *72*, *73*, *74*, 75, 92.
   4.5 litre. 51, *72*, *73*, 75, 77, *78*, *79*, 81, 87, *92*, *100*, *102*, 103, *104*, 105, *108*, 109, *116*, 117–119, *128*, 129, *130*, 133, 137, *138*, 139, *140*, 141,*164*, 165, 169, *170*, 171, 193, *194*, *212*, *220*, 229, *234*, 235, 237, 239.
   'Old Mother Gun'. (4. 5 litre). 51, *236*, 237.
   4.5 litre 'Blower' (supercharged) & Team. 47, 53, 77, *78*, *79*, 81, 83, 85, 87, *104*, 105, 107, *108*, 109, *110–111*, *112*, 113, *114*, 115, *116*, 117, *118*, 119, 121, 129, 165, *166*, 169, *170*, 171, *172–173*, 175, 177, *180*, 181, 193, 195, 197, 229, 231, 239, 241.
   6.5 litre. 105, 183, 195, 229.
   Speed Six. 52, 53, 77, *78*, *80*, 81, *92*, 105, *166*, 169, 195, *196*, 197, *198*, 229, 239, *240*, *241*.
   'Old No. 1'. (Speed Six). *50*, 51, 53, *106*, *108*, 109, *170*, 171, 175, 177, 181, 193, *194*, 197, *198*, 211, 237, *238*, 239, *240*, 246.
   8 litre. 229.
   'SCRAP'. 15.
   Engines. 53, 105, 225, 237, 246.
   4.5 litre Derby Car. 243.
Bentley Motors & Bentley Motors Ltd. 13, 15, 31, 53, 61, **67-69**, 85, 87, 91, 93, 107, 127, 225, 229, 231, 235, 239, 240, 246, 247.
Bentley Motors (1931) Ltd. 229.
Benz,
   18.8 litre. 29.
   Blitzen/Burman. 21.5 litre. 27, 91, 167.
Berengaria, Liner. 199.
Bertelli. *220*, *224*, 225, 227.
Bertelli Ltd. 225, 227.
Bignan, 2 litre. 41.
Birkin-Comery
   Car. 103.
   Engine. *98*, 99.
Birkin & Couper Ltd. , H. 103.
Birkin Lace Co. 99, 103.
Birkin-Morgan Clutch Control. *98*, 103.
Black Hawk Stutz. See Stutz.
Bleriot Plane. 141.
Bligh Bros. 27.
BNC. 39.
Bollee, Leon & Co. 157.
British Anzani. See Anzani.
British Mercedes Co. See Mercedes.
Bugatti & Team, 15, 27, 44, 115, 133, 135, 141, *154*, 157, 167, 169, *176*, *212*, 213, 219.
   Brescia. 39.
   2 litre. *140*, 141.
   Type 30, 2 litre. 27, 41, 44, 70, 85, 235.
   Type 35, 2 litre. 115, 129, 155, 189, *190*, *191*, *192*, 213.
   Type 35B, 2.3 litre. *154*, 155, *158*,

255

159, *166*, 175, 177, 178.
Type 35C, 2 litre. 115, *154*, 155.
Type 37, 1.5 litre. 153.
Type 37A,1.5 litre supercharged. 159, *212*, 213, 215
Type 39, 1.5 litre. 61, *152*, 153, *154*, 155, 157.
Type 39A, 1.5 litre. 61, 75, 153, *156*, 157, 159.
Type 40. *198*.
Type 43. *79*, *104*, 135, 137, 139, 141, 177, 182.
Type 51, 2.3 litre. 119.

C.

Calthorpe. 51, 231, 233, 234.
Camper & Nicholson. 97.
Castrol Oil. 246.
CAV Co. 233.
Charmian, Schooner. 7, 135, *136*, 243.
Chenard-Walcker. 39, 63.
Chitty I/Chitty Bang Bang. 15, 23.
  No I. 15, *24*, *26*, 27-29, 33, 45.
  II. *26*, 29.
  III. *28*, 29, 33.
  IV. 29.
Chris-Craft. 209.
Chrysler. *100*, 237, 239.
Clerget Engine. 24.
Clyde Shipping Co. 185.
Clyno Motor Cycles. 103.
Cobham/Blackburn Airways. 203.
'Consuta system'. 99.
Cooper-Clerget. 24.
Courageous, HMS. 187, *188*, 189.
Coventry-Climax. 246.
Cressy, Cruisers. 185–187.
  HMS. 185.
Crossley. 37.
Cunard Shipping Line. 220.
'Cynara'. Schooner. *94*, 97.

D.

Daedulus, HMS. 246.
Daimler-Benz. 181.
Daimler Works. 71.
Danae, HMS. 187.
Darracq, 27.
  Works. 71.
Dartmouth College. 185.
Dauntless, HMS. 187, *188*.
Davey, Paxman & Co. 33.
Day Summers & Co. 97.
De Beers.
  Consolidated Mines. 217.
  Mining Co. 217.
de Havilland Aircraft Co. 145, 197.
  Gypsy Moth. 183, 189, 197, *200*.
  Puss Moth. 197–199, 201, 203, 209.
  Comet. 246.
  Gypsy engine. 155.
Delage,
  1500cc Straight 8, GP. 75, 141, 155, 159.
  V12. 121.
  Straight 6. 237.
Delaney Gallay. 83.
Delaunay-Belleville. 83.
Delhi, HMS. 187.
DFP. 27, 45, 87, *98*, 99.
Dorsey-Calthorpe. 233.
Dragon, HMS. 187.
Dreadnought, HMS. 187.
Drummond's Bank. 3.
Duff and Adlington. 87, 91.
Du Pont. 239.
Duesenberg, 85.
  Straight 8. *142*, 143.
Dunedin, HMS. 187.

E

Eileen, Yacht. *10*.
Elfin, Motor Launch. 97.
Empress of Britain. *228*.
Enfield-Allday. 225,235.
Enfield-Allday Co. 225.
ERA. 27, 246, 247.
Eric-Campbell. 85
Europa, Liner. 199.

F.

Fairy Aviation. 135.
Fiat (FIAT) & Team, 91, 133, 143, 191.
  501. 3.
  1500cc. 147, 149.
  10 litre. 27, 91.
  'Mephistopheles'. 91.
'Flat Iron' Thomas Special. *See* Thomas Specials.
Fokker Aircraft. 141, *142*, 143.
Frazer Nash & Team, 3, 15, 37, 38 39, 133, 137, 177, 183.
  1100cc 'Rodeo' Special. *38*, 153.
  1500cc. *36*, 37, *38*, 41, 55, 61, 133, *154*, 157, 159.
Freestone & Webb Co. 243.
'Frothblower'. 223.

G

GN. *38*, 51, 143.
'Green', Hydroplane. 151.
'Grey Mist', Motor Yacht. *94*, 97.
Guyot 'Indy' Special. *154*, 155.
Gwynne. 37, 135.
Gurney Nutting Co. 13, 15, 195, *196*.
Gypsy Moth. *See* de Havilland.

H.

Halford Special. 155.
Hawke, HMS. 187.
Hawker,
  Tempest. 155.
  Typhoon. 155.
HE. *100*.
HFB Special. *212*.
Higham Special. 23, 27, *28*, 29, *48*, 49.
  'Babs'. 29, *48*, 49.
Hillman. 165.
Hispano-Suiza. 127, 190, 233.
  H6B ('Boulogne'). 27, 37, *190*, 191.
  H6C ('Monza'). 27, *34*, 37, 71, 235.
Hogue, HMS. 185, *186*.
Hood, HMS. 187.
Hooker, Peter, Ltd. 49.
Hooker Thomas Engine. *48*, 49, 149, 234.
Hooker Thomas, Peter.
  See Thomas Specials.
Hooper Co. 183, 191.
Hornby Trains. 25.

I

'Ida', motor launch. 99, 125.
Imperial Airways. 195, 203.
Invicta, 4.5 litre. *82*, 83, 85.
Isotta-Fraschini,
  10. 6 litre. 163.
  Tipo 8ASS. 177.
Itala. 117.

J.

Jaguar. 3, 246.
Jarvis Co. 66, 67, *232*, 235, 237.
'Jason & Portia', Schooner Yacht. 97.
Junkers Co. 193, 199.

K

Kellner Co. *34*, 37.
Kestrel engine. 162.
Kidston & Co, AG. 185.
KLG (Sparking Plugs). 68, 69, 137.

L.

Lagonda & Team. *78*, *132*, 133, 135, 175.
Lea-Francis & Team, *76*, 83, 133.
  Supercharged 1500cc. 53, 77, 81–83, 103, 133, 139, *156*, 159, 169, 171, 175, *176*, 177, 183, 237.
Leon Bollee, Paris. 157.
Leyland Motors Ltd. 43, 47, 49.
  Leyland Eight. 37, *46*, 49, 63, 65, 85, 147, 191.
  Leyland Thomas. 33, 37, *48*, 191, 237.

INDEX.

Liberty Aero Engine, 27 litre V12. 29.
LNER. 33.
Locomobile. 27, *230*, 231.
Lockheed Aircraft & Factory. 199.
    Vega. 199, *200*, 201, *202*, 203, 205.
Lorraine-Dietrich.
    15CV. 59, *90*.
Love Co. 37.
Lucas Co. 233.
Lynx engine. 141.

M.

'Magic Midget'. See MG.
Malborough. 49.
Malborough Special.
    See Thomas Specials.
Marechal. 151.
Marendaz. 149.
Marseal (Marseel). 149.
Martin Walter Co. 15, 34, 37, 59,
    166, 183, 243.
Maserati & Team. 85, 123.
    Tipo 8C,
        2.5 litre. 119.
        3 litre. 121, 123–125.
Maybach, 23 litre, 300 hp engine. 27.
Meadows engine. 82.
'Mephistopheles'. *See* Fiat.
Mercedes & Team, 1, 15, 27, 31, 59,
    95, 97, 105, 107, 115, 133, 141,
    143, 177, 178–179, 181, 211.
    1914 GP, 4.5 litre 4 cylinder. 25, 27.
    60 hp 4 cylinder. 25.
    2 litre 4 cylinder 'Targa Florio'. *12*,
        37.
    2 litre straight eight, 170hp. 31,
        113, 119.
    33/180. 141.
    S-36/220. *x*, 7, 61, 103, *104*, *108*,
        109, *130*, 131–141, *132*, *138*,
        166, 167, *168*, 169, *170*, 171,
        172, *173*, 175, *176*, 177, *178*,
        180, 183, 193, 213.
    S-38/250. 81, *108*, 109, *111*, *112*,
        115, 131, *140*, 141, *166*, 167,
        169, *176*, 177, *179*, 183, 197,
        212, 213, 215, *240*, 241,
        244–245.
    SSK-38/250. *112*, 123.
    Chassis. 24, 27, 29.
    Engines.
        15 litre. 29.
Mercedes, British, Co. 37, 131, 133.
Miller, 2 litre. 27, 31, *70*, 71.
Miller, Golden. 117.
MG & Team, 85, 123, 133, 161, 246.
    850cc. *80*.
    EX 120. 161, 163.
    EX 127 ('Magic Midget'). *160*, 163.

    K3. *120*, *122*, 123.
MG Car Co. 161.
Morgan. 3.
Morgan Giles Dinghy. 189.
Moth. See Wolseley.
Mowlems. 3.

N.

Napier. 37, 91.
Napier Campbell. 49.
Napier & Son, 87, 229.
    Sabre Engine. 155.
'Newg' Hydroplane. 225.
Norton. 233.
Norton Motor Cycle Co. 233.

O.

'Ocean Rover', MV. 68.
'Olga', Miss. *150*, 151, 225.
OM, 17, 169.
    Straight 8. 159.
    2 litre six cylinder. 133, *156*.
Orion, HMS. *186*, 187.
Osborne, HMS. 185.

P.

Pacific Locomotives. 33.
Pacey-Hassan Special. 246.
Packard. 71.
Pamela, Yacht. 199.
Park Ward Co. 191.
Peter Hooker Ltd.
    See Hooker, Peter, Ltd.
Peugeot. 45.
'Poo, Mr'. 225.
Powerplus Ltd. 145, 153, 161.

R.

'Ratcatcher', Motor Launch. 97.
Ratier. 63, 161.
Renwick & Bertelli Ltd. 227.
Repulse, HMS. 187.
Ricardo Co. 91.
Riley & Team, *132*, 133, 139, *158*, 159,
    235.
    1100cc. *156*, 161, 171, *176*, 177.
    Brooklands Speed Model. 51, 75,
        77, *79*, 133.
Rhodesian Aircraft Co. 203.
RM. 247.
Rolls-Royce. 31, 162, 229, 231, 246.
Roots Supercharger. 43.
Ropner Shipping Co. 3.
Rothschild Bank. 217.
Rubery Owen & Co. 45.
Rudge-Whitworth. 7, 55.

S.

Salmson, 27, 51, 133, 141, 156.
    Grand Sports Special. 51.
    San Sebastian. 51, 85, 157.
SARA. 75.
Saunders Roe Co. 99, 151, 223, 225.
Scalectrix. 103.
SCAP Engine. 39.
Scott, Liner. 217.
'SCRAP'. 15.
Shell Petroleum. 91.
Shelley Ltd. RT. 233.
Silver Hawk. 85.
Singer Sewing Machine Co. 33, 97.
Skoda. 190.
Smith & Sons, S. 68.
Soper, JM & Son. 135.
Sopwith Camel. 155.
Speedcraft. 215.
'Speed of the Wind'. *162*.
Speedway, Miniature. *98*, 103.
Standard Oil. 151.
Star Engineering. 87.
Straker Squire. 87.
    Co. 87, 144.
Stutz, 197, *198*, *236*, 239, 241.
    Black Hawk. *102*, 237.
    Splendid. *104*, *130*.
Submarine,
    U-9. 185, 187.
    U-29. 187.
    L-24. 187, *188*.
    L-3. 187, *188*.
    X-1. 187, *188*.
    U-173. 187.
    H-48. 187.
Sunbeam & Team, 117, 127, 145, 147.
    350 hp, V12 (Blue Bird). 27, 29, 37.
    1000 hp Land Speed Car. 49.
    2 litre, 4 cylinder. 127.
    2 litre, 6 cylinder supercharged, GP.
        51, 53, 68, *82*, *106*, 109, 137.
    2 litre, 'The Cub'. 83, 161.
    3 litre, 4 cylinder. 127
    3 litre, 6 cylinder. 71, *72*, 85, 87,
        90, *112*, 129, 171, 175.
    3 litre, 8 cylinder. 27, 127.
    3.25 litre, 1914 TT. 137.
    4 litre, 12 cylinder ('Tiger'). 63, 65,
        81, *154*.
    4.5 litre, 4 cylinder GP. 67–69, 127.
    4.5 litre, 6 cylinder GP. 127.
    4.9 litre 'Indy' engine, 1921 chassis.
        27, 51.
    4.9 litre TT. *126*, 127.
    9 litre, 'Toodles V'. *126*, 127.
    18.3 litre, 12 cylinder. 127, 137.
    Engines. 151, 225.
Sunbeam Motor Co. 127, 145.

T.
Talbot & Team, 133, 147.
    70. 129, 191.
    90. 197, 239.
    105. *79*, 81.
    1.5 litre. 145, 155, *156*, 169.
    2.6 litre. 233.
    3 litre. 27.
    4³/₄. 3, 233.
Talbot-Darracq & Team. 127, 129, 145, 147, 153.
Theo. Schneider. 75.
Thin-Wall Bearings. 3, 235.
Thomas Inventions Development Co. 49.
Thomas Specials, *48*, 49, 149, *234*.
    'Babs'. See Higham Special.
    'Flat Iron'. *40*, 41-45, *42*, *48*, 49, 55, 61, 65–67, 153, 159.
    Hooker. *48*, 49.
    Leyland. See Leyland.
    Malborough. *48*, 49, 85.
Thorneycroft Co. 97.
Thunderbolt. 246.
Titania, HMS. 187, *188*.
Tracta. 135.
Triumph Motor Cycle. 143.
Trojan. 3.

U.
Union Airways. 203.

V.
Vanden Plas Co. 15, 191.
Vandervell Products Ltd. 3, 233–235.
Vanwall. 3, 235.
Vauxhall,
    Prince Henry. 163.
    4.5 litre. 145.
    30-98. *34*, 35, 37, *38*, 39, 40, 41, *46*, 55, 71.
    'Rouge et Noir'. 27, 35, *162*, 163, *164*, 165.
    'Silver Arrow'. 3, 35.
    3 litre TT. 165.
    3 litre (Superspecial) Villiers. 165, 169, 183, 213.

Vauxhall Motors. 87, 165.
Vickers Co. 45.
Villiers superchargers. 165.

W.
Walter, Martin. See Martin Walter.
Walton-on-Thames Launch Works. 151, 223.
White & Son. 199.
Windsor Castle, Liner. 203.
Wolseley, 225.
    Ten. 230.
    Moth 1. 233, 235.
    Moth 11. 227, *230*, 233, 235.
    Engine. 223, 225, 230.
Wolseley Motor Co. 233.

Z
Zenith Carburettor Co. 144.

CIRCUITS, INSTITUTIONS, LOCATIONS, RACES & VENUES.

Plate pages in italic.

A.
Aberdeen. 91.
Acton. 3, 229, 233.
Adriatic Coast. 123.
Africa. 9, 215.
Ainsdale Beach. 213.
Alps, The. 141.
America(n). 23, 25, 44, 70, 77, 97, 143, 199, 217, 231, 233, 237, 239.
Amersham, Bucks. 33.
Amiens. 127.
Amsterdam. 193.
Antibes. 209.
Ardenrun Mansion. 3, 221–223, *224*, 225, *226*, 227, 231, 246.
Ards Circuit. See Tourist Trophy Race.
Argentian. 44.
Arromanche, France. 83.
Aston Clinton Hill Climb. 87, 165.
Aspley Grange Mansion. 107.
Avus Circuit, Germany. 129, 181.
Australia(n). 33, 65, 117, 187, 223, 246.
Austrian. 181.
Automobile Club de l'Ouest. 155.

B.
Bahamas, 151.
    Governor. 151.
Baker Street, London. 45.
Bangor Bay, N. Ireland. 135.
Baragwanath Airfield. 203.
BARC. 21, 163.
Barnes. 153.
Basingstoke. 97.
Belfast. 7, 135, 175, 181, 193.
Belgian. 141.
Belgian Grand Prix,
    1929. *158*, 159.
    1931. 119.
    1932. 121.
Belgian 24 Hour Race. 119, 123.
'Bentley Corner'. 227.
Bentley Drivers Club. 3.
Berlin. 129, 155, 193, 195, 199.
Billericay. 233.
Blackpool. 107.
Blakeney. 125, 223.
Bodicote House. *200*, 201, 243.
Boer War. 9.
Bold Faced Stag Public House, The. 68.
Bologna. 119.

Bonneville Salt Flats, Utah. *162*, 246.
Boulogne. 36, 37, 39, 127, 139, 141, 147.
Boulogne (sur Mere) Circuit. 36, *38*.
    Automobile Race Week,
    incl. Hill Climbs & Speed Trials.
    Grand Prix de Boulogne &
    Concours d'Elegance,
    1923. 93, 147.
    1924. *148*, 149–151, 155.
    1925. 19, 21, 37–41, *38*, 59, 151–153.
    1926. 33, *60*, 61-65, *62*, 69, 75, *152*, 153.
    1927. 141, *154*, 155-157.
    1928. 139-141, *140*.
    Georges Boillet Cup Race,
    1923. 147.
    1925. 39.
    1926. 61, 63, 65.
    1928. *104*. 105, 141.
    Cup Grand Prix, 1925. 19.
Bourne. 247.
Bournemouth. 145.
BRDC. See British Racing Drivers Club.
Brent Reservoir. 225.

INDEX.

Brescia, Italy. 113, *120*, 123.
Bridge Village, Nr Canterbury. 19, 25.
British. 123, 131, 141, 187, 201, 231 239.
   Olympic Fencing Team. 93.
   (Brooklands) Grand Prix. 61, 75.
   Motor Boat Club. 225.
   Navy. *See* Royal Navy.
British Racing Drivers Club. 85, 124.
Brooklands, 3, 11, 13, 17, *20*, 21, 25, 29, *34*, *46*, 47, *48*, 49, 64, *68*, 83, 91, 99, 109, *114*, 124, 125, *126*, 127, 133, 137, 145, *146*, *162*, 163, 169, *192*, *220*, *230*, 233, 237, 239, *240*, 246.
   Automobile Racing Club.
     See BARC.
   Racing Circuit. *20*, **21-23**, 49, *88*, 91, 98, *118*, *144*, 147, 151, 161, 219, 221, 223,*230*,*234*.
   Race Meetings. 24, 25, 27, 29, *44*, 51, 61, 67, 69, 75, *82*, 83, *84*, 91, 97, 99, 113, 119, 121, 127, 141, 145, 153, 155, 159, 161, 163, 165, 167, 191, 227, *230*, 231, 233, *234*, 235, 241.
   200 Mile. 22, 23, 65, *146*, 147–149, 153, *156*, 157, 159, 225, 227, 233, 235.
   500 Mile. *50*, 51, 53, 77–81, *82*, 83, 87, 109, 117, 123, 161, 193, *220*, 237, *242*.
   Double Twelve Hour. 23, 51, 52, 53, 77, *78-79*, 81, 85, 109, *110*, 113, 129, 159, 161, 165, 195, 211, 220, 237, *238*, 239, 240.
   Mountain Handicap. *82*.
   Six Hour Endurance. 23, *50*, 51, *72*, 75–77, 85, 87, *100*, 103, *108*, 109, 117, *156*, 165, *166*, 169, 182, 193, *220*, *234*, 235, 236, 237, *238*, 239, *242*.
Brooklands
   Estate. 3.
   Society. 3.
Broome, Aus. 117.
Brownsea Island. 69.
Brussels. 143.
Bucks. 33, 219.
Burnham-on-Crouch. 225.
Bursledon, Hants. 69.
Bwlch, Breconshire. 206.

C.

Caerphilly Hill Climb, Cardiff. 145.
Café de l'Hippodrome. 75.
California(n). 231.
Calshot, The Solent. *150*.
Cambridge, 143, 217.
   University. 223.
Canada/Canadian. 91.
Cannes. 199, 208, 209, 211.
Canterbury. 19, 21, 25, 27.
Cape Town. 199, 200, 201, *202*.
Cardiff. 117, 145.
Carshalton. 195.
Caterham, Surrey. 193.
Chamonix. 155.
Channel Sea, English. 69, 71, 113, 121, 142, 143, 147, 195.
Charterhouse School. 217.
Cheltenham. 85, 95.
Chicago. 69.
China. 91.
China Naval Station. 187.
Colchester. 33.
Colden Common, Hants. 246.
Coldstream Guards. 69.
Copa Catalunya, 127.
Coppa Florio. 68.
   1922. *126*, 127.
Coupe d'Ostend, 127.
Coupe des Voitorettes, Boulogne. 127.
Coupe de l'Auto, Boulogne, 127.
Coventry. 71.
Cowes, IOW. 199.
Cricket, HMS. 243-246.
Cricklewood. 95, 225, 232, 235.
Croydon Airport. 141, *142*, 143, 193, 195, 199, 201.
Cuban. 67, 225.
Czecholovakia(n). 190.

D.

D-Day. 83, 243.
Dartmouth College. 185.
Daytona Beach. 49.
Dessau. 199.
Detroit, USA. 199.
Devenport. 187.
Donington Circuit. 21, 247.
Double Twelve Hour Race,
   See Brooklands.
Drakensberg Mountains. 203.
Dublin. 135, 168, 171, 193.
Duff and Aldington. 91.
Duke of York Trophy Races. 151, 153, 222, 225.
Duke's Meadow, Barnes. 153.
Dungeness. 33.
Dunstable. 247.
Durban. 203.
Dutch (Men). 187.

E.

Edgware. 197.
Eden Roc. *See* Hotels
Elham, Kent. 35.
Embassy Club. 219.
England. 11, 91, 93, 117, 125, 135, 187, 199, 203, 246.
Englefield Green. 246.
English(man) 45, 145, 147, 151, 171, 177, 247.
English Channel. *See* Channel.
Epsom. 85.
Essex Motor Car Club. 231, 233.
Eton College. 25.

F.

Fareham, Hants. 143.
Finlaystone, Renfew. 185.
Fitzroy Lodge Boxing Club. 223.
Florida. 151.
Folies Bergere. 219.
Folkestone. 33, 37,41, 59, 166, 247.
France. 28, 191, 217.
   Northern. 99.
   South of. 131.
French(men). 27, 45, 49, 63, 115, 143, 151, 155, 161, 177, 209, 225, 237.
French Grand Prix,
   1913. 127.
   1914. 127, 143.
   1921. 127, *142*, 143.
   1922. 22, 127.
   1924. 31, *70*, 71, 129.
   1927. 155.
   1928. 177.
   1929. 177.
   1930. *114*, 115.
   1931. 119.
French Riviera. 209, 211, 223.

G.

Geneva, Lake. 99.
German(s). 27, 95, 105, 115, 143, 185, 187, 193, 213.
German Grand Prix.
   1926. 129.
   1928. 105.
   1931. 119.
   1933. 181.
Germany. 199.
Gibraltar. 189.
Glasgow. 185.
Goodwood. 3, 23.
Gordon Bennett Races. 171.
Gorsley House, Bridge. 19.
Gosport. 97.
Grand Prix,
   d'Endurance de 24 Heures Le

Mans. Coupes Rudge-Whitworth.
   See Le Mans.
de Monaco. 123.
de Paris. 87, 236.
de Provence. 191.
de Tourisimo Guipusca. 93.
of Tripoli, 1933. *122*, 123–125.
Grosvenor Sq. *190*, 201, 227.
Gt. Britain. 201.

H.
Hamble,
   Airfield. 201.
   River. 69, 243.
Hamburg. 199.
Hampshire. 6,7, 11, 243, 246.
Hampstead. 217.
Hampton-on-Thames. 97.
Hanworth Airfield. 199.
Harley Street, London. 83.
Hartlepool, West. 3.
Hermitage Bungalow, The. 49.
Heston Airport. 199, 201.
Higham House & Park. *18*, 19, 25, *26*, 31, 33, 95.
Highland Court. *See* Higham House.
Holland. 187.
Hollywood. 199.
Holme Moss Hill Climb. 165.
Hook of Holland. 185.
Hotels,
   de Paris. 59, 75.
   Eden Roc. 208, 209.
   Excelsior Paris. 211.
   Hermitage. 209.
   Majestic. 209.
   Moderne. *54*, 59, *72*, 75.
   Palm Beach. 209, 211.
   Savoy. *73, 74,* 75.
Huddersfield. 165.
Hyde Park. 199.
Hythe. 33, 151, 222, 223.

I.
Indianapolis ('Indy') 500,
   1914. 127.
   1915. 67–69.
   1920. 127.
   1923. 27, *44*, 70.
International Club. 219.
Ireland. 181.
   North. 133.
Irish Free State. 171.
Irish Grand Prix (Phoenix Park). *168*, 211.
   Eireann Cup & Saorstat Cup.
   1929. 51, *76*, 77, *108*, 109, 119, *158*, 159, 165, *168, 170*,
   171–175, *172–173*, 181, 193, *194, 242.*
   1930. 53, 81, *112*, 115, 129, 161, 213, 215.
   1931. 119.
Irish Sea. 7.
Irondown Hill. 165.
Isle of Man, 125, 135.
   Motor Cycle Races. 71, 99.
   Tourist Trophy Races,
   1914. 87, 137.
   1922. 127, 133.
Italian. 113, 115, 119, 123, 125, 143.
Italian Grand Prix,
   1921. 127.
   1924. 31.
   1926. 115.

J.
Jockey Club. 21.
Johannesburg. 11, 203.
John O'Groats. 155, 195, 196.
Juan-les-Pins. *208*, 209.
Jutland, Battle of. 187.

K.
Kensington Gardens. 2.
Kent(ish). 21, 29, 35, 49.
Keyna. 142, 143.
Kimberley Mine. 217.
Kings Cup Air Race. 199.
King's,
   Own Scottish Borderers. 69.
   Royal Rifles. 19
Kingston-on-Thames. 37, 68.
Kinsale. 19, 21.
Kisumu, Lake Victoria. *202*.
Kop Hill Climb. 25, 27, 163, 165, 233.

L.
Laindon Two Church Hill. 233.
La Baule. 155.
   Grand Prix. 1927. 155.
La Turbie Hill Climb, Nice. 25.
Langley Vale Village. 85.
Lasarte Circuit. 137.
Le Bourget Airport. 201.
Leander Rowing Club. 143.
Le Mans. *72, 76, 89, 92,* 125.
Le Mans Circuit & races, 2, 21, 23, *56–57*, 71, 83, 107, 127, *142*, 143, 171, 211.
   1923. 83, *86*, 91–93.
   1924. *88–89*, 93.
   1925. 59, 71, 72–75, 85, *90*, 93, 129.
   1926. 1, 2, 7, 13, 15, 21, 47, *54, 55*–61, *58*, 75, 87, 92, 93.
   1927. 72, *73*, 75, *84*, 85, 87, *92*, 93, 235, 236.
   1928. 76, 77, *92, 93, 100, 101, 102,* 103–105, *116,* 117, *128,* 129, 157, *236,* 237.
   1929. 51, 85, *92, 93, 106,* 109, 119, *128,* 129, 165, 171, *184,* 193, *194,* 236, 237, *238,* 239, *242.*
   1930. 53, *80,* 81, *92, 93, 110–111,* 113–115, 129, 193, 195–197, *198,* 231, 239, *240,* 241.
   1931. *118,* 119.
   1932. 117, 121.
   1933. 117, 125.
Le Touquet (-Paris-Plage), 113, 121, 139, 155, 209.
   See Boulogne.
Liffe, River. 158.
Lingfield. 221, 226.
Lithunia. 117.
London. 9, 11, 13, 25, 31, 41, 87, 91, 95, 117, 135, 147, 183, 199, 201, 202, 207, 217, 219, 221.
   Airport. 199.
   City of. 11.
   East End. 11, 215.
   Motor Show. 131.
   South. 13.
   University. 47
London Life Association. 229.
Loos, Battle of. 143.
Luton. 163.
Lyons, 70, 71, 127, 129.
   Circuit. 31.

M.
Madresfield Speed Trials. 165.
Maiden Erlegh Estate & Stud. *10,* 11.
Maitland Aerodrome. *202.*
Malta. 187.
Mandelieu Polo Ground. 211.
Manhattan, New York. 25.
Marseilles. 191.
Mayfair, London. 31.
Medina River. 199.
Melbourne, Aus. 33, 117.
Melton Mowbray. 25.
Meon Valley. 9.
Merthyr Tydfil. 207.
Mesopotamia. 99.
Milan. 119, 123.
Mille Miglia, 171.
   1930. 113.
   1933. *120, 122,* 123.
Miramas Circuit. 191.
Molsheim Factory. 27, 44, 198.
Monaco Grand Prix,
   1929. 177.
   1933. 123.

INDEX.

Monte Carlo, 123.
    Rally. 195, 196.
    Motor Boat Racing Fortnight. 223.
Montlhery, 59, 87, 93, 161, 163, 246.
    Formula Libre Race 1927. *154*, 155,
Monza, 115.
    GP. 31, 153.
Mortlake. 151, 225.

N.
Natal. 204.
National Motor Museum. 3.
Netheravon Airfield. *200*, 201.
Newcastle. 93.
New York. 25, 217.
New Zealand. 187.
Nice. 25, 155.
Norfolk. 99, 125, 223.
Nottingham(shire). 97, 99.
Nurburgring. 105, 181.

O.
Old Burseldon, Hants. 243.
Old Surrey Barstow Foxhounds. 223.
Olympia, London. 183, 191.
Oxford. 243.
    University. 223.

P.
Palestine. 217.
Palm Beach. *See* Hotels.
Paris. 31, 155, 157, 181, 201, 209, 219.
Paris to Venice, 1902. 25.
Pau. *114,* 115.
Pendine Sands. 29, *48*, 49.
Pesaro, Italy. 123.
Phoenix Park. See IGP.
Pietermaritzburg. 203.
Poole Harbour, 214, 215.
    100 Mile Speed Test. 214, 215.
Porthcawl Speed Trials. 145.
Portsmouth. 187.
Powerboat Craft & Racing. 7, 67, 151, 153, 223.
Putney. 151, 225.

R.
RAC. 23, 75.
RAF. *156*.
ROAC. 83.
Rathmore, Kinsale, Co. Cork. 19, 21.
Reading. 11.
REME. 83.
Rhine, River. 83.
Rhodesia. 201.
Riviera. *See* French Riviera.
Rome. 113, 123.
Romney, Hythe & Dymchurch Railway. **33**.
Royal Automobile Club. See RAC.
    Berkshire Rifles. 91.
    Engineers. 87, 217.
    Field Artillery. 143.
    Flying Corps. 45, 99.
    Highlanders. 185.
    Motor Yacht Club. 151, 153, 223.
    Navy. 151, 185, 187,189, 193.
    Warwickshires. 99.
Rudge-Whitworth (Triennial Cup). 7, 55.
Rumanian. 157.
Russia/Russian. 91, 123, 171.

S.
Sahara Desert. 29.
Salisbury Plain. 201.
Sandown. 85
San Sebastian, 93.
    Grand Prix. 68, 129, 137.
Sarajevo. 181.
Sarthe Circuit. *See* Le Mans.
Savoy Hotel. *See* Hotels.
Shadwell Court. 113, *118*, 201.
Shelsley Walsh Hill Climb. 107, 163, 165, *182,* 183, 191, *192*.
Sherwood Foresters, 7th. 99.
Sicily. 68, *126*.
Sienna. 123.
Six Hour Endurance Race. See Brooklands.
Skegness, Sand Races/Speed Trials. 165.
    1925. 37.
    1930. *212,* 213–215.
SOE. 177.
Solent, The. *150,* 189.
South Africa. 11, 201, 203, 215.
Southend Regatta. 151.
South Harting Hill Climb. 145, 165.
Southport Sand Races.
    1927. 107.
    1928. *106,* 109.
    1929. 167–169.
    1930. *212,* 213.
    1931. 215.
Southsea Esplanade Speed Sprints. 145.
Southampton. 83, 97, 135, 155, 199, 217, 225, 228.
    Water. 135, 151.
Southwick House, Estate, Priory & Village. *6, 7, 8, 9,* 11, 207.
Spa, Belgium. 119, 123, 169, 171.
Spanish. 190.
    Grand Prix, 1924. 137.
Spread Eagle Hill Climb. 145, 147.
St James Court, London. 25.
St Malo. 155.
St Margaret's, Westminster. 189, 207.
St Radigunds, Canterbury. 27.
St Raphael, France. 209, 211.
St Tropez. 209.
Staughton Manor. 32, 33.
Stock Exchange, London. 51, 209.
Strand, The. 207.
Strasbourg, 127.
    GP, 1922. 22, *144*, 145.
Sudan. 143.
Sunningdale. 219.
Surrey. 21, 193, 221, 226, 227.
Surrey Cricket Club. 223.
Sutton Bank Hill Climb. 165.
Switzerland. 32, 99, 125.
Sydney, Aus. 117.

T.
Tacolneston Hall. 109.
Targa Florio, 1927. 115.
Tempelhoferfeld Airport (Tempelhof), Berlin. 195, 199.
Thames River. 225.
Thetford. 118.
Three Cocks, Breconshire. 185.
Tor Bay. 225.
Tourist Trophy Race (Ards Circuit, Belfast). 7, 23, 125, 171, 211.
    1928. 77, *104,* 105, *132,* 133–139, *134,* 138, *164,* 165, 171, 175, 220.
    1929. 77, *108,* 109, *116,* 119, 141, 161, 169, 175–183, *178–179, 180,* 182, 193, *194*.
    1930. 81, *112,* 115.
    1932. 121.
    1933. 125.
    Isle of Man. See IOM.
Tourist Trophy Races – pre 1928. *See* IOM.
Trans-Siberian Railway. 91.
Tring. 87.
Trinity Hall College, Cambridge. 143, 217.
Tripoli. 124.

U.
Ulster(man). 3, 133, 175.
Upper Heyford. 201, 243.
Upper St Martin's Lane, London. 87, 91.
USA. 33, 93, 97, 162, 199, 227, 228, 229, 231, 246.

V.
Venice. 25.
Vintage Sports Car Club (VSCC). 3, 83, 233.

W.
Wallington. 195.
Walthamstow. 49.
Wandsworth. 51.
Welsh Harp Reservoir. *222*, 225.
Welwyn Garden City Works. 47, 103, *104*, 105, 107, 113.
Wembley Stadium. 225.
Westcliffe-on-Sea. 231.

Westminster, 189, 207.
   School. 71.
Weybridge, Surrey. 21.
Whaddon Chase. 219.
Whale Cay, The Bahamas. 151.
Whitehall Shipyard, Whitby. 169.
Wimbledon. 66.
Wimille Hill Climb, See Boulogne.
Wimpole St, London. 85.
Windsor Great Park. 246.

Y.
Yachting World Challenge Cup. 215.
Yangtze River. 91.